ASIA'S FLYING GEESE

A VOLUME IN THE SERIES

CORNELL STUDIES IN POLITICAL ECONOMY

edited by Peter J. Katzenstein

A list of titles in this series is available at www.cornellpress.cornell.edu.

Asia's Flying Geese

HOW REGIONALIZATION SHAPES JAPAN

Walter F. Hatch

Cornell University Press ITHACA AND LONDON

First published 2010 by Cornell University Press
First printing, Cornell Paperbacks, 2010

Printed in the United States of America

Library of Congress Cataloging-in-Publication Data
Hatch, Walter, 1954–
    Asia's flying geese : how regionalization shapes Japan /
Walter F. Hatch.
        p. cm. — (Cornell studies in political economy)
    Includes bibliographical references and index.
    ISBN 978-0-8014-4868-3 (cloth : alk. paper)
    ISBN 978-0-8014-7647-1 (pbk. : alk. paper)
    1. Business networks—Japan.   2. Regionalism—Economic
aspects—Japan.   3. Elite (Social sciences)—Japan.   4. Manu-
facturing industries—Japan.   5. Japan—Economic policy—1945–
I. Title.   II. Series: Cornell studies in political economy.
    HD69.S8H379 2010
    338.8′7—dc22   2009038042

Cloth printing   10 9 8 7 6 5 4 3 2 1

Paperback printing   10 9 8 7 6 5 4 3 2 1

To Kenji, Maya, and Teshika

Contents

Acknowledgments   ix

Introduction: External Sources of Continuity and Change   1

Part One BASELINE
1 Social Networks and the Power They Produce   13
2 The Postwar Political Economy of Japan   40
3 Leading a Flock of Geese   71

Part Two THE 1990S
4 Maintaining the Relational Status Quo   105
5 Elite Regionalization and the Protective Buffer   142
6 The Costs of Continuity   175

Part Three THE NEW MILLENNIUM
7 Grounding Asia's Flying Geese   203
8 Some Change . . . at Last   223

Conclusion: Beyond Asia   246

References   257
Index   285

Acknowledgments

Japan's political economy has come a long way. Although it continues to be characterized by remarkably stable networks of social exchange, it is no longer the institutionally rigid structure it once was. Changes in East Asia— or rather, in Japan's ties with the region—have helped bring about this shift at home. In these pages, I use an outside-in perspective to explain both the long-standing continuity and the more recent discontinuity in the political economy of Japan.

Talk about a long journey! I began thinking about this project in the mid-1990s, when I was a PhD student in Seattle. I started to research it when I moved to Tokyo with my family in 1996 as a Fulbright Fellow and started to write it when I returned to Seattle in 1999 to teach in the Jackson School of International Studies at the University of Washington. A year later, the project was submitted in the form of a dissertation.

And then, as I took up a new position at Colby College in Maine and gyrated through a period of turbulence in my life, the project sat idle. Predictably, though, history did not. Japan, which had seemed stuck in an institutional rut, gradually began to change in ways I had not contemplated. I feared that I had been overwhelmed by events.

Over the last few years, however, I have been able to return to this project, make several new visits to Japan and the rest of East Asia, retest and revise my argument, and produce this book. The journey is complete, but I would be remiss if I did not express gratitude to the many fellow travelers who helped me at various stages along the way.

The usual caveat applies here: I am responsible for the final product, including any possible errors.

I have been blessed to learn about Japan, as well as the science (and art) of political economy, from two extraordinary masters.

Kozo Yamamura, perhaps the world's leading expert on the economy and economic history of Japan, helped me launch this project. I met him in 1990, when I suspended my career as a journalist to return to graduate school at the University of Washington. I eventually became his research and teaching assistant in the Jackson School of International Studies. With his stratospheric standards and no-nonsense manner, Yamamura scared the hell out of his students, including me. But he also offered more support (intellectually, emotionally, and financially) than anyone could ever ask for.

T. J. Pempel, perhaps the world's leading expert on the political economy of Japan, helped me reshape and complete this project. He encouraged me to think harder and, even when he did not agree with my conclusions, provided invaluable feedback. He also invited me to participate in another project that contributed to my knowledge about Japan's role in Asian regionalism.

At the University of Washington, I have also benefited from the guidance of James Caporaso, Joel Migdal, John Haley, and the late Dan Lev.

Many of Japan's finest scholars helped me during my extended stay there. For example, at Keio University, Yakushiji Taizo sponsored me as a visiting researcher, while Kimura Fukinari and Suzanami Yoko invited me to participate in a graduate seminar on regional trade and investment flows. At the University of Tokyo, where I became an associate professor and editor of an academic journal, I received help from Suehiro Akira, Hiwatari Nobuhiro, Fujiwara Kiichi, and Greg Noble. Urata Shujiro of Waseda was also an endless source of good advice.

In addition to my UW mentors, several colleagues and friends read all or part of the manuscript; others listened patiently as I tried to talk my way over mental hurdles. These included Dan Slater, Dave Leheny, Ellis Krauss, Richard Samuels, Saori Katada, Jayantha Jayman, Robert Pekkanen, and Glenn Hook.

I could not have completed this project without the cooperation of numerous government officials (especially at METI, JETRO, and JBIC), business executives (especially at Toyota, Nissan, Mitsubishi Electric, Hitachi, and Fujitsu), and labor leaders (especially Rengō) in Japan and the rest of Asia. Most of these individuals should remain anonymous, but Miwa Naomi and Tejima Shigeki can handle, and justly deserve, special mention.

A small army of smart, competent research assistants helped make contacts, follow the news, dig up data, and prepare charts. In Japan, for example, I relied heavily, maybe too heavily at times, on my dear friend Naruse Takatoshi. I also turned frequently to Hitomi Kaoru for help. At Colby, I was aided by Jonathan Devers, Christoph Nguyen, Anna Simeonova, Tammi Choi, and Shiga Kyoko.

I received generous financial support from the Fulbright Foundation, the Association for Asian Studies, and the Division of Social Sciences at Colby College. I received either technical or moral support from Steve Motenko, Mikiko Amagai, and Susan Eastgard. I am especially indebted to my partner, Laurie Mann, who lifted me up as I labored to resurrect this project, and to my father, Willard Hatch, who prodded me to finish. Without them, I would be lost.

I also am grateful to Cornell University Press for its good work moving this manuscript through the process. From the very beginning, Peter Katzenstein, the editor of this series, has been a wonderful and influential mentor. He has shown interest in, and support for, my work over many years, providing invaluable guidance on this and other projects. Professor Katzenstein and an anonymous reviewer made a number of helpful suggestions here. Roger Haydon, executive editor of Cornell, offered wise counsel, good humor, and solid leadership. Candace Akins, senior manuscript editor, was both competent and kind in the final stages of production. Thanks to all of you.

This book, however, is dedicated to my three children, who had no choice but to join me on this long journey when they were still in different stages of innocence. They are now immensely wise. I am very proud of each of them and am grateful for their patience in putting up with me, the imperfect but perfectionist papa, as I kept stumbling forward.

NOTE: In this book, I present Japanese names in the Japanese style—family name followed by given name. But I use the Western style for Japanese authors whose work is published chiefly in English.

Introduction

External Sources of Continuity and Change

Japan's model of capitalism has, until quite recently, stood apart. In the last half of the twentieth century, it tended to be organized around social relationships, and thus acquired characteristics that made it different from the mostly laissez-faire systems that emerged in the United States and England, but also different from the more corporatist systems of northern Europe.[1] In Japan, government bureaucrats, acting in collaboration with and often at the behest of industry executives, routinely have used not only formal means such as rules and regulations but also informal means such as "administrative guidance" to organize markets. Private firms have maintained long-standing, mutually reinforcing ties with one another, manifested by cross shareholdings, interlocking directorates, personnel transfers, and interfirm transactions. Meanwhile, core employees in large corporations have stayed with one employer for most if not all of their working lives, acquiring new skills and receiving incrementally higher wages inside rather than beyond that firm.

Surprisingly, the Japanese political economy remained distinctive through the 1990s—despite massive pressure, both economic and political, for change. Indeed, near the end of that decade, a report commissioned by the Economic Planning Agency of Japan (Economic Planning Agency [EPA] 1998a, 23) concluded that Japanese capitalism, unlike other market systems,

---

1. I thus assume greater variety among capitalist economies than most others who have written about "varieties of capitalism." For example, Hall and Soskice (2001) distinguish between "liberal market economies," including the United States, Canada, Australia, and the United Kingdom, and "coordinated market economies," including Germany, France, Italy, and Japan. Likewise, Yamamura and Streeck (2003) acknowledge important differences between Germany and Japan, but still lump them together as leading examples of "illiberal capitalism" standing in binary opposition to "liberal capitalism."

continued to emphasize "the merits of cooperation based on long-term relationships between economic actors and within economic institutions. In this way, each economic actor has been able to avoid the risks associated with fierce competition, maximizing its self-interest by forging alliances within the market."

This continuity is surprising, even perplexing, because in 1989, a financial bubble in Japan began to reveal its fragility, exposing Japan's political economy to a tsunami of pent-up forces for structural transformation. For almost a decade, Japan largely resisted such forces, clinging to relationship-based institutions that seemed, at least to outsiders, hopelessly anachronistic in an era of increasing market integration. To understand this recent history, I explore the domestic politics of Japan but then go further. I highlight an external factor that has, until now, been ignored—Japan's political and economic ties with East Asia—to help explain the remarkable continuity of the Japanese political economy during the 1990s, as well as its more recent, and still tentative, movement in a new direction. Voters helped shape this new direction in 2001 to 2006 when they rallied behind the economic reforms of Prime Minister Koizumi Jun'ichiro, and again in 2009 when they endorsed the insurgent campaign of the Democratic Party of Japan (DPJ), which wrested political control from the Liberal Democratic Party (LDP) after more than a half century of nearly uninterrupted hegemony. Although the DPJ campaigned against the market liberalism of the Koizumi wing of the LDP, it also pursued pro-consumer policies that could reduce the economy's reliance on export-led manufacturing. This represents a break from tradition.

Explaining Japan's Inertia

Scholars have used three main approaches to explain Japan's stubborn resistance to change in the 1990s. The first one emphasizes incentives. Japanese economic actors (producers and consumers alike), and thus policymakers as well, did not face a crisis severe enough to cause them to abandon longstanding patterns of behavior. The macroeconomy may have been weak, but it was not so weak that it kept Japan from "muddling through" in the 1990s. As Lincoln (2001, 69) asks rhetorically, "Unless and until a broader segment of the population feels economically inconvenienced, why change?"

The second approach focuses on "vested interests" who are predisposed to support the status quo: conservative politicians in the ruling LDP, entrenched bureaucrats in antireform ministries, and weak, generally inefficient industries in the private sector.[2] Japan's policy-making apparatus,

---

2. See also Katz (1998) and George Mulgan (2002).

according to Sheard (2007, 7), is characterized by "dysfunctionality," because it privileges these opponents of reform and thus stifles initiatives for change.

The third approach highlights the overriding force of ideas, norms, and values, suggesting that Japanese political actors are unable to detach themselves from institutions with which they identify. Since those actors regard the political economy of Japan as culturally unique, they are disinclined to abandon it, no matter how poorly it performs, in favor of a model that is viewed as alien (or Western). Japan, according to Lee (2005, 3), "is now in a paradigmatic crisis, a crisis in the beliefs held by many Japanese about their own political-economic system, and is in need of finding an alternative paradigm that the people can accept—a process that inevitably takes a long time."

All of these explanations fall short—indeed, they are overwhelmed by a set of empirical facts that, added together, suggest a rather different causal analysis.

With respect to the first approach, for example, we know that real economic growth dropped precipitously in the early 1990s, from the 5 percent per year average that had prevailed in the late 1980s to less than 1 percent in 1992 and 1993, and barely 1 percent in 1994. The Tokyo stock exchange lost more than 65 percent of its value, with the Nikkei index falling from above thirty thousand in late 1989 to about ten thousand in 1992. This added up to a profound economic shock. Yet Japan shunned change during the 1990s, even as its previously robust economy skidded to a near halt.

With respect to the second approach, we know that vested interests were on the defensive inside Japan throughout the 1990s. The LDP was toppled from power in 1993 and had to rely on other parties to cobble together a majority in the Lower House beginning in 1994. Bureaucrats were suddenly facing criticism from the media and the public, which blamed them not only for a growing number of scandals but, more critically, for the substandard performance of the economy in general. And weak firms in inefficient industries began going bankrupt. Given that they had to devote so much energy to merely surviving in a hostile political and economic environment, it seems highly unlikely that "vested interests" alone could have done what was required to defend the status quo.

Finally, regarding the third approach, we know that a vigorous debate has raged inside Japan over the structure of the political economy. Critics, especially outsiders, have complained that the close ties between government and business elites, as well as the ties between firms in corporate groups or *keiretsu* and the ties between managers and lifetime employees within firms, are both economically corrosive and politically exclusionary. Nonetheless, despite the lack of a broad consensus in favor of the status quo, the institutions of the Japanese political economy survived largely intact throughout the 1990s.

There are also analytical problems with these explanations. One is that they do not appear to grasp the underlying dynamics of power in Japan (a problem I discuss in the first chapter). But another problem may be even more serious: the conventional explanations consider Japan in isolation and overlook the impact of external factors (both challenges and opportunities) on the domestic environment. My own approach views the Japanese political economy in the context of globalization, which in the 1990s was beginning to exert extraordinary pressure—what Pempel (1999) called "structural *gaiatsu*" (pressure)—on Japan's relationship-based institutions; and in the context of regionalization, which served at the same time as a kind of relief valve, reducing the structural pressure on those institutions.

In this book, I argue that Japanese bureaucratic and business elites avoided, or more precisely forestalled, change in the domestic political economy by regionalizing Japan's core networks of political and economic exchange. They were able to buy themselves some time, in the face of global market and political forces, by extending into East Asia the administrative and production networks that had come to dominate Japan's political economy.[3] For most of the 1990s, the region grew rapidly as an increasingly integrated but hierarchical group, a group of what Japanese diplomats and economists came to call "flying geese." The "lead goose" or most developed economy, Japan, supplied the capital, technology, and even developmental norms to second-tier geese such as Singapore and South Korea, which in turn supplied capital and technology to third-tier geese such as Thailand, Malaysia, and the Philippines, which in turn supplied capital and technology to fourth-tier geese such as Indonesia and coastal China, and so on down a V-shaped line. This informal regional order was, however, far from a self-contained trading bloc. Although most of the capital, technology, and norms that fueled this order originated in Japan, a large share of its finished goods ended up as exports destined for Western markets, especially in the United States.

Regionalization, in sum, trumped globalization—but only for a while. In the late 1990s, two things happened: a fiscal crisis spread like wildfire through the region, undermining the central position of Japanese elites in East Asia; at the same time, China emerged from its role as laggard goose to become an economic dynamo, challenging Japan for regional hegemony and helping to topple the vertically layered, "flying geese" pattern of regional development. It was then, in the late 1990s and early part of the new

3. Unless identified otherwise, "East Asia" means China, the four Asian newly industrializing economies, or NIEs (Hong Kong, Singapore, South Korea, Taiwan), and the four core members of the Association of Southeast Asian Nations, or ASEAN (Thailand, Malaysia, Indonesia, and the Philippines).

millennium, that regionalization began to lose its ability to act as a buffer for domestic networks under attack from global market and political forces.

I am not the first to emphasize the effect of external factors on the political economy of Japan in the 1990s; Pempel (1998), Tiberghien (2007), and Schoppa (2006) have already done so. On the surface, Schoppa's argument seems to resonate most closely with mine. He suggests that domestic actors (including multinational corporations) helped bring about a decade of remarkable continuity in Japan by exercising "exit" (literally abandoning the country) rather than "voice" (engaging in political action to bring about change). This is a useful characterization, but ultimately reflects an excessively narrow and territorial interpretation of the boundaries between what is "domestic" and what is "foreign." In regionalizing the Japanese political economy, domestic elites did not "exit" Japan; they took it with them. That is, they transplanted homegrown institutions and relational structures into the rest of Asia, where they had come to expand operations.

The common and problematic denominator in previous efforts to consider the impact of external forces on Japan is a tendency to equate such forces with globalization, ignoring the sometimes countervailing force of regionalization. As a result, these efforts have failed to accurately pinpoint the timing of continuity and change in the Japanese political economy. Unless we distinguish regionalization from globalization, we cannot adequately understand how the status quo persisted in Japan, in the face of global pressure for change, until early in the new millennium.

My argument, then, challenges conventional views of both globalization and regionalization—two important concepts that deserve closer scrutiny.

Understanding Globalization

I define globalization as (1) the increasingly unconstrained, cross-border flow of capital, labor, technology, and information that tends to integrate otherwise disparate communities; and (2) the spread of U.S.-inspired neoliberal ideology and U.S.-led neoliberal institutions ("Americanization")—the hegemonic force behind such otherwise "neutral" flows. Globalization is, without a doubt, a powerful force in the international system. But it is described too often, too glibly, as *overpowering*, capable of wiping away national differences and compelling illiberal states to adopt market-oriented policies—or suffer the consequences of nonconvergence. States, according to this view, are losing their *capacity* as agents of history that can make things happen or stop things from happening.[4] Ohmae (1990, x–xi), a Japanese pundit, tells us for

---

4. Fukuyama (2004) distinguishes between state capacity (the ability to coherently make and carry out policy; i.e., its effectiveness) and scope (the range of activities; i.e., its size).

example that globalization "has swallowed most consumers and corporations, made traditional national borders almost disappear, and pushed bureaucrats, politicians, and the military toward the status of declining industries." More sober scholars, such as Strange (1996), Kurzer (1991), and Cerny (1995), have largely embraced this view, if not the apocalyptic prose. They note that high capital mobility can dramatically undermine a state's ability to effectively use macroeconomic policies to stimulate consumption or investment or to use distributional policies to protect the weak.

In truth, though, the state is far from powerless in the face of globalization. One obvious example is China's communist state, which has managed to maintain a very tight grip on society during more than three decades of economic liberalization. Whether it follows the lead of bureaucrats (Vogel 1996), interest groups (Garrett 1998), "political entrepreneurs" (Tiberghien 2007), or party cadre, the state can mediate, if not completely deflect, global market forces, using them selectively to reshape but not necessarily transform the domestic environment. Weiss (1998) goes so far as to suggest that a state, depending on its own capacity vis-à-vis nonstate actors at home, may actually be able to "reconstitute" and thereby strengthen itself by playing a critical role in the globalization process. It can, for example, cooperate with other states to forge regional trade and development agreements, or forge ties with its own multinational corporations to establish successful operations overseas: "Far from relinquishing their distinctive goals and identity, states are increasingly using collaborative power arrangements to create more real control over their economies (and indeed over security). As such these new coalitions should be seen as gambits for augmenting rather than shedding state capacity" (209).

I generally endorse Weiss's perspective, though with one important exception. In arguing that states can broaden their authority by cooperating with neighbors or with home-based firms looking to invest in neighbors, she makes the common mistake of conflating globalization and regionalization. These often are different phenomena, different processes. Only a global superpower such as the United States can dramatically shape the process of globalization. Smaller powers that enjoy some measure of regional hegemony, such as Japan and Germany in the 1990s, can guide or at least influence the process of regionalization.

Understanding Regionalization

Weiss is not alone. Many scholars, including economists such as Lawrence (1996) and political scientists such as Milner (1997) and Mattli (1999), view regionalization, like globalization, as a process driven almost exclusively by market forces, but operating on a geographically smaller scale. This characterization, however, is too narrow. One need only consider the diversity of regional orders in the world today to recognize that, in the case of regionalization and regionalism, political power also matters, and that it may matter as much as economic efficiency. If it is sufficiently powerful, a regional hegemon can influence the terms of social exchange and make the region look more or less like the hegemon itself. This helps explain why the European Union—the mother of all regional orders—emerged as one that subsidizes farmers, distributes funds to poorer regions, and protects the "fundamental rights of workers" even as it liberalizes trade; or why its commission in Brussels had, as of 2007, a staff of more than twenty-three thousand civil servants; or why Turkey, a mostly Muslim nation that has petitioned for many years to be a member of this group of predominantly Christian nations, still does not belong. France and Germany, as co-hegemons in Europe, played a critical role in shaping these outcomes.

For the same reason, a U.S.-led NAFTA (North American Free Trade Agreement) is focused on promoting trade and capital flows, not a "social market," and lacks a bureaucratic infrastructure. And a Japan-led Asia was, until recently, organized around informal business and administrative networks—clearly a regional alternative to "Americanization."

Power thus creates the terms of exchange, which in turn produces collective identity. Regionalization must be understood not only as the cross-border flow of capital, labor, technology, and information within a geographical area but also as the consolidation of social ties that build up over time within that area. This definition is influenced heavily by Deutsch (1981), who argues that a region is historically and epistemologically constructed through social interaction: "It is the multiplicity of common cultural elements and links of horizontal and vertical communication and potential understanding that makes a region, somewhat as—on a smaller but more intensive scale—such links often including language, religion, or way of life, can make a people."

This, however, does not mean that a region is a fixed or static entity, a "bloc" in a geographically fractured world. Although it is shaped largely by interactions between its constituents (private actors such as business executives and labor leaders, as well as public actors such as state officials), it also is reshaped by interactions with the outside world. As Katzenstein (2005) notes, global forces penetrate regions that are more or less "porous."

Regionalization versus Globalization

Not only are regionalization and globalization different phenomena, but the former may be, for certain actors in the international system, preferable to the latter. In the case of Europe, Schmidt (2002, 45) describes the political impulse creating the single market and monetary union as "a regional foil to globalization," and as "a countervailing force in its own right." The former thus can serve as a shield to protect domestic actors from the latter. Katzenstein and Shiraishi (1997, 344) believe states may sometimes pursue regional integration "to regain some measure of political control over processes of economic globalization that have curtailed national policy instruments." Hurrell (1995, 346) has a slightly different explanation for the same result. National policymakers, he suggests, may choose regional rather than more broadly multilateral schemes for economic integration because "commonality of culture, history, homogeneity of social systems and values, convergence of political and security interests, and the character of domestic coalitions all make it far easier to accept the necessary levels of intrusive management, in terms of standard setting and regulation, and even more of enforcement and effective implementation."

Likewise, Nesadurai (2002) finds that firms headquartered in a particular region may resist globalization, at least temporarily, as they pursue a "developmental regionalism" that gives them a short-term advantage vis-à-vis extra-regional and usually larger competitors. Finally, neo-Marxist scholars such as Amin (1999) and Mittelman (2000) have encouraged third world states to embrace regionalization (and its institutional counterpart, "transformative regionalism") as an antidote to globalization, a way to mitigate its ill effects, especially its power to polarize and thus destabilize societies.

Some Third World leaders seem to have followed this advice. In October 2003, Luiz Inacio ("Lula") da Silva and Néstor Kirchner, the left-leaning presidents of Brazil and Argentina respectively, unveiled a joint economic agenda that they called the Buenos Aires Consensus to draw a sharp contrast with the neoliberal agenda, the Washington Consensus, promoted by the United States and the International Monetary Fund (IMF). They pledged to strengthen Mercosur, a trade agreement for South America, while resisting efforts by the United States to expand the multilateral General Agreement on Services to include the privatization of some public services. Likewise, in a January 2004 speech to the Economic Cooperation Organization, which includes ten Muslim states in the Middle East and Central Asia, President Mohammed Khatami of Iran embraced regionalization as "a crucial mechanism for preserving national identity in the face of globalization" (*Iran Daily,* January 27, 2004).

Regionalization, then, can take the form of rearguard action, a defensive response to global market and political forces for change. However, this response is effective only under limited conditions, and only for a limited time. I am not as sanguine as Amin and Mittelman about the ability of smaller states in the developing world to successfully carry out rearguard regionalization. This option may be available only to regional powers, such as Brazil in South America, Nigeria in West Africa, and of course, Japan in East Asia.

As I will demonstrate, Japanese elites did occupy a central position in the region's social networks during most of the 1990s, and thus were able to use the protective buffer of regionalization to thwart the otherwise overwhelming force of globalization. But as Japan's economy grew weaker and China's grew stronger, this status quo could not hold. By the dawn of the twenty-first century, Japan's political economy began to undergo significant change. For better or worse, global forces battered once-solid domestic institutions. One could argue that this was a step in the right direction, a triumph of pluralism: Networks that for years had privileged dominant insiders began to unravel, allowing previously marginal political actors in Japan to enjoy more authority. But one could also argue that this was a step in the wrong direction, that the unraveling of those networks was akin to the thinning of the ozone layer. Indeed, more than ever before, Japan became exposed to the ultra-violet rays of the global marketplace. This became painfully evident in 2008, when a financial crisis that began in the United States hit Japan as hard as any other economy in the world. Exports eroded, industrial production plummeted, and the Japanese economy experienced its most severe recession in decades. This book documents the continuity and the change in Japan's political economy, and offers a plausible explanation for both.

PART ONE
Baseline

1 Social Networks and the Power They Produce

Why on earth would Japanese elites in the 1990s want to extend the shelf life of an economic system that yielded little or no growth? In this chapter, I introduce a sociological model of network politics to begin answering that question, arguing that Japanese elites sought to preserve relational structures that privileged them. In the process of answering that question, I engage overlapping debates in three fields: political economy (technological and economic development); comparative politics (institutional change); and international relations (power and dependency in a region of the world). My model is driven primarily by two concepts: selective relationalism, the extent to which social relationships dictate the character and conduct of political and economic exchange; and positional power, the relative access to resources, including capital, labor, and technology, but especially information, enjoyed by elites in an exchange network. And these concepts, in turn, are populated by two important actors: networks and elites. I proceed below by briefly introducing the actors in the cast and then, in much more detail, explaining the concepts before finally summarizing how we can apply these concepts to the case study.

The Cast

A network is a relational structure composed of individuals or groups of individuals. It is an intermediate form of social organization, somewhere between the shapeless anarchy of the market and the centralized hierarchy of the state or the firm. Simple or complex, highly plastic or highly cohesive, it always has the following characteristics:

1. *Three or more connection points.* This means that a network tie, unlike a dyadic relationship, affords additional linkages beyond an immediate nexus.

2. *Relative reciprocity.* This means that each party in the network is able to gain access to another party, although in most cases not instantly and not without passing through other nodes; and this suggests a form of interdependency, or mutual hostage-taking, but does not imply "equality."

3. *Longevity.* This means that relations among network members are not ad hoc; they endure for relatively long periods. A network is thus not equivalent to a "coalition," which represents an always fragile alliance or marriage of convenience between otherwise competing interests, such as political parties or corporations. Instead, it is an organic unit —akin to a nervous system—that facilitates the internal movement of resources such as information.[1]

An elite is an individual or group of individuals occupying a central position in a network of relationships, allowing he, she, or it to more easily gain access to resources in the network. Put differently, elites enjoy a measure of structural autonomy because they are less dependent on other individuals or groups; conversely, of course, those other individuals or groups are more dependent on elites. Depending on the structure of the network (open or closed), elites may be able to exploit this relative autonomy by behaving as oligopolists if not monopolists, limiting if not completely controlling access to resources in the network. The influence or privilege held by elites comes directly from these socio-institutional ties, and only indirectly from other factors such as class, race or gender.[2]

The Concepts

Selective Relationalism

This is, I concede, a neologism constructed for want of anything better.[3] Although far more concrete, it is similar in meaning to "embeddedness," a term coined by Mark Granovetter in 1985 that has since lost much of its original meaning.[4] Granovetter argues that all transactions, even those in modern, highly marketized economies, are—to some degree—embedded in and

---

1. My definition draws on the exchange theory of Emerson (1972) and the communications theory of Deutsch (1963).

2. See Field and Higley (1980) or, for a more rigorous and technical definition, see Laumann and Knoke (1986). Sonoda (1999) applies a definition of this kind to the Japanese case.

3. Kumon (1982) uses a Japanese term, "*aidagara-shugi,*" which he translates as "contextualism," to mean something quite similar.

4. Scholars now use this term more often to explain why institutions tend to vary from one setting to the next. Hollingsworth and Boyer (1997), for example, suggest that institutions are embedded in different "social systems of production."

thus constrained by ongoing social relations.[5] There is a simple, intuitive logic at work here: we generally prefer to do business with those we trust. "Better than the statement that someone is known to be reliable is information from a trusted informant that he has dealt with that individual and found him so. Even better is information from one's own past dealings with that person" (Granovetter 1985, 490).

In Granovetter's analytic, the least embedded transactions are those envisioned in the "undersocialized" world of neoclassical economic theory—spot market deals in which buyer and seller meet only at the point of sale and communicate merely on the basis of price. At the opposite end of the spectrum, the most embedded transactions take place within a single institution, such as the vertically integrated firm, and thus bypass the market altogether. This, according to Granovetter, is the "oversocialized" world envisioned by Williamson (1975) and other neoinstitutional economists. It seems clear that most transactions take place somewhere between these two extremes in quasi markets or quasi hierarchies; in fact, they often take place in that large gray area that includes various forms of networking.

There is, however, a key ingredient missing from Granovetter's otherwise brilliant analysis: human volition or intention. In his generally sympathetic critique of the "embeddedness" approach to analyzing markets, Fligstein (1996, 657) refers to this missing ingredient as "agency":

> The major limitation . . . is that networks are sparse social structures, and it is difficult to see how they can account for what we observe in markets. Put another way, they contain no model of politics, no social preconditions for the economic institutions in question, and no way to conceptualize how actors construct their worlds.

In other words, the "embeddedness" approach tends to assume an a priori level of sociability that does not depend on human agency. In reality, of course, actors embed themselves in relationships with some but not all of the actors with whom they interact. Indeed, they often choose quite intentionally to exclude others by *not* forging ties with them. This is why I stress here that relationalism is selective; actors, operating within an institutionally bounded context, make choices about the kinds of relationships they are willing to enter into.

When they forge mutually reinforcing ties with others and thereby create stable network structures, actors are behaving rationally; they are trying to

5. Although heavily influenced by the "substantivist" (Polanyi 1944) and "moral economy" (Thompson 1971) schools of economic history, Granovetter distinguishes himself from them in this manner. That is, he does not envision a radical break between the level of embeddedness in premarket economies and modern, market economies.

reduce the risks associated with political and economic exchange. In particular, actors seek to protect themselves from opportunism on the part of exchange partners who are looking after their own best interests. Strong ties are more effective than weak ties in reducing the costs of gathering information about prospective partners and in monitoring contracts with existing partners.

On the other hand, strong ties may generate costs as they become exclusionary, cutting insiders off from outside sources of information. This is what Granovetter (1973 and 1974) found when he asked working people how they learned about their current jobs. Information about job opportunities rarely came from a close friend or, in other words, a source with whom the respondent shared a strong tie. When it came from another person, such information tended to come instead from a friend of a friend, or a more distant acquaintance; that is, it tended to come from someone with whom the job seeker shared only a weak tie. Granovetter's logic is deceptively simple: members of very cohesive networks tend to already know what other members know.

Burt (1992) extends this logic by introducing the concept of "structural holes," which he defines as "a relationship of non-redundancy" between two actors/nodes in any human network. Nonredundancy implies both disconnection and opportunity. Two actors/nodes either have no direct contact with one another or, more often, they have contacts that do not include the other. A very dense network, one with few structural holes, yields fewer information benefits than a sparse network, according to Burt (17). "Because the relations between people in that network are strong, each person knows what the other people know and all will discover the same opportunities at the same time."

On a micro level, then, exchange networks seem to reduce transaction costs and raise opportunity costs as they grow more and more cohesive. At this level of analysis, however, we cannot determine—a priori—the cost-benefit ratio of any particular network.

A micro-analysis of selective relationalism can be easily extended to the macro level, and political economies can be evaluated along a continuum. Some political economies are thus only "thinly" relational not only because they operate more on the basis of political opportunism and arm's-length transactions, rather than reciprocity, but also—more fundamentally—because individual actors in those political economies, responding to structural incentives created by institutions of their own making, are less inclined to forge long-lasting social ties. In today's United States, for example, people move relatively freely from job to job, from city to city, and often do not plant themselves deeply in a community. They often seem to eschew longstanding relationships. Other political economies, meanwhile, are more embedded or "thickly" relational.[6] In Japan, for example, people tend to stay put for longer periods of time in employment and thus in residence; long-term, reciprocal relations or networks form the foundation of business and politics.

Jeffrey Broadbent, a sociologist, conducted comparative research in the 1990s on Japan and the United States that appears to confirm my argument with respect to political exchange. In a survey of 122 Japanese organizations and 117 U.S. organizations that seek to influence labor policy in their respective polities, Broadbent (2000, 14) found that Japanese groups expected reciprocity from others in the labor policy domain far more often than U.S. groups did:

> Many organizations [in Japan] are densely woven together by bonds of (expected) reciprocal obligations. Fully 75 organizations out of 122 (61 percent) acknowledge and mutually confirm such ties with others. These bonds interweave the labor sector as extensively as in the United States, if not more so. But they also weave together the business sector, and connect the state to both business and labor.

To evaluate my argument with respect to economic exchange, we can use proxies to measure the level of relationalism. For example, in a 1992 survey of firms manufacturing finished goods in Japan, Europe, and the United States, the Mitsubishi Research Institute asked about the strength or weakness of interfirm ties. It found that a) Japanese firms engaged in more "repeat" transactions with parts suppliers (76 percent of respondents in Japan, 64 percent in Europe, and 37 percent in the United States reported that most of their transactions were carried out on a long-term or "repetitive" basis); b) Japanese firms invested more heavily in subcontractors (96 percent of respondents in Japan, 77 percent in Europe, and 16 percent in the United States reported they owned shares in one of more of their suppliers); and c) Japanese firms used personnel exchange more intensively (88 percent of respondents in Japan, 22 percent in Europe, and 6 percent in the United States reported that they dispatch officers to work alongside their parts suppliers).[7] Likewise, one could consider intrafirm ties. Kato (1998), using OECD data, finds that the average length of employment is significantly greater in Japan than in most European countries (with the exception

6. The distinction here between "thin" and "thick" relationalism has an interesting parallel in the distinction made by some rational choice theorists between "thin" and "thick" rationality. The latter is rationality embedded in social norms and values. See, for example, Ferejohn (1991).

7. These findings from Mitsubishi Research Institute ("Purchasing Behavior of Major Producers of Finished Products in Japan, the United States, and Europe") are reported in Tsuru (1995, 68–70.)

of Germany), and almost double that in the United States. Japan would certainly come out on the "high" end of almost any comparative study of relationalism.[8]

Observing this kind of cross-national variation, some scholars have attempted to develop a general theory of "social capital"—the largely horizontal networks of trust and reciprocity that they claim enrich communities.[9] Putnam (1993) argues that social capital makes government institutions more effective by encouraging civic engagement, while Fukuyama (1995) suggests that it does much the same for economies by unleashing entrepreneurial energies. This approach would be highly useful for our analysis were it not for two significant problems. One is that we never really learn the origin of social capital. In most formulations, it appears to be an exogenous variable that emerges automatically, effortlessly from the deep, dark recesses of "culture."[10] The second problem is that scholars too often present social capital as an immutable public good, when in fact—as Mauricio Rubio (1997) has shown in his analysis of Colombia—it also can assume a "perverse" form characterized by collusion, rent-seeking, and even criminally syndicalist behavior. To overcome these problems, we need an analytical model that demonstrates a) how networks of cooperation, which yield positive externalities, actually come to exist; and b) how such networks may degenerate over time into exclusionary networks for private gain.

At the outset, we should recognize that a society's institutional characteristics are always a function of contested politics, not "culture" (defined exogenously), and are thus subject to change. For example, as Gourevitch (1996, 239–40) notes, the political economy of the United States at the end of the nineteenth century resembled postwar Japan and postwar Germany much more than it does today. Although in a nod to Albert (1991), he calls it more "Nippo-Rhenish," we might instead simply say it was more "relational." In those days, the U.S. government collaborated with business to build railroads and canals and to promote large, export-oriented industries. Giant banks and industrial firms organized themselves into oligopolistic "trusts" or "combines." Craft unions served the interests of skilled and thus elite employees, but did not—or could not—organize rank-and-file workers across an entire industry.

To understand how this institutional pattern of selective relationalism got

---

8. It is, I concede, far more difficult to quantitatively measure relationalism along the state-industry nexus. But qualitative studies invariably show that Japan scores "high" on this indicator as well.

9. The concept was developed first by Coleman (1988).

10. To his credit, Putnam (1993) does try to tackle this question. His answer, however, only pushes the question back in time. All the way back, in fact, to the twelfth century, when the division he finds between northern and southern Italy was still evident.

started in the United States, we have to go all the way back to the quarter century following the Civil War, when—as Skocpol (1998, 29–30) notes—large numbers of translocal civic associations were launched: "American association builders were determined to link North and South, just as much as East and West. They thought in terms of national unity and regeneration, and worked hard to make this vision real." And in the devastation following the Civil War, the victorious coalition of Northern industrialists and small-scale, family farmers in the West pursued an ambiguous reconstruction program—much less radical than some Republican proposals for land reform, but obviously more progressive than the system of slavery that had previously existed. At the same time, manufacturing interests secured for themselves long-coveted protective tariffs, but also persuaded the state to compensate their allies, the Western farmers, by opening public domain via the Homestead Act of 1862. This was the genesis of what Moore (1966) has called "democratic capitalism" in the United States.

The U.S. case suggests that elites can create "social capital" by investing in relationships. That is, they build networks of cooperation by choosing to eschew short-run, interest-maximizing behavior and instead forging ties with others outside their immediate zone of interest.[11] These may take the form of broader, corporatist alliances—or what Olson (1982) has called "encompassing coalitions"—or they may take the form of narrower, intraelite groupings. In the case of the latter, elite insiders may use a portion of the gains they capture from cooperation to make side payments designed to compensate nonelite outsiders. These forms of credible commitment to cooperative behavior have a "demonstration effect"; others in society, persuaded that their trust will not be violated, return the favor by committing themselves to cooperative behavior. Miller (1992, 232) expresses this view of social capital–creating elites in the context of management-labor relations in the modern firm. Managers, he writes, "must create appropriate psychological expectations, pay the 'start-up costs' for appropriate cooperation norms, kick-start the secondary norms that will be the primary enforcers of cooperation norms, and create institutions that will credibly commit the leader to the non-exploitation of employee ownership rights in the organization."

This helps explain the origin of selective relationalism in a given political economy, but does not explain why or how these relational networks of cooperation unravel. To do this, it might help to return briefly to the U.S. case. In the late nineteenth century, network capitalism in the United States (se-

---

11. This begs a further question, which will not be pursued in detail here. That is, why do elites choose to invest in relationships/build social capital in the first place? One suspects they do so in response to an exogenous shock, such as a domestic or international crisis that threatens to erode the central positions they occupy in exchange networks.

lective relationalism on a macro level) spawned impressive economic growth, but—as it became ever more exclusionary and collusive—eventually also triggered political discontent. By the Progressive Era of the early 1900s, farmers, consumers, workers, and others mobilized to break up the powerful trusts and protect their own interests through regulations on everything from food labeling to bank lending, from working hours to occupational safety. A different kind of system, one characterized more by arm's-length business transactions and adversarial relations between state and industry, one much closer to what we now view as the Anglo-American system of capitalism, began to emerge as a result of this political conflict.

It may be, as Olson (1982) asserts, that selective relationalism inevitably turns collusive in time. Indeed, relational structures created to overcome some collective action problem do seem to have a built-in incentive to survive beyond their usefulness to society. But is this always true? Furthermore, can we predict precisely or even vaguely when this will happen, or do we only know post hoc, when we see it with our own eyes? In other words, Olson's concept—applied broadly, or universally—seems frustratingly difficult to operationalize. However, applied to the specific case of development or industrialization, it does in fact provide some explanatory reach. At the most superficial level, we can see that the slower growth experienced by mature, developed economies denies elite insiders the opportunity to use side payments to compensate outsiders. And at a more fundamental level, we should recognize that the costs of selective relationalism will begin to outweigh the benefits once industrializing economies have reached the global technological frontier, once—that is—they have achieved "catch-up" development by adopting all there is to adopt from the global supply of existing technology. Defending this assertion requires a brief excursion into economic theory.

In separate critiques of neoclassical economic analysis, Hirschman (1958) and Murakami (1992) distinguish between mature or developed markets, which they believe the theory is quite adept at modeling, and developing markets, which they contend the theory is woefully unable to comprehend. Hirschman focuses on what I call "proto-development," an early phase in the process when capital markets are characterized by problems of contract enforcement and product markets are afflicted with imperfect or incomplete information—the makings, in short, for a classic prisoners' dilemma. In this environment, risk-taking activities are impeded, Hirschman writes (26), "not by physical obstacles and scarcities, but by imperfections in the decision-making process," meaning institutions. Undeveloped economies become swamped by uncertainty due to a dizzying array of "unexploited opportunities." To overcome these market failures, the state can provide an important, even catalytic, function. It can virtually jump-start a stalled economy, provide the needed spark, by building stable, growth-oriented institutions.[12]

Murakami focuses on a later phase of the process—what I call "dynamic development"—in which firms adopt successively more sophisticated technology from the global pool of established know-how, thereby achieving declining long-run average costs (LRAC) or, in other words, increasing returns. Neoclassical theory, he argues, cannot grasp this process because it largely ignores the variable of technological change.[13] It assumes that all markets are like those in mature or developed economies, where firms *do* face increasing LRAC, and thus diminishing returns (which create the upward sloping supply curve drawn in modern economics textbooks), because they operate at the global technological frontier and thus cannot simply adopt existing know-how.

For developing economies, the trick is not merely how to launch this dynamic process of technological absorption but how to sustain it. That is because development spawns social instability and economic inefficiency as firms race to invest larger and larger sums in industries characterized by declining LRAC. If left unchecked, this "investment race," which Japanese bureaucrats used to call "excess competition," will lead first to excess capacity and later to bankruptcies and unemployment, both of which impose deadweight losses on a developing economy.[14] In the end, this "excess competition" is likely to produce monopolistic or highly oligopolistic industries.[15]

Murakami, echoing the views of Johnson (1982), Amsden (1989), and Wade (1990), recommends that autonomous, technocratic regimes in developing economies embrace an aggressive program of state-centered "developmentalism" (*kaihatsu-shugi*), nurturing and guiding innovating industries and, above all, managing the "investment race" by—for example—authorizing temporary cartels. It is here, where he joins the Weberian campaign to "bring

12. Aoki, Murdoch, and Okuno-Fujiwara (1996, 9) make a similar point when they assert that "the government's role is to facilitate the development of private sector institutions that can overcome these [coordination] failures."

13. This remains largely true despite valiant efforts by "new growth theorists" such as Romer (1986) and Lucas (1988). New growth theory has sought to endogenize the variable of technological change. Unfortunately, however, this approach is still not very useful in that it is highly abstract and comes with a number of strong assumptions designed to improve its mathematical tractability.

14. In neoclassical economic theory, the market autonomously and automatically reallocates surplus factors of production to their highest and best use. In reality, though, physical and human capital represent sunk costs that are not so easily reallocated.

15. Western economists have ridiculed the concept of "excess competition," an oxymoron in neoclassic theory. They are certainly correct that, for a fully developed economy, competition nearly always yields social benefits by reallocating resources to their most efficient use. However, they often do not seem to appreciate the fact that, for a developing economy in which firms are able to achieving declining LRAC by adopting successively more sophisticated technology, this "investment race" or "excess competition" may indeed generate net costs.

the state back in," that Murakami slips. He fails to recognize that collective action problems are often exacerbated, if not created themselves, by what can only be called "hierarchical" (as opposed to market) failure. Institutions, including the state, are neither omniscient nor selfless; rather, they are the products of human beings, reflecting the same mix of good and bad intentions as the actors who helped create and maintain them. Indeed, a truly autonomous state is one that is free to pursue its own interests, which may include power, plunder, prestige, or a combination of these, and such interests are unlikely to be as broadly inclusive as excitable speechwriters imply when they use the term "public (or national) interest." For this reason, Granovetter advises us not to lurch from neoclassical theory's undersocialized conception of economic action to the oversocialized conception used by many state-centered political scientists and neoinstitutional economists.

If neither the market nor Leviathan is the driving force behind long-run economic development, then what is? I argue that mutually reinforcing linkages—"synapses"—between the principal socioeconomic actors in a developing economy are needed to sustain the virtuous cycle by which successively more sophisticated technology is adopted and capital is accumulated. In other words, what is needed is relationalism—a thick web of non- (or hyper-) market ties between business and government, between upstream and downstream firms, and between labor and management. At the macro level, ties between government and business foster a stable environment for firms to invest, step-by-incremental step, in more advanced technologies.[16] Ties between and within firms combine the benefits of internalization (reduced transaction costs through constant information exchange) with the benefits of marketization (reduced governance costs). In particular, these micro-level ties encourage the rapid diffusion of existing technology—at least within the socially constructed networks. If successful, relationalism sustains growth in a developing economy and creates a relatively even distribution of the benefits of growth.

But selective relationalism, as I hinted earlier, can easily outlive its utility. Although it facilitates the adoption of existing know-how, it tends in the long run to inhibit more radical ("breakthrough") or basic ("broadly applicable") innovation. At the micro level, highly cohesive network structures—especially ones characterized by hierarchy—become dense, inward-looking, and thus resistant to new, external stimuli.[17] In his study of technological devel-

---

16. State-industry cooperation, as neoclassical economists note correctly, often leads to rent-seeking activities. But this is not a predetermined outcome; when state officials are motivated by a sense of national urgency or crisis, they are likely to refrain from paying rents.

17. Silicon Valley is quite different—at least according to Saxenian (1994) and Micklethwait (1997). The subregion is organized around horizontal exchange networks that are decentralized, outward-looking, and highly fluid. Thus, it was able to quickly retool during the economic slowdown of the early 1980s—unlike the Route 128 technology corridor west of Boston.

opment inside an industrial network, Håkansson (1987, 92) describes a "lock-in" effect that blocks change, especially "structural" as opposed to incremental change: "If a product is changed, other relationships might also have to be changed. This can only be done at a certain cost. Thus, when dependencies have to be altered, this always entails the cost of such a change."

Uzzi (1996, 675), who examined exchange networks within the apparel industry in New York City, found that firms characterized by "embeddedness" (strong, mutually reinforcing ties with other firms) outperformed other, more independent firms—but only up to a "threshold point," when the positive effect suddenly turned sharply negative:

> A crucial implication is that embedded networks offer a competitive form of organizing but possess their own pitfalls because an actor's adaptive capacity is determined by a web of ties, some of which lie beyond his or her direct influence. Thus a firm's structural location, although not fully constraining, can significantly blind it to the important effects of the larger network structure, namely its contacts. (694)

At the macro level, we can define the "threshold point" as the time when a developing economy finally achieves technological "catch-up."[18] At that point, the costs of cohesive network structures—manifested in collusive or rent-seeking behavior and extremely rigid markets—begin to outweigh the benefits. The bottom line is this: what worked so well in the past suddenly becomes dysfunctional.

Positional Power

Positional power, accrued by centrally placed actors in structurally cohesive networks, is the second key concept in the model of network politics presented here. It, too, is a new (or at least revamped) formulation, and thus warrants some explication.

Not so long ago, scholars regarded power as an individual attribute, a stock of capabilities. In the field of international relations, for example, structural realists such as Waltz (1979) defined power as the aggregate military and economic resources—measured in warheads and industrial output—that individual nation-states possess and thus can mobilize in their defense. Today, however, power is viewed more often as a relational attribute. Thus, we talk about the power one has in relation to, or over, another; the power to "compel another actor to do what it would not otherwise do." Baldwin (1980) defends this definition artfully, citing the example of a per-

---

18. It makes more sense, though, to think of this as a moving target rather than a once-and-for-all destination. If an economy falls dramatically behind others in the adoption of state-of-the-art technology, it will find itself again in a period of "catch-up." I thank Kozo Yamamura for this insight.

son who threatens another with a gun and then utters the eerie cliché, "Your money or your life." If the robber's target is suicidal or places little value on his own life, the threat loses its coercive authority. Thus, an instrument of potential power becomes an instrument of actual power only when its coercive value is recognized by the ultimate target. In other words, power cannot be understood by reference to the presumed power-holder alone; it is a relational attribute.

Economists, typically agnostic about power, have begun to recognize that imperfect markets, and more specifically markets characterized by incomplete information, create opportunities for the exercise of power by one actor over another. This imbalance frequently emerges in a dyadic relationship, whether it is the implicit contract relationship between a principal (such as a stockholder) and an agent (such as a company's chief executive officer), or the explicit exchange relationship between a buyer and seller. "In isolation, knowledge is only productivity," notes Bartlett (1989, 101). "It becomes power only when other persons do not have it."

In neoinstitutional economic analysis, this kind of power is modeled through the concept of information asymmetry. North (1990, 186) tells us, for example, that

> not only does one party (sometimes the buyer and sometimes the seller) know more about the valued attribute than the other party, but that person may stand to gain by concealing that information, which takes us to the behavorial assumptions we use in economics. Following a strictly wealth-maximizing behavorial assumption, a party to an exchange will cheat, steal, and so on, when the payoff to such activity exceeds the value of the alternatives available to that person.

Thus, when information is unevenly distributed, those who have it can maximize the potential gains from trade at the expense of those who do not have it.[19]

These conceptions of "relational power" mark a significant improvement over earlier notions of power as a stock of capabilities. Unfortunately, though, they cling to the fiction that exchange, whether political or economic, involves only two actors. In fact, exchange is almost always nested in a social system, a network of opportunities and—if those opportunities are utilized—a network of exchange relationships.[20] Consider these scenarios

19. This simple insight is the basis for important work done by neoinstitutional economists on problems such as "adverse selection." See, for example, Akerlof (1970).

20. I concede that game theorists have tried to model these more complex exchange relationships by using "n-person games." These models, however, typically have produced multiple equilibria, which in turn have prompted analysts to impose ever more unrealistic assumptions (about, for example, the rationality of actors). In other words, the results are often disappointing. See Gerard Van der Laan and Xander Tieman, "Evolutionary Game Theory and the Modeling of Economic Behavior," in *De Economist* 146, no. 1 (1998): 59–89.

in buying a car: (1) after looking at two different vehicles from two different sellers, A opts to purchase the one from B rather than the one from C; and (2) A buys from B with the expectation of reselling it to C, who (in this scenario) does not own a car and is eager to purchase one. In both cases, A has engaged in an exchange relationship with B that clearly involves C. A's relationship with one is thus integrally connected to its relationship with the other. This "connection" is defined by Cook et al. (1983, 281) in the following way: "Two exchange relations between actors A-B and actors A-C are connected to form the minimal network B-A-C to the degree that exchange in one relation is contingent on exchange (or non-exchange) in the other relation."

This feature of exchange (that it is often contingent on, or embedded in, a larger network of relationships) makes possible the attribute I am calling "positional power." (Indeed, on a macro level, the likelihood that elites will possess positional power is positively correlated with the density of relational networks in any political economy.) For the sake of simplicity, assume that the network described above is indeed as minimal as suggested (that is, it includes only those three actors: A, B, and C), and assume further that B and C are linked only indirectly through A. In that network, A enjoys positional power or what Burt (1992) calls "structural autonomy." Under either scenario, A has alternatives that B and C do not have—*solely as a result of its position in the network structure.* Under Scenario 1, it is a monopsonist that can play the two sellers off against one another. Under scenario 2, it can inform B that his asking price is too high for C, the ultimate buyer, and then—after B relents—inform C that his offer is too low given B's initial price. If they wish to make a deal, B and C must go along with A; by virtue of their positions, they have no choice.[21]

The position an actor occupies in any network structure determines his power relative to others in that structure. If he commands a central position through which others must "pass" to gain access to resources within that network, then he enjoys positional power. In the words of Knoke (1990, 9), power

> emerges from [an actor's] prominence in networks where valued information and scarce resources are transferred from one actor to another. Positions are stratified according to the dependence of other positions on them for these es-

---

21. Hirschman (1970) counters that actors dissatisfied with market conditions almost always have two choices: they can "exit" (take their business elsewhere) or they can exercise "voice" (seek redress in the political arena). But under both of the scenarios above, the "exit" option is unavailable. There is no "there" to exit to. And what about "voice"? Hirschman himself (40) concedes that "voice" is a costly option, and that it relies on a given level of bargaining power. But it also relies on a given level of knowledge, which is exactly what B and C— under both scenarios—do not have.

sential resources. Not only the direct connections are important in determining positional power, but the indirect connections are critical because they comprise limits and opportunities for obtaining desired ends.

Emerson (1962), a sociologist, tried years ago to develop a network model for use in analyzing this kind of power. He began with an elegantly simple proposition: power is the inverse of dependence; that is, a particular actor's power is measured by the extent to which others in an exchange network rely on that actor to achieve outcomes, or—conversely—by the extent to which that actor can achieve outcomes without relying on others. This is similar to the concept of "substitutes" in consumer economics; one's power increases as the number of equally accessible but alternative paths ("substitutes") to a goal (utility) increase. Marsden (1983) refined this model further to show that centrally positioned actors may act as discriminating monopolists, as price-makers, restricting the flow of resources (including capital, labor, and technology, but especially information) and thereby increasing the value of resources under their control by "capitalizing on the fact that their trading partners lack valuable alternatives to an exchange relationship" (714).[22] In other words, they may engage in hoarding; in particular, they may engage in what I call "information hoarding."

As a practical matter, elites should find it easier to hoard resources embedded in networks that are, at their core, more cohesive than open. Thus, as relational ties become stronger, the opportunity to exercise positional power increases commensurately.

Later in this chapter, and in chapter 6, I discuss in some detail how Japanese elites have used (or abused) their positional power to hoard resources, including capital and labor, but especially information, from nonelites. Here I offer only one telling example. In the early days of this new millennium, the administration of Prime Minister Koizumi held a series of what it called "town meetings" (or "TMs") across the country, ostensibly to receive input from the public on polices that the government should consider. But a subsequent investigation revealed that this was not the example of Jeffersonian democracy it pretended to be. Indeed, the government later was forced to acknowledge that

---

22. Marsden has been joined by several other sociologists trying to use network analysis to develop a model of resource dependency. They include Jeffrey Pfeffer, "A Resource Dependence Perspective on Intercorporate Relations," in *Intercorporate Relations: The Structural Analysis of Business*, ed. Mark S. Mizruchi and Michael Schwartz (Cambridge University Press, 1977), 25–55; Wayne Baker. "Market Networks and Corporate Behavior," in *American Journal of Sociology* 96, no. 3 (November 1990): 589–625; and Matthew Mahutga, "The Persistence of Structural Inequality? A Network Analysis of International Trade, 1965–2000," in *Social Forces* 84, no. 4 (June 2006): 1863–89. Oddly, political scientists have contributed very little in this area. Even Christopher Ansell, one of the few political scientists to use network analysis, tends to ignore power in his study of political organization. See, for example, his "The Networked Polity: Regional Development in Western Europe," in *Governance* 13, no. 3 (July 2000): 303–33.

it had manipulated at least 115 (or 66%) of the 174 "town meetings," primarily by paying people to ask prepared questions that supported the government's policy positions. Organizers mobilized participants in seventy-one meetings, going so far as to exclude troublemakers who had emerged at previous meetings. Bureaucrats themselves posed as audience members with questions in twenty-nine meetings. And organizers carefully coached audience members in another fifteen meetings.[23]

In this regard, Japanese elites are by no means unique; indeed, in political economies marked by high levels of relationalism, this behavior is quite common. Pastor and Wise (1994, 480–1) offer an example from Mexico, where the regime of Carlos Salinas de Gortari won domestic support for the North American Free Trade Agreement in the early 1990s by forging stronger ties with big business, while working with these corporate executives to exclude likely opponents in small business and labor. The authors discuss eighty different studies commissioned jointly by a business lobby and a government trade ministry in Mexico, and in the process they reveal a great deal about the correlation between exclusionary networks and positional power:

> Although debates over the findings of these studies have gone on at the highest levels of the state-business coalition, the results themselves have been held under virtual lock and key. Thus, those few industrialists with access to this information have a more accurate idea of the likely macroeconomic consequences of NAFTA than have small and medium-sized producers or labor leaders. Due to their close working relationship with the state economic bureaucracy, larger firms also have had much more knowledge about and input into the specific sectoral adjustments that are part of the NAFTA. Financial capital, which played a leading role in [the pro-trade lobby], has been especially well-placed; our interviews with top bank officials revealed an uncanny foreknowledge of the details of the financial aspects of the treaty (helped along perhaps by their monthly joint meetings with the Ministry of the Treasury), while representatives of smaller industrial and service companies seemed much less aware about the trade treaty details and even complained about being less informed.

In his seminal analysis of the political deals that led the U.S. Congress to approve the Smoot-Hawley Act, Schattschneider (1963, 212) provides another good example of the correlation between relationalism and positional power. Specifically, he reveals how lobbyists for corporate interests seeking tariff protection used their status as "insiders" to secure privileged access to information and thereby rewrite the rules of the game:

---

23. See *Yomiuri Shinbun,* "Taun Mītingu chōsa hōkokshuo" (A Report on Town Meetings), December 14, 2006; or *New York Times,* "Japan's Leaders Rigged Voter Forums, a Government Report Says," December 13, 2006.

The activity of economic groups in the tariff revision of 1929 was variable, in part because they were not equally well informed of the event. The public authorities aggravated this situation by two varieties of negligence. The committees did not circulate the notice of the hearings with sufficient energy and published the specific proposals made to them too late to be useful to interests adversely affected, in most cases. On the other hand, the government did not maintain a discipline sufficiently stringent to prevent favored groups from obtaining confidential information in its possession by private channels. The groups affected by the tariff may be divided, therefore, into two categories: outsiders who knew too little, and insiders who knew too much.

Positional power, then, is a kind of structural power that is determined by relative *access* to information and other resources embedded in a network of relationships rather than actual *possession* of such resources. Insiders, those who are centrally positioned in the network and thus able to tap its embedded resources with relative ease, have power over outsiders who must rely on the insiders to gain access to those resources, which help insiders maximize gains and minimize risks. The concept of positional power, however, should not be confused with the more amorphous concepts of "structural power" advanced by Strange (1988), "meta-power" advanced by Krasner (1985), or tacit power advanced, in different ways, by several others.[24] Unlike these concepts, which tend to obliterate agency (and thus defy measurement—and sometimes even empirical observation), the concept of positional power specifies actors and intentions and the shape of the structures in which they operate.[25]

Application: Relationalism and Positional Power

In this book, I use these theoretical insights to pursue a case study of exchange networks in the Japanese political economy during the postwar period. Although the case study touches on other sectors such as banking, it tends to focus on manufacturing, particularly machine manufacturing.[26] This is not accidental. Manufacturing has occupied, and still occupies, a central—even privileged—position in the Japanese economy. Today, more than

24. For an insightful discussion of the problems with both neorealist and structuralist conceptions of power, see Guzzini (1993).

25. The careful reader will note that my critique does not include Gramsci's (1992) concept of "hegemony." Although this concept encompasses intersubjective meaning ("consent") and is thus rather broad, it also is nested in the material conditions of a so-called historic bloc.

26. One could, I am sure, argue that this represents "selection bias," claiming that Japan's tertiary sector—particularly financial services—underwent dramatic change in the mid-1990s as a result of liberalization. But this assertion, itself quite arguable, may signify nothing more than just how woefully troubled and inefficient—compared to manufacturing—Japan's service sector has been. Without the changes that took place in the late 1990s, the financial services industry might well have become completely protected by the government, or might have been overtaken in the global marketplace.

three decades after Japan achieved technological "catch-up," manufacturing continues to account for more than one quarter of its GDP. (Comparative figures compiled by the U.S. Central Intelligence Agency show that industrial activity was 26.5 percent of all economic activity in Japan in 2007, 23.4 percent in the United Kingdom, and 20.5 percent in the United States.) And when Japanese elites discuss the Japanese economy, they invariably emphasize the pivotal role of manufacturing. For example, Jin (1996, 3), managing director for the Japan Bank for International Cooperation, voices the common view that manufacturing is the engine of Japanese economic power, the locomotive that drives the service and commercial sectors: "If the ability to produce things is neglected, and if the technological capacity and competitiveness associated with that skill begins to disappear in Japan, the impact will not stop at manufacturing. All industries, including service industries, will lose their vitality."

In the next chapter, I demonstrate that selective relationalism served Japan well in the early part of the postwar period (1945–73), when it was still trying to achieve technological parity with the West, but not well at all in the later part of this period, when Japan had achieved its goal of catching up. In other words, Japanese firms (particularly manufacturing firms) used a web of cooperative networks in the 1950s and 1960s to move to the edge of the global technological frontier; once they got there, however, they found themselves unable to push aggressively beyond it. The structural weakness of the Japanese economy was not readily apparent after 1973 because its firms continued to invest heavily, even though they received lower and lower rates of return on capital. In the 1990s, of course, this weakness became painfully obvious, and was evidenced by a sharp drop in total factor productivity (MITI 1997, 252–56), a rising deficit in intellectual property royalty payments, lagging sales growth in key industries such as computers, and rising un- (and under-) employment. Japan's network capitalism suddenly, and dramatically, began to show its age.[27]

This represented a very real crisis for Japanese elites, from the politicians in Nagatachō, to the bureaucrats in Kasumigaseki, from the industry executives in Ōtemachi, to the factory foremen in Hitachi City and the lifetime blue-collar employees in Toyota City.[28] It was, even for private sector elites,

27. One might argue that these symptoms were the result of the massive volume of nonperforming bank loans following the collapse of Japan's economic bubble in the early 1990s, not the result of "system fatigue." But I agree with Katz (1998) who argues that the maintenance of a high and increasingly inefficient level of capital investment masked the structural problems of the Japanese economy for many years and contributed to the bubble of the late 1980s.

28. Nagatachō is the legislative district in Tokyo, home to the Diet; Kasumigaseki is the neighborhood in Tokyo where ministries and agencies are located; Ōtemachi is the financial and corporate center of Tokyo. Hitachi City, where the electronics firm has most of its domestic manufacturing, is located in Ibaraki Prefecture, north of Tokyo; Toyota City, where the automaker conducts much of its domestic manufacturing, is located in Aichi Prefecture near Nagoya.

more than an economic problem of diminished profits and leaner paychecks; it also was a *political* problem. The political and market forces of globalization threatened to rip apart the web of strong ties those elites had sewed together over the years, and that they continued to dominate.

For more than a decade, Japanese elites employed a variety of schemes to try to shield their exchange networks from the forces of globalization, to try to maintain the status quo as much as practically possible. Chief among these was an effort—documented in chapter 3—to extend existing production and administrative networks into East Asia. They chose this region for an economic reason, as well as an overarching political reason. The economic reason was simple: The region, not yet operating at the global technology frontier, could accommodate selective relationalism without incurring unacceptable costs. Even though this model of capitalism was creating more costs than gains in a developed Japan, it still could be effective and yield overall net gains in developing Asia—at least for a time. The political reason was even simpler: Japanese business and political elites could do it. That is, they could cling to positional power in Japan by extending relationalism into Asia, where they were just beginning to accumulate positional power on a regional level. In the 1990s, Asian countries became dependent on Japan, the "lead goose" in an increasingly integrated and networked region, for manufacturing technology, private capital, foreign aid, and administrative guidance. Thus, Japanese elites could get away with replicating their homegrown institutions in Asia. By moving offshore, they could prop up their threatened positions at home.

Anderson (1983, 150), using Gramscian logic, not network analysis, finds a similar motivation on the part of European elites who established or consolidated colonial empires in Asia and Africa in the mid-to-late nineteenth century after coming under political attack at home from groups mobilized by the revolutionary spirit of 1848:

> One is tempted to argue that the existence of late colonial empires even served to *shore up* domestic aristocratic bastions, since they appeared to confirm on a global, modern stage antique conceptions of power and privilege. . . . It could do so with some effect because . . . the colonial empire, with its rapidly expanding bureaucratic apparatus and its "Russifying" policies, permitted sizeable numbers of bourgeois and petty bourgeois to play aristocrat off centre court.

In taking the step into Asia, Japanese elites resorted to a longstanding, well-studied practice of trying to overcome a challenge by reconfiguring the political space in which that challenge presents itself. Crozier (1964, 156) notes that a threatened group "fights to preserve and enlarge the area upon which it has some discretion," while Schattschneider (1960, 3–7) suggests that a threatened group often will strive to increase its leverage by reducing the scope of conflict. In this case study, we can see Japanese elites struggling to survive a crisis in the 1990s by "going regional" into Asia, where they enjoyed positional power in a set of emerging administrative and production networks. Whether they were expanding or contracting space, the motivation was the same. If one chooses to view the crisis of the 1990s as a purely domestic matter, then one would say Japanese elites were following Crozier's dictum by trying to enlarge the area of contestation; and if, as I contend, this was instead a crisis of globalization, we should then say they were following Schattschneider's dictum by trying to shrink (regionalize) the area of contestation, resisting the forces of change by moving the struggle from the global to the regional level.

Yamazawa Ippei, a neoclassical trade economist who now serves as president of Ajiken (the Institute of Developing Economies) and JETRO (Japan External Trade Relations Organization), notes that Japan in the 1990s found itself suddenly "exposed" to the outside world and a cross-current of external pressures. Globalism, he suggests, was likely to rip apart the nation's institutional fabric; but regionalism was not: "People must become 'fully naked' to move toward globalism, but only 'half naked' for regionalism. The Japanese hate being 'naked.' "[29]

This, of course, merely begs the question I asked at the beginning of this chapter: Why would Japanese elites want to hang on to the gown of selective relationalism in the first place, particularly if—as demonstrated already—it no longer fits? In broader terms, we must ask: Why would the principal actors in a society attempt to preserve a set of anachronistic institutions (policies and practices) that produced net benefits in the past but that now produce net costs? This is a puzzle worth pondering from different theoretical perspectives.

Utilitarians would call this a classic collective action problem in which individuals seek to maximize their own narrow, short-term interests at the expense of the larger, longer-term interest of society. The state, in this case, becomes "captured" by rent-seeking interests, such as business executives and labor leaders in a declining industrial sector, that are able—by virtue of their small numbers—to organize themselves effectively for collective action. Large groups within society, such as consumers, taxpayers, and employees in general, are unable to organize themselves so effectively and thus are penalized as the market's invisible hand is cuffed (Olson 1982; Bates 1981).

Institutionalists, meanwhile, would call this a classic example of "path de-

---

29. *Daily Yomiuri*, "Japan Sees Priorities Changing amid Conflict between Regionalism, Globalism," May 20, 1997.

pendence" in which individuals, rather than calculating their own interests at every turn, stumble forward out of historically formed and institutionally reinforced custom. They do so because they have invested heavily in particular polices and practices that create common expectations about the future, thereby reducing uncertainty (Krasner 1984, 235). These institutions, then, represent "sunk costs," and serve to constrain the actions of individuals and inhibit their ability to undertake change—even when such change, as in this case, may yield a positive result (Steinmo, Thelen, and Longstreth 1992; Evans and Stephens 1988).

These approaches offer valuable insights. The utilitarian school, for example, notes correctly that actors are motivated by competing interests, and often behave strategically in pursuit of them. Institutionalists, on the other hand, remind us that actors cannot easily secure those interests; in reality, they must operate within limits created by their environment. Both approaches, however, fail to answer the question adequately because they: (1) rely on a unit of analysis that is, as noted already, either undersocialized (the atomistic, individual utility maximizer of utilitarianism) or oversocialized (the Leviathan of hierarchy in institutionalism); and (2) ignore the critical variable of power.

My answer, which addresses these shortcomings, flows from network analysis: elite actors who occupy central positions (critical nodes) in exchange networks enjoy positional power, which allows them to limit if not control access to resources, including information, in any given political economy. In addition, positional power affords those who hold it a significant amount of prestige. That is, elites are able to confirm their exalted status as "insiders" by exploiting their positions. It is no wonder, then, why the principal actors in a society would resist institutional change even at the risk of jeopardizing that society's economic well-being and thus, in the longer run, their own economic well-being. In serving as gatekeepers who control the flow of resources, particularly information, elites acquire not only a political advantage but also a social privilege they are reluctant to relinquish—despite any diminution in the total volume of resources under their control. Rational choice theory, emphasizing utility maximization, and historical institutionalism, emphasizing path dependence, overlook this motivation in their equations.[30]

---

30. Rational choice advocates, members of the utilitarian school, might counter that their approach can accommodate this analysis, asserting, for example, that Japanese elites—as self-interested actors—act to maximize power, not economic well-being. One can certainly accept this assumption in the case of bureaucratic elites, whose utility must have something to do with expanded turf or jurisdiction, but not in the case of private sector managers, whose utility must have something to do with the economic performance of the firm (even if performance is measured in terms of market share rather than profits). If an actor's utility can be defined in an entirely post hoc fashion, then the rational choice model becomes so plastic, so inclusive that it can explain everything—and nothing.

But this begs yet another, perhaps even more difficult question: What about nonelites or outsiders? These include nonregular workers, consumers, independent business proprietors, individual investors, and all the others who do not occupy central positions in Japan's tightly networked political economy. They do not enjoy positional power. Yet they have, until recently, acquiesced to a system that has not only produced low returns, high prices, and systemic corruption, but that also has marginalized them. Why? This question, too, should be pondered from different perspectives.

Utilitarians, particularly neoclassical economists and advocates of rational choice theory, like to plumb the psyche of individual players in the economic and political "game." Japan's outsiders have been tolerant of the status quo, according to this view, because they have utility functions that favor safety or security. For example, Sato (1997a and 1977b) documents a process of financial deepening in which households hold fixed-claim assets, such as savings accounts and annuities, and leave large industrial conglomerates to gobble up variable-claim assets, such as stocks, which offer both higher risk and higher returns. Japanese individuals, he argues, tend to be risk averse —a tendency that has allowed Japanese corporations, especially the financial institutions that stand at the center of horizontal keiretsu, to increasingly control the nation's assets or wealth. "Corporate capitalism," writes Sato (1997b, 17), "is the devil's child born of people's risk aversion. It is people who must blame themselves. They are getting what they deserve."

Institutionalists, on the other hand, tend to view political and economic actors as creatures of habit; their preferences are shaped by the distinctive policies and practices that become entrenched (institutionalized), over time, in a particular community. Vogel (1999a) thus argues that Japanese consumers are quite unlike American consumers; they often prefer tariffs and regulations that serve the interests of fellow outsiders such as farmers and small businessmen—even if those preferences help maintain high prices.

Again, these explanations advance our understanding, but ultimately fall short by relying on an oversocialized or undersocialized unit of analysis and by ignoring power. That is, advocates of these competing approaches disregard the allocation, or misallocation, of resources embedded in Japan's dense networks of exchange. More precisely, they disregard the ability of actors who have occupied central positions in those networks to access and mobilize resources, and the lack of ability of actors who have occupied peripheral positions to do the same. Japanese outsiders have, until quite recently, put up with selective relationalism for two reasons. First, they typically did not incur unreasonable costs, at least during Japan's rapid growth period. This is because insiders, both public and private elites, used some of the assets generated by relational capitalism to compensate outsiders, often handsomely. From 1955, when it was created in response to demands from big business for a merger of Japan's leading conservative (pro-status quo) parties, the ruling Liberal Democratic Party was preoccupied with providing these side payments.

For example, the LDP generously subsidized rice farmers by purchasing their output at a mark-up well above the market price. And it protected small businesses, particularly "mom-and-pop" retailers outside the interfirm linkages in the Japanese political economy. Finally, the LDP used the Fiscal Investment and Loan Program (FILP), which draws on funds in the government's massive postal savings system, to finance new bridges, railway lines, sewers, and the like in less populated and underdeveloped areas in Hokkaido, Kyushu, Shikoku, and along the Japan Sea.[31] The Construction Ministry was the conduit for this massive income transfer. In the mid-1960s, public works projects consumed up to 19 percent of the total government budget.[32]

By the late 1990s, when it faced a growing budget deficit, the LDP found it could no longer afford to make such generous side payments. This generated resentment among outsiders, especially as the nation's media began reporting a plethora of scandals involving longtime insiders.

Outsiders put up with relationalism for a second reason: They were denied access to information that would have allowed them to assess reasonable alternatives. To the extent that it is selective, and thus closed, relationalism inevitably excludes outsiders through the hoarding of network resources, including valuable information. Outsiders were largely unaware of the opportunity costs they were paying to help maintain relationalism.

Consider the case of Japanese consumers who were, for many years, kept in the dark about artificially high domestic prices for many manufactured goods, including televisions.[33] In 1956, Japanese TV manufacturers formed a cartel to maintain high prices for sets marketed in Japan, and used the profits to subsidize cheap exports to the United States. For several years, the appliance makers controlled wholesalers and retailers through their exclusive distribution keiretsu, coaxing them with rebates and threatening them with supply restrictions if they failed to maintain listed prices. A decade later, in 1967, Japanese housewives finally learned about the price-fixing cartel—

31. Calder (1988) devotes a chapter to farmers (231–73), to small business (312–48), and to rural areas (274–311).

32. See Pempel (1998, 62).

33. This fact goes further toward a plausible explanation of the apparently "irrational" behavior of Japanese consumers (who, as Vogel notes, have supported certain protectionist policies that keep prices high and have opposed some forms of deregulation designed to increase competition and reduce prices) than Vogel's own institutionalist/cultural explanation (see Vogel 1999a). They behave as they do because they are locked out of network structures that contain useful information. Given more "data" about alternatives, Japanese consumers tend to behave much like consumers elsewhere.

but not from their own government, which had sanctioned the practice. The information came from the U.S. government, which had filed an antidumping lawsuit on behalf of American TV manufacturers. Furious that they had to pay twice as much for a Japanese product as their counterparts in the United States, Japanese housewives organized a nationwide boycott of Japanese TVs. But this action, like the U.S. antidumping suit, came too late. By then, Japanese manufacturers all but dominated the global market.[34]

Or consider the example of consumers harmed by poorly designed or defective products that are, therefore, dangerous. In much of the postwar period, the Japanese state maintained a set of liability laws that required manufacturers to compensate individual consumers for damages from such products, but that also allowed those manufacturers to withhold (hoard) information about such products from the public-at-large (or from consumers as a class). This was possible because product liability cases were handled primarily as private matters, not as legal matters, and were resolved through face-to-face negotiations (*aitai kōshō*) between manufacturers and complaining individuals, not through court proceedings.[35]

Consider also the experience of communities affected by industrial pollution. In the 1960s, the state collaborated with manufacturers in their frantic, almost monomaniacal pursuit of rapid growth, allowing them to continue to build and operate factories that badly polluted the environment—despite the vocal warnings of scientists and the mounting fears of citizens. Not only did state and business elites refuse to listen to any outside testimony on the risk of environmental degradation and the danger to public health, they exercised what Broadbent (1998, 95–6, 281, 355) refers to as "soft social control" (or social hegemony) to silence local critics who dared to question them. Information hoarding here led to rather tragic consequences as Japan experienced some of the worst environmental disasters in history.[36]

Or consider the plight of individual investors. Disarmed by annual reports that disclosed little or nothing, they typically were unable to acquire useful information about the financial standing of Japanese corporations, especially when insiders dominated the boards of such corporations. According to Tsuru (1995, 19–20), during the mid-1990s less than one quarter of the directors of listed companies in Japan hailed from outside the firm. This compared with 71 percent in the United States.

34. This narrative draws on Yamamura and Vandenberg (1986).
35. See Maclachan (2002, chap. 8) and Kitamura (1992, 23).
36. These included a widespread case of mercury poisoning that became known as Minamata disease, as well as a case of cadmium poisoning (*itai itai* or "ouch ouch" disease) that caused bones to become brittle and break easily. In both cases, critics—including the doctors who identified the source of the health problems—were initially discredited as rabble-rousers. The company responsible for the mercury poisoning in Kyushu hired gangsters to bully (and, in at least one instance, even assault) such rabble-rousers.

Japanese firms sometimes went to extraordinary lengths to keep individual investors in the dark, hiring gangsters to attend a firm's annual stockholders' meeting and muzzle anyone trying to ask about questionable investments, low earnings, and other unpleasant matters that management would prefer to keep secret. In the Japanese press, these gangsters (*sōkaiya*) are usually cast as villains who extort money from corporations by threatening to disrupt those annual meetings. New research, however, suggests they also are fulfilling a market demand for limits on the disclosure of corporate information.[37]

Ogino (1997, 17–18) describes his experience attending NTT's annual meeting for shareholders in 1994:

> As I entered the room, I was struck by the fact that all front seats close to the podium were taken while about 30 percent of the remaining seats were open. . . .
>
> After the proceedings began, however, I realized why I could not take a front seat. Those seated in the first three rows were all men picked by management—employee shareholders and delegates from subcontractors. Those "bodyguards" and "mercenaries" had cornered the seats early in the morning, long before ordinary shareholders arrived.
>
> Every time the chair of the meeting . . . put forth an item from the agenda, someone in the front shows shouted, "Igi nashi" (no objection) or "Sansei" (aye). About a dozen people, including a few men in gaudy suits—possibly *sōkaiya*—as well as bona fide shareholders attending for the first time, asked several questions. Among them were these: Why is the company making less profit than before? What are you going to do about the counterfeit telephone cards? Will the company plow back the profits from listing its subsidiaries?
>
> The question-and-answer proceeded smoothly in a businesslike manner. . . . In due course, the chairman called an end to questions and answers, although there was a man at the microphone waiting for his turn to ask a question. "We now proceed to voting," declared the chairman, and then one item after another was voted on in rapid succession amid shouts of "Igi nashi" from the planted shareholders. The meeting ended before noon. I came away with a sense of emptiness, wondering whether an annual meeting like this was really worth holding.

Finally, consider the everyday reality of ordinary citizens who rarely learned the messy details about the mutually reinforcing ties between bureaucrats and industry. Until the late 1990s, the Japanese press exposed corrupt practices only when they involved outsiders (i.e., firms such as Lock-

---

37. At annual meetings, management routinely will nominate and secure "approval" for its own slate of candidates for the corporation's board directors in a carefully orchestrated "*shan shan*" (as in the sound of brisk clapping) maneuver. The company president will read the candidate's name, the *sōkaiya* will shout its approval, and the president will move on quickly to the next nominee. For more on *sōkaiya* see, for example, Szymkowiak (2001).

heed, Recruit, and Sagawa Kyūbin that are not well integrated into the core networks of the Japanese political economy). This, however, has begun to change as marginal players in government-business networks have begun to receive fewer side payments for their ongoing cooperation, or—in this case —silence. Whistle-blowers have emerged into this void, putting pressure on the media to tell these previously untold stories.

Challenging and Defending the Status Quo

Unless they are sufficiently compensated, outsiders will, sooner or later, take steps to acquire knowledge and challenge a system that keeps them on the outside. Indeed, this is already happening. In recent years, frustrated outsiders have demanded (and occasionally even secured) new policies and practices that are slowly beginning to pry open Japan's once exclusionary networks. At the same time, these changes have been stubbornly resisted by bureaucratic, business, and labor elites who cling to positional power in the political economy of Japan.

Some of the biggest battles have been waged outside Tokyo, with local residents increasingly mounting campaigns to challenge large-scale development projects that threaten the environment.[38] For example, activists in Kagoshima Prefecture went to court to demand that local officials release the contents of an environmental impact statement about possible toxic runoff from a proposed golf course development in Kyushu. In the same year, residents of the city of Tokushima on the island of Shikoku demanded that local government officials give them a chance to vote on a proposal to build a dam across the nearby Yoshino River.

Bureaucrats, backed by business interests, routinely resist such citizen pressure; that is, they either refuse to allow a public vote or they ignore the outcome. For example, Japan's construction minister was unmoved by a public vote in Tokushima, where citizens opposed the dam project by a 12–1 margin: "As long as the experts don't revise their views, I am in no position to change my stance."[39]

But the tide may be turning. In 2002, for example, voters in Nagano Prefecture overwhelmingly reinstalled Tanaka Yasuo as governor after the prefectural assembly removed him from office for canceling work on two large dam projects. I return to this story, a major victory for the opponents of selective relationalism, in chapter 8.

Even in Tokyo, where elites are most entrenched and thus enjoy the most

38. *Asahi Shinbun* (March 23, 1999, 4) documented this trend by providing a long list of initiative campaigns by Japanese citizens.

39. See Sonni Efron, "Economy-Boosting Effort in Japan Isn't Worth a Dam," *Los Angeles Times,* January 26, 2000.

positional power, outsiders are banging, harder than ever, on the closed doors of exclusionary networks. Here I highlight two examples that will be discussed more fully in chapter 8:

- In 1999, citizen activists finally persuaded the Diet to approve a Public Disclosure Law to promote transparency in government by granting citizens access to many public documents.[40] The law, which took effect in 2001, followed a number of failed cover-ups, including the Ministry of Health and Welfare's effort to conceal its role, and the role of pharmaceutical companies, in decisions that caused nearly two thousand hemophiliacs in Japan to become infected with HIV-AIDS through the transfusion of tainted blood.
- In 2001, local members of the LDP demanded an end to the traditional method of selecting the party's president, a method in which faction leaders met behind closed doors to anoint one of their own. Koizumi Jun'ichiro, a party maverick, rode this grassroots movement to victory in the party's presidential election and became prime minister of Japan. He promised to carry out structural reform of the Japanese economy "with no sacred cows."

In both cases, of course, Tokyo-based elites worked hard to defend the status quo. That is, the relational empire struck back:

- Before approving the Public Information Law, LDP politicians in the Diet opened several large loopholes. For example, they voted to exempt information provided voluntarily by corporations with the understanding that it would not be disclosed; information related to the burgeoning number of public corporations in Japan; and information whose disclosure might be deemed to be "detrimental to the interests of the nation and its relations with other countries." In 2002, the Diet amended the law to further restrict its use in monitoring the expenditure of public funds. Then, to add insult to injury, the Defense Agency began using the new law as an excuse to conduct background investigations on 142 information requesters. It used its own intranet to inform agency staff about those requesting information, categorizing them as "suspicious citizens," "group members," "overly curious journalists," or "anti-war Self Defense Force members." Agency officials then tried to cover up their illegal spying activities. The scandal was first reported by the *Asahi Shinbun* on May 29, 2002.

---

40. See Information Clearinghouse Japan, "Japan: Breaking Down the Walls of Secrecy," on the freedominfo.org website, posted July 26, 2002. Also see Maclachlan (2000).

- Despite his pledge to pursue reform in every area of the political economy, Koizumi faced strong resistance from party veterans and bureaucrats, and thus managed to achieve only limited success. In what was, admittedly, an early assessment, George Mulgan (2002, 238) concluded that Koizumi led a "failed revolution," producing change that was merely "superficial, partial, incomplete, and unconsolidated." Indeed, virtually all of the prime minister's reform proposals, including one to privatize the financial services of Japan's postal system, were significantly watered down by opponents within the LDP.

None of this should surprise us. Insiders inevitably strive to hold onto positions of power. In the next two chapters, I show why and how they resorted to desperate measures.

2 The Postwar Political Economy of Japan

The Japanese political economy of the 1950s and 1960s performed magnificently, despite the presence of illiberal institutions fostering cooperation between government and business, between firms, and between labor and management—a fact that has raised serious questions about the laissez-faire prescriptions of neoclassical economic theory. But the Japanese economy of the 1990s performed miserably, despite the presence of the same set of illiberal institutions—a fact that has undermined the so-called revisionist theory that often seemed to champion cooperative capitalism. What shall we conclude, finally, about Japan's postwar system?

I have two goals in this chapter. First, using a consistent analytical model, I try to explain why Japan's system of network capitalism fared so well in the early postwar period only to fare so poorly at the end of the twentieth century. Second, I strive to establish a baseline against which to measure (in chapter 4) the extent of change or continuity in the postbubble political economy of Japan.

Political economies are products of contested politics, not manifestations of ontological coding or "pure" reflections of cultural identity. As a result, they are never completely static, even though they may enjoy periods of remarkable stability. The Japanese political economy, which has evolved over time to assume its current form, is no exception. It is tempting to believe we can determine the precise moment when it began to assume the shape it had in the 1990s as a complex set of institutions. Many indeed have searched for the genesis of this distinctive form of capitalism.[1] A handful of scholars,

---

1. Because I am restricting my analysis to *political economy,* I do not consider here any of the many efforts to explain the origins of contemporary Japanese *society*. The most important (and certainly the most ambitious) of these efforts was undertaken by Murakami, Kumon, and Satō (1979). They trace the collectivist nature of Japanese society all the way back to the twelfth century, when agro-military communities in Japan began to organize themselves according to what they call the "*ie*" (literally "household") principle.

including Harada (1998) and Tabata (1987), say the current system did not emerge until the mid-1970s, when Japan was trying to regain economic stability after it was rocked by the first oil crisis. Others, such as Pempel (1998) and Hashimoto (1996), trace its origins back to the early postwar period, when Japanese bureaucrats mobilized the nation to rebuild its devastated economy and catch up with the West.[2] Still others, including Noguchi (1995) and Dower (1990), point to the wartime planned economy of the 1940s. Finally, some experts, such as Baba (1986) and Dore (1973), go back even further to the interwar period, particularly the 1920s, to find the roots of Japan's contemporary capitalist order, often referred to as "companyism."

This disagreement over historical origins flows from a more fundamental disagreement over how to characterize the Japanese political economy. Which institution or institutions serve as its locomotive? One is reminded of the six blind men who touch different parts of an elephant—the legs, tail, trunk, ears, belly, tusk—and then attempt to define its essence. Here, too, some scholars emphasize bureaucratic guidance of industry; others focus on informal business linkages (especially *keiretsu*); still others point to cooperative labor–management relations. This debate, however, turns out to be just as fruitless as the one over history. When one digs more deeply, one finds the same sociopolitical dynamic—selective relationalism—driving all of these institutions, and in turn driving the Japanese political economy throughout much of the postwar period.

In chapter 1, I suggested that Japan was a "thickly relational" political economy because long-term reciprocal ties, or networks of affiliation, exert inordinate influence over the terms of political and economic exchange. This is not an altogether new concept. Gerlach (1992), as well as Imai and Kaneko (1988), have written about the Japanese economic system as a "network," while Okimoto (1989) uses the same modifier to describe the Japanese state. All of these authors are referring to cooperative sinews that entangle major actors in the fate of the other.

This does *not* mean, however, that Japanese society is "group-oriented" or marked by inordinately high levels of social capital, civic participation, and undifferentiated trust. Indeed, Yamagishi (1998 and 1999) describes Japan as a society in which "reassurance," maintained through participation in long-standing relational networks, substitutes for "trust," a more diffuse quality that transcends particularistic relationships. Cross-national surveys bear him out. Nishihara (1987), for example, found that Japanese (29%) were far less likely than their counterparts in the United States (60%), Germany (43%), and South Korea (38%) to offer assistance to someone on the street

2. Samuels (1994) fits squarely in this camp. But because he is interested in the intellectual/ideological roots of Japanese "technonationalism," he traces the origins of this system all the way back to the mid-nineteenth century.

needing help, and have less trust in broadly constructed institutions with which they may not be personally connected, such as labor unions, the legislative branch of government, business enterprises, and religion.

How can Japan's political economy be characterized by "networks of affiliation" while its social system is apparently plagued by general suspicion and mistrust? This riddle is answered in part by those sociologists who emphasize the highly localized, particularistic context in which exchange occurs in Japan. Kumon (1982), for example, argues that contemporary Japanese tend to behave neither as individualists nor as collectivists (individualists who have submerged their individual selves into a collective self), but as "contextualists" who define themselves according to the particular context, the specific relational setting, in which they find themselves at any one time.[3]

> A contextual, when separated from or not in a context, is like an amoeba and has no definite shape because he does not possess a hard "shell." However, once he joins a certain context and occupies a specific *bun* ["part"], his shape is determined. He then becomes himself, or in Japanese, he becomes *jibun,* which literally means "my share." (19–20)

Kumon's analysis of "contextualism" is inspired by Hamaguchi (1977), who used the term *kanjinshugi* or "relationalism" to characterize Japanese society. Likewise, Rohlen (1989) describes Japanese society as a set of overlapping "patterns of connectedness" that do not rely on a legally sanctioned and abstractly acknowledged center.[4]

Although this sociological/anthropological model illuminates the paradoxical nature of relationalism in Japan (which is simultaneously inclusionary and exclusionary), it also obscures the political forces that created it and served to maintain it for several decades. It may be correct to assert that the weblike political economy of Japan lacks a "center," a unitary power that oversees the entire grid, but it is incorrect to say that it also lacks a "spider" (or, more properly, "spiders"),[5] or a purpose (a raison d'être). Japanese manufacturing interests initially spun these ties to help them adopt technology from the global reservoir of developed know-how and, consequently, allow them to keep expanding output. As the web expanded over time, how-

3. Kumon's analysis puts some meat on the rather thin or facile observation that sociologists often make about the sharp line between *uchi* (inside) and *soto* (outside) in Japanese society. Indeed, it is the confluence between individual identity and reciprocal relationships that makes this line visible at all in Japan.
4. Rohlen, however, envisions this order as somehow organic ("intensely socialized"), rather than as politically constructed to benefit elites.
5. Although this metaphor is most often associated with Karel van Wolferen (1989), it was first used in an analysis of the Japanese political economy by William Lockwood (1965).

ever, this goal became subordinate to the broader objective of preserving network ties from which "nodal" members derived positional power and thus access to valuable resources, such as capital, labor, and information. For this reason, centrally positioned actors have continued to invest in network ties they dominate.

Although he does not use social network analysis, Vogel (2003, 330) hints at this same objective of maintaining positional power when he attempts to explain why potential agents of economic reform in Japan have been slow to embrace the Anglo-American model of laissez-faire capitalism—even slower than state officials, business executives, and labor leaders in Germany, the other leading example of an alternative model of capitalism, which he calls the "organized market economy." Japanese firms, he notes, "are linked to banks, other firms, and government agencies in even denser networks of inter-relationships than their German counterparts, making them more reluctant to undermine these ties or to support reforms that might jeopardize them."

Three-Legged Stool

Relationalism in Japan today sits on a three-legged stool of cooperation between elite actors: bureaucrats and business executives; legally independent firms (in particular, assemblers and suppliers); management and labor.[6] Each leg (or part) is indispensable in supporting the stool (the whole). Business interests cooperate with the state, allowing centrally positioned firms to forge long-term ties with others, which in turn allows management inside those larger firms to collaborate more closely with their workers. And these overlapping networks support overlapping institutions. For example, high-ranking bureaucrats routinely retire (via *amakudari,* an institution I outline below) into firms that share capital, technology/information, and personnel with one another (via *keiretsu,* another institution I explain below), and which themselves are held together by intrafirm institutions such as life-time employment and seniority-based wages.[7] The result is a complex, politically constructed system that is biased in favor of producers seeking to expand market share rather than to maximize profits, a system that runs on what Dore (1986, 77) refers to as "relational contracting."

The interests of elite actors converge neatly on only the most fundamental, salient issues of economic growth and economic security, creating a centralized or corporatist political structure. Labor policy includes a number

6. Elsewhere, Kozo Yamamura and I have called this "the triangle of cooperation." See Hatch and Yamamura (1996, 75, 78).

7. Colignon and Usui (2003, 72) provide statistics showing that "a disproportionate share of amakudari go to keiretsu-affiliated firms."

of such issues—from collective bargaining rights to labor standards. Kume (1998, 37) refers to a cross-class "accommodationist alliance" on labor policy that encompasses conservative but conciliatory representatives of the state and the business community, as well as private sector union representatives who shun left-wing ideology. This is buttressed by the findings from a comparative study of labor policy networks in Japan, Germany, and the United States. Knoke et al. (1996, 219) report that "peak" organizations representing the most powerful government, business, and union interests form a unified "center" in Japan, and that "all other positions revolve around this single center of gravity." The authors find less compact networks of elite interaction in Germany and the United States.

On many other issues, however, Japan's three-legged stool of relationalism does not represent a broad, corporatist platform that encompasses all elite interests at all times. In other words, it often looks quite unlike the mythical, unitary actor caricatured in the phrase "Japan Inc." In those instances, it looks much more like a bundle of relatively narrow networks that overlap from time to time. Such a compartmentalized but overlapping structure or *tatewari gyōsei* (vertically divided or segmented administration) exists inside the Japanese bureaucracy, where—as Muramatsu (1981, 96) noted—"each ministry and agency has different interests, and each takes a stand on the battlefield of political competition." Indeed, it has even existed within the Liberal Democratic Party, where policy "tribes" (*zoku*) in the Diet have jostled with one another to bring home the bacon for their particular "clients," whether general contractors or doctors. In all cases, however, the cohesiveness of these networks of economic and political exchange is maintained by limiting access to selected "insiders" and thereby hoarding resources that are embedded in these networks.

Although embryonic forms of relationalism did surface during prewar and wartime years, especially within innovating and expanding manufacturing firms hoping to protect their investments in human capital, the system as a whole did not actually begin to take shape until the early postwar period. It developed incrementally, in a series of accretions, over the two and a half decades following World War II.

U.S. occupation policy, which veered sharply from "reform" to "reconstruction" in the late 1940s, served as the lathe that turned the first leg of the stool: government-business cooperation. In its quest to democratize and pacify Japan, the U.S. government undermined most elements of the old, prewar regime—the military, landholding elites, the *zaibatsu* (financial cliques)—sparing only the civil bureaucracy and, of course, the emperor. Then, in its subsequent effort to rebuild Japan as a "bulwark against communism," the United States pushed Japanese bureaucrats to collaborate with their counterparts in big business. Pempel (1998, 103) notes how American authorities in Tokyo, under the direction of the Supreme Commander of the Allied Powers (or SCAP, embodied in the person of Gen. Douglas MacArthur), promoted "fusion" among economic bureaucrats and business executives. For bureaucrats, cooperation with business became increasingly necessary because the U.S. occupation's economic austerity program (the Dodge Line) had reduced the size of government, leaving them dependent on frontline actors for information about factor and product markets that could be used to kick-start a stalled economy.[8] For business executives, co-operation with the bureaucracy was vitally important because, crippled by the war, they required help in securing resources such as capital and technology and in repelling rival imports. The result of this interdependence was a form of government-industry collaboration that Samuels (1987) aptly calls "reciprocal consent."

In the 1960s, an increasingly liberal trade regime began to impinge on Japan's protectionist policies. Deemed a developed country, Japan had to generally relinquish the use of quantitative import restrictions under Article XI of the General Agreement on Tariffs and Trade and then had to elimi-nate most foreign exchange restrictions under Article VIII of the Interna-tional Monetary Fund's charter. It was the threat posed by this earlier incarnation of globalization that pulled together so many anxious Japanese firms in horizontal and vertical networks and thereby created the second leg of this three-legged stool (Aoki 1987). But the government was not an in-significant player in this process. Indeed, the Ministry of International Trade and Industry (MITI), which today is known as the Ministry of Economy, Trade and Industry (METI), then faced pressure to reduce tariffs that had protected domestic markets from foreign imports and the Ministry of Fi-nance (MOF) faced pressure to reduce capital restrictions that had shielded domestic industries from inward foreign direct investment. In response, these agencies actively encouraged major firms to cement existing interfirm ties through intensified cross-shareholding, personnel and technology ex-change, and other forms of "hostage-taking" (Vestal 1993, 53). In the auto-mobile industry, for example, Tate (1995, 55) notes that MITI "made extensive efforts to encourage rationalization of automobile suppliers that supported the formation of vertical keiretsu."

These efforts were referred to unabashedly as "liberalization counter-measures" (Katz 1998, 158). But while they functioned as private barriers to

---

8. Toeing the Dodge Line, the Yoshida administration in 1949 reduced the number of ad-ministrative personnel in the central government from 1.6 million to 1.4 million. More per-sonnel cuts followed in 1951 and 1954. See Ito (1995, 239). I should note, however, that bureaucrats had shown a willingness to cooperate with business executives even before these dramatic cuts came into effect. For example, in 1946 they collaborated with industry on pro-grams such as reconstruction financing and "weighted production" (*keisha seisan hōshiki*).

foreign goods, services, and capital, they also served to insulate members of newly emerging relational networks from domestic "outsiders" in the Japanese political economy. For example, MOF set up quasi-governmental organizations such as the Japan Joint Securities Corporation and the Japan Securities Holding Association, which bought publicly traded shares and resold them to "stable" shareholders. And MITI revised the Japanese commercial code to make it easier for firms to "stabilize" holdings of their stock by (a) raising capital through private, undisclosed sales of equity, often at bargain prices, to selected individuals or firms, including trusted suppliers and distributors; and (b) limiting stock purchases to preferred insiders. Electronic and automobile manufacturers, just beginning to enjoy a boom in the 1960s, were heavily represented among firms capitalizing on this new opportunity. Toyota, for example, changed its articles of incorporation to limit shareholding to Japanese nationals and corporations (Suzuki 1977).

Following the extraordinarily bitter labor strife of the early postwar years, Japanese employers, particularly large, export-oriented firms, tried desperately to isolate radical, industry-level unions and nurture moderate, enterprise unions. But it was not until the 1970s that they managed to achieve a general understanding or implicit contract that swapped employment security for wage restraint.[9] As Hiwatari (1996) demonstrates, this was possible with the help of state intervention in the market and the expansion of interfirm ties, especially vertical keiretsu ties between assemblers and their parts suppliers. The former spurred the creation of oligopolistic industries that could control wage competition, while the latter allowed employers to protect "core" employees by transferring older or surplus workers to subcontractors. With the consolidation of this system of enterprise unionism, a system of stable wages and long-term employment, the third leg of relationalism, was finally attached.

Having laid out a chronology of the evolution of selective relationalism in Japan, it may be useful here to examine more closely the specific institutions that make up these three distinct but occasionally overlapping networks of cooperation.

State-Industry Cooperation

Observers, especially American observers, of the Japanese state used to view it as remarkably similar to the U.S. state—a vessel to be claimed by different

---

9. According to both Kume (1998, 175) and Price (1997, 255), the turning point came in 1975. Labor's spring offensive (*shuntō*) that year achieved an average wage increase of 13 percent —even though inflation was running even higher, at around 15 percent. Price, who adopts a Gramscian perspective, views this wage entente as the beginning of "market hegemony" and the end of militant unionism in Japan. Kume, like me, is less pessimistic. He views it as the beginning of an accommodation between labor and management to jointly defend job security in Japan.

interest groups at different times in a wide-open, pluralist competition for power.[10] In his seminal work, Johnson (1982) repudiated this view. Japan, he argued, was ruled by its elite, "plan-rational" bureaucracy, particularly MITI, which enjoyed autonomy from nonstate actors in society. Although Johnson exposed the shortcomings of the prevailing wisdom, his "corrective" also missed the mark—particularly in the era of slower growth and creeping globalization/liberalization in which he wrote. In the 1970s and '80s, when depressed industries were particularly vocal and the tools of industrial policy[11] were suddenly blunt, MITI did indeed try to coordinate the interests of industries and firms—but largely at the behest of the "coordinated" interests.[12] Even earlier, in the 1950s and '60s, when the interests of state and capital more neatly converged, one must ask: "Who co-opted whom?"[13]

The answer is not clear, but much of the recent literature suggests that the Japanese state was never as autonomous as Johnson asserted.[14] Okuno-Fujiwara (1997, 396–97), for example, refers to Japan's as a "relation-based" government that engages routinely in efficiency enhancing, ex post bargaining with business interests (i.e., bargaining that takes place after formal rules have been established). This is possible, he writes, because bargaining is iterative (repeated constantly over a long term) and is carried out by familiar "insiders" with sufficient resources to make side payments to concerned but marginalized actors (outsiders) who otherwise might try to sabotage agreements. These insiders often are representatives of "lower" levels of government (for example, officials in sections or bureaus that oversee specific industries or even sectors) and representatives of "peak" organizations (such as trade associations) that can aggregate the competing interests of different firms.

It is true, of course, that government has heavily regulated business in Japan—so heavily, in fact, that input costs in the mid-1990s greatly exceeded

10. This view is expressed most articulately in Patrick and Rosovsky (1976), especially 43–54.

11. Industrial policy is any measure used by the government to change relative prices in any industry and thereby induce greater or less investment in that industry. Typical examples are subsidies or import barriers.

12. This same point is made by those using Marxist analysis (see, for example, Watanabe 1987), as well as those relying on pluralist analysis (see Uriu 1996).

13. Gourevitch (1978, 907) asks this question of those who view Japan as a bureaucratic-led polity.

14. In his account of efforts by Fairchild Semiconductor to do business in Japan in the early 1970s, Flamm (1996, 56–57) shows that the Japanese state sometimes *looks* more autonomous than it really is. After failing to win MITI's approval for its proposal to build a Japanese production facility, Fairchild tried to license its chip technology to NEC. It finally reached an agreement with NEC—but only after dramatically reducing its fee schedule. Fairchild believed it had no choice; MITI, it was told, would review the terms of the proposed agreement and insist on such a change. Fairchild learned only after the fact that NEC's president also chaired the MITI licensing approval advisory committee that would conduct the review.

costs in other industrialized economies. MITI (1995a, 140) estimated that Japanese prices for basic inputs (raw materials, parts, and capital goods) were, on average, 30 percent higher than in the United States, 19 percent higher than in Germany, and 46 percent higher than in South Korea. The gap in prices for services, which in Japan has been regulated even more doggedly than manufacturing, was found to be even wider (51 percent, 96 percent, and 475 percent relative to the United States, Germany, and South Korea, respectively).[15]

But what really distinguishes the relationship between government and business in Japan is not the heavy load of formal rules that the public sector imposes on the private sector. Most other industrialized nations, even those imposing less onerous regulations, have larger bureaucracies.[16] Rather, what distinguishes Japan is the informal and iterative bargaining between state and industry, or what Iwata Kazumasa, a respected Japanese economist, called "participatory interaction."[17] In other words, representatives of these two interests engage in an unusual amount of mutual consultation.[18] Moreover, they rarely allow outsiders (those who are peripheral to this "interaction") to participate. A survey by the Management and Coordination Agency confirms the exclusionary nature of this bargaining process: The government introduced, revised, or abolished ten thousand regulations between April 1986 and July 1998, but issued a public notice before acting in only one hundred of those cases, and considered public comment in only sixteen cases.[19]

In his study of the regulation of private utilities, Kishii (1999, 56) provides an example of this sort of exclusionary consultation, which he argues is "peculiar" to Japan and which, as he puts it, ultimately can "fuse the interests of the regulator and the regulated."

> Bargaining is not held between an individual utility operator and a government office, but collectively between a trade association or a group of utility operators and a government office. Direct involvement in the bargaining process

15. One Japanese electronics manufacturer reports that government rules and regulations accounted for half of the costs generated by its factory supervision unit in the 1990s. See Yamada and Okumura (1997, 111).

16. In the mid-1990s, only 6.5 percent of the Japanese labor force worked in what the OECD (2000) calls the "limited public sector" (central and local government)—a small amount compared to France (20.2%), Italy (18.2%), the United States (14.2%), Germany (14.1%), or the United Kingdom (11.9%). Government expenditure as a share of GDP is also relatively small. Employment statistics collected by the OECD are available at http://www.oecd.org/puma/mgmtres/hrm/pubs/table.pdf.

17. Iwata was speaking at a symposium on economic cooperation sponsored by the Economic Planning Agency in November 1994. Terry (2002, 308) quotes him: "The government played the role of catalyst, giving incentives to a dynamic private sector. That function as catalyst means that in economic development one plus one equaled three or four instead of two."

18. See Schaede (1995).

19. *Yomiuri Shinbun,* October 15, 1998.

by representatives of consumers, the ultimate beneficiaries, only seldom occurs; from the outset, information about the process, let alone effective participation in it, is off-limits for consumers and the general public. Thus, the bargaining is done almost invariably behind closed doors, involving only the existing utility operators, or their trade associations, and government offices.

This mutual but exclusionary consultation has been carried out through a host of institutions—all of which represent credible commitments to manage the inevitable conflicts that plague government and business. One of the most important of these consultative institutions has been "administrative guidance" (*gyōsei shidō*), a highly informal, flexible system of bureaucratic rule-making and enforcement. Some view it as an example of unbridled state authority; indeed, the economic ministries (particularly METI and MOF) enjoy broad, discretionary powers under the so-called establishment laws that created them.[20] But administrative guidance does not—in spite of its name —allow bureaucrats to unilaterally control the bargaining process. Indeed, business interests appear to prefer such informal regulation because of the greater opportunity to negotiate and renegotiate outcomes.[21] But the system would not work so effectively, so flexibly, were if not for the fact that outsiders are kept on the outside. Upham (1987, 202) makes this point bluntly: The relationship of mutual trust between "guiding" bureaucrats and "guided" firms "is maintainable only because of the closed, informal nature of the industrial policy process whereby interim decisions are rarely challenged publicly and are frequently unknown outside the industrial policy community until they have become a fait accompli." Likewise, Young (1984, 947–49) refers to a process that systematically excludes outsiders—the inevitable flip side of a process that binds participants together via reciprocal ties.

State-industry ties have been reinforced by the practice of amakudari, literally "descent from heaven," in which bureaucrats retire into management positions in the private sector, and often at firms they used to regulate. This reflects neither state domination of industry nor the reverse, but rather a system of hostage-taking and embedded information exchange that benefits both parties.[22] The state can utilize retired employees who have "descended"

---

20. Kato Hideki, a former MOF official who now serves as president of Koso Nippon, a Tokyo think tank, expressed this opinion in an interview with the *Daily Yomiuri,* June 9, 1998. He has called for the repeal of these "establishment laws."

21. See Young (1984).

22. This means that I steer a middle road between those, like Okimoto (1989), who see amakudari as a bureaucrat-led system designed to improve the implementation of industrial policy, and those who see it as an industry-led system designed to tap public resources. On the other hand, the evidence does not appear to support Calder (1989), who sees amakudari as a system used by smaller firms seeking greater access to government information. Colignon and Usui (2003) show that, in 1995, firms with fewer than one hundred employees received only 12.1 percent of all amakudari transfers.

into the private sector (including the rapidly expanding not-for-profit sector) as conduits for information about rules and regulations. From the other side of the network, firms can deploy them as well-connected lobbyists for whatever cause they are promoting.

These ties also have been reinforced by the routine installation of *shingikai* (deliberation councils), in which affected parties negotiate over policies proposed by bureaucrats. As Schwartz (1998) has shown, *shingikai* serve to mediate conflicts or coordinate competing interests in Japanese society, particularly those between bureaucrats and industry. In this way, as Abe (1978, 8) notes, they reflect the long-standing weakness of Japan's legislative process:

> In regimes marked by a representative government, the legislative branch has traditionally assumed responsibility for managing conflicts among different interests and promoting political integration. But with the bureaucratization of the state, this function of political integration has often come to be played by the administrative branch. One problem for bureaucrats is the lack of a proper mechanism to perform those functions otherwise performed by means of the legislative branch, including the collection of information necessary for coordinating various interests in society. As the Japanese state has become bureaucratized, *shingikai* have proved useful by performing this coordination function.

Bureaucrats staffing *shingikai* not only provide the informational grist for the deliberation mill, they also hand-pick members. Widely divergent or strident views are unwelcome (Harari 1986, 32). In the past, *shingikai* considering economic policy consisted almost exclusively of industry and government officials, particularly bureaucratic OBs ("old boys" from a certain ministry or agency), but now typically include representatives from other circles, such as academia. These presumed "outsiders" bestow legitimacy—a cover, according to Kusano (1995)—on a relatively closed system of bargaining without, in most cases, ever really challenging its fundamental operating principles. As experts in the particular policy arena being discussed, the "outsiders" are in fact closely aligned with the insiders from business and government.[23] Indeed, they are sometimes referred to as "*zoku* scholars" or academics who belong to a particular policy tribe.[24]

23. Schwartz (1998, 40–47), adopting what he calls a "neo-pluralist" view, is much more sanguine about the evolution of *shingikai,* which he says are now heavily influenced by different interest groups. He concedes, however, that outspoken critics of the established system (selective relationalism) are rarely invited to participate.

24. By itself, the word *zoku* simply means "tribe." But in the context of Japanese politics, it refers to different groups of Diet members belonging to the Liberal Democratic Party who work with bureaucrats and interest groups associated with a specific policy issue. There are, for example, "agriculture zoku," "construction zoku," "finance zoku," and so on. Each works to promote the interests of that "tribe."

Sekimoto Tadahiro (1996, 104), the former chairman of NEC, has justified these relatively closed policy circles of the past, saying they should have been called "golden triangles" rather than "iron triangles" because they contributed greatly to information exchange and thus economic development. At the same time, however, he has praised the new configuration of cooperative ties that characterize many present-day *shingikai*. In place of the former "golden triangle," he writes, Japanese policy now is commonly constructed by what he calls a "neohexagon" that includes representatives from academia, labor, and the media—in addition, of course, to those from industry, the bureaucracy, and the Diet. Sekimoto's "neohexagon" model is clearly more inclusive than previous (neocorporatist) models of interest mediation in Japan, but it is powered by the same elitist philosophy that policy-making should be conducted within closed networks dominated by "experts."

Business–Business Cooperation

Japanese firms compete aggressively—but not always in terms of price, and not always as atomistic agents in the market. That is, business competition in Japan often revolves around nonprice factors such as quality and service, and often occurs between affiliated blocs of firms rather than individual companies. Indeed, Japanese elites have been so skeptical about unbridled price competition that, as noted in chapter 1, they invented a concept—"excess competition" (*katō kyōsō*)—that one would never find in a modern economics textbook in the United States. Morozumi (1966, 61), one of many Japanese economists who viewed the market with suspicion, explains this seemingly radical concept: when firms compete so fiercely and cut prices so low that one or more of them can no longer survive in a strategic industry, then "the losses to the national economy exceed the gains from that competition."

The antidote for "excess competition" is, of course, cooperation, and Japanese firms cooperate with one another in a variety of ways. For example, erstwhile rivals in an industry characterized by overcapacity will often form a cartel to guard against lethal price-cutting. Firms in basic industries such as steel and petrochemicals, struggling to keep pace with lower cost competitors in less developed countries, routinely engage in such collusive behavior. And construction firms typically rig their bids on public contracts, using an informal practice of consultation (*dangō*) whereby they divide the market among themselves and exclude outsiders. These collusive structures overcome collective action problems in the market, but are nonetheless unstable because they present a classic prisoners' dilemma—members face powerful incentives to cheat. For this reason, the state plays a pivotal role as a third party guarantor over the tacit agreement to cooperate. Thus, to cite only one example, the Fair Trade Commission of Japan outlaws retail discounting that it believes could, if continued for an extended period, harm competitors.[25]

Business collusion is often justified in contemporary Japan as a function of culture. Far from viewing it as a crime, many apologists view it as "a beneficial trait of Japanese society" that reflects a "spirit of harmony" and a belief that "everyone can live peacefully together," argues Funabashi Haruo (2005), a historian and chief executive officer of the Sirius Institute, in an article about a bid-ridding scandal in Japan's construction industry. He sarcastically dismisses this way of thinking as "charming," and notes that it fails to recognize the undemocratic consequences of collusion, the perverse consequences of what I have called "positional power."[26]

> The fact is that the benefits of such harmony can only be enjoyed through the sacrifice of those who are outside the circle of collusion. In the current case, the victimized outsiders are the taxpayers. Those in the inner circle—the administrators, bureaucrats, and companies—do not take these victims into consideration.

Japanese firms with complementary assets are able to cooperate more freely through keiretsu, the controversial "lineage groups" that are largely misunderstood outside of Japan. Members of these groups are legally independent but bound together over time by a set of tangible and intangible commitments that may include cross-shareholding, interlocking directorates, and intragroup trade, as well as technology and personnel transfers. Keiretsu do not operate within the framework of hierarchy directed by a central power (the "visible hand" of Alfred Chandler's ideal bureaucratic organization), nor as autonomously self-regulating and impersonal units (the "invisible hand" of Adam Smith's ideal market organization). Rather, they function as "hands interlocked in complex networks of formal and informal inter-firm relationships" (Gerlach 1992, 3).

There are three different kinds of "lineage groups," including the relatively famous (or even infamous) horizontal or intermarket keiretsu. Some of these horizontal keiretsu are offspring of the prewar *zaibatsu* that emerged in the late nineteenth and early twentieth centuries to capitalize on new opportunities created by Japan's massive campaign to industrialize and catch up with the West. After World War II, the U.S. occupation force in Japan

25. *Nihon Keizai Shinbun* (web version), May 29, 2000.
26. Ironically, in the same article in which he assails collusive behavior, Funabashi defends the practice of amakudari. "Government bureaucrats and private industry operate in a mutually cooperative relationship aimed at achieving the goals of the nation as a whole," he writes. Making it harder for bureaucrats to retire into the private sector would "do harm to Japanese society as a whole."

dissolved the family-owned holding companies that controlled each group. But as soon as the occupiers left, the Japanese state encouraged the largest, most strategic members of these now disbanded groups to cluster again—this time around a "city bank" (a large commercial bank) that would serve as a conduit for the allocation of cheap credit.[27] Four former *zaibatsu* groups —Sumitomo, Mitsui, Mitsubishi, and Yasuda (now called Fuyo)—re-created themselves as keiretsu, and two new groups—Dai-ichi Kangyo and Sanwa (named after their main banks)—eventually followed suit.[28]

Each group tries to maintain one and only one company in every sector of the Japanese economy—a practice that has come to be called *Wan Setto Shugi* ("one settism"). Thus, the Sumitomo Group has a major automaker (Tōyō Kōgyō, better known as Mazda), a major electronics firm (NEC), a major chemical manufacturer (Sumitomo Chemical), a major brewery (Asahi), and so on. In addition, each group has a general trading company (GTC) with its own worldwide network of branches and stations; it handles exports and imports, coordinates complex logistics, and serves as the international intelligence unit for the entire keiretsu. Finally, a large commercial bank not only allocates capital to group members; it also performs an oversight or monitoring function that, for Western firms, is typically provided by a board of directors.[29] In the late 1970s, when Mazda's financial health was jeopardized by its ill-timed decision to produce gas-guzzling rotary engines, Sumitomo Bank grabbed control of the automaker. It used a combination of no-nonsense management and abundant group resources to rescue the firm.[30]

Cooperation in this kind of keiretsu is achieved through different means, including the presidents' club (*shachō-kai*) that meets each month to exchange information on employment, production, and marketing issues. These meetings, according to Imai and Kaneko (1988, 40–41), serve to "reduce uncertainties, meet growing mutual demands and settle investment decisions":

> Moreover, as a result of such information exchange, affiliated firms feel confident in making joint investments; investment decisions are made easier; and risks are reduced in an environment that calls for interdependent development. Because of potential competitive relations within the same group in the sector of the new venture, information exchange has an accelerating effect on investment decisions.

27. This was done primarily through the use of a subequilibrium interest rate policy, which allowed the state to engage in a practice known as "window guidance." I discuss this further below.

28. The Dai-ichi Kangyo group was not actually formed until 1971, when two banks—Dai-ichi and Kangyo—merged.

29. See Sheard (1994, 333–338).

30. Pascale and Rohlen (1983) do a fine job of telling (and analyzing) these events.

Nakatani (1984), as well as Lincoln, Gerlach, and Ahmadjian (1996), have demonstrated empirically that horizontal keiretsu serve a useful purpose—at least in the event that the economy is still developing or maturing. That is, they function as a kind of insurance mechanism, easing or distributing risks (and thus curtailing and reassigning profits) within the group. Kim, Hoskisson, and Wan (2004) have confirmed and extended this finding, showing that stronger members of the group capture a greater share of the network's gains, using product and international diversification to expand their sales. Like independent firms, weaker members of the group tend to concentrate instead on earning profits. Tsuru (1995, 40), focusing on the main bank in the keiretsu, has identified an additional purpose for these groups: they encourage financial institutions to produce and use information about member firms/borrowers: "With a greater amount of lending, the advantage associated with information production becomes greater, and the cost of failing to produce information is also greater. This provides incentives for costly monitoring. Long-term and sustained business relationships are also likely to result because the production of information about companies by financial intermediaries becomes possible only under relationships of this kind."

Although firms belonging to a keiretsu may share information readily with their group bank, as well as with other group members, they generally disclose less information on their financial statements than non-keiretsu or independent firms, according to Covrig and Low (2005). This finding supports a claim, made by Cooke (1996), among others, that keiretsu, as exclusionary groupings, withhold information from outsiders.

A second form of "lineage group"—vertical or supply keiretsu—links the assemblers of machinery and the suppliers of parts. Of all the different patterns of business–business cooperation, this one receives the most attention in this book because it has played a critical role in shaping the political economy of Japan. Vertical keiretsu emerged in the 1960s as manufacturers hoping to reduce transaction costs began to rely more and more heavily on subcontractors for parts production.[31] Automakers and electrical appliance manufacturers, in particular, constructed and dominated their own supply clubs. Toyota was one of the first to do so. It built a massive pyramid, using a number of first-tier subcontractors who called on a larger number of second-tier subcontractors, who relied on an even larger number of third-tier subcontractors, and so on. Nishiguchi and Beaudet (1999) have documented the solidarity of Toyota's supply club. In 1997, when a fire destroyed

---

31. Surveys by the Small and Medium Enterprise Agency show that the ratio of subcontractors to the total number of small and medium firms in Japan's manufacturing sector climbed steadily between 1966 and 1981. See SME Agency, *Kōgyō Jittai Kihon Chōsa Hōkokusho* (Basic Survey Report on the State of Industry). Tokyo: MITI, various years.

production capacity at Aishin, a major producer of brake parts, other Toyota suppliers rushed to the automaker's defense. They used Aishin's drawings and, within days, came up with suitable brake parts for Toyota.

To be sure, resources flow in both directions inside a vertical keiretsu. In most instances, parent firms—the assemblers—provide their trusted suppliers with capital and technology, as well as a relatively stable market. In exchange, they receive high-quality parts "just in time" through the so-called *kanban* system. Kodama (1991. 144–46 and 151–52) has called this a "national system of demand articulation," a system of linkages that allows for the rapid integration of market requirements into a product concept and the equally rapid decomposition of that concept into development projects. It is an interactive system that relies on instantaneous feedback and results in shorter production cycles.

Mindful of this two-way flow of resources, some scholars have concluded that vertical keiretsu represent another mechanism for sharing risks and redistributing profits from assemblers to suppliers. It is, they say, a system characterized by mutual restraint and nonexploitation, a system that therefore enhances efficiency.[32] In a statistical study, Okamuro (1995) produced evidence supporting the conventional view that a Japanese automobile assembler typically absorbs some of his supplier's risk of increasing production costs. However, he found that assemblers perform this function "selectively" (217) —that is, only for large and favored suppliers; and he also found that the assembler routinely shifts onto the supplier some of what he calls the "much more important" (211) risk of softening demand for finished goods. One might also note that prices for parts are rarely negotiated upward. In a personal account, Sakai (1990, 40) argues that electronics suppliers like him actually lose their freedom when they enter into a subcontracting relationship:

> [The supplier] is told what to make, when to put it on line, and how much it will get for it on delivery. If the company that placed the order feels a profit squeeze, it can easily order the subcontractor to reduce its final price. If hard times continue, the larger company can demand yet another cut. If it gets to the point that the subcontractor is losing money on each unit it is producing and has cut expenses and streamlined production to the utmost, the "parent" company could demand that it buy some new piece of equipment to increase productivity. And even if the subcontractor neither needs nor wants the equipment, it has no choice: if it refused, the flow of orders from the parent would dry up overnight—and its business would be gone.

The third and final kind of "lineage group" is the distribution keiretsu, a legacy of the early postwar years, when the growth of the manufacturing in-

---

32. See, for example, Asanuma (1984) and Ahmadjian (1997).

dustry in Japan outstripped the capability of wholesalers and retailers to move and sell all the newly produced goods. Manufacturers, particularly those producing consumer electronics, automobiles, cosmetics, and pharmaceuticals, overcame this obstacle by setting up and maintaining their own distribution networks. Each one established a complete marketing channel, investing in and providing management and technical support to selected members of the network. And each secured nearly absolute control over that channel, using rebates, territorial sales restrictions, single-outlet–single-account systems and other mechanisms to exert ongoing pricing authority. Although this is less true today, manufacturers in those days had "life and death power over dealers, who [had] no alternative but to agree to the regressive practices effected by such standard terms of trade as 'application sales' and blank promissory notes," writes Ishida (1983, 324), a former official of the Japan Fair Trade Commission.

In the late 1980s, one newspaper (*Japan Economic Journal,* November 25, 1989) identified seventy thousand wholesalers and retailers that were tied exclusively to a single manufacturer. And in the early 1990s, a study carried out jointly by MITI and the U.S. Commerce Department found that Japanese manufacturers controlled a majority of the shares in 32 percent of the members of the Japan Automobile Dealers Association. In the United States, by contrast, a study conducted as part of the MOSS (market-oriented sector-specific) trade talks, found that "equity participation by vehicle manufacturers is very uncommon. A Big Three vehicle manufacturer participates in equity, either entirely or partially, in only about 1.5 percent of its dealerships."

On top of these semiformal groupings (horizontal, vertical, and distribution keiretsu), the political economy of Japan is sewn together by scores of more loosely organized alliances. Even nominally independent firms (that is, firms that are unaffiliated with any particular keiretsu) tend to cooperate with one another more than their counterparts in other industrialized economies. Consider just one industry: medical equipment sales. A June 1996 study by JETRO found that Japanese dealers of such equipment routinely provide extensive after-market service to their customers (hospitals and clinics), and that this "standard practice" serves to build "long-term, stable relationships" between seller and buyer. Price becomes merely one among many considerations, and it is often a secondary consideration.

Itami (1989, 57) argues that Japanese firms are more likely than Western firms to steer clear of the spot market:

> One can hardly say that trading relations among Japanese firms are based on the principle of free market trade. Once a trading relationship is begun, it usually lasts for a long period of time, and thus trading partners as a rule be-

come fixed. In most cases, the number of trading partners does not grow. What Japanese firms attempt to do is maintain intensive, cooperative, and long-term relations with a limited number of firms.

Scher (1997) has attempted to build a sociological framework, which he calls the "relational access paradigm," to explain the relatively high levels of interfirm cooperation in Japan. In his framework, which is similar to the model of relationalism presented here, network ties are graded along an *uchi* (insider)—*soto* (outsider) continuum ranging from "belonging" to "no relationship" (41). Japanese firms tend to land on the *uchi* side of the continuum, where implicit and opaque rules govern access to information. Thus, Scher argues that the ideal-typical Japanese firm represents a "nexus of implicit relational contracts, indicative of a high-context, communal form of industrial organization," while its Western counterpart represents a "nexus of linear contracts in a freely negotiated market" (131).

Labor–Management Cooperation

The nature of interfirm relations in Japan has been determined in part by the nature of intrafirm ties; that is, the ties between labor and management. Managers in Japan have a tendency to foster ties with outside firms that will serve to protect their own interests and those of their peers. This is because they tend to be promoted from within the firm, and thus identify with the firm. In an analysis of 520 companies listed on stock exchanges in Japan, Suehiro and Wailerdsak (2004) found that nearly 90 percent of the directors and executives rose to their positions from within the ranks of their current firm or came from an associated firm. In other words, managers may have been socialized by the Japanese employment system to maintain long-standing interfirm relationships, such as keiretsu ties, that serve to reduce risks, secure market share, and preserve jobs in the firm, even if this means sacrificing some amount of profit taking.[33] Kester (1996, 112) describes this as an "incentive to act prophylactically against whatever broader organizational impulses may exist to take advantage of implicit agreements through opportunistic behavior."

But causality also runs in the other direction. That is, intrafirm relations in Japan have been determined in part by the nature of interfirm ties. If the entrepreneur or stockholder (the presumed "principal") loses hegemony over a firm, as happened increasingly in postwar Japan with the emergence of a system of stable or cross-shareholding, managers (the presumed "agents") are freer to aggressively represent the interests of other concerned "stakehold-

33. For more on the "socialization" of managers, see Dore (2005).

ers," including—of course—longtime employees. Kester (1996, 122) notes that many of the shareholders in the ideal-typical Japanese firm (that is, the large innovating Japanese firm) also serve as creditors, customers, and suppliers: "Not surprisingly, therefore, Japanese managers tend to view their proximate task as the preservation and enhancement of these complex relationships rather than an immediate, direct pursuit of any one stakeholders' interests." Aoki (1988, 101) agrees, but tries to simplify what is a complex image. Unlike the ideal-typical Anglo-American firm, he argues that the Japanese firm is "dually controlled" by stockholders and employees. Management serves as an arbiter, carefully balancing the interests of these two parties. It pursues a long-run growth strategy that defies the "Western" law of short-run profit maximization and thereby delivers extra benefits to employees.

Japan's Economic Planning Agency (1998c, 16) has captured this distinction in terms that resonate with my own analysis—that is, in terms of selective relationalism. It calls Japan's an "insider model" of corporate governance that privileges employees, and calls the U.S. and U.K. corporate governance an "open model" that privileges shareholders. We can hear this distinction again in a discussion moderated by the *Nihon Keizai Shinbun* (December 3, 1996, 1), with Toshiba's former president Nishimuro Taizo defending the Japanese model and General Electric's former CEO Jack Welch defending the Anglo-American model. After Welch notes that profit margins generally are much lower in Japan than in the United States, Nishimuro responds:

> Of course, no business should be loss-making, but there are low margin businesses that are socially meaningful, such as satellites or power equipment, and our top mission is not to give up on them but to try to improve them. . . . It is not the Japanese custom to cut personnel in one fell swoop. Neither the employees nor the shareholders demand exclusive pursuit of profit maximization. ROE [Return on equity]-only management is not suitable for firms that want to be respected and that employees can be proud of.

Likewise, Miyauchi Yoshihiko, the chairman of Orix, used a symposium on corporate governance sponsored by the *Asahi Shinbun* (April 12, 2000, 17) to express serious doubts about a U.S.-style system that gives ultimate authority to shareholders. "Whom are we [in management] supposed to work for?" he asked. "Shareholders who have stayed with us from the very beginning? Or those who only wish to make a killing? And what about foreign investors?" Miyauchi acknowledged that Japanese firms should pay more attention to shareholders, but insisted they should not neglect other stakeholders, such as company employees and long-time transaction partners.

To understand these views on the proper role of management, we need to go back in time, all the way back to the 1920s, when Japan's industrial sector was divided neatly into two pieces: a traditional sector made up of thousands of small, labor-intensive firms, and a modern sector made up of a handful of large, capital-intensive firms trying to adopt Western technology.[34] The oligopolistic firms at the top end of this dual economy were spending a great deal to train their workers to operate the new machinery, and they did not want to lose their investment in human capital. So they made an informal pact with labor, a pact that could be called the innovation bargain. In exchange for the loyalty of their skilled employees, management offered two important benefits: long-term if not permanent employment (*shūshin koyō*) and a related system of seniority-based pay (*nenkō jōretsu*) that rewarded those who remained with the firm.

But the innovation bargain of the 1920s did not yield cooperation between labor and management. In those days, labor agitated for political influence, and management persuaded the state to respond with all its repressive power, using both the police and the law. It was not until the postwar period—and more specifically, not until the 1970s—that the two sides found a way to collaborate through the vehicle of the enterprise union. (Unlike a Western industrial union, which represents coal miners, machinists, or other occupationally specific workers who perform the same function across an entire industry, an enterprise union represents the entire spectrum of long-time or "core" workers inside one firm, including those with white, pink, and blue collars.) Keiretsu had, by that time, become a solid fixture in the Japanese political economy, and members increasingly cemented intra-group ties via cross-shareholding. In the process, management gradually acquired more and more autonomy to act on behalf of—and to bargain directly with—employees. This bargaining takes place within the firm at the level of the enterprise union.

Although management and labor, like assemblers and suppliers, cooperate closely in Japan, they, like assemblers and suppliers, do not function as equal partners. Employees are important but subordinate members of the team. Through QC (quality control) circles, factory workers frequently get a chance to suggest ways to improve the production process. And through the *ringi* system of widely circulating draft policies for the company, lower-level managers often can participate in the decision-making process. In return, however, employees are expected to work hard, unflinchingly, for the welfare of the firm—even if that means bowing to a sudden request from management to stay late to meet a critical deadline.

In addition to tangible benefits such as firm-specific training and seniority-based pay, management uses the ideology of "familism" to instill in workers a sense of belonging, a spirit of "we the company." This often takes on

34. This section relies heavily on Yamamura (1986).

the character of a political campaign, complete with buttons and banners urging workers to identify with the corporate "family" and its goals.

Although the large manufacturing firm operates as a "family," and thus sets up a barrier between insiders and outsiders, it also is internally divided into different groups—some of which are more "inside" than others. In his case study of a VCR manufacturing plant, Nakamura (1996, chap. 1) shows that "core workers" in product innovation teams are set apart from less permanent, basic production work groups. The former, which enjoy the full range of company benefits, are predominantly male; the latter, which include many women, tend to be "contract" or temporary workers who are, by definition, not fully vested in the team.

Other Examples

Although selective relationalism shapes the Japanese political economy through these three nexuses of cooperation, it may emerge in other forms as well. Japanese journalists, for example, have organized press clubs (*kisha-kai*) that bargain over access to information with the government agencies their members are supposed to monitor. The watchdogs of the press, in this case, tend to behave more like guard dogs (if not lapdogs), officially restricting the flow of information to members only.[35] Another example is the way in which large corporations cultivate personal ties with academics to recruit new talent from elite schools. In an interview, a Sony official tells how his firm, known as an organizational maverick in Japan's otherwise clubby corporate world, polished this image by announcing in the 1990s that it would consider job applicants "blindly"—that is, only on the basis of individual merit, not the name of the university they attended.

> That was true—but only for our nonengineering staff. Just like all the big machine manufacturers, we continued to negotiate with engineering schools over the allocation of their graduates. For years, you see, individual professors have parceled their top students out on an equitable basis—one to Sony, one to Hitachi, one to Toshiba, and so on. That's how the system has worked, and we felt we had to continue to play along. We worried that if we cut off our ties with those professors and tried to recruit students on our own, we would be locked out of the arena altogether.[36]

Although I have restricted my discussion here to selective relationalism in the political economy of Japan, one could cite numerous examples of

35. See Yamamoto (1989).

36. Interview, Tokyo, Feb. 25, 1999. This long-standing practice of relational recruiting is described unfavorably by a Sony manager in Kobayashi (1966, 165–68). Thus, despite its ardent opposition, even a maverick like Sony was—three decades later—unable to buck the system.

such networks in other spheres of Japanese life. In traditional music, dance, Noh, kabuki, and even flower arrangement, for example, artists/performers belong to hierarchical organizations or schools led by a master (*iemoto*) who directs that organization, but who also intervenes in the personal lives of his (or, far less often, her) disciples, even serving as a matchmaker.[37] And in elementary and junior high school, students forge social ties through their club activities (*bukatsu*), and relate to one another as *senpai* (senior partner, or leader) and *kōhai* (junior partner, or follower).

Relationalism Succeeds

The mutually reinforcing linkages of selective relationalism served Japan exceptionally well during the 1950s and 1960s (the rapid growth period), when it was trying to rebuild an economy devastated by World War II. Like all industrializing countries, Japan in those days faced a critical shortage of both capital and technology. The government was able to solve the more tractable of these two problems; it promoted capital accumulation by using tax incentives to encourage household savings, and by keeping itself relatively lean (thereby leaving room for private investment).[38] On its own, however, the government could do little to eliminate Japan's yawning technology gap; only selective relationalism, as it turned out, could correct that.

To appreciate the severity of this problem, some background is necessary. Until the mid-1960s, Japanese economic growth bumped into an intermittent barrier in the form of a balance of payments (BOP) crisis. Whenever the economy began to grow rapidly, imports would outpace exports and a trade deficit would result. To maintain the fixed exchange rate of the time (360 yen to the dollar), the Bank of Japan was obliged on those occasions to raise interest rates and thereby cool down the economy. This slowed the flow of imports, and gradually restored balance to the current account. But it also interfered with the momentum of industrialization, which relied on a heavy flow of imported raw materials.

For Japan to truly achieve catch-up development, it needed to break through this macroeconomic barrier. And to do so, it had to somehow upgrade its industrial structure, and thus enhance the composition of its exports, so that it could earn more foreign exchange and thus more easily finance its imports. Japan had to reduce its emphasis on the production of low-value-added goods such as textiles (its largest export in the 1950s) that

---

37. See Nakane (1970, 58–59)

38. One such incentive, the so-called *maruyū* program, exempted interest earned on bank deposits from the income tax. More broadly, the government allowed the tax system to become increasingly regressive, taxing wage earners far more heavily than self-employed businesspeople or farmers. A regressive tax system benefits the wealthy, who tend to save more.

had low income and price elasticities of demand and only limited positive spillovers, and increase its emphasis on the production of higher value-added goods with higher income and price elasticities and more positive spillovers. In other words, Japanese firms had to find a way to innovate more aggressively. Selective relationalism made this possible.

Consider, first, the government-business nexus. Close ties between bureaucrats and industrialists, many of whom graduated together from a handful of elite universities such as the University of Tokyo, allowed information about market conditions and possible policy responses to flow smoothly in both directions, minimizing transaction costs between the private and public sectors.[39] The state did not oversee a unilaterally scripted "master plan" for the structural adjustment of the Japanese economy. To borrow a useful expression from Evans (1995, 13–16), it served instead as a "midwife" in the birth of these new industries. It not only offered a temporary, protective cover from imports but also provided scarce resources to them—in exchange for meeting certain performance criteria related to export volumes, product quality, and product variety.

The Ministry of Finance, for example, set a lid on interest rates, which created excess demand for capital. Its proxy, the Bank of Japan, then supplied that demand by overlending to the city banks, the financial hubs of the keiretsu; specifically, it did this by authorizing them to make loans that exceeded their reserves (i.e., deposits held with the central bank) and equity. In doing so, MOF acquired enormous leverage over those banks. The banks, eager to gain access to artificially cheap credit, obediently followed MOF's "window guidance" by loaning money to the targeted ("strategic") industries that needed capital to import technology: shipbuilding, chemicals, steel, automobiles, and electronics.

In this sense, the state provided little more than what economists have long recognized as infant industry protection. As exports grew steadily, firms achieved economies of scale that allowed them to earn increasing returns. This produced the "investment race" that Murakami (1992) described and that I discussed in chapter 1. As early entrants in these markets began to enjoy declining long-run average costs, they moved to expand capacity; others, meanwhile, sought to join the fray by building their own plants. Due to the phenomenon of declining costs, the market was not clearing. Rather, it appeared likely that firms would engage in forward pricing (or what one

39. Although, as I asserted earlier, the state in postwar Japan was never as "autonomous" as Johnson (1982), Wade (1990), and many others have suggested, it was relatively "cohesive." That is, economic bureaucrats in rival ministries and agencies aligned themselves with rival industries, but generally shared a conviction that they were working on behalf of the national interest of Japan as a whole. As Samuels (1994) has demonstrated, state actors imbibed and then promoted an ideology of "techno-nationalism" that was not far from the Meiji era mantra of *fukoku kyōhei* (rich country, strong country). The goal was to catch up with the West. This helps explain why relationalism did not lead to massive rent-seeking in the rapid growth era.

might call "domestic dumping"), a mad dash to drive rivals out of the market by expanding output and cutting prices until one firm survived as the triumphant monopolist or as one of a small number of oligopolistic enterprises. A third party was needed to play a mediating role in organizing an institutional solution to this rather obvious problem of collective action. MITI played this role by coordinating the pace of investments. It "guided" each oligopolist in a market to invest an amount proportionate to its current market share, and thereby maintain the stability of that market. In many cases, especially those in which firms adopted new technology providing economies of scale in production, MITI authorized the use of cartels to reduce or eliminate excess capacity. This was particularly true during the late 1950s and the 1960s.[40]

The steel industry presents perhaps the classic case study of state efforts to coordinate competing business activities. In the first half of the rapid growth period, the "Big Six" steel companies organized themselves into the Japan Iron and Steel Federation and independently coordinated their pricing. But this system began to break down in 1965, when overcapacity in the industry threatened to bankrupt some of the major producers. MITI stepped in, using administrative guidance to try to get the Big Six to reduce output and stabilize prices.[41] Only Sumitomo Metals resisted, and it gave up after a short but highly public fight. The others, which had former, high-ranking MITI bureaucrats on their boards, happily went along.[42] Indeed, the former chairman of Yawata Steel (and later Nippon Steel), Inayama Yoshihiro, became known as "Mr. Cartel" for his strong advocacy of ordered markets.

This cozy arrangement proved durable, outliving even the rapid growth era, as evidenced by an article in the *Nihon Keizai Shinbun* (January 7, 1981):

> Welcome to the Iron-Steel Building in Nihonbashi, Tokyo. Around noon every Monday, elderly gentlemen arrive in black cars. . . . They go to Room 704, where a sign reads, "Regular Monday Club Meeting." The members consist of the senior executives of eight major steel producers. They sit at a rectangular table around the section chief of the Ministry of International Trade and Industry, who is seated at the head of the table.

The computer industry provides another example of the state acting as a mediator for potentially competing interests. In 1961, MITI helped set up

40. See Yamamura (1982). Many economists have argued, by contrast, that MITI was never so smart, and that it authorized cartels only in declining industries (i.e., ones marked by rising average costs). For a nuanced view, see Kosai (1997).

41. See Yamawaki (1984, 268–72).

42. Johnson (1982, 268–71) provides a wonderful description of the Sumitomo-MITI conflict. He notes that Sumitomo was the only one of the Big Six that did not (then) have amakudari bureaucrats in its boardroom, but he also notes that, three years after accepting defeat and bowing to the terms of the steel cartel, Sumitomo invited a retired MITI official to serve on its board of directors.

the Japan Electronic Computer Company (JECC), which was jointly owned by the country's up-and-coming computer manufacturers—Hitachi, Fujitsu, NEC, Mitsubishi, Toshiba, and Oki. Over the next two decades, the government provided about $2 billion in low-interest loans to JECC, which in turn used the money to buy computers from its member firms and rent them to users (primarily corporations hoping to computerize their operations) for low monthly fees. JECC thus served as the institutional nexus between the state and the industry.[43]

In the early 1970s, when IBM introduced its new 370 series, MITI jumped into action again by organizing a national research project. Fujitsu and Hitachi agreed to collaborate on the development of large IBM-compatible computers; NEC and Toshiba worked together to build medium-sized Honeywell-compatible computers; and Oki and Mitsubishi cooperated on the development of small, specialized computers.

The "New Series" project (1972–76) allowed Japanese computer manufacturers to overcome many of their technological problems and begin to compete seriously, for the first time, in global markets. But in the next project (1976–79), they made an even bigger leap by achieving very large scale integration (VLSI) of semiconductor circuits. This time, MITI organized reluctant firms into two groups. Fujitsu, Hitachi, and Mitsubishi maintained one lab; NEC and Toshiba maintained another. In the end, the cooperating firms were able to produce 64K RAM and ultimately the 1 megabit chip. And they began producing computers that matched or outperformed IBM's top of the line machines, while beating them in price.[44]

A Japanese newspaper describes how the government coaxed, cajoled, goaded, and guided firms into cooperating on the VLSI project. Nebashi, the MITI official who headed the project,

> did his best to eliminate the egoism of member firms and to create the harmony among researchers necessary for joint research. In the evenings, he went to the rooms and listened to the researchers' opinions and any dissatisfactions they had. At times, he drank *sake* with researchers. . . . The monthly meetings, attended by senior officers of the member firms, were intentionally held at the joint research institute. . . . The purpose was to let these officers become familiar with the different projects and boost the morale of the researchers. In time, tennis and golf clubs were organized among the researchers . . . and the walls of secrecy dividing the research rooms were gradually removed.[45]

In both cases, government-business cooperation was a critical but not a sufficient factor behind the growth of Japanese manufacturing. One cannot

---

43. See Anchordoguy (1988, 517–22).
44. Ibid., 526–30.
45. *Asahi Shinbun,* June 22, 1981, 9.

forget the business–business nexus, which created a steeper trajectory of technological growth in Japan. Large manufacturers cooperated with one another, and also cultivated close but vertical ties with suppliers who belonged to an interfirm network or division of labor. This allowed technical know-how to diffuse upstream.[46] Likewise, the labor–management nexus played a key role. It sanctioned informal agreements within the innovating firm to promote and protect human capital.[47]

Viewed in total, selective relationalism allowed large manufacturing enterprises to sustain the otherwise destabilizing process of development, the process of adopting successively more sophisticated technology and thereby achieving declining long-run average costs. Because costs continued to fall over the long run, these innovating firms were able to maximize market share and profits at the same time. A virtuous cycle of innovation and growth and innovation followed: In the short span of fifteen years, Japan was able to increase its GDP per worker from $3,600 in 1955 to $11,500 in 1970 (Katz 1998, 133). It achieved catch-up development faster than any other large economy in the postwar period.

Relationalism Fails

Because it fosters iterative bargaining and exchange over the long run, selective relationalism reduces the transaction costs associated with the execution and enforcement of explicit and implicit contracts. This tends to promote investment. On the other hand, because it ignores or discounts exogenous sources of capital, labor, and knowledge, selective relationalism also increases opportunity costs. This tends to create inefficiency. As discussed in chapter 1, rising opportunity costs begin to outweigh savings in transaction costs when an economy achieves catch-up development and thus enters an environment of technological uncertainty. Firms continue to invest heavily, but those investments are less and less efficient.

In Japan, relationalism generated net economic benefits in the 1950s and 1960s. Manufacturers, in particular, were able to use the web of administrative, interfirm, and intrafirm networks to successfully adopt technology from outside Japan and diffuse it throughout the domestic economy. As studies by Denison and Chung (1976), Kuroda (1996), and Cameron (1997) have shown, Japan enjoyed sustained and rapid economic growth because it was able to generate large increases in total factor productivity (TFP)—the weighted average of labor and capital productivity.[48]

46. See Imai and Yamazaki (1992).
47. See Koike (1981).
48. In his now famous growth model, Robert Solow identified a residual that is unexplained by increases in labor and capital inputs. This residual is often regarded as a proxy for TFP.

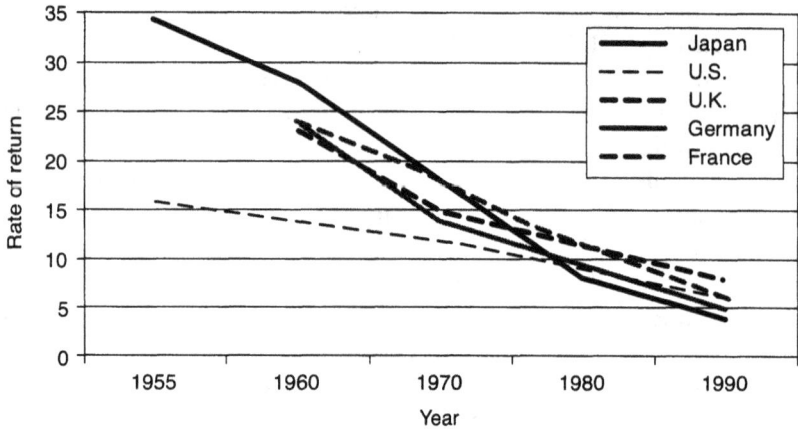

Figure 2.1. Rate of return on capital: A cross-national comparison
Source: Alexander (1997), 8. Reproduced in Katz (1998).
Note: The information in the table is the real aggregate rate of return on gross nonresidential fixed capital stock.

But TFP growth faltered in the mid-1970s. It averaged a measly 0.8 percent a year between 1973 and 1980, after reaching 2.2 percent a year between 1955 and 1973.[49] In part, this reflects the simple fact that, by the early '70s, Japan had caught up technologically with the West; that is, Japanese firms had, for the most part, adopted all they could from the global reservoir of existing technology. But it also reflects the fact that the institutions of Japanese capitalism had become increasingly obsolete. This assertion is counterintuitive to many scholars and journalists, who note that Japan was the first industrialized country to recover from the first oil crisis and the stagflation it wrought. What they do not appreciate is that Japanese firms disguised their problems during this period by investing phenomenal amounts of capital—as much as 39 percent of GDP in 1973—far more than other industrialized countries at the time.[50] These investments, however, proved less and less efficient, generating lower and lower returns. As figure 2.1 demonstrates, the rate of return on Japan's gross fixed capital stock fell precipitously—from 34 percent in 1955 to 18 percent in 1970, and continued to fall. Or, to use a slightly different measure, a $1 increase in Japan's capital stock yielded less than a 20 cent **increase** in its GDP in the mid-1970s

---

49. These figures come from Cameron (1997), but they are very close to those found in Kuroda (1996).

50. This estimate comes from Yuki Naito, Robert C. Norrington, and Keiko Yamaguchi, "A Multi-Country Evaluation of Trade Imbalances," April, 1999. Available at http://international econ.com/tradeimbalance/japan.html. The estimate might seem absurdly high, but it is actually conservative. Katz (1998), using the Penn World Tables compiled by Robert Summers and Alan Heston, estimates that Japan invested an even larger share of GDP (41%) in 1973.

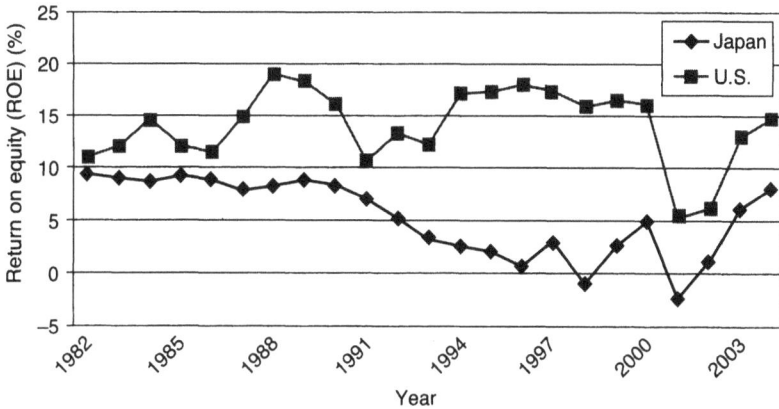

Figure 2.2. Diverging gains: Profit rates for large firms in Japan and the United States
Sources: Nomura Research Institute, "Nomura 400," Tokyo; and Standard & Poor's Corporation, "Standard & Poor's Analyst's Handbook," New York.
Notes: The U.S. data register return on book value for the "Industrials" in the S&P 500; the Japanese data, return on equity for Nomura's top 400 firms.

—a miserable fraction of the $1.20 cent increase it earned in the late 1960s.[51]

Today, in retrospect, we can clearly see the signs of underlying weakness in Japan's political economy. It was during this period, the mid- to late 1970s, that Japanese firms began to earn profit rates well below their counterparts in other industrialized countries, mostly notably the United States. (This is revealed rather starkly in figure 2.2.) It was also during this period that the consumer price index jumped more than 20 percent a year, making the cost of living in a city like Tokyo much higher than in other major cities around the world. And, finally, it was during this period that political scandal became a commonplace event, recorded almost daily in the newspapers.

Capital investment remained high in the 1980s, eventually fueling a financial "bubble" characterized by massive asset inflation, but Japan's technological development did not keep pace. The value-added-to-sales ratio in the computer industry "plunged steeply"—from 30 percent in 1982 to 22 percent in 1991, according to Yamada and Okumura (1997, 114). This industry, once imbued with great expectations for high growth, "joined the ranks of ordinary manufacturing industries . . . and is no longer a lucrative undertaking."

What caused this poor performance? Some, like Katz (1998), blame the

---

51. In general, firms in an economy that has achieved technological catch-up can expect some decrease in their marginal productivity of capital. But this decrease was exceptionally dramatic in Japan's case. Data on returns to capital come from Robert Summers and Alan Heston's *Penn World Tables* (1995), and are reported in Katz (1998, 69).

state, saying it quit supporting "sunrise" industries in the mid-1970s and began protecting only "sunset" industries. The protected, inefficient sectors of the Japanese economy, including many upstream suppliers of inputs such as steel and petrochemicals, dragged down the competitive, export-oriented sectors that use these inputs. This perspective, which is quite insightful as far as it goes, misses the larger picture: finished goods producers, which themselves continued to receive government support, willingly paid the inflated prices of intermediate goods industries. They agreed to "buy high," as Elder (1998) puts it, because they wanted to maintain relational ties that yielded access to network resources and that thereby provided them with positional power.[52]

Even though it reached the end of its catch-up phase by the early 1970s, the Japanese political economy did not begin to undergo a major transformation until very late in the 1990s. Instead of structural reform, Japanese elites used what Sheridan (1998, 27) calls the "tried and true methods" of the past to restart the stalled economy:

> Approval of the superficial economic recovery worked to delay the much-needed reform of the foundations of the economic system. Rather than "flexible and creative," the method of achieving recovery could as well be seen as a retreat, with a loss of the will and vision that were needed to adapt the economy to its new conditions of affluence and labor shortage.

Thus, as a new millennium approached, Japan's political economy was held together by the same web of network ties that had held it together for years. Indeed, that was the problem: selective relationalism, which had worked so well for firms facing declining long-run average costs, no longer worked for firms that had already adopted much of the existing technology in the global supply of existing know-how, and that therefore faced increasing long-run average costs. The system, in other words, had begun to run its course. Once blessed but now cursed by a high level of "societal coordination," the political economy of Japan, according to Witt (2006), ran into a dramatically different, more dynamic environment to which it could not properly adjust. It was, he writes, like "a car with the parking brake engaged" (186), chugging mightily but unable to keep up. To borrow terms used by Yamamura (1997, 301–2), "institutional symbiosis" gave way to "institutional collusion," and selective relationalism became a net drag on the economy.

As I suggested in chapter 1, such collusion imposes costs on insiders, who

---

52. Elder's argument is similar to, but not the same as, the argument presented here. He suggests that large, export-oriented Japanese firms have tolerated government policies that push up input prices because they, too, have benefited from such protection and promotion and because protection for upstream suppliers of inputs has been kept relatively moderate.

ultimately suffer from "information impactedness"—an inability to pick up signals outside network channels. And it imposes costs on outsiders, who suffer from information asymmetry—an inability to access the resources locked inside network structures. Harari (1998, 40–41) believes these latter costs are especially high; they can overwhelm a political system by undermining trust in its institutions. In suggesting ways for the Japanese state to regain public confidence in its handling of economic policy, he emphasizes

> the necessity to not only increase the scope of participation in policy processes without undermining political stability, but also create the conditions under which participation in policy processes equals sharing information and participating in creating and diffusing knowledge. Transparency is essential for lowering "agency costs" [in business], which are considered relatively high in the Japanese mode of *corporate* governance. It is just as essential for making national governance more effective from the point of view of both domestic and international "stakeholders."

The 1990s crisis in Japan's financial industry dramatically illustrates this problem. Amyx (2004) examines the regulatory policy networks centered on the Ministry of Finance, which had functioned smoothly in the past but became "paralyzed" in the 1990s, when partial liberalization, increasing capital flows, and political instability conspired to distort what she calls "relations-based regulation" (32). Instead of promoting multidirectional communication, Japan's exclusionary and opaque financial networks restricted the flow of information ever more tightly. MOF clung desperately to its central position in those networks, concerned above all for its own bureaucratic survival, allowing a string of financial setbacks to spread steadily into a systemwide financial crisis.

The "institutional collusion" in finance was not restricted to government-business relations; it also existed in the private networks linking main banks to their keiretsu clients. A study by Wan et al. (2008) shows that social bonds contributed to the banking industry's debt crisis in the 1990s because main banks refused to reduce or end their presumed obligations to related clients after those borrowers had become weak or "zombie" debtors. "Instead of acting as efficient monitors of client firms' operations and performance, relationship banks appear to act as keen supporters of client firms by consistently supporting them" (423), even during a dramatic macroeconomic contraction. This was evident as late as 2001, when Kanno Akira, vice-chair of the Japan Bankers Association, argued that it would be suicidal for banks to pull the plug on nonperforming loans because they would be reneging on "vital corporate relationships" (Bremner 2001).

Collinson and Wilson (2006, 1359) document other cases of "institutional collusion"—this time in the manufacturing sector, where firms have shown themselves to be "ill equipped to deal with the changing Japanese and international economic contexts" because of "embedded routines," characterized by internal network structures and external relational ties, that reduce their adaptability. Under previous and more propitious market conditions (including long-term growth in domestic demand and increased productivity), these routines had given Japanese firms a competitive advantage. But under more challenging conditions, Collinson and Wilson (2006, 1377) conclude that these routines produced inertia, "making [the firms studied] less able to respond to the radical changes in their competitive environment." In a nutshell, they lost much of their innovative capacity.

In the 1990s, this pattern of institutional failure was repeated throughout the political economy of Japan. Indeed, in countless public agencies and private firms, the costs of selective relationalism grossly outweighed the benefits; and yet network ties persisted through virtually the entire decade. Political and business elites continued to cooperate in the formulation and implementation of industrial policies, but their collaboration often generated disappointing results. As Callon (1995, 148) notes, MITI "discovered that pushing out on the technology frontier was much more difficult than the catch-up policies that targeted existing technologies that had been perfected by the United States." Meanwhile, business elites continued to cooperate with one another and with their core employees; that is, they continued to pursue market share maximization, as they had all along, but they no longer seemed able to maximize profits (see figure 2.2).[53]

By the 1990s, the economic costs of relationalism had created a political crisis for Japanese elites. But they were not entirely bereft of options. Instead of dismantling selective relationalism, a model of capitalism that had run its course at home in Japan, they chose to regionalize it.

---

53. Many studies have shown that Japanese firms fail to maximize profits, relative to their counterparts in the West, particularly the United States. For example, see Odagiri (1989) and Watanabe and Yamamoto (1992). Fewer studies, however, have managed to demonstrate, once and for all, that this is due to the preferences of managers whose goal is expanding market share rather than raising the rate of return on investment. Kagano et al. (1983, 25) do, however, offer convincing survey data in support of this assertion.

3 Leading a Flock of Geese

In the summer of 1990, Japan's financial "bubble" began to stretch thin and crack, signaling an end to the happy days spawned by runaway asset inflation. Business and government elites faced mounting pressure, both economic and political, as the Japanese economy, like Snow White, fell into a deep sleep that would last throughout the 1990s.

Much of this pressure came from an increasingly competitive global market. Manufacturers struggled to hang onto sales volumes as labor productivity declined slowly but steadily to the point that, by 1994, Japan's rate was about 34 percent lower than the U.S. rate.[1] Profits suffered as a result; returns to capital were lower in Japan than anywhere else in the industrialized world. But pressure also came from a highly politicized international system. In the first half of the 1990s, the United States pursued a new "results-oriented" and "managed trade" policy that took especially careful aim at Japanese automobiles and electronics goods.[2] Other countries, although not as aggressive, also criticized Japan for its persistent trade surplus. In the latter half of that decade, the United States pushed Japanese government officials to roll back regulations that inhibited the development and expansion of new business activities.

1. Productivity in manufacturing actually decreased 0.1 percent a year, on average, between 1990 and 1994. By 1994, labor productivity in Japanese manufacturing was second from the last in a ranking of twelve industrialized countries. Only South Korea was ranked lower. See Seisansei Kenkyūjo (1997, 4). This fall was due in large part to the excess capacity created by reduced demand.

2. Although the Clinton administration's approach was new, U.S. pressure on Japan had been building for some time. In September 1989, the two governments began negotiations on the "structures" of their respective economies. The United States pushed, for example, for stronger enforcement of Japan's Anti-Monopoly Act and elimination of exclusionary keiretsu ties. For the most part, these negotiations were unsuccessful. See Schoppa (1997).

Japanese elites, informed by their own experience and by reform-minded groups such as the Maekawa Commission, understood the underlying cause of their malaise: selective relationalism, an inappropriate system for a highly developed economy like Japan, had run its course and now was producing more costs than benefits.[3] Elites also recognized they had to move in one of two directions: (1) they could dismantle this obsolete system, relying more on unfettered markets and less on firmly established relationships to carry out exchange, or (2) they could try to expand the scope of the system; that is, they could try to rescue relationalism by extending its social networks into a new and more fertile environment in which firms might still be adopting existing technology, and thus one in which selective relationalism might yield net gains.

From the entrenched positions occupied by Japanese businessmen and bureaucrats, Asia—with its young, still developing economies—loomed on the horizon like a life-giving oasis. The region's developmental promise was, in the early 1990s, palpable: land was cheap and plentiful; labor was cheap and, better yet, relatively literate. But best of all, business and government officials in host countries typically had longstanding ties with their Japanese counterparts, and—in most cases—wanted to strengthen or deepen such ties.[4]

As Shiraishi (1997, 171) notes, this was not the first time that Japanese elites had turned to Asia, particularly Southeast Asia, in a moment of distress:

> The region has repeatedly figured as a "solution" for Japan in crisis. It appeared to offer a way out of the mess Japan found itself in China toward the end of the 1930s. It seemed to offer a solution for Japan's economic recovery when China was closed in the 1950s and 1960s. And the region is again seen in Japan as a way out of the current predicament.

This chapter documents the way in which Japan has come to engage Asia, and the way it came to embrace the region, again, in the 1990s as a solution to its economic crisis. Just as before, no one this time needed to convene a meeting. No one needed to forge a written agreement. Japanese manufac-

---

3. In fact, relationalism had run its course much earlier—in the 1980s. But continued high rates of capital investment, and the bubble economy fueled by that investment, helped mask this reality. The Maekawa Commission, set up by former prime minister Nakasone and chaired by a former governor of the Bank of Japan, highlighted this situation in its 1986 report. It was not until the 1990s, however, well after the bubble burst, that other prominent government officials and business leaders paid much notice.

4. Due to the legacy of Japanese imperialism, China and South Korea have been the most reluctant to deepen ties with Japan. In the 1990s, however, bitter memories did not stop the Chinese government from relying on Tokyo for most of its bilateral ODA, or Korean firms from obtaining almost half of their technology imports from Japanese firms.

turing firms that had invested in Asia were enjoying economic success (i.e., earning profits that generally were far higher than elsewhere), and Japanese bureaucrats who had moved or visited there as advisers were enjoying political success (i.e., winning friends and profoundly influencing people). Thus, to those elites most affected by the unfolding crisis in Japan, the future opportunities presented by regionalization were rather obvious.

Government officials quickly became cheerleaders for a process of economic regionalization that had begun slowly in the 1980s and that soon would accelerate. "Japan's main target [of trade and investment] must be Asia," declared Hosoya Yuji, deputy director of MITI's industrial policy bureau.[5]

Keidanren, Japan's big business federation, noted that Asia was becoming "an indispensable part of the business and procurement activities of Japanese companies." Those economic ties between Japan and other countries in Asia benefit both sides, and thus should be strengthened. "Japanese companies will have to form a closer cooperative relationship in an effort to secure their international competitiveness."[6]

Many Japanese academics soon joined the chorus. One of them, Seki Mitsuhiro (1993), wrote that Japan had no choice but to regionalize its economy:

> [It] finds itself no longer able to support its old habit of thinking of itself as a small, weak country striving for its own prosperity. Japan must discover a fundamental new raison d'être in a mutual interdependence with its neighbors who desire industrial modernization and economic development. . . . Japan needs to place the highest priority on figuring out how to contribute to this general tide of events in East Asia; how to ensure smooth technical transfer; and, further, how to foster the regionalization, or geographical diversification, of Japanese business.

Takahashi (1997, 44–49), meanwhile, called for the construction of an "Asian Superhub," a kind of federation of economically interdependent states, to replace the region's loose and broadly inclusive grouping—APEC, which spans five continents and includes twenty-one members. APEC stands for Asia Pacific Economic Cooperation, but Takahashi facetiously called it "Asia Pacific Economic CONFLICT," because he believes it gives its biggest member, the United States, too much leverage and undermines the economic sovereignty of Asian countries in the region. Due to its pivotal position in the emerging regional economy, Japan, he writes, should serve as the leader of this new "Superhub," which could be called "PEACE" (Pan

5. Quoted in *Financial Times*, December 21, 1992, 23.
6. *Keidanren Review*, special issue, 1993, 8.

East Asia Coastal Economies) or "AREA" (Asian Regional Economic Alliance).

Unlike Takahashi, however, most writers were interested in regionalization, the informal or business-led process of integration, and not regionalism, the formal-legal process. A leading business scholar, Itami Hiroyuki (1993, 93), commented that Japanese manufacturers were hemmed in by two walls: the "wall of the system" (Japan's outmoded political economy), and the "wall of the world," which he says the West built to keep out Japanese manufactured imports. Asia, he wrote, offered a way for Japanese manufacturers to clear both walls, and he urged them to build more factories in that region.

Firms in high-tech, export-oriented industries were especially receptive to such advice—for obvious reasons. While U.S. computer firms such as Gateway, Dell, and Compaq enjoyed explosive sales growth in the first half of the 1990s (1,232, 790, and 310 percent, respectively), Japanese firms stumbled. Sales at Fujitsu and Sony increased by only 11 and 3 percent, respectively, from 1990 to 1995. NEC, Japan's leading computer maker, did better, reporting sales growth of 116 percent during this period.

This revenue crisis—a result of declining productivity, reduced consumption at home, and higher prices for exports—encouraged firms to step up their regionalization initiatives. Yamada and Okumura (1997, 115) note that

> Japanese computer makers are now compelled to reconsider a vertical division of labor with Southeast Asia, which could serve as an outlet for exports. They will also need to pursue a horizontal division of labor and strategic alliances to facilitate the expansion of local markets and economic growth in foreign regions into which they have made significant inroads.

Looking back from the perspective of today, one can easily see why Japanese elites would choose to regionalize their production and administrative networks. At the time, however, this move—elite regionalization—was actually quite daring, even radical.

Recent History of Japanese Regionalization

In the late 1960s, Japan began accumulating a trade surplus that gave Japanese firms the opportunity to engage in foreign direct investment (FDI). But those firms remained, nonetheless, reluctant to invest outside their home country. Even as recently as 1980, the stock of Japanese foreign direct investment represented less than 4 percent of Japan's GDP, compared with 43 percent for the United States and 16 percent for the United Kingdom.[7]

7. See OECD, *International Direct Investment Statistics Yearbook.*

It is true, of course, that Japanese firms invested in resource extraction activities in Asia, primarily Southeast Asia, in the 1950s, and that automobile and electric appliance producers began to shift simple "screwdriver" or assembly operations to the region in the 1960s. It is equally true that the Japanese state aggressively promoted external investment—more aggressively, in fact, than any other government in the world; between 1953 and 1999, the Japan Export-Import Bank (which in 1999 became the Japan Bank for International Cooperation) provided $72 billion in public loans for overseas investment, or more than 10 percent of all postwar Japanese FDI (JFDI). By comparison, the German government provided only $2.6 billion in such financing, or 0.53 percent of German FDI during the same period (Solis 2004, 15–18). Despite all of this, the scale of JFDI—especially in manufacturing, which receives most of my attention here—remained limited, especially in light of the size and maturity (or technological sophistication) of Japanese industry. Those firms had invested heavily in selective relational ties at home that, in their calculations, represented both sunk costs and—at one time— competitive advantages. They were extremely reluctant to abandon them (Tejima 1996, 372).

Caution began to evaporate, however, in 1985, when the finance ministers of Japan, Germany, the United Kingdom, France, and the United States met at the Plaza Hotel in New York and agreed to an "orderly appreciation of the main non-dollar currencies against the dollar." Within nine months, the yen jumped in value from 250 per dollar to 150. The impact on Japanese overseas investment was massive: the country that had been such a reluctant source of FDI suddenly became one of the world's leading capital exporters. In 1985, Japan accounted for only 6.4 percent of the global stock of outward FDI—a tiny fraction of the U.S. share (36.4 percent); by 1990, Japan accounted for 11.8 percent—almost half the U.S. share of 25.5 percent (United Nations 1998).[8]

During those heady years in the late 1980s, 60 percent of Japanese man-

8. This turnaround is even more dramatically revealed in figures on the annual *flow* of direct investment. In the 1978–80 period, Japan accounted for only 5.6 percent of the total FDI flows from developed countries. The United States, the United Kingdom, and Germany, by contrast, accounted for 43.2, 14.6, and 9.0 percent, respectively. In the 1988–90 period, Japan accounted for 21.1 percent, larger than that for the United States (12.9), the United Kingdom (15.1), and Germany (9.9). Using a different yardstick, however, we must conclude that Japanese manufacturers remain relatively cautious about producing overseas. Compared to their counterparts from the United States and Germany, who in 1994 produced 36 and 23 percent, respectively, of their total output in foreign countries, Japanese manufacturers had an overseas production ratio of only 8.6 percent that year—the latest year for which comparable data could be obtained (MITI 1998a). Although low in comparison to manufacturers from other industrialized countries, the 1994 rate for Japanese manufacturers represents a big increase from earlier years. The rate in 1985, for example, was 3 percent.

ufacturing FDI went to North America.[9] This was due in large part to the Plaza Accord, which slowly but steadily shifted relative prices and made Japanese exports less competitive. However, it also reflected the fact that Japanese manufacturers had been finding it increasingly difficult to export to their favorite overseas market, the United States, which—since the early 1970s—had gradually adopted a new and more aggressive trade policy including demands for "voluntary" export restraints on automobiles and other products.

To avoid high domestic production costs and circumvent export restrictions, Japanese manufacturers invested overseas—and not only in North America. Indeed, much of the JFDI that flowed to Asia in the late 1980s was motivated by this goal; Japanese manufacturers built export platforms that sent relatively cheap goods, especially electronic products, to the United States. In those days, Japanese electronics manufacturers in Asia exported about 10 percent of their total production to North America.[10] A triangular pattern of trade developed in which Japan shipped capital goods and intermediate products (often relatively high-value-added parts or specially processed materials) to Asia, where they would be assembled into final goods for export to the United States, and increasingly to Europe as well. Urata and Kawai (1996) document this triangular trade pattern in their econometric analysis of U.S. imports from 1990 to 1992.[11] And Chia (1997, 51), in her survey of twelve Japanese electronics manufacturers in Singapore, finds a similar trading pattern.

In 1991, as the domestic economy began to stall, Japanese manufacturers —especially machine manufacturers[12]—fixed their sights more firmly on Asia than ever before. One company, Matsushita, established seventy-eight of its regional production facilities there in the 1990s—or 85 percent of the ninety-two plants that it had, by the end of that decade, built in the region.[13]

9. Ministry of Finance, *Taigai chokusetsu tōshi no kyoka todokede jisseki* (Statistics on the Approval/Notification of Overseas Direct Investment). Tokyo: MOF Printing Bureau, various years.

10. See MITI, *Wagakuni Kigyō no Kaigai Jigyō Katsudō*, various years.

11. This study used a gravity model, testing the effect or "weight" of different variables (such as the GNP of a trading partner and the distance from a trading partner) on U.S. bilateral imports. The key explanatory variable was the cumulative stock of Japanese FDI in a particular country exporting to the United States. The coefficients of this variable, when disaggregated for machine industries, were positive and statistically significant at the 5 percent level. For general machinery, the authors used eighty-five observation points and achieved an adjusted R-squared of 0.867. For electrical machinery, the corresponding figures were 90 and 0.781; for transportation machinery, they were 79 and 0.884.

12. In the 1990s, more than 70 percent of Japanese manufacturing FDI in Asia was carried out by firms in the four machinery industries: electronics, automobiles, general machinery, and precision machinery. See MITI (1999a, 159).

13. Interview with Matsukawa Yoshihiro, Matsushita corporate planning, Osaka, March 26, 1999.

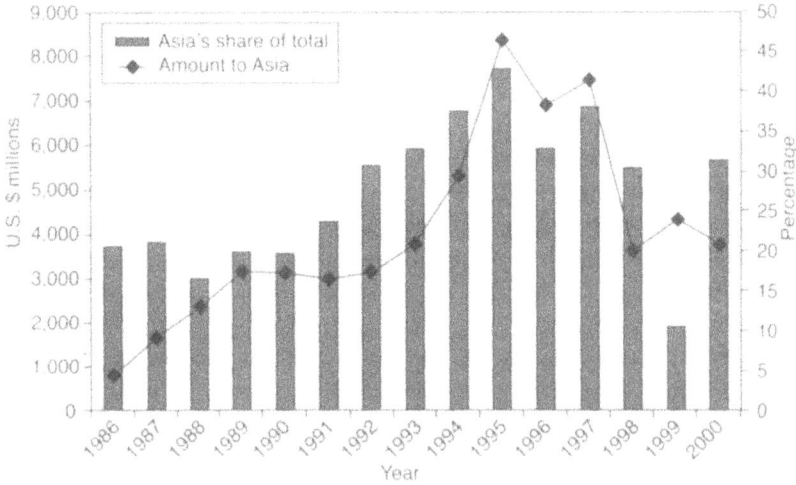

Figure 3.1. Japanese manufacturing FDI to Asia
Source: Calculated by the author from Ministry of Finance, *Kokusai Kinyū kyoku Nenpō,* various years.
Note: For years 1989–2000, exchange rate is based on the number in "International financial statistics," IMF.

As figure 3.1 shows, Asia attracted 23.7 percent of Japan's total manufacturing FDI in 1991, and continued to receive an increasing share until 1995, when it attracted almost 43 percent ($8.3 billion of $19.4 billion in total manufacturing FDI). Given the relatively small size of the regional economy of Asia (compared with North America and Europe), this was an extraordinarily large amount.[14] Even in 1997, when the region became engulfed in a deepening financial crisis, Asia continued to receive nearly 38 percent ($7.4 billion) of Japan's total manufacturing FDI. And such figures actually understate the volume of Japanese FDI in the region because they do not include reinvestments by existing affiliates enjoying profits there. MITI has estimated that, between 1992 and 1996, reinvestments by Japanese affiliates in Asia—which are unreported—actually exceeded officially new (reported) investments from Japan by about 14 percent.[15]

Figure 3.2 breaks down the location of Japanese manufacturing affiliates, and demonstrates how elite regionalization steadily advanced over the decade. By the end of the 1990s, more than 60 percent of those affiliates were in Asia. If we break this down further, considering Japanese manufacturing *facilities,* rather than manufacturing *affiliates,* Asia accounted for an even larger share: about 70 percent of the total number of overseas facto-

14. One must acknowledge, of course, that FDI often has a regional bias. Just as Japanese manufacturers invest heavily in Asia, U.S. manufacturers invest heavily in Canada and Mexico, while European manufacturers invest heavily in other countries in Europe.
15. See MITI 1998a, 53; and JETRO 1997a, 32.

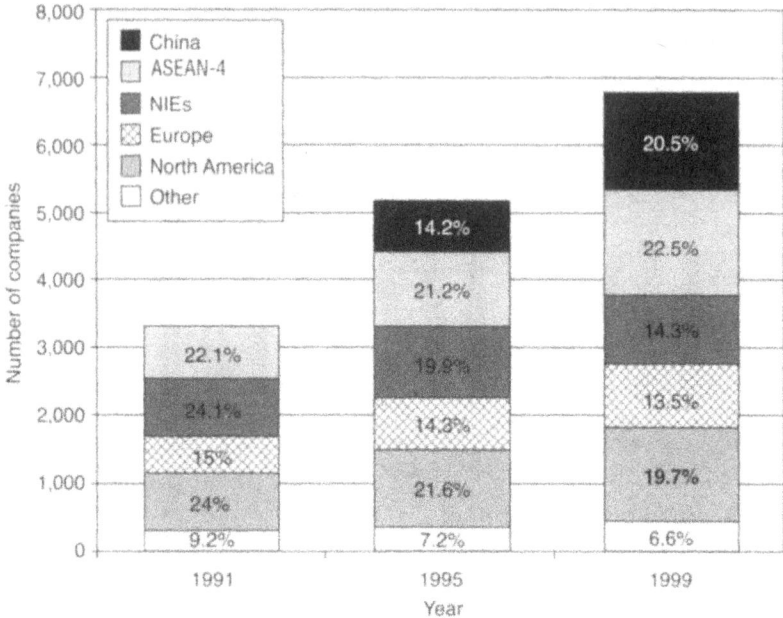

Figure 3.2. Location of overseas Japanese manufacturing affiliates
Source: MITI, *Kaigai Jigyō Katsudō Kihon Chōsa*, #22, #26, #30.

ries.[16] This is simply because many manufacturing affiliates in Asia operate more than one factory.

The discrepancy between figures on the value of Japanese manufacturing FDI to Asia and the number of affiliates (or factories) in the region is due to the remarkably large investment by small and medium-sized enterprises (SMEs), particularly parts producers. These component manufacturers dramatically increased their presence in Asia in the early 1990s. Consider the spurt in sales by Japanese affiliates in Asia between 1992 and 1994 in the following manufacturing sectors:[17]

- audiovisual components, 28 percent;
- parts for "white goods," such as refrigerators, washers and dryers, 30 percent;
- computer components, 101 percent;
- parts for office automation equipment, 58 percent;
- semiconductor parts, 99 percent;
- electrical/electronic components, 26 percent;

16. See JETRO (1998, 4).
17. See Japan Machinery Exporters Association (1994). This was a survey of 144 Japanese machinery manufacturers with factories in China, the Asian NIEs, the ASEAN-4, and Vietnam.

- camera parts, 25 percent;
- parts for telecommunication equipment, 57 percent;
- industrial machinery components, 14 percent.

Just as explosive was the expansion of Japanese automobile parts suppliers into Asia. In the thirty-five years from 1962 through 1997, Japanese auto parts producers made 405 investments in the ASEAN-4 countries of Southeast Asia (Thailand, Indonesia, Malaysia, and the Philippines); but they made 223 of those investments (or 55 percent) in just the final seven years, from 1991 through 1997.[18] The peak year was 1996. If we look at new production bases created in that year throughout Asia (i.e., in China and the Asian NIEs, as well as in the ASEAN-4), we find that auto parts manufacturers moved heavily into this region. Of the 124 overseas factories newly established in 1996, 94 (or 76 percent) were in Asia.[19]

By the mid-1990s, then, the region had emerged as the overseas base for Japanese subcontractors in a variety of machine manufacturing industries. Indeed, Asia at that time accounted for 100 percent of the consumer appliance parts, 84 percent of the electronic and electrical components, 74 percent of the computer parts, and 59 percent of the audiovisual components manufactured by the overseas affiliates of Japanese firms (Yamamoto 1996, 25). In general, SMEs preferred to invest in Asia rather than in other regions of the world; in 1994, 81 percent of small and medium-sized enterprises expanding overseas chose Asia; even in 1997, 55.3 percent chose this region in spite of its sudden economic woes.[20]

In the mid-1990s, China began to rival the ASEAN-4 economies as the favorite destination for Japanese SMEs, especially suppliers generating "reverse imports," goods produced overseas for the Japanese market. These suppliers built scores of factories along the coast, particularly in northeast China (Manchuria), where Japan had established a puppet state (Manchukuo) in the 1930s. Indeed, they had—by 1996—established more than fifteen hundred joint venture operations in Dalian, which had been the major port city in Manchukuo.[21]

On top of traditional forms of FDI, Japanese manufacturers began to heavily engage in what Oman (1984) has called "intermediate forms" of overseas

18. This is taken from Fourin (1998a).
19. See Japan Finance Corporation for Small Business (1997, 35). In 1994 and 1995, Asia received a smaller, but still substantial share (about 50%) of all of the overseas investment projects by Japanese auto parts producers. See Watanabe (1996, 23).
20. SME Agency 1998, 73.
21. The Japanese state has encouraged this second, but entirely peaceful, invasion by providing loans to SME investors and by spending $60 million to develop land and infrastructure in and around Dalian. See *The Nation* (Bangkok), September 5, 1997.

Table 3.1. Japan's bilateral ODA to Asian countries

Country	1989	1991	1993	1995	1997	1999
China	832.2	585.3	1,350.70	1,380.20	576.9	1,226.00
	(55.7)	(46.3)	(60.2)	(54.5)	(47)	(67.3)
Indonesia	1,145.30	1,065.50	1,148.90	892.4	496.9	1,605.80
	(67.2)	(60.9)	(60.1)	(68.5)	(62.9)	(74)
Thailand	488.9	406.2	350.2	667.4	468.3	880.3
	(74.4)	(63.5)	(62.2)	(80.7)	(77.9)	(88.5)
Philippines	403.8	458.9	758.4	416.1	319	413
	(53.3)	(53.2)	(56.8)	(55.6)	(56.2)	(67)
Malaysia	79.6	199.9	none	64.8	none	122.61
	(60.3)	(73.2)	(n/a)	(60.7)	(n/a)	(87.5)

Source: MOFA, *Wagakuni no Seifu Kaihatsu Enjo no Jisshi Jōkyō,* various years.
Note: Upper number: Japan's contribution in $U.S. millions.
Lower number in parentheses: Japan's share of recipient's total bilateral aid.

investment, particularly franchise contracts and technology licensing agreements with Asian partners.[22] For example, Japanese technology exports to Asia doubled between 1986 and 1991 (from less than $700 million to nearly $1.4 billion), and then doubled again to $2.75 billion by 1996, when they began to plateau. In the mid-1990s, Asia received roughly half of Japan's technology exports.[23]

Finally, in addition to these private capital and technology flows, the Japanese state itself began to invest large sums in the region via official development assistance (ODA), or foreign aid. Japanese ODA, which began in the 1950s as war reparations to Southeast Asian nations occupied during World War II, was always just one piece of a broader program of "economic cooperation" (*keizai kyōryoku*) that included both public aid (as a pump primer) and private investment. But from the end of the 1980s until the start of the new millennium, Japan served as the world's leading aid donor, and it tended to reserve well over half of its ODA for developing countries in Asia. Most of this aid was delivered in the form of yen loans for dams, bridges, electricity transmission lines, telephone lines, and other infrastructure projects that are needed to support industrialization. Indeed, it was routinely criticized by other wealthy donor countries for focusing on such development projects rather than humanitarian programs. As table 3.1 shows, the leading recipients of Japanese aid in the 1990s were China, In-

22. Even though MNCs engaging in such "intermediate forms" of FDI do not acquire a majority equity stake in an offshore business, they often gain de facto control over the business. This is why Oman and other economists treat them as variants of foreign direct investment.

23. See Science and Technology Agency, *Kagaku Gijutsu no Shinkō ni kansuru Nenpō Hōkoku* (Annual Report on the Promotion of Science and Technology), various years.

donesia, Thailand, India, and the Philippines—often in that order. In the late 1990s, when the currency crisis washed across Asia, the Japanese state stepped up its commitment to these and other struggling countries in the region. The $30 billion Miyazawa Initiative, a special funding package designed to prime Asia's jammed economic pump, reflected this commitment. In 1998, the first year of that plan, Asia received $5.37 billion in aid from its wealthy neighbor—62.4 percent of Japan's total ODA (and 90.7 percent of its total package of yen loans).

We should recognize, however, that in its effort to promote the economic development of Asia, the Japanese state did far more than merely provide cash. Through the Japan International Cooperation Agency (JICA), which then was one of the two main government agencies (and since 2008, the only one) implementing Japanese ODA, a large number of Japanese advisers—known as "experts"—were dispatched to the region every year to offer technical assistance on everything from effective methods for fertilizing crops to strategies for improving the productivity of manufacturing. By the mid to late 1990s, 60 percent of all JICA experts heading overseas were going to Asia (3,351 in 1999, up from 1,292 in 1991).[24] Moreover, this did not include the experts dispatched through JICA's Japan Senior Volunteers Program or through the Japan Overseas Development Corporation (JODC). Asia received the lion's share of these Japanese technicians and engineers who have retired from jobs in the private sector. Indeed, JODC—an arm of MITI—then operated only three overseas offices, all of them in Asia (Bangkok, Jakarta, and Beijing).

In the 1990s, the common strategic objective of both Japanese state officials and industry executives vis-à-vis Asia was the construction of a regional division of labor based on the different technological levels of member countries. That is, they attempted to promote economic integration through capital, technology, and merchandise flows that reflected the different but complementary factor endowments and industrial structures, and thus the different but complementary comparative advantages, of trading partners in Asia. Such a division of labor, according to several Japanese scholars, was bound to yield a dynamic process of "industrial sequencing" as more advanced economies in the region "pass down" industries in which they no longer enjoy a comparative advantage—much as an older sibling passes down outgrown clothes to a younger sibling.[25] They called this the "flying geese" pattern of regional economic development, a tightly linked or V-shaped pat-

---

24. See Ministry of Foreign Affairs, *Wagakuni no Seifu Kaihatsu Enjo no Jisshi Jōkyō* (Japanese ODA: The Actual Situation), various years; also see Japan International Cooperation Agency, *JICA nenpō* (annual report), 2002.

25. Ojima Yoshihisa, a former high-ranking MITI official, actually used this analogy in a 1970 speech to a group of Asian government officials.

tern with Japan as the "lead goose," followed by the Asian NIEs, followed further by ASEAN (Association of Southeast Asian Nations) and China.[26]

By the early 1990s, this concept had come to sit at the center of Japanese foreign economic policy toward the region. Thus, Prime Minister Kaifu Toshiki told a Southeast Asian audience that

> Japan will . . . continue to seek to expand imports from the countries of the region and promote greater investment in and technology transfer to these countries, in line with the maturity of their trade structure and their stage of development. And as the necessary complement to this effort, I hope that the host countries will make an even greater effort to create a climate receptive to Japanese investment and technology transfer.[27]

From time to time, MITI tried to coordinate this effort to construct a regional division of labor (or what it called "complex international work sharing" based on "agreed specialization"[28]), using policies such as the New AID plan (discussed in chapter 5) to identify specific industries that individual countries should promote and develop. In one study, the Japan Research Institute (1988, 126–27) described the Japanese state as the throbbing "Asian Brain" at the center of the region's evolving neural architecture. Ultimately, however, the process was driven as much by the business strategies of individual corporations—or networks of corporations—as by the far-flung schemes of bureaucrats in Tokyo.[29]

Japanese electronics firms pursued such strategies most aggressively, creating vertically layered intrafirm or intranetwork supply chains using technology-intensive production from Japan, capital-intensive production from the Asian NIEs, and labor-intensive production from China and the ASEAN-4. More specifically, the Asian affiliates of these Japanese multinational corporations (MNCs) assembled finished products with high-tech components im-

26. The "flying geese" concept was first used by Akamatsu Kaname ("A Historical Pattern of Economic Growth in Developing Countries," in *Developing Economies,* vol. 1, 1962) to describe the process of technological assimilation that allowed a single industry in a developing economy to "graduate" from dependence on imports and eventually become a producer of internationally competitive exports. He was describing the turn-of-the-century textile industry in Japan. The concept was later used by Japanese economists such as Kojima Kiyoshi (1978) to describe the pattern of trade and investment within Asia that carried technology from mature to maturing economies. The concept was appropriated again in the 1980s by Japanese government officials, such as Okita Saburo (1986), who used it to promote Japanese trade and investment in the region.

27. The speech is reproduced in the *ASEAN Economic Bulletin* 8 (1991).

28. MITI, *White Paper on International Trade,* 1992 (English version). Tokyo: JETRO, 101–18. For more on the role of the Japanese state in this process, see Hatch and Yamamura (1996, 117–22, and 138–41), and Machado (1995), 35–36.

29. Urata (1996b, 10) does a fine job of describing this strategy of "breaking up the entire production process into several sub-processes and locating labor-intensive sub-processes in labor abundant Asian countries."

ported from Japan, slightly less complex parts imported from the Asian NIEs, and the most simple, standardized parts from China and the ASEAN-4. For example, to manufacture VCRs (videocassette recorders) at its assembly plant in Bangi, Malaysia, Sony imported integrated circuits and other high-tech components from Japan and printed circuit boards from Singapore. It also purchased tape decks, as well as many other standard parts, from local suppliers in Malaysia, many of them Japanese.[30]

Automobile manufacturers built their own supply networks in Southeast Asia, taking advantage of such ASEAN regional programs as the 1988 Brand-to-Brand Complementation (BBC) scheme and the ASEAN Industrial Cooperation (AICO) scheme to reduce tariffs on certain kinds of intraregional, intraindustry trade. In general, these programs induced firms to swap parts produced in larger volumes at specified factories across the region, and then assemble them in finished vehicles in each country. Toyota, for example, used its affiliate in the Philippines as a base for specialized production of transmissions, its affiliate in Indonesia for gasoline engines, its affiliate in Malaysia for steering gears and electronic components, and its affiliate in Thailand for diesel engines and pressed parts.[31] In 1996, only four years after it had set up its regional production network, Toyota moved nearly $200 million in parts between its plants in Southeast Asia (Matsuoka 1997, 22).

Tamura (1996, 22) wrote that Japanese MNCs are building a regional division of labor that emphasizes "prototype" production in Japan and mass production of standardized products in Asia. These manufacturers, he concluded, "view Japan and Asia as one interconnected zone of activity, and carefully allocate production facilities to the most suitable location in this zone."

For a time, capital and technology flows did seem to bind the region together in a single, vertically layered unit organized by Japan. The Economic Planning Agency of Japan (1995, 279–81) described it this way: "Parent companies in Japan have built extremely tight (*kinmitsu na*) ties of interdependence with their affiliates in Asia. As a result, domestic sales (in Japan) and exports to Asia have become closely correlated." In addition, capital and technology flows did seem to promote a virtuous cycle of industrial sequencing within and between the various host economies of Asia—much as the "flying geese" model predicted. For one thing, the sales and procurement practices of Japanese producers in Asia drove higher and higher levels of intraregional trade. MITI (1998a, 188–89, 202–3) reported that, in 1995, 13.3 percent of sales by Japanese manufacturing affiliates in the region consisted of exports to other countries in Asia, and 14.4 percent of pro-

---

30. Hatch and Yamamura (1996, 25), based on interviews with Sony officials in Tokyo (July 1992) and Penang (April 1993).
31. Hatch and Yamamura (1996, 26–27).

curements consisted of imports from other countries in Asia. Much of this intraregional trade was conducted through intrafirm channels: 49.9 percent of the exports and 44.9 percent of the imports to/from other countries in Asia went to/came from other affiliates of the parent company.[32] But Japanese manufacturers also incorporated independent Japanese suppliers, as well as ethnic Chinese capitalists in Taiwan, Hong Kong, Singapore, and Southeast Asia, into their relatively tight production networks.

In 1997, a severe financial crisis spread through much of Asia, dramatically slowing economic growth and disrupting the virtuous cycle of industrial sequencing.[33] Japanese manufacturing affiliates, especially those—such as automakers—who sold most of their goods in domestic markets across Asia, became saddled with excess production capacity. Most of them were able to hang on, for months in some cases and for years in others, with the prodigious help of their parent companies, the Japanese state, and their own regional networks. Automakers responded by trying to transform their domestic manufacturing bases into quasi-export platforms, thereby taking advantage of depreciated local currencies, while electronics manufacturers moved to deepen the regional division of labor even further by concentrating the production of specific goods at different plants across Asia, and then exporting those items to the rest of the region and world.[34] In the end, however, even these heroic measures could not rescue the flying geese pattern driven by elite regionalization.

The region's financial crisis ultimately helped undermine the positional power that Japanese bureaucrats, manufacturers, bankers, and traders had come to enjoy in Asia. Multilateral financial institutions, especially the International Monetary Fund, emerged as highly influential, albeit equally controversial, sources of funding and policy advice. Japanese manufacturers, struggling to reduce costs at production sites throughout the region, began to import less from the parent company and Japan-based suppliers. And they suddenly found themselves challenged by reinvigorated rivals from the United States, Europe, and even the new dragons of Asia, which had learned

32. Data come from MITI (1998a, 213 and 220).

33. Most economists have blamed the crisis on premature moves to liberalize Asian financial markets. This argument has plenty of merit: banks and security houses were ill equipped to handle the wash of capital into—and, unfortunately, out of—these countries in the mid-1990s. But exchange rate movements also played an important role. China devalued its currency in 1994, making its labor-intensive exports highly competitive relative to those from the ASEAN-4. And the yen lost 18 percent of its value against the dollar between 1995 and 1996. This undermined the "virtuous cycle of development" anticipated in the flying geese model. Many Japanese manufacturers shifted export-oriented production from Southeast Asia to coastal China, or back to Japan. This analysis is developed more completely in Hatch (1998).

34. *Asahi Shinbun* described these strategies in a three-part series, "Ajia Kiki Ni-nen" (The Asian Crisis, Year Two), June 3, 4, and 5, 1999. *Business Week* also carried an informative article ("Japan's Asian Comeback") in its November 1, 1999 edition.

to tap into the emerging China market. As I explain in chapter 7, the era of Japanese economic domination was coming to an end.

The Paradox of Japanese Regionalization

Japanese manufacturing affiliates in Asia have inspired wildly different responses. On the one hand, one invariably hears loud, sometimes even strident, complaints, especially from academics and government officials in the host country, but occasionally from local entrepreneurs as well, about how those "stingy" Japanese multinational corporations refuse to freely transfer their technology. For example, Park Woo-hee (1992), former president of the Korean Academy of Industrial Technology, called Japan the "black hole" of the innovating universe, forever sucking in technology (from the West) but never spitting it back out (to Asia). And a high-ranking official in Indonesia's Office of the Coordinating Minister for Economy, Finance, and Development Supervision argues that Japanese automobile and electronics assemblers in that country use unfair quality standards and inspections to discriminate against local (i.e., Indonesian-based) parts suppliers. "Just rejecting and rejecting parts doesn't teach anyone anything."[35] These kinds of complaints have been widely noted by researchers outside Japan, from Taylor (1995) to Hatch and Yamamura (1996), and increasingly by researchers within the country such as Ichikawa (1996) and Kono (1997). On the other hand, one cannot help but come across abundant evidence that local firms in Asia quite often *prefer* doing business with Japanese MNCs.[36] This was especially true in the early and mid-1990s, when alternative sources of technology (from the United States, Europe, South Korea, and Taiwan) were still rather limited. How can we explain this paradox?

The answer is that, while Japanese technology does indeed come with strings tightly attached, it also comes with network ties that bring opportunities for local capitalists who seek profits rather than technological autonomy.[37] Indeed, the restrictive strings are equivalent to the supportive ties. By

35. Interview with Miranda Goeltom, Jakarta, September 16, 1997.

36. The government of South Korea has tried valiantly to persuade domestic manufacturers to rely on other foreign technology sources besides Japan. But despite this effort, between 1962 and 1995 48 percent of South Korea's technology imports came from Japan. See Korea Industrial Technology Association (KITA), "Major Indicators of Industrial Technology," 1996, 180–81.

37. Seki notes that many Asian capitalists who forge ties with Japanese MNCs come from the real estate or financial sectors, not from manufacturing, and thus have very little knowledge about or interest in the technology being transferred. "What this means is that the Japanese partner is stuck with the burden of doing virtually all the work; but at the same time, it also means that he can enjoy the luxury of making his own decisions without worrying about the local partner." See *Nihon Keizai Shinbun*, "Kigyô no shinshutsu wa tomaranai" (FDI Won't Stop), an interview, January 5, 1997, 11.

purchasing technology from a Japanese manufacturer, the Asian capitalist typically is forced to abide by sometimes mind-numbingly detailed conditions on the use of that technology.[38] In doing so, however, he also typically secures access to a broader set of social relationships, including long-standing customers, suppliers, distributors, and political allies of the Japanese manufacturer—all of which may help him reduce his transaction costs over time.

In her comparative study of technology transfer by American and Japanese multinationals in Indonesia, Allen (1994, 24) argues that different kinds of learning—"managerial learning" versus "organizational learning" —occur in U.S. versus Japanese MNCs. Local managers in U.S. MNCs acquire individualized skills they can take with them as they move on in their careers, while local managers in Japanese MNCs learn about "the institutionalization of systems and structures" (303), and about how they may fit in to wider networks of relationships.[39] Likewise, Lin (1995, 65–66) notes that Japanese technology comes in a package of human relationships that, once unwrapped, may be difficult if not impossible to utilize: "To be able to adopt this kind of technology, one must be willing to work with the technology provider for a very long time."

These analyses dovetail neatly with my own, suggesting that the regionalization of Japanese manufacturing entails, for better or worse, the regionalization of firmly embedded network ties. Two stories, one with a happy ending and one with an unhappy one, help illustrate this phenomenon.

In 1997, I met a Thai auto parts producer who had forged a highly successful joint venture with a Japanese MNC and thereby gained access to Japanese-dominated supply clubs in Thailand. He launched the manufacturing enterprise with $400,000 he earned from his original business, an auto dealership, and was expecting to achieve $50 million in annual sales. He attributed his success to humility, to a recognition that he will never be able to do what his Japanese partner does. "Our mentality should be, 'Let them take the lead.' I take the lead on finance and personnel, but when it comes to technology, I let them take the lead. If they want to buy a machine, that's fine. I just ask them to make sure it gets used once in a while."[40]

A member of supply clubs maintained by Honda and Toyota, the Thai parts producer said he was seeing fewer and fewer local faces at club meet-

38. These include requirements to purchase specified products or raw materials, or to sell through identified agents or distributors, and include restrictions on the export of goods to particular markets. For more on this, see Hatch and Yamamura (1996, 108).

39. This difference could also be characterized as one between social (therefore tacit) knowledge and individual (therefore explicit) knowledge. A clear example of this is the use of routinized "apprenticeship" (on-the-job training) in Japanese firms versus a reliance on manuals in American firms. See Kitajima 1998.

40. Interview, Ayutthaya, Thailand, September 10, 1997.

ings. "It's become an increasingly Japanese show. I'm one of the few locals left. The others lack understanding. They are getting wiped out by their own ignorance."

Later that same year, I met another auto parts supplier, this one in Indonesia, who had had a very different experience. This capitalist, who began his industrial career as a textile manufacturer, was anxious to acquire technical skills because he hoped to become an automobile assembler himself one day. First, however, he wanted to gain valuable experience producing components. To that end, the firm had supplied flywheels to a major Japanese automaker—until a rival supplier, a member of the automaker's own keiretsu in Japan, arrived on the scene. "Once the Japanese supplier moved in, [the Japanese assembler] dropped us right away," complained the Indonesian business executive. "They cooked up some story about quality and delivery problems. But when I examined the records, I found only one problem that had been reported early on, corrected immediately, and never again repeated."[41]

As these examples suggest, Japanese MNCs in Asia can make excellent business partners/customers—at least in certain cases, and under certain conditions. For those local capitalists willing to go along with the fundamental rules of the networking game, the payoffs from cooperation are sufficiently large. But for local capitalists hoping to acquire technology and become autonomous actors in the market, the costs may be too large.

The Japanese Difference

I suspect that this discussion will trouble those, including neoclassical economists, who prefer highly portable, even universal, models of analysis. But such models tend to ignore the role of socially constructed institutions, which—being social constructs—vary, by definition, from place to place. Because they have been conditioned over time by institutions (i.e., distinctive policies and practices) in the home country, Japanese multinational enterprises can be expected to behave differently from non-Japanese MNCs.[42] And this should be particularly true as they expand into Asia, where Japanese affiliates often serve, as discussed earlier, in a regional network or division of labor organized and supervised by the parent company in Japan.

In his comparative study of MNCs in Malaysia, Aoki (1992, 91) is struck by

41. Interview, Jakarta, Indonesia, September 20, 1997.
42. This insight, while a bold one, is hardly novel. In attacking the "myth" of the global corporation, Doremus et al. (1998, 3) find evidence of "the enduring influence of national structures within the home states of the world's leading corporations," national structures that "continue to account for striking diversity in the character of core operations undertaken by those corporations." For an abridged version of this argument, see Pauly and Reich (1997).

how much Japanese electronics manufacturers rely on such regional and local business networks. This "is in sharp contrast with U.S. multinationals in Malaysia, which do not form networks in spite of the fact that nearly all are producing ICs [integrated circuits] and semiconductors."

But this contrast is a function of a more fundamental difference between Japanese MNCs and non-Japanese MNCs in Asia: the former remain tethered tightly to the parent company in Japan for much longer periods of time. Since 1992, I have interviewed more than fifty local managers at Japanese manufacturing plants across China, Taiwan, Korea, and Southeast Asia, and have heard this same message over and over again. One Thai manager at an electronics plant outside Bangkok lowered his voice to a whisper as he spoke about management at the parent company in Tokyo: "They pretty much want to control everything."[43] A forty-something Malay who supervises personnel for a large Japanese manufacturing affiliate in an industrial suburb of Kuala Lumpur took me aside to say the parent company is not comfortable with "outsiders" managing departments other than human resources. "What they really want are 'yes men'; it's easier to get compliance from Japanese staff."[44]

I also have visited the headquarters of dozens of Japanese MNCs, most headquartered in Tokyo, where I interviewed executives in charge of regional corporate planning. Many view themselves as guardians of a set of business relationships that must be protected as much as possible as the firm expands overseas. One company executive, who supervises a machine tool manufacturing operation in Beijing, said he and his colleagues in Tokyo are considering a proposal to turn over limited authority to local managers in China.[45]

> We make all the decisions now—not only on behalf of ourselves at the parent company, but also on behalf of all the insiders (*miuchi*) who belong to our extended family. This way of doing business worked quite well in the past, when our operations were tightly concentrated in Japan. But now, as we regionalize, it is taking much longer for us to make important decisions. So I have suggested a hybrid approach that would allow us to immerse ourselves in the local environment without abandoning our extended family.

If one reads the literature on this subject, one quickly discovers that the results of my fieldwork are neither extraordinary nor groundbreaking. For example, Ernst (2006, 179), who has spent years studying the overseas operations of electronics manufacturers, notes that Japanese affiliates in Asia

43. Interview, Chonburi, Thailand, September 9, 1997.
44. Interview, Shah Alam, Malaysia, January 13, 2004.
45. Interview, Tokyo, July 26, 1999.

typically are managed in a "top-down, bureaucratic way. The main objective is to make sure that the subsidiary responds faithfully to orders from Japan, which requires hard taskmaster managers." And Fukao (2006) shows that Japanese MNCs have moved at a relatively sluggish pace to localize their operations in Asia. They continue to rely heavily on Japanese managers and Japanese suppliers. Likewise, Legewie (1999, 18) finds that Japanese manufacturers in Southeast Asia, compared to their U.S. and European counterparts, have maintained "an unusually strong linkage" with the parent company and thus have "a relatively low level of decision-making autonomy." And Itami (1998, 21) confirms that, in East Asia, "overseas production by Japanese corporations is closely integrated with Japan's domestic production systems (that is, they are not very independent)."

Others who have conducted country-level studies reach much the same conclusion[46]:

- In Thailand, Sedgwick (1996, 29–30) finds that Japanese manufacturing affiliates "are part of a tightly controlled and rigorously hierarchical organizational structure extending down from Japan." And Nakashima (1998, 14), focusing more narrowly on a single automobile assembler in the Bangkok area, finds that the affiliate has adopted many of the parent company's management policies "without modification." Why? "This is not because local department and other managers lack the ability to devise a new system, but because they are not given the authority to do so."
- In Singapore, Singh, Putti and Yip (1998, 155–79) use a case study to compare Japanese MNCs (Kao and Ajinomoto) and Western MNCs (Unilever and Philips), and conclude that the former are controlled much more firmly by their parent companies.
- In Indonesia, Takahashi (1996, 58) describes the hierarchical division of labor between the Japanese parent and its local affiliate, a manufacturer of desalinization systems. "The parent company in Japan draws up the project proposal, does the engineering and design work, and fabricates the major components of the system, with the subsidiary in Indonesia performing final assembly and installation work. The work

---

46. Beechler (1995) is an exception to this rule. In the 1995 study, she finds "very few differences in the coordination and control mechanisms used by Japanese and American affiliates" in Southeast Asia. This is surprising in light of survey findings she reported only three years earlier. Beechler wrote then (1992, 163) that respondents—Japanese managers in charge of Japanese consumer electronics plants in Southeast Asia—"felt under increasing pressure from both local governments and employees and from third parties, such as Japanese and Western academics, to transfer technology, localize management, decentralize control, and 'de-Japanize' authority. However, they also believed that this process would put their operations at risk and would therefore not be carried out until all other alternatives were exhausted."

performed by the subsidiary is about one quarter of the total value of the project."

- In Hong Kong, Chen and Wong (1997, 96) examine transactional ties between the parents and affiliates of Japanese and non-Japanese manufacturers.[47] "All Japanese firms indicated strong to medium linkages with their parents. In contrast, five out of nine US firms, as well as other foreign firms, indicated weak linkages with their parents."
- In Taiwan, Tu (1997, 73) finds that Japanese manufacturing affiliates are more likely to have ongoing technical ties with their parents.[48] "Of the Japanese firms, 73 percent maintained close technical relationships with their parents, whereas only 45 percent of U.S. firms and 33 percent of 'other' firms did."
- In Malaysia, Ali (1994, 121) notes that Japanese manufacturing affiliates, relative to non-Japanese firms, tend to rely more heavily on their parent companies for basic research and new product designs.

If, as I have attempted to demonstrate, the ideal-typical Japanese manufacturing affiliate in Asia tends to be tied rather tightly to its parent, we should expect its behavior to reflect—more or less—the institutions of selective relationalism in the home country, where the parent operates. And indeed, each leg of the three-legged stool discussed in chapter 2 seems to have been replicated, at least partially if not always wholly, in the elite regionalization of Japan's highly networked but industry-centered political economy.

Intrafirm Ties

To be sure, Japanese manufacturing affiliates in Asia have not aggressively transferred the more "democratic" features of their homegrown management regimes, such as quality control circles and the *ringi* system of bottom-up communication.[49] Most, however, have adopted—albeit in modified form—other, more fundamental features that encourage long-term employment, loyalty, and "companyism." For example, in a comprehensive survey of 132 Japanese manufacturers in Thailand, Malaysia, and Singapore, Kitajima (1997, 37) found that 90 percent of the respondents had fully or

---

47. Conclusions are based on the findings of a survey of seven Japanese and nine U.S. MNCs in Hong Kong. The authors asked the firms to indicate how much of their total exports they ship to their parent company, and also how much of their capital and technology, as well as machinery, material, and parts, they source from their parent company.

48. Respondents to this survey included twenty-one MNCs from Japan, eleven from the United States, and ten from other countries or economic areas.

49. This point has been made previously by Sedgwick (1996), Smith (1993), and Yamashita et al. (1989).

partially adopted the on-the-job training system they used in Japan, and about 55 percent had adopted the seniority-based pay system.

Indeed, one scholar has suggested that successful Japanese manufacturing affiliates have achieved such positive results by thoroughly adopting their homegrown management regimes. Specifically, the overseas affiliates of Toyota and Honda have outperformed Nissan, according to Kagano (1999, 60), because they have "spent a lot of time in transplanting their distinctive cultures, their distinctive way of management, a very homogenous one."

In adopting their management regimes, however, Japanese MNCs have been relatively unwilling to entrust local staff with important positions in sales, procurements, finance, and corporate planning. Let me give just one example: In 2004, while touring a Japanese plant in Malaysia that produces "white goods" (household appliances), I was told that Japanese managers head up every department except human resources. In fact, I was told that 17 percent of the affiliate's managerial staff was Japanese. "What was the ratio ten years ago?" I asked. The answer was unsurprising: "Pretty much the same."

Even the Japanese government has fretted openly over this lack of progress. In its tenth annual survey of the Japanese manufacturing affiliates in Asia, JETRO noted that more than 40 percent of respondents in 1997 acknowledged they did not have even one local (Asian) person sitting on the board of directors supervising that affiliate. "Such hiring is not progressing," it groused.[50]

Mingsarn (1994, 84) notes that Thai managers are less likely to rise to the top of Japanese affiliates in Thailand; in her survey, only fifteen of eighty-four Japanese MNCs (18 percent) had a Thai managing director, while fifty-two of 153 non-Japanese MNCs (33 percent) had a local person in that slot. These findings have been duplicated in numerous cross-national studies throughout the region.[51] I quote here from just one, Chia (1997, 55), which concludes with this comment on multinationals in Singapore's electronics industry: "Localization of senior personnel has been proceeding faster in U.S. than in Japanese firms. Most of the senior management of companies surveyed were completely non-U.S., with positions filled by Singaporeans and other Asians. For the Japanese firms, however, top management was invariably Japanese."

---

50. The quote is from a JETRO press release dated April 23, 1997.

51. See, for example, Ali (1994, 119), Sedgwick (1996, 20), and Stewart (1985, 13–14). The slow pace by which Japanese firms localize their overseas management is not a purely "Asian" phenomenon. A study by Hal Gregersen and J. Stewart Black found that only 23 percent of the top management jobs in Japanese affiliates all over the world were held by non-Japanese, while 55 percent of the top management jobs in U.S. overseas affiliates were held by non-Americans. (See *Daily Yomiuri*, November 6, 1999).

How can we explain such results? Some economists, noting that Japanese manufacturers are relative newcomers to the game of global business, believe they reflect nothing more than inexperience. Citing a presumed "vintage effect," they suggest that Japanese manufacturing affiliates will localize their operations more thoroughly as they gain more experience operating overseas. In an econometric study of technology transfer by Japanese MNCs in Asia, Urata (1996a, 19) finds a positive correlation between the length of operation in a host country and the localization of simple management and technical skills such as maintenance and inspection of machinery. Interestingly, however, he concludes that "the vintage effect does not have a significant impact on transferring more sophisticated technologies," such as the design and development of new products.

For their part, Japanese manufacturers tend to blame linguistics for the slow pace of localization.[52] That is, Asian managers and technicians are usually able to function well in English, but rarely can do so in Japanese. As a result, they say, these local staffers are excluded from important intrafirm communications, particularly those between the parent company and the affiliate. However, as should be readily apparent, this argument is hopelessly circular. If Japanese expatriates did not exercise such exclusionary control over the affiliate, it seems unlikely that intrafirm communications would need to be conducted so routinely in Japanese.

I think the most persuasive answer comes from Itagaki (1997, 372–73):

> This tendency [to move slowly, if at all, toward localization] stems from one particular characteristic of Japanese companies, at home or abroad, which is to rely to a considerable extent on human networks within companies and on information shared by employees, rather than on a standardized and integrated mechanism. Even if an affiliate enjoys strong autonomy, there are often cases where Japanese expatriates, who are most familiar with Japanese methods, exercise full discretion.

To sum up, large manufacturing enterprises in Japan are characterized by longstanding relational ties inside the firm. When they expand into Asia, these firms tend to replicate such ties, giving an advantage to managerial insiders and a big disadvantage to outsiders, including local candidates for supervisory positions. To rise in the ranks, these management candidates must first become insiders; but to invest the time in becoming insiders, they face enormous opportunity costs—namely, the better positions and higher incomes they could achieve more quickly at non-Japanese affiliates in the host economy.

---

52. Interviews, Bangkok, Beijing, Jakarta, Kuala Lumpur, Seoul, Singapore, Taipei, 1992–2004.

Interfirm Ties

Japanese parent companies exercise authority over more than just the personnel matters of their manufacturing affiliates in Asia; they also have a lot to say about the direction of sales and the source of procurements. As one machine manufacturer puts it, "All of the important stuff—quality control, decisions on which parts to use, and where to source them—is handled in Japan."[53]

This helps explain why the ratio of reverse imports from Japanese manufacturing affiliates in East Asia has been lower than from U.S. manufacturers in the region. As noted in chapter 2, selective relationalism protects well-connected firms in Japan from competing imports. Kimura (1996, 12) suggests that Japanese parent firms have used their authority to limit such reverse imports with the goal of protecting domestic employment in Japan. It also helps explain why Japanese manufacturing affiliates in the region have not moved quickly—or, in some cases, have not moved at all—to sever long-standing ties with home-based suppliers of raw materials and components after setting up their Asian factories. A MITI study (1996, 73–74) found that even Japanese manufacturing affiliates with fifteen or more years of experience in Asia continued to import an unusually large share of their intermediate products from the parent company's suppliers in Japan.[54]

In their local and intraregional transactions, Japanese manufacturing affiliates in Asia often follow the relational contracting patterns first established at home by their parents. Tejima (1996) suggests, correctly, that this is a rational attempt to exploit a competitive advantage they enjoy in networking. I discuss this issue in greater depth in chapter 5; for now, it is sufficient to note that one can easily find evidence of both horizontal and vertical keiretsu ties being replicated in the manufacturing operations of Japanese affiliates in Asia.

In the Philippines, where it established a joint venture to manufacture consumer electronics in 1982, Sharp, a Japanese giant, secured financing for its overseas operation from the Rizal Commercial Banking Corp., owned in part by Sanwa Bank (now Mitsubishi UFJ), the financial hub of the hori-

---

53. Onishi Akira, vice-president of Mabuchi Motor, as quoted in Katayama (1996, 246).

54. This controversial finding is based on a survey of nearly nine hundred Japanese manufacturing affiliates in Asia in 1994. MITI organized the data according to the time period in which respondents actually began operating in the region (1992–94; 1989–91; 1986–88; 1983–85; and up to 1982), and then evaluated how heavily the affiliates in each group relied on Japan for imported parts. MITI fully expected to confirm the so-called vintage effect; i.e., that overseas affiliates will, over time, procure an increasingly large share of their parts from local suppliers and—conversely—procure a smaller and smaller share from the parent company, or the parent company's suppliers, back in the home country. But the results defied MITI's expectations.

zontal keiretsu to which Sharp's parent company then belonged.[55] Toyota, which has been affiliated with the Mitsui keiretsu, also pulled on horizontal strings when it set up its production plant in the Philippines in 1988. Mitsui Bussan, the group's giant trading company, directed Toyota to industrial real estate, introduced it to local political and business leaders, and even helped underwrite the automobile manufacturing project.[56]

Just as common is what is known as "follow-the-leader" investment (*zuihan shinshutsu*) carried out by subcontractors from an assembler's vertical keiretsu in Japan. China has attracted a large amount of such Japanese investment by parts suppliers following their home country assemblers.[57] Kikai Shinkō Kyōkai (1995, 94) gives the example of subcontractors in the metalworking industry moving one after another into northeast China to service their Japanese customers. In the automobile industry, Toyota established an assembly plant in Tianjin in 2000, and induced most of its major subcontractors to come along and establish parts production plants in the area. Thailand also has received an enormous amount of such "follow behind" investment; in 1995, more than half (56 percent) of all Japanese FDI in that country was carried out by subcontractors.[58] Anuroj (1995, 113) argues that Japanese manufacturing affiliates in Thailand are far more likely than their non-Japanese counterparts to use transplants from the home country as "local" suppliers. Suehiro (1998, 31) goes even further. He writes that "existing local components suppliers [have been] forced out of the market by Japanese ones who advance into this area to supply their products to Japanese assemblers."

Political Ties

Compared with U.S. and European MNCs, Japanese manufacturing affiliates in Asia cooperate closely with government officials from the home country. They receive more public support than other MNCs, operating as "a system of enterprises cum government," according to Mingsarn (1993, 24), a Thai economist. And Panglaykim (1983, 17), an Indonesian economist, has described the Japanese MNC as "a formidable integrated system" that straddles the private and public sectors. This is because the Japanese state traditionally has used its bilateral ODA to promote private investment flows to Asia, and also because the state traditionally has used industrial policies to support Japanese firms that have established operations in the region, or that are considering doing so.

---

55. *Far Eastern Economic Review,* May 2, 1991, 46.
56. See Sender (1996, 48).
57. See Japan Small Business Corporation (1997, 8).
58. JETRO (1997a, 190). Also see Mukoyama (1996, 7), who cites statistics from the Thai Board of Industrialization indicating that nearly one-third of JFDI in 1994 went into supporting industries.

In Asia, it is sometimes difficult to tell where the activities of the Japanese public sector end and those of the Japanese private sector begin. Consider two examples.

General trading companies (GTCs, or *sōgō shōsha*) have served as a proxy for the Japanese state in dealings with the region's political outcasts. In 1991, when Tokyo was still honoring a U.S.-led trade embargo against Hanoi, the Mitsubishi Corp. delivered to Vietnamese officials a "master plan for the automobile industry in the Republic of Vietnam."[59] It included a long list of recommended policies to develop a domestic industry with Japanese assistance by, among other things, limiting the number of local manufacturers and protecting them from imports. Japanese assemblers and parts suppliers, many of them members of the Mitsubishi keiretsu, were highlighted. More recently, Mitsui Corp. conducted studies for the military regime in Myanmar (Burma) on the feasibility of various development projects.[60] (In its more traditional role, the company also has collaborated with the repressive regime to establish the Mingaladon Industrial Park and help construct the Yadana natural gas pipeline.) The Japanese state, which normally might carry out such activities, turned over the duty to Mitsubishi and Mitsui in these cases.

Another example of public-private cooperation in Asia is the Japan International Development Corporation (JAIDO). It was established in 1989, when the Japanese government—operating through the Overseas Economic Cooperation Fund (OECF), the agency that then provided low-interest loans to developing countries—teamed up with Japan's big business federation (Keidanren).[61] In fact, OECF provided one-third of JAIDO's start-up capital. It did so in part because it felt obliged to compensate private Japanese firms for lost business opportunities as the state in the late 1980s moved away from "tying" all of its yen loans to the purchase of equipment made in Japan or to the use of Japanese engineers and contractors.[62] Since the early 1980s, Japan had been under growing pressure from Western nations to "untie" more of its foreign aid.

In the 1990s, JAIDO actively invested in joint venture projects, particularly export-oriented enterprises, in developing countries. About half of the projects financed by the organization were in Asia. For example, it invested almost $3 million in a steel plant in the Philippines, more than $2 million in a joint venture in China to produce Japanese-language computer software, and $8.7 million to build an office complex at Chulalongkorn University in Thailand.[63]

---

59. The document is discussed in Hatch and Yamamura (1996, 34–35 and 136–37).

60. Sender (1996, 48).

61. OECF later merged with the Japan Export Import Bank to form the Japan Bank for International Cooperation (JBIC).

62. Interview, OECF headquarters (Tokyo), June 24, 1999.

63. "JAIDO," a company brochure.

Positional Power in Asia

It is rather simple to demonstrate that, during most of the 1990s, the Japanese state, as well as Japanese MNCs, wielded enormous influence in Asia. Indeed, host economies throughout the region depended heavily on resources provided by Japanese government and business interests:

- Japan was the number-one source of bilateral ODA for most countries in Asia. Indeed, in the mid-1990s, China received 50–60 percent, Thailand received 70–80 percent, and Indonesia received 60–90 percent of its government-to-government aid from Japan (see table 3.1).
- JICA experts served as insiders in capitals throughout the region, providing valuable advice to host government agencies on industrial and macroeconomic policies. For example, in the 1980s and 1990s Japanese officials helped draft all of Thailand's five-year national development plans. In addition, they encouraged Thai officials to liberalize trade and investment rules to lure more Japanese MNCs into targeted sectors. And they pushed the Thai government to follow Japan's example by creating public institutions that cooperate with private industry, such as the Thai Export-Import Bank, and private sector groups that cooperate with the state, such as the Thai Dye and Mould Industrial Association.[64]
- Japan was the leading source of manufacturing FDI in Asia, especially the ASEAN-4, where it accounted for more than a quarter of all such flows in the decade from 1987 through 1996.[65]
- Japanese producers dominated important markets in host countries, from machine tools to bearings, from household appliances to automobiles. Indeed, until the late 1990s, they manufactured and sold an estimated 80–90 percent of the passenger and commercial vehicles produced in the ASEAN-4 countries.[66] And Japanese subcontractors in Southeast Asia became the chief source of auto parts for those assemblers. In 1997, forty-six of the fifty-three major (foreign) joint ventures

64. Interviews with Thai and Japanese officials, July 1992, April 1993, July 1995, September 1997. For more on these personal networks between Japanese government officials and their counterparts in Southeast Asia, see Hatch and Yamamura (1996, 130–45).

65. See also Legewie (1998, 10), who notes that country-level data on FDI flows grossly exaggerate the significance of intraregional investment from the Asian "tigers," particularly Hong Kong and Singapore, and from the "new tigers," particularly Malaysia. Much of the FDI attributed to these countries actually comes from Japanese firms with operations there, or from local firms who move domestic capital offshore and then invest it back into the home country to take advantage of incentives offered to foreign investors.

66. This estimate comes from Automotive Resources Asia, a Bangkok-based consulting company. The *Nikkei Weekly* ("Japan's Share of Car Production in ASEAN to Fall, Says Study," March 9, 1998) put the figure at 76 percent of total production in ASEAN.

in Indonesia's auto parts industry were Japanese.[67] Even if one includes purely local suppliers (i.e., firms with no foreign capital), which generally produce only low-value-added parts, Japanese affiliates made up nearly half of all auto parts manufacturers in Indonesia.[68]

- Japanese manufacturing affiliates were major employers—with more than 1.1 million Asian workers on their payrolls in 1995. In Thailand, Japanese firms employed 7 percent of all production (shop floor) workers in 1997, according to the Japanese Chamber of Commerce and Industry (Bangkok). In Malaysia and Singapore, they employed 45 percent and 25 percent, respectively, of all workers in the electronics/electrical machinery industry (Okamoto 1996, 20).

- Japanese MNCs generated a significant share of the exports from different host countries in Asia. For example, the Japanese Chamber of Commerce and Industry (Bangkok) noted that its members produced nearly a quarter of all exports from Thailand in 1997.

By generously supplying such resources (ODA, policy advice, FDI, production and process technology, jobs, foreign exchange via exports), Japanese state and business interests gained relative power in bilateral negotiations with their counterparts in Asia. Although they rarely needed to use it, they held an awesome trump card—the threat of withdrawing the supply of such resources.[69] Hatch and Yamamura (1996, 144–45) show how the Japanese government persuaded the Thai government to cast off its budget concerns and move ahead with the Eastern Seaboard Development Program, a major construction project favored by export-oriented manufacturers from Japan. Tokyo tamed Bangkok by threatening to cut off the flow of ODA. Likewise, Legewie (1998, 32–33) documents how Matsushita persuaded the Malaysian state to go along with its AICO proposal to reallocate the regional production of electric fans and to reduce tariffs on the intraregional trade of parts used to assemble those fans, even though Malaysia would lose production capacity and jobs under the proposal. Matsushita got its way by threatening to move all of its fan production in Malaysia to Thailand.

Japan, according to a number of Japanese scholars, was the driving force behind the economic success of the Asian "tigers" and "new tigers" in the 1980s and the first half of the 1990s. In his econometric study of international backward linkages, Inomatsu (1998, 57) concludes that "Thai indus-

---

67. Interview and association directory, Gabungan Industri Alat Mobil & Motor (GIAMM/Indonesia Auto Parts and Components Industries Association), Jakarta, September 15, 1997.

68. See Fourin (1998a).

69. In discussing the ability of transnational investors to move capital into and out of developing markets, Winters (1996) has called this "power in motion."

tries have fallen into chronic dependency on Japanese goods and services, no matter how costly they may be due to the persistent appreciation of the yen." And Kanō Yoshikazu, president of the Kokumin Keizai Kenkyū Kyōryoku Kai (National Economic Research Cooperation Society), wrote in the mid-1990s that "in reality, manufacturing industries in Asia are completely dependent on Japan. In product and process technologies, Japan is way ahead, and in all the countries in the region, local firms are eager to forge joint ventures with Japanese firms" (1996, 81).

But Watanabe Toshio, a well-known economist at the Tokyo Institute of Technology, has argued passionately against this assertion. "It is sheer arrogance to imagine that Japan plays such a larger-than-life role" in the region (1996, 57). He argued that, even by the mid-1990s, the regional economy of Asia had become largely independent of Japan's national economy, and was driven by intra-Asian trade or what he refers to as an "intra-regional circulation mechanism" (*ikinai jiko junkan mekanizumu*).

If we treat "Japan" as a unitary actor (one economy in the global economy, or one nation in the international system), and if we consider only "Japan's" relative power (the relative amount of resources it brought to its bilateral economic relations with individual Asian countries in the 1990s), Watanabe may have a point. For example, by 1996, the increasingly integrated economies of Asia *had* begun to reduce their reliance on Japan as an export market and became, instead, more dependent on one another for trade and investment. However, even Watanabe acknowledges in the end (65) that Japanese interests have played a critical role in bringing about— or fostering—this emerging Asian regionalism.

In other words, Japanese elites did much more than bring considerable resources to bear on their activities in individual countries in Asia; they also acted as agents of a remarkably informal, extralegal form of regional integration, occupying central nodes in an integrated structure of administrative and production networks linking political and economic actors in the region. Japanese elites thus served as gatekeepers controlling access to resources (public goods associated with regional cooperation) that were locked inside that network structure. They were, as Takenaka (1996, 133) put it, "the glue holding together a complex web of relationships." In this way, Japanese elites enjoyed *positional* power (control over access to network resources) and not merely relative power (coercive authority that comes with possessing relatively abundant resources) in Asia. Using different terminology with, nonetheless, much the same meaning, we might say that these elites acquired "structural autonomy" (Burt 1992, 44–45) by embedding their regional exchange partners in networks they dominated. A few examples from this period may illustrate my point.

The State: Exercising "Coordinatorship"

In the 1990s, Japanese bureaucrats occupied central positions in the expanding and deepening linkages that characterized the regionalization (that is, the informal, extra-legal integration) of Asia. Rather than outright "leadership," they exercised what Yanagihara (1987, 418) called "coordinatorship," a forceful but largely behind-the-scenes effort "to achieve an alignment of diverse interests and to form a consensus, or at least an appearance of it, among the region's countries with respect to intra-regional and global economic issues."

More specifically, economic ministries managed to coordinate competing economic interests in Asia by creating new industrial federations that functioned as the regional equivalent of trade associations. And MITI (now known as METI) organized its counterparts throughout the region into a group—the ASEAN Economic Ministers (AEM)–MITI Economic and Industrial Cooperation Committee—to pursue industrial policies and coordinate development plans on a regionwide basis. As I discuss further in chapter 5, MITI supplied both the financing and the staff for this organization. One of the goals of AMEICC, as well as the new industrial federations, was to harmonize standards, accounting rules, certification requirements, and other programs that individual states in the region had otherwise implemented on an ad hoc, unitary basis. JETRO, meanwhile, established a program to encourage the deepening of economic linkages, especially between parts suppliers and assemblers.

Trading Companies: Regional Distribution and Deal-Making

Blessed with their own warehouses and customs clearance centers at major ports throughout the region, Japanese GTCs became, by the 1990s, pivotal players in Asia's distribution networks. Itōchu, alone, claimed to handle 10 percent of the trade between China and Japan.[70] Mitsui Soko, a logistics firm, created a regional distribution system, a replication of the vaunted just-in-time delivery system, for Sony in Malaysia and Thailand. It stored and sorted parts and materials, as well as finished products, at local warehouses, pushed them through customs, and then purchased discount space on container ships headed to the desired port. At each step in this process, a complex satellite system monitored the progress of parts headed for Sony plants, or finished goods shipped from Sony plants.[71]

By the mid-1990s, many scholars and many more journalists began to

70. See Sender (1996, 47).
71. See Tokunaga (1992).

focus attention on the "overseas Chinese" in Taiwan and Southeast Asia who presumably used their family or kinship ties to set up joint ventures on the mainland.[72] But even then, some of those with the best connections in China had been known to rely on Japanese trading companies to make those deals come to life. For example, the Salim Group, Indonesia's largest conglomerate, owned by Chinese-Indonesian capitalist Liem Sioe Liong, used Marubeni to broker an agreement to establish a textile factory in southern China. "It is safer for the overseas Chinese to go in with us," explains Nishida Ken'ichi, head of the trading company's Hong Kong office and deputy chief representative in China. "If the Chinese don't fulfill the agreements, we can ask the Japanese government [for help.] We also have purchasing power to resell their products in our market."[73]

Manufacturers: Regional Production Networks

As discussed earlier, Japanese manufacturers in the 1980s and 1990s set up regional networks to assemble finished goods in one particular location using components imported from other factories in Asia. These networks tended to be exclusionary, consisting largely of the regional affiliates of the parent company in Japan, or of the regional affiliates of the parent's keiretsu suppliers in Japan. This was particularly true of the electronics industry. Just as the Asian financial crisis was beginning to spread, MITI (1998a, 213 and 220) reported that nearly 60 percent of intraregional exports by Japanese electronic firms in Asia moved through intrafirm channels, while 46 percent of intraregional imports came from such intrafirm channels.

Nonetheless, the regional production networks of Japanese MNCs did occasionally include truly local suppliers—and they always held the *possibility* of including more. Furthermore, these networks often accommodated non-Japanese MNCs, particularly contract manufacturers from Taiwan, in significant supporting roles. For example, Jinbao Electronics assembled calculators in Thailand for Sharp on the basis of an original equipment manufacturing (OEM) agreement.[74] And Dai Hwa Electronics assembled audio components in Indonesia for Sony on a similar OEM contract.[75] In both cases, the Taiwanese MNCs slavishly followed the Japanese parent's technical specifications, using only parts manufactured by the parent's suppliers.

---

72. See, for example, Weidenbaum and Hughes (1996), Haley et al. (1998), Kao (1993), and *Fortune,* October 5, 1992.

73. See Sender (1996, 47). Sender notes that Marubeni was brought in partly because company president Toriumi Iwao had befriended Liem many decades earlier when he worked as a young trader in Indonesia.

74. Bernard and Ravenhill (1995, 186–87).

75. Interview, Sony Electronics Indonesia, September 19, 1997, Jakarta.

In the process, however, they gained valuable experience in this contract-assembler role.

Finally, and most important, these Japanese production networks fostered the economic integration of Asia and thereby generated network resources (as well as income, employment, and exports/foreign currency reserves) for host economies in the region. Specifically, they contributed heavily to Asia's growing intraregional trade (which was 45 percent of the region's total trade in 1995, up sharply from 26 percent in 1985).[76] From Pusan to Bandung, government and business officials in those host economies recognized this fact, and thus competed fiercely with one another to attract Japanese manufacturing investment.

Embracing Asia

In the early and mid-1990s, Asia nicely served the interests of Japanese elites who dominated the region's emerging administrative and production networks, providing a kind of cushion during hard times at home. Bureaucratic elites secured new turf (*nawabari*) upon which they could operate just as reformers sought to reduce their policy discretion in Japan. Business elites, meanwhile, acquired efficient production sites that strongly buttressed their domestic operations. In a report, MITI (1998b, 260–61) noted that Japanese manufacturing affiliates in Asia contributed to Japan's trade surplus in the mid-1990s (that is, they imported more from Japan than they exported back to the home country), and did not contribute to the technological "hollowing out" of Japan (that is, R&D operations generally remained at home).[77]

For these elites, Asia suddenly became an extension of Japan, an expanded zone of production and administrative networks. Ichikawa (1996, 4–5), a consultant in a Tokyo think tank, described an "Asia-wide Full-set Industrial Structure" in which "Japan exercises leadership while linking arms with the various countries of Asia." Likewise, Inoue argued in 1997 (61) that Japanese firms had evolved into "Asian" firms. And an arm of MITI (Zenkoku Shitauke Kigyô Shinkô Kyôkai 1997b, 49) concluded in the same year that "domestic production must now be viewed as part of an Asia-wide division of labor, a regionally organized specialization system."

This new reality was clearly evident in the way that Japanese bureaucrats set up shop in Asian capitals, helping to write development plans for differ-

---

76. Calculated from IMF, *Direction of Trade Statistics,* various years.

77. MITI thus concluded that, for Japan, investing in Asia was a better deal than investing in the United States or Europe.

ent industries. And it was evident in the way that manufacturers used the region as a hedge mechanism; whenever the yen appreciated sharply, they shifted a larger share of the production of standardized goods to Asia.[78] Harada Tamotsu of the Electrical Industry Association of Japan summarized the new reality in a simple sentence: "Asia is no longer 'overseas'."[79]

78. See JETRO (1997a, 28) and EPA (1995, 295–6).
79. Japan Small Business Corp. (1997, 8).

PART TWO
The 1990s

4 Maintaining the Relational Status Quo

In 2001, a year that should have been filled with hope and anticipation, many Japanese looked back on the 1990s as a "lost decade" characterized by slow or no growth. Income and wages had remained flat throughout those years. But more than the economic stagnation, what really caught the eye of Japanese observers was the remarkable stagnation in the institutions of their own political economy. Those institutions had defied the odds, remaining surprisingly constant in the face of political and market pressure for change.

This may seem surprising in light of the head-spinning tumult in electoral politics. During the 1990s, Japan had seven different prime ministers; the ruling Liberal Democratic Party lost power for the first time in thirty-eight years before regaining it a year later; the leading opposition Japan Socialist Party virtually imploded after forging a power-sharing coalition with its longtime nemesis; voters screamed about the scandals associated with "money politics"; and the Diet completely overhauled the rules for elections to the Lower House.

But for all these new developments in the political halls of Nagatachō, many journalists looking back on the last (lost) decade of the twentieth century found nothing but the same ol' same old in the bureaucratic offices of Kasumigaseki or the corporate boardrooms of Ōtemachi. An editorial writer for *Yomiuri* (April 2, 2001) noted that the Japanese government suffered from "institutional fatigue," and called for an administrative shake-up, while a columnist for *Nikkei* (November 25, 2001) blamed institutional "rigidity" for persistently low earnings posted by Japanese electronics manufacturers. Yes, he wrote, they are trying to restructure their operations, but only rather timidly. "The companies remain inflexible in their strategies and have failed to implement serious cost-cutting, despite repeated calls for sweeping efforts to do so since the collapse of the bubble economy a decade ago."

In reality, Japan's political economy had begun to undergo change as early as 1998, but those changes were still very weak and halting—like a car engine with too much air and not enough gas—and thus not immediately obvious. No one could have expected a break from the status quo: the domestic institutions that had emerged in the wake of World War II had stubbornly survived through most of the 1990s and appeared as solid as cold steel.

In this chapter I do not offer an explanation for the surprising durability of the relationship-based political economy that characterized postwar Japan, nor for the implications of such continuity; those tasks will be taken up in chapter 5 and chapter 6, respectively. In addition, I do not describe why or how the ancien régime finally began to give way to something new— a significant relaxation of once tight relational ties; that task will be taken up in chapters 7 and 8, respectively. Instead, I try here to measure the extent of continuity and change during the lost decade, the 1990s. I do this by comparing the institutions of selective relationalism in the 1970s and 1980s (before Japan was subjected to intense stress from the market and political forces of globalization) with the institutions of political economy existing in the 1990s. This chapter thus builds upon chapter 2, which offered not only a baseline for analyzing the extent and nature of change but also offered a model for doing so.

Although Japan's political economy did not undergo significant *structural* change in the 1990s, it did experience significant *distributional* change during that decade. Relationalism became even more selective, distributing benefits to a narrower slice of Japanese society. Many subcontractors were squeezed on prices or were simply cut loose from the web of interfirm ties; large numbers of women ended up in part-time or temporary employment; and income inequality worsened dramatically.

But relationalism, which had defined the structure of Japan's postwar political economy, remained alive and well through most of the 1990s—a fact that even the Japanese government came to acknowledge. In its 1998 white paper, MITI (now METI) argued that the rigid structure of Japan's highly networked economy now limited its ability to achieve dynamic technological change. Another arm of the government, the Economic Planning Agency (1998a), wrote that "to improve productivity, induce energetic behavior by various economic actors, and return to increasing production capacity, we face an urgent need for structural reforms that create institutions based on the market mechanism and free competition" (159).

Before considering the evidence in detail, you deserve to know what I would view as "structural change." I can answer this most clearly in response to a counterfactual question: What would Japan have looked like at the end of the 1990s if it had actually undergone structural change? In general, I think we would have witnessed a breakdown in the reciprocal and informal relational ties that had sewn together the Japanese political economy over so many years. This, in turn, would have manifested itself in several rather specific ways, including—among many other possible examples—a reduction in the number of amakudari "descents" from the bureaucracy, an unraveling of cross-held equities among well-connected firms, and an across-the-board increase in labor mobility.

In the following sections, I look for continuity or change in the three legs of relationalism—state–industry ties, business–business ties, and management–labor ties—and I confirm that structural change was not yet evident as the twentieth century came to an end.

State and Industry

In chapter 2, I noted that the Japanese state cooperated quite closely with industry in the postwar period, so closely in fact that it often became difficult to draw a neat dividing line between the public and private sectors. For example, bureaucrats—invoking the threat of "excess competition" as a rationale—intervened routinely in the market, regulating everything from plant-siting decisions to personnel policies. Did they continue to do so in the 1990s, or did globalization compel them to back off?

No one can deny that the government, in response to considerable pressure from sources inside and outside Japan, sought to liberalize markets and promote competition. As early as the 1980s, the Suzuki and Nakasone cabinets focused on privatizing state-run monopolies such as NTT (Nippon Telegraph and Telephone), JNR (Japan National Railway), and JTB (Japan Tobacco Bureau).[1] But Vogel (1996) has shown that liberalization can actually lead to reregulation—and this was particularly true in the privatization of NTT. The Ministry of Posts and Telecommunications (MPT) emerged from the process more powerful than ever, armed with an extraordinary arsenal of formal and informal regulations over the telecommunications industry.

The non-LDP coalition that grabbed power in 1993, interrupting nearly four decades of conservative rule, raised anew the promise of deregulation by organizing an Economic Reform Study Group headed by Hiraiwa Gaishi, president of the Keidanren. But the Hosokawa and Hata cabinets lasted only a year, and were replaced by a coalition including the LDP, its longtime rival, the Social Democratic Party of Japan, and the reform-minded New Party

---

1. Sumita (1997), a former bureaucrat, provides a fascinating insider's account of the privatization of Japan National Railways. We should note that Sumita "descended" (via amakudari) from his position as administrative vice-minister of the Ministry of Transport to eventually become the head of Eastern JR Railways, one of the newly privatized companies.

Sakigake. This coalition established a three-year deregulation promotion plan, targeting thousands of different rules. Future cabinets, particularly that of Hashimoto Ryūtaro, also set targets and thereby raised expectations about regulatory relief.

With only a few exceptions, however, the results were unimpressive.[2] Despite all the promises and plans, the Japanese government not only failed to curb its regulatory reach, it actually has expanded it. In 1986, when the Management and Coordination Agency began collecting such statistics, there were 10,054 regulations on the books—from licensing and permitting requirements to quality standards. Thirteen years later, in 1999, there were 11,581 rules, an increase of 15 percent.[3] We shouldn't be surprised to learn that the Ministry of Construction or the Ministry of Agriculture, Forestry and Fisheries added to the overall regulatory burden. Less expected, the Ministry of Finance, along with the newly created Financial Supervision Agency,[4] which was carved out of MOF in 1998, contributed a net additional 731 regulations during a period in which Japanese financial markets were being liberalized.[5]

One result of this lack of progress on easing Japan's regulatory burden was a commensurate lack of progress on reducing Japan's high domestic price structure. This is surprising because the recessions of the mid- and late 1990s created a strong deflationary pressure, lowering prices for certain goods. But Japanese prices remained quite high relative to prices in other countries. In every one of its biannual cost-of-living surveys conducted during the 1990s, the Economist Intelligence Unit found that Tokyo and Osaka were the world's most expensive cities, with prices as much as 40 percent

2. By the end of the millennium, LaCroix and Mak (2001, 232) conclude that "Japan's transportation, public utility and communication industries are still moderately to highly regulated." One exception, one area of progress toward deregulation, might be the repeal of the Large Store Law, which had been routinely used to protect mom-and-pop retail establishments by restricting the development of supermarkets, department stores, and big chain stores (including foreign ones—most notably, Toys 'R Us). But the law was replaced by a package of new rules allowing local governments to do what MITI alone used to do—that is, wield powerful authority over retail development. And critics such as Sato (1998) warned that the new rules would constrain competition just as much as the old law had.

3. Of the total, 39.3 percent are classified as "strong regulations" (requiring government permission, approval, or licensing); 12.7 percent are considered "medium-term rules" (calling for authorization, inspection, or registration by the state); 43.9 percent are referred to as "weak regulations" (requiring only notification or disclosure to the state); and 4.1 percent are dubbed "other." See Management and Coordination Agency, "Kyoninka nado no Tōitsuteki Haaku Kekka (Dai 13-ka) ni tsuite" (Results of a Consolidated Accounting of Permits, Licenses, and Regulations, No. 13), March 1999.

4. The administrative reshuffling that began in 1998 with the creation of the Financial Supervision Agency continued in July 2000, when the new agency was merged with MOF's Financial System Planning Bureau to form the Financial Services Agency.

5. It is worth repeating the point, highlighted by Vogel (1996), that liberalization may actually create a need for increased regulation, or reregulation.

higher than New York's. Even the annual survey by the Cabinet Office found that, on the basis of purchasing power parity, goods and services in Tokyo in 2000 still cost 22 percent more—on average—than in New York, 21 percent more than in London, 60 percent more than in Paris, 71 percent more than in Berlin, and 23 percent more than in Geneva.[6]

Who was responsible for the slow pace of regulatory reform in Japan? In the 1990s, observers frequently pointed fingers at the bureaucrats, especially those who staffed the advisory panels on deregulation and were then supposed to implement their proposals. These officials, we were told, did not truly believe in free competition[7] or they had a vested interest in the status quo and thus routinely sabotaged reforms.[8] It is true that government agencies occasionally have supported proposals to deregulate activities supervised by other agencies, but have adamantly opposed any that might threaten their own positional power.[9] Consider the Ministry of Finance, which resisted change throughout the 1990s. In the early part of the decade, it fought hard to block reform proposals that it believed would curtail its ability to service the national debt (Mabuchi 1994); in the mid-1990s, it opposed a measure to create an independent body to supervise financial institutions (Mabuchi 1997); and as the decade came to end, it rallied against legislation to nationalize ailing banks because it preferred to maintain its discretionary authority to negotiate bailout schemes with the industry as a whole. A coalition of politicians, feeling pressure to act, pushed through watered-down versions of these proposals.

In most cases, however, the political parties—particularly the LDP—shared the bureaucracy's reluctance to embrace deregulation. Although

---

6. Cabinet Office, *Seikei chōsa ni yoru kōbairyoku heika oyobi naigai kakakusa no gaikyō*, 2001.

7. Kikai Shinkō Kyōkai (1998, 8), an arm of MITI, openly expressed such skepticism about the merits of competition. In a report, it noted that some Japanese machine manufacturers were suffering from sluggish consumption, "and making matters worse by engaging in price competition and price cuts, making it difficult for them to revamp unprofitable divisions."

8. Japanese newspapers, which waged a kind of public relations offensive against the bureaucracy in the 1990s, often carried articles that alleged sabotage. See, for example, *Daily Yomiuri*, "Ministries Drag Feet over Reform Plan" (May 18, 1999). But what critics referred to as "sabotage" was often nothing more than aggressive, albeit often questionable, lobbying—not only of influential Diet members but also of the general public. In October 1997, for example, I joined hundreds of Tokyo residents in attending a revival concert of "The Wild Ones," a folk music group popular among the Japanese baby boomers that came of age in the 1970s. It was not until I entered the auditorium, where I was greeted by a long line of smiling civil servants and handed a bag of "gifts," including promotional brochures about the Ministry of Posts and Telecommunications, that I realized the "free" concert was sponsored and financed by MPT, which was at the time one of the targets of the administrative reform movement.

9. MITI, which has been a forceful advocate for deregulation of business activities it does not oversee, is the agency most often accused of hypocrisy on this issue. See Vogel (1999b, 13) and *Nikkei Business*, "Kisei Kanwa Suishinshō ni Henshin" (Transforming Itself into the "Ministry for the Promotion of Deregulation"), October 24, 1994, 14–18.

Japan's electoral system received a face-lift in 1994, it continued to encourage candidates to compete as "personalities," not as representatives of a particular policy perspective, and thus reinforced what Kitschelt (1999, 32) properly calls "clientelist voter-politician linkages."[10] A leading LDP reformer, Shiozaki Yasuhisa (1999, 13), laments that his party and its allies in the Diet were unwilling to seriously grapple with this issue:

> There is no active policy debate among rank and file LDP politicians. Commonly, only a handful of higher-ranking party leaders of the LDP, Liberal Party, and sometimes Komeitō, decide most of the policies. These days, policies have been negotiated—and often motivated—to maintain the parties' political position. I seriously doubt that we can confront structural reform if the current policy-making practices continue.

As recently as 2000, the ruling party was deeply divided over the wisdom of regulatory reform. About 180 LDP legislators formed a working group to study the negative effects of deregulation on small retailers and other longtime political allies. The "Forum to Reconsider Deregulation," which called for several changes to the government's reform agenda, was made up of LDP heavyweights, including secretary-general Mori Yoshiro (who became Japan's prime minister in April 2000), Policy Research Council chairman Kamei Shizuka, Education Minister Nakasone Hirofumi, and Muto Kabun, head of the administrative reform promotion committee. Muto, who had served as director-general of the Management and Coordination Agency under Prime Minister Hashimoto, and thus had been on the front lines of the deregulation initiative, actually chaired the group. He apologized for "overemphasizing the market mechanism and individual responsibility" in his earlier role. "I should have approved more exceptions (to the principle of laissez-faire). Too much deregulation could have a bad effect" (*Asahi Shinbun,* January 9, 2000, p. 2).

Although it appears that bureaucrats and politicians were not enthusiastic about regulatory reform, one could be forgiven for assuming that representatives of big business were. But this was not the case. Nukazawa Kazuo, former managing director of Keidanren, said that most of the trade associations making up his business federation in the 1990s were opposed to aggressive deregulation because they had benefited handsomely in the past

10. The new election system approved in 1994 combines single member districts and proportional representation (PR). But Kitschelt (1999, 33) notes, among other things, that parties can field the same candidate in both a single member district and on the PR list: "Electoral rules continue to make politicians seek their electoral fortunes as individual entrepreneurs, in competition with candidates of their own party." Ōtake (1997) is equally pessimistic about the prospects for change under this new system. For a more optimistic view, see Krauss and Pekkanen (2004).

from cooperative ties with government agencies.[11] "In the business community itself, the voices calling for deregulation are few and far between," he told me. Furthermore, he said many of those who strongly advocated deregulation only did so because they viewed it as an alternative to Keynesian-style spending programs that would expand the government's budget deficit and thereby jeopardize its pledge to reduce corporate tax rates.

Nukazawa's opinion is supported by polling data showing that, in the mid-1990s, large Japanese firms wanted government to allow them to compete more freely, but did not want government to remove itself from the ring. Only 6 percent of respondents to a 1996 *Nikkei* survey expressed support for changing the pattern of government-business cooperation in Japan.[12] Indeed, they were neatly divided, about half and half, over whether Japan "definitely needs" an "economic system based on market principles" or merely needs such a system "to a limited extent."

This skepticism about laissez-faire economic principles was reflected in meetings between MITI and semiconductor manufacturers in the autumn of 1996, shortly after Japan and the United States signed a new trade agreement. MITI, concerned that Fujitsu and other chip producers might be accused of dumping exports on the U.S. market, organized the meetings in an effort to "guide" firms to maintain existing price levels. "Japanese manufacturers continue to hand over to MITI chip production and marketing data at their meetings," one newspaper reported.[13] "Some executives of the major chip makers want even more guidance from MITI. The 10-year U.S.-Japan semiconductor agreement nurtured a sense within the industry and its regulators that administrative guidance is to be taken for granted."

By the late 1990s, even some in academia and the media, both of which had pushed most vigorously for deregulation, seemed to have lost their enthusiasm—especially in the wake of liberal reforms in the financial sector that were called precipitous and excessive. Kasahara Hidehiko, a political scientist at Keio University, argued that Japan must find its own model of deregulation, and avoid borrowing too heavily from the United States or the United Kingdom.[14] Japan's regulatory regime, he concluded, had "functioned as a brake on the extraordinary and excessive levels of competition" in the society, while its "convoy system of coordination between the government and private sector deserves some praise for maintaining order within industry and restraining the impulse to abandon the weak." In a similar vein,

11. Interview, November 11, 1997, Tokyo.

12. *Nihon Keizai Shinbun*, October 19, 1996, 8. The survey is also discussed in Tilton (1998), 187–88.

13. *Nikkei Weekly*, October 21, 1996.

14. Kasahara Hidehiko, "The Bureaucracy in Japan: Historical Ruminations," in the *Japan Foundation Newsletter*, January 1997.

the editors of *Asahi Shinbun* concluded that, yes, the government had intervened too much, too often in the marketplace, but called the deregulation effort a "backlash that has given too much influence to market forces" (January 1, 1998). And Ota Hiroshi, business editor for the pro-business *Yomiuri Shinbun*, described a new, more cautious attitude about deregulation in Japan: "The feeling now is that it is unwise to let market forces reign" (March 17, 1999).

This renewed old "feeling" was particularly evident in the government's mounting concern over the financial health of small business. To counteract the effects of a lending squeeze, MITI moved to supply emergency funds to the SME credit guarantee associations: twenty trillion yen in 1998 and another ten trillion yen in 1999 (Reuters, March 25, 1999). With MOF's support, MITI also moved to beef up the activities of the three state-controlled institutions that lend money to small business—the People's Finance Corporation (Kokumin Kinyū Kōko), the Japan Finance Corporation for Small Business (Chūshō Kigyō Kinyū Kōko), and Shōkō Chūkin. The volume of lending by these institutions jumped sharply in the late 1990s; indeed, in the case of the Japan Finance Corporation for Small Business, it jumped 221 percent from January 1997 to January 1998 (*Yomiuri Shinbun*, February 20, 1998). This represented a Lazarus-like turnaround for government banks that were supported in large part by the Fiscal Investment and Loan Program (FILP), which in turn was funded by postal savings, public pension funds, and postal insurance funds. Just a few years earlier, these government banks had been slated for consolidation or elimination under various reform proposals.

It should be noted, however, that SMEs and their financial benefactors were not the only ones to benefit from this renewed suspicion about unfettered market forces. Politicians rallied behind the Japan Development Bank, a government-affiliated institution that earlier had been a leading candidate for privatization. Rather than privatizing the JDB, the Diet actually expanded the bank's public mandate, allowing it to absorb the functions of the highly political Hokkaido Tohoku Development Finance Corporation without forcing it to make any personnel cuts.[15] The bank, in turn, continued to loan money to some of Japan's biggest corporations—including eighty-five billion yen in early 1999 to Nissan, the heavily indebted vehicle manufacturer that was then negotiating a mega-merger deal with French automaker Renault.[16]

15. In 1998, before the merger, the JDB and the Hokkaido Tohoku Development Finance Corp. collectively employed 1,389 people. In 2000, after the merger, the new Development Bank of Japan employed 1,387 people. See Lincoln (2001, 169).

16. *Economist*, February 6, 1999, 17. Renault did ultimately agree to bail out Nissan, spending $5.6 billion to acquire a one-third interest in the ailing Japanese firm. Carlos Ghosn, the Brazilian-born Renault executive, became Nissan's new president.

Indeed, the late 1990s witnessed a dramatic upsurge in the Japanese state's use of industrial policies to promote investment by targeted industries and firms. Here I cite only a few of the many possible examples:

- In 1998, MITI unveiled a seven-year plan to aid the Japanese satellite industry by organizing joint research projects to reduce the cost of manufacturing key components (*Asahi Shinbun,* September 16, 1998).
- In 1998, MITI renewed its pledge to help Japanese manufacturers launch their own commercial aircraft industry—this time with an eighty-seat passenger plane. The announcement came in the wake of Boeing's decision to drop out of a project to develop a slightly larger plane (the YSK) (*Daily Yomiuri,* August 20, 1998). In addition, MITI indicated it would launch a joint R&D project to develop higher quality carbon-fiber materials for use in aircraft bodies (*Daily Yomiuri,* February 4, 2000).
- In 1999, the ministries of international trade and industry, agriculture, education, and health and welfare jointly announced a "national strategy" of catching up with the United States and Europe in biotechnology. They signaled their intent to promote commercial applications of genetics research (*Japan Digest,* February 19, 1999, 5).
- In 1999, MITI proposed legislation that would give it new tools to promote increased productivity through "industrial revitalization." Under this law, target firms would receive money and guidance to focus on "core activities," carry out restructuring, and develop new products (*Nihon Keizai Shinbun,* July 13, 1999, 5).
- In 1999, MITI, MPT, the Ministry of Construction, and the National Police Agency indicated they would work with one hundred private firms to jointly develop technology for intelligent transportation systems (*Nihon Keizai Shinbun,* July 8, 1999, 1).
- In 2000, MPT initiated a plan to build up Japan's e-commerce software industry by giving away free Internet lines to targeted software developers (*Japan Digest,* February 1, 2000).

The list goes on and on. But ultimately, the number of government regulations, the volume of government subsidies, and the amount of industrial policy initiatives represent imperfect measures of structural change or continuity in the state-industry nexus of relationalism. Indeed, neither a strong commitment to formal rule making nor a heavy reliance on "corporate welfare" is unique to Japan or other highly relational political economies. Relationalism, as discussed above, has to do with reciprocal ties that cast a shadow of the future over otherwise one-time political and economic transactions. Thus, a more telling measure of relationalism might be the extent of informal, reciprocal rule making (administrative guidance). Unfortunately, the use of such guidance, which can take the form of a simple phone call to advise a firm about a particular regulation or a lunch meeting to discuss future investments in an industry, is extremely difficult to quantify.[17]

On the other hand, one only had to pay casual attention to the Japanese press in the 1990s to recognize that exceptionally close, reciprocal ties continued to bind regulators and the regulated in Japan, often in ways that undermined both the impartial oversight of corporate activities and public trust. For most of the postwar period, political scandals in Japan involved politicians, not central government officials. But in the late 1990s a succession of high-ranking bureaucrats captured headlines (and, in many cases, court dates) by trading preferential treatment for money, gifts, and favors from business interests under their jurisdiction. This obviously was nothing new; Japanese bureaucrats had been engaged in such corrupt practices for years. What changed was the tolerance level of government underlings and big-city reporters, who suddenly began to blow the whistle.

For example, a top official of the Ministry of Health and Welfare was sent to jail for accepting sixty-five million yen in bribes from the operator of a nursing home for the elderly. MITI officials were implicated in a corruption scandal involving oil wholesalers and prospectors. MPT was questioned over its handling of contracts for gasoline sales to postal service bureaus. Officials of the Japan Highway Public Corporation were charged with accepting bribes from underwriters seeking a contract to manage the corporation's bond issues, as well as from the manufacturers of lighting equipment and components for signal controls. Officials in the Defense Agency's procurement department ran into trouble for the cozy deals they made with suppliers (*Yomiuri Shinbun*, September to November, 1998).

While all of these scandals rocked the nation, none made as big a splash as one involving the Ministry of Finance and Bank of Japan, whose bank inspectors and policy planners received bribes in the form of lavish entertainment, including golf outings and excursions to Tokyo's most expensive "hostess" bars and restaurants.[18] As it turned out, at least twenty commercial banks, long-term credit banks, and trust banks had special units whose staff —known as "MOF *tan*" or "MOF liaison"—devoted themselves to wining and dining public officials to gain inside information on upcoming inspections, applications from competitors, and new policy initiatives being pur-

---

17. On May 12, 1999, one newspaper (*Yomiuri*) expressed concern that MITI was aggressively seeking to expand its use of administrative guidance. For example, it noted that the ministry had, in its role as secretariat of a commission on competitiveness, pushed a proposal to oversee the process by which manufacturers could dispose of excess production capacity.

18. MOF and BOJ were particularly embarrassed by salacious reports of late-night trips to "*no pan*" (no panties) pubs, where the serving staff went bottomless.

sued by the ministry (*Yomiuri Shinbun,* January to April, 1998). Occasionally, the cozy ties between banks and banking regulators had direct and disastrous consequences, such as the collapse of the Long-Term Credit Bank. MOF and BOJ officials conspired with bank officials to conceal the actual scale of the bank's massive portfolio of nonperforming loans (*Yomiuri Shinbun,* October 13, 1998, May 26 and 27, 1999).

In nearly all of these cases, the reciprocal ties between regulators and the regulated were solidified through the practice of amakudari ("descent from heaven"). As discussed in chapter 2, government officials retire from public posts at a relatively early age (usually fifty-five) and often take up posts in the private firms they once regulated, or in one of the 26,275 different "public interest corporations" (*kōeki hōjin*) that often coordinated activities carried out by private firms in the late 1990s.[19] Consider, for example, these scandals:

- *MOF and the BOJ.* After they broke the first stories, Japanese newspapers reported that 164 former MOF officials and ninety-six former BOJ officials had "descended" into high-ranking posts in financial institutions that they used to regulate (*Yomiuri Shinbun,* February 21, 1998). Many of them worked in the "MOF-*tan*" units, wining and dining their former colleagues in the public sector (*Yomiuri Shinbun,* January 28, 1998).
- *Japan Highway Public Corporation.* It was a former MOF official who, in his amakudari post at the public corporation, accepted more than seven million yen in bribes from companies looking for underwriting contracts with the public corporation (*Yomiuri Shinbun,* July 1, 1998.)
- *Japan National Oil Corporation,* a *tokushū hōjin* (or special—i.e., government-funded—corporation) affiliated with MITI that finances oil exploration and that, in the late 1990s, found itself holding more than one trillion in bad loans. Newspapers reported that retired MITI officials traditionally run the JNOC and also "descend" routinely into private oil companies. In late 1998, fourteen former MITI officials held amakudari posts at seven different oil companies doing business with JNOC (*Daily Yomiuri,* March 2, 1999).[20]
- *The Defense Agency,* which ran afoul of the law for questionable pro-

19. These public interest corporations include nonprofit corporations (*zaidan hōjin*), special corporations (*tokushū hōjin*), and authorized corporations (*ninka hōjin*). The number given above comes from *Daily Yomiuri,* December 9, 1998.

20. On this score, JNOC is hardly exceptional. A survey by the Management and Coordination Agency found that nearly half of the directors of *tokushū hōjin* "descend" from central ministries, while more than half of the companies and organizations that do business with the *tokushū hōjin* are amply stocked with former ministry officials. See *Nihon Keizai Shinbun,* March 8, 1987, 5.

Table 4.1. Amakudari "Descents" (1979–98)

	1998	1997	1996	1995	1994	1993	1992	1991	1990	1989
National Police	43	54	44	37	38	38	32	16	18	18
Defense	9	15	19	18	18	16	16	13	15	13
MOF (Finance)	111	130	153	161	165	165	153	139	144	153
National Tax	124	116	113	83	86	84	83	43	46	47
MAFF (Agriculture)	46	50	48	53	53	55	57	52	50	53
MITI (Trade)	90	99	92	88	92	97	86	89	96	89
MOT (Transportation)	69	68	66	67	58	59	59	49	49	49
MPT (Posts)	25	30	32	33	33	28	28	24	25	24
MOC (Construction)	152	150	144	151	151	154	151	130	123	124
Bank of Japan (*)	77	94	100	96	97	97	98	104	114	109
(Former) JNR (**)	56	68	64	74	80	90	88	100	101	102
Urban Planning (**)	32	38	40	42	45	48	48	52	45	40
Japan Roads (**)	73	70	71	71	66	68	63	63	59	60
Highways (**)	7	12	12	13						
Japan Railways (**)	26	25	25	29	27	26	28	29	27	23
JDB (***)							18	19	22	22
NTT (****)										
JT (Tobacco) (*****)										
TOTAL (x)	940	1,019	1,023	1,016	1,009	1,025	1,008	922	934	926
Retired Officials (y)	35,235	35,465	35,782	35,427	37,283	38,088	40,438	42,288	43,433	42,118
Ratio (x/y)	0.0267	0.0287	0.0286	0.0287	0.0271	0.0269	0.0249	0.0218	0.0215	0.0220

	1988	1987	1986	1985	1984	1983	1982	1981	1980	1979
National Police	21	19	21	23	21	20	23	21		
National Defense	13				15	16				
MOF (Finance)	137	131	119	123	126	124	124	120	114	99
National Tax	49	57	59	73	78	75	76	72	68	66
MAFF (Agriculture)	48	38	38	40	36	34	35	29	31	29
MITI (Trade)	82	76	76	70	68	75	73	76	78	80
MOT (Transportation)	39	40	46	55	50	52	47	48	46	39
MPT (Posts)	22	23	20	16	17	20	21	21	21	21
MOC (Construction)	117	109	112	117	109	115	98	90	83	83
Bank of Japan (*)	111	112	104	111	110	114	117	117	116	117
(Former) JNR (**)	109	114	114	134	141	150	150	147	130	124
Urban Planning (**)	41	42	45	40	39	36	39	38	36	29
Japan Roads (**)	56	51	55	59	58	55	52	47	42	37
Highways (**)										
Japan Railway (**)	24	19	20	22	21	20	17			
JDB (***)	19	22	22	23	31	30	28	26	26	26
NTT (****)				209	207	187	180	175	179	176
JT (Tobacco) (****)				19	19	18				
TOTAL (x)	892	857	858	1,142	1,146	1,141	1,080	1,027	970	926
Retired Officials (y)	40,723	40,568	36,713	41,307	50,575	38,431	36,444	36,256	34,657	32,446
Ratio (x/y)	0.0219	0.0211	0.0234	0.0276	0.0227	0.0297	0.0296	0.0283	0.0280	0.0285

Sources: Tōyō Keizai Shinpōsha, Kigyō Keiretsu Sōran, various years.
National Personnel Authority (Jinji-in), Kōmuin Hakusho, various years.
Notes: * Authorized Company (Ninka Hōjin); ** Special Corporations (Tokushū Hōjin);
*** JDB (Japan Development Bank); **** NTT and JT were privatized in 1986

curement practices. Of the top-ranking officers who retired from the agency between 1993 and 1997, 225 landed amakudari positions with twenty private contractors that received most of the agency's defense work (*Yomiuri Shinbun*, November 29, 1998).

- *MPT's regional postal service bureaus,* which showed preference for one firm in its award of contracts for a variety of goods and services. The president of the company, Sogo Shizai Service, is traditionally a former MPT official, and other top managers tend to be former post office officials (*Yomiuri Shinbun*, May 12, 1999).

This list falls far short of exhausting all the many examples of amakudari-related corruption in the 1990s. But it should suggest that the practice of "descending from heaven," a tangible manifestation of relationalism in the state-industry nexus, thrived—albeit in a sometimes virulent form. Fortunately, I need not rely solely on newspaper coverage to follow movements in the use of this practice. Since 1979, a private research firm has conducted an annual survey of ministries and agencies, collecting data on the number of officials who have "descended" from the central government. The results, assembled in table 4.1, show remarkably little change in the use of amakudari. In the eight years between 1979 and 1986, there was an average of 1,036 "descents" per year. In the eight years from 1991 to 1998, there was an average of 955 "descents" per year. This very small difference is caused by a reduction in the number of retirements, not by a reduction in the proportion of bureaucrats "descending" into the private sector. (To confirm this, please note the ratio of amakudari cases per retirements.)[21] In other words, this practice has continued, virtually unabated, despite the privatization of numerous public corporations and the liberalization of several industries.[22] Indeed, Nakano (1998, 105) has demonstrated that, in the aftermath of the privatization of NTT and the liberalization of the telecommunications industry, the Ministry of Posts and Telecommunications managed to *increase* its use of amakudari: "Practically every major common carrier has at least one MPT amakudari board member."

Business and Business

As noted in chapter 2, firms in postwar Japan have cooperated with one another far more closely, and for longer periods of time, than their counter-

---

21. Tōyō Keizai Shinpōsha, *Kigyō Keiretsu Sōran* (Directory of Corporate Groups), various years. The company quit publishing this volume in 2000, and did not provide any statistics on "descents" after 1998.

22. Using a slightly different measurement stick, Schaede finds that government "old boys" increased their presence in large firms in Japan during the first half of the 1990s. See Schaede (1995), 293–317.

parts in other market economies. This cooperation has taken many forms, from market-sharing agreements between otherwise rival enterprises (cartels) to quasi integration tying together legally independent corporations (keiretsu). Did globalization erode these forms of interfirm cooperation in Japan during the 1990s? The evidence suggests that it did not. At the most fundamental level, we must note that Japanese firms showed little interest in abandoning such cooperation; while 54.5 percent of large firms surveyed in 1996 by Japan's leading business newspaper called for change in the system of "side-by-side" competition (*yokonarabi taisei*, a negative term implying collusion by rivals in the marketplace), only 9 percent expressed opposition to the long-standing practice of "industrial cooperation" (*gyōkai kyōchō*, a more positive term that nonetheless means much the same).[23]

In late 1999, Toyota Motors persuaded four other major companies, including Matsushita, to join forces on a marketing campaign aimed at young and fickle consumers. The companies sold everything from automobiles to refrigerators, from beer to computers, under the common "WiLL" logo. "Young people these days are interested in too many things for a company to keep up with," complained Homma Hideaki, a marketing executive for Toyota. "Then it occurred to us to share this frustration with other companies."[24]

It is true that in the 1990s the Fair Trade Commission, the government agency charged with enforcing Japan's Anti-Monopoly Act, began to crack down on some of the numerous cartels that had, in the past, been ignored if not blessed or even coordinated by the government. For example, it took aggressive action against producers of pharmaceuticals and cosmetics (Iyori 1995, 10–14). At the same time, however, the FTC was less aggressive against politically powerful interests such as construction companies and steel manufacturers that continued to collude on prices.

To combat such collusion in the construction industry, the government in 1994 launched a new system of open bidding for public works contracts. But this system was used in only 20 percent of the four trillion yen in contracts awarded in fiscal 1997, according to a survey by the Board of Audit. It found that contracting agencies, by and large, continued to use the old system in which they listed construction companies according to their size and technical ability, and then authorized a limited number to submit bids (*Yomiuri Shinbun*, November 26, 1998). Given this lack of change in the established process, no one should have been surprised by a report in 1999 that five

23. *Nihon Keizai Shinbun,* October 19, 1996, 8. The newspaper surveyed the heads of ninety-one of Japan's largest firms and eighty-seven of its medium-scale firms. For another view on these survey results, see Tilton (1998, 187–88).

24. Kobayashi Kakumi, "Firms Hope Fewer Products, One Label Cure Recognition Woes," *Japan Times,* December 30, 1990.

firms—Mitsubishi Heavy Industries, NKK Corp., Kawasaki Corp., Hitachi Zosen Corp., and Takuma Co.—continued to engage in bid-rigging (*dangō*) on public contracts to build stoker incinerators. Representatives of the firms allegedly met on numerous occasions each year to reach agreement on how to allocate work on those contracts. They, as well as two other manufacturers, had been told to stop colluding in 1979–twenty years earlier—but apparently restarted the practice in 1989 (*Yomiuri Shinbun,* August 9, 1999).

More surprising, perhaps, is the continuation of collusive, price-fixing behavior that boosts the costs of steel, petrochemicals, and other basic inputs used by assemblers, such as automakers, facing fierce competition in global markets. A marketing executive for a large Japanese steel producer told Tilton (1998, 176) that his firm and its rivals are still "violating the Anti-Monopoly Act every day. . . . [We] get together and talk about what the price ought to be." *Nihon Keizai Shinbun* (May 10, 1994), Japan's leading business newspaper, came to the same conclusion when it reported that domestic steel makers continue to "use tacit pressure to keep out imports and support the price structure." This begs the question: Why would the producers of finished goods continue to tolerate such practices? After all, they—unlike government officials—do not receive campaign cash or bribes from their suppliers. But Elder (1998, 15) argues that downstream users of basic inputs such as steel, petrochemicals, and semiconductors have indeed received compensation in the form of predictable pricing over the long run. "Upstream industries sometimes compensate the downstream industries by providing a certain degree of price stability or price smoothing. In periods of slack demand, the price for domestic users may be higher than the world prices, but in periods of tight demand, it might be lower and/or domestic users will get preferential access to suppliers." In other words, relational ties matter.[25]

This brings us to the question of keiretsu, which—as I argued in chapter 2—should be viewed as a manifestation of largely informal and invisible ties between independent firms, and should not be reified as a concrete "being." In the 1990s, journalists and even many academics repeatedly announced the pending collapse of such interfirm ties. But events repeatedly proved them wrong.

Let us begin by looking at the vertical keiretsu linking large assemblers of

25. It should be noted that Elder explicitly (and, it is argued here, inadvisably) dismisses keiretsu ties as an alternative explanation for how Japan managed to reconcile the conflicting interests of upstream suppliers and downstream users of basic inputs. He focuses more heavily on compensation provided by the government, particularly nonenforcement of the Anti-Monopoly Act. But Elder seems to acknowledge (22) that this emphasis may be misplaced for the 1980s and '90s, when "downstream user industries were much less dependent on government protection and promotion policies," but when prices in Japan for such inputs continued to be significantly higher than foreign prices.

machinery and smaller suppliers of parts. As late as 1997, the government (SME Agency 1997, 147) reported that subcontractors, who traditionally have supplied a high proportion of the value-added in production, continued to make up more than half of all small and medium sized manufacturing firms in Japan. And the majority of these subcontractors continued to rely on a single "parent" (a major assembler with whom they have done business for at least twenty years) for more than 50 percent of their total sales (SME Agency 1997, 149).

But change—distributional change—clearly did take place in this form of interfirm networking. For one thing, many subcontractors reported to me and to others conducting research that they have less and less bargaining power with their parents.[26] Indeed, in the 1990s they often remarked that they were "squeezed" by their major customers, who in some industries (particularly automobiles) tried to reduce their costs by as much as 30 percent and thus demanded that their suppliers reduce parts prices by an equivalent—or greater—amount.[27] The goal was to achieve what many parent firms referred to as "Asian prices"—the cheaper prices charged by parts suppliers in Taipei or Kuala Lumpur.

Even during a brief moment of economic recovery in 1996, subcontractors were continuing to slash prices—much faster and deeper than their parents, according to a survey by Japan's machinists union (Zenkoku Kinzoku Kikai Rōdōkumiai 1997). It found that, as a result of these precipitously steep price cuts, subcontractors in the auto parts industry earned extremely low profits that year (1.7 percent of sales, compared to 2.3 percent for assemblers). Indeed, it found that only 55 percent of small manufacturers in the machinery industry—compared to 91 percent of large manufacturers—operated in the black during that short-lived recovery. This led the union to issue the following appeal: "In an effort to preserve Japan's manufacturing base, we ask that major companies take the attitude that they should tie themselves to, and grow together with, their subcontractors, accepting proper prices that reflect the skills that subcontractors possess" (2).

Some subcontractors, especially smaller, less technologically sophisticated ones, found themselves unable to keep up with these new and increasingly harsh demands from their parents. In one survey, nearly 84 percent of third-tier suppliers in the automobile industry reported they were receiving fewer

---

26. During the mid- and late 1990s, I interviewed about a dozen parts suppliers/subcontractors, most of whom mentioned this problem. See also Japan Finance Corporation for Small Business 1996, 29; Japan Finance Corporation for Small Business 1997, 38; Shōkō Chūkin 1995, 20.

27. This experience of "*shiwayose*" (squeezing) was also cited frequently in interviews, and is well-documented in written materials. See, for example, Jichirōrento Shokurō Keizaishibu, "Baburu Hōkaigo no Machikōba no Keiei Jittai," July 1997, 8; Ikeda 1996, 132–33; Nakazawa 1997, 74; Zenkoku Shitauke Kigyō Shinkō Kyōkai 1997a, 72.

orders than in the past (Japan Finance Corp. for Small Business 1997, 38) On the other hand, a much smaller percentage (59 percent) of first-tier suppliers reported a drop in orders. Likewise, in the consumer electronics industry, 55.5 percent of first-tier suppliers expected to maintain (44.4 percent) or even strengthen (11.1 percent) the long-term ties they enjoyed with their customers, while only 42.9 percent of third-tier suppliers expressed similar optimism. Indeed, none (0.0 percent) of those smaller suppliers in the consumer electronics industry anticipated stronger ties (Japan Finance Corp. for Small Business 1997, 62).

What this means is that a fundamental shakeout occurred in Japan's vertical keiretsu. Japanese government and business officials referred to it as "*nikyoku bunka*" or polarization. In other words, while some subcontractors were jettisoned by their parents, others were pulled even more tightly into supply networks through a process of selection (*senbetsu*).[28] Or, as the SME Agency (1996, 199) put it, "Some subcontractors are leaving their keiretsu, becoming independent, and seeking orders from multiple customers, but many others—especially those with superior skills—are forging even tighter relations with their parents."[29]

As figure 4.1 shows, this process of selection was not new. From the early 1970s, parent firms moved slowly but steadily in the direction of relying on a single trusted supplier, rather than multiple and competing suppliers, for a particular part. In other words, subcontracting orders became increasingly concentrated in the hands of a smaller and smaller group of elite suppliers, who maintained extremely close relations with their customers.[30] What was new in the 1990s was the accelerated pace at which this selection process unfolded.

In the automobile industry, this process often assumed the form of "modularization," the procurement of an entire set or package of parts from a single subcontractor. Nissan, for example, announced a plan in 1998 to reorganize its parts supply network over a five-year period, cutting in half the number of first-tier suppliers with which it routinely did business, and en-

28. In addition to the large number of survey and press reports on this process, NHK contributed an outstanding television documentary that focuses on Mazda: "Keiretsu ga Kuzureru Toki: Hiroshima-Machi Kōjō no Sentaku" (May 1997).

29. If survey results are any indication, subcontractors did not expand their list of customers in the 1990s. One study (SME Agency 1998, 98) found that 83 percent of subcontractors had the same number of parent firms, or even fewer, than they had three years earlier. Another study (Japan Finance Corporation for Small Business 1997, 89) reported that 69.5 percent of subcontractors were either maintaining the same number or reducing the number of customers with whom they did business.

30. In a survey of automobile parts suppliers, 12.2 percent of first-tier subcontractors expressed the belief that ties with their parent firm would grow stronger in the future, while none of the third-tier subs could predict this. See Japan Finance Corporation for Small Business (1997, 42).

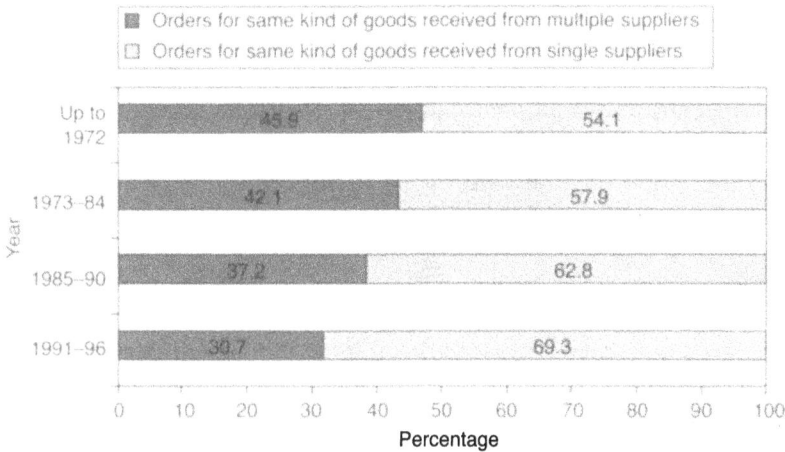

Figure 4.1. Subcontracting: From multiple to single suppliers
Source: Small and Medium Enterprise Agency, *Chūshō Kigyō Hakusho,* 1996, 189.

trusting the "survivors" with enhanced responsibilities.[31] (After Nissan's 1999 merger with Renault, new company president Carlos Ghosn floated another, even bolder reorganization plan that involved selling the parent firm's equity shares in all but a handful of core subcontractors.[32]) Suzuki and Mitsubishi Motors (MMC) pursued their own modularization strategies, each with the goal of cutting costs by as much as 25 percent.[33] In the electronics industry as well as the auto industry, the selection process also led to a new pattern in which assemblers and first-tier suppliers worked together to develop critical components. The motivation behind such joint development projects was to reduce the time it takes to move new products or models from the design stage to full production. Parent firms recognized that, to achieve this goal, they must forge even stronger bonds with their key suppliers.[34]

One can cite numerous examples of continuing, close cooperation between assemblers and suppliers in Japanese manufacturing industries. Between 1995 and 1999, for example, Toyota actually *increased* its equity stake in its three largest parts suppliers: Denso (in which Toyota boosted its share

31. *Nihon Keizai Shinbun,* July 22, 1998, 1.

32. See Ikeda (1999). At the same time, however, Nissan encouraged some of its key suppliers to strengthen their financial positions through horizontal tie-ups. Thus, Tachi-S and Fuji Kiko merged, while Unisia Jecs, Calsonic, and Kansei moved to forge a three-way alliance. Internally, Nissan management was sharply divided between "traditionalists" who believed the assembler should retain its close transactional ties with these core subcontractors and "radicals," led by Ghosn, who believed it should loosen or even cut such ties. See *Nikkei Weekly,* September 6, 1999. As we shall see, Ghosn won this battle but later retreated.

33. See Japan Finance Corporation for Small Business (1997, 34).

34. This became a common refrain in the literature on restructuring in the automobile and electronics industries. See Shimokawa 1995, 8; Shimokawa 1997; Altbach 1997, 9.

to 24.6 percent); Toyoda Gosei (42.4 percent); and Aishin (24.4 percent). Japan's leading automaker solidified those interfirm ties further by sending its own representatives to serve on the suppliers' corporate boards.[35] And it drew a formerly independent supplier into its keiretsu camp, becoming the largest shareholder of Art Kinzoku, a major producer of pistons (Whittaker 1997, 103). Finally, the behavior of assemblers during the darkest days of the financial crisis provides additional testimony to the importance they placed on maintaining established supply networks. Daikin, which assembles air conditioning equipment, and Komatsu, a manufacturer of heavy machinery used in construction and agriculture, were among those providing special loans to favored suppliers that otherwise struggled to obtain investment capital during a particularly severe credit crunch (*Nihon Keizai Shinbun*, February 4, 1998).

In the 1990s, then, parent firms continued to value mutually reinforcing ties with a defined set of suppliers, even as the size of that set shrank. The most comprehensive survey of subcontracting in Japan's machinery industries showed that, as of 1995, only 11.6 percent of assemblers were routinely conducting business with suppliers outside their established subcontracting networks.[36] What was happening was not so much the "unraveling" as the "re-raveling" of keiretsu ties. While the bonds between some firms loosened, those between others tightened. This was a clear case of distributional but not structural change.

I turn now to an examination of horizontal keiretsu, the pan-industrial groups organized around a major city bank, with a related firm in nearly every industry. In 1989, these groups were targeted by U.S. trade negotiators, who called them "exclusionary" and said they represented a "structural impediment" blocking access to the Japanese market. The Japanese side, which had its own complaints about U.S. impediments to free trade, pledged to take action to open up Japan's cozy business world. Four years later, the Diet amended the commercial code to require every firm listed on the Tokyo Stock Exchange to appoint at least one *kansayaku* (an "independent" auditor; i.e., someone who is not a current or former employee) to its board of directors to carry out a review of the company's compliance with various laws, as well as a review of the company's financial health. The legislation was

---

35. In 1999, a former Toyota vice president became chairman of the board at Aishin. Honda used a similar personnel transfer to tighten ties with a core subcontractor; it sent a former executive director to Keihin, where he became president. See Tōyō Keizai Shinpōsha (*Kaisha Shiki-hō*, vol. 3, summer 1999).

36. Shōkō Chūkin 1995, 23. This survey also showed that breaking keiretsu ties is a low priority for parent firms reorganizing their operations. On a list of eleven restructuring options, this one was ranked tenth.

heralded as evidence that Japan was becoming more open by adopting the emerging global (or, more precisely, American) standards of corporate governance. Instead, however, it provided an opportunity for large firms to forge even closer ties. When they studied the on-the-ground implementation of the new law, Sato and Yamauchi (1994, 68) discovered that 66.5 percent of the *kansayaku* appointed by firms belonging to a keiretsu were actually affiliated with another firm in the same group. They implied that group members had tried to sabotage the new law.[37]

No one, including me, can deny that these corporate groups came under enormous stress later in the 1990s, when financial market liberalization and bad loans combined to force Japanese banks to scramble for new ways to remain competitive. Indeed, some of the city banks that had stood at the center of rival horizontal keiretsu began to merge operations, thereby allowing them to raise much more capital and sell new financial instruments. Fuji Bank (of the Fuyo group) and Dai-Ichi Kangyo Bank (of the DKG group) merged with the Industrial Bank of Japan in October 2000 to become the Mizuho Financial Group (with assets, then, of $1.5 trillion). Likewise, Sumitomo Bank and Sakura Bank (the former Mitsui Bank) merged across keiretsu lines in April 2001 to create a new Sumitomo-Mitsui Bank with assets, then, of about $937 billion.[38]

This did not, however, spell the end of business relationships within particular horizontal keiretsu.[39] Indeed, companies not only hinted that they would eventually realign into four rather than six bank-centered groups, they actually moved on a couple different fronts to strengthen interfirm ties. First, the new bank combines (Mizuho and Sumitomo-Mitsui, as well as Tokyo-Mitsubishi and UFJ) jumped at the opportunity to build more tightly coordinated groups resembling the prewar *zaibatsu* and organized around a holding company.[40] This opportunity came in the form of a 1997 amend-

37. A more charitable interpretation might be that large firms could not, arithmetically, embrace the spirit of the law. In the mid-1990s, Japan had only about eight thousand accountants—one-thirtieth as many as in the United States (250,000)—capable of serving as "independent" auditors. See Taggart Murphy, "Don't Be Fooled by Japan's Big Bang," in *Fortune*, December 29, 1997.

38. Two other big bank mergers did not span rival keiretsu. These were the marriages between the Bank of Tokyo and Mitsubishi Bank in 1996 (Bank of Tokyo–Mitsubishi) and between the Sanwa, Tokai, and Asahi banks in 2001 (UFJ). In 2005, the two financial combines were merged to form Mitsubishi UFJ Financial Group.

39. In rejecting the conventional wisdom that keiretsu ties unraveled during the 1990s, I am joined by McGuire and Dow (2003, 384), who studied the business activities of four hundred group members and concluded that, despite all the pressure to delink, "the keiretsu system remained intact."

40. *Ekonomisuto* (March 28, 2000) devotes a special issue to bank mergers and holding companies.

ment to the Anti-Monopoly Act, which the Diet thought would help industrial conglomerates improve performance through restructuring. But by consolidating various functions under one roof, the big financial institutions created what one newspaper (*Asahi Shinbun*, April 28, 2000, 11) called "full-settism . . . a strengthening of cooperation within city bank groups." In the case of Mizuho, four members of the Fuyo group began to solidify their intra-keiretsu ties even as Fuji Bank studied a merger with Dai-Ichi Kangyo. Fuji bought $2.6 billion worth of new shares in Yasuda Trust, increasing its stake in the affiliate from 17 percent to just over 50 percent. In addition, the two firms began to collaborate with Yasuda Mutual Life Insurance and Yasuda Fire and Marine Insurance on plans to enter new business fields (*Yomiuri Shinbun*, July 17, 1998). Likewise, the Bank of Tokyo–Mitsubishi decided it would, in spring 2001, form a giant holding company (Mitsubishi Tokyo Financial Group) to oversee its own operations and also those of Mitsubishi Trust and two smaller trust banks in the Mitsubishi keiretsu (*Asahi Shinbun*, April 19, 1 and 11).

On a different front, large manufacturers in the automobile and electronics industries began strengthening established keiretsu ties through new technology-based alliances. For example, Fuyo members—including Nissan, Hitachi, and Unisia Jecs (a smaller supplier affiliated for years with Nissan and now, through a joint venture with Valeo SA of France, affiliated with Renault as well)—agreed to collaborate on the development of intelligent transport systems (ITS), the guts of new high-tech automobiles (*Yomiuri Shinbun*, December 8, 1999).

Given the harsh climate in the financial sector, where a glut of nonperforming loans created a massive credit crunch, we should not be surprised to learn that a number of firms scrambled in the 1990s to raise cash and beef up sagging balance sheets by, among many other things, selling shares they held in other firms, including some of the mutually held shares that traditionally cemented keiretsu bonds. The dissolution of cross-shareholding proceeded at a modest pace until the middle of the decade, when it apparently began to accelerate. This happened in spite of the fact that, in a 1994 survey, nine out of ten Japanese corporations indicated they would continue the practice of cross-shareholding—even though they saw no particular economic benefit to doing so (EPA 1996, 374). And it happened in spite of the fact that, in a 1999 survey, 98 percent of 731 large firms indicated that they owned shares they generally did not trade; of these firms, 66.5 percent indicated that such "stable shareholdings" accounted for at least half of their total shareholdings (Inagami 2000).

Based on the trend line of the late 1990s, as well as press releases from cash-strapped corporations, business reporters prematurely forecast the demise of cross-shareholding.[41] Even otherwise sober-minded think tanks often went too far. In its 1998 report on financial market activity, Nissei Life Insurance (NLI), for example, argued that cross-shareholding had become increasingly "irrational"; in its 2001 report, an NLI researcher, Kuroki Fumiaki, stuck his neck out even further and suggested that the practice was doomed.[42]

By 2002, that researcher had to retreat from his bold prediction. Evidence was beginning to show rather clearly that, while cross-shareholding among unrelated firms was down, it was holding steady among members of horizontal keiretsu. Kuroki acknowledged that "despite instances of unwinding and revision of cross-holding relationships within groups, fundamental changes have not yet occurred."[43] In other words, no matter how economically "irrational" the practice might have become, it continued to have sociopolitical salience for the executives of Japan's largest firms who occupied positions of power in business networks.

Using data from the Japan Fair Trade Commission (2001), figure 4.2 offers a clear picture of this continuity. Members of horizontal keiretsu bucked the general trend by hanging on to cross-held shares, despite financial pressure to unwind them: in 1989, those shares represented 21.64 percent of the outstanding shares owned by keiretsu members; in 1999, they represented 20.05 percent. This picture of continuity is painted yet again in an analysis of cross-shareholding data collected by Tōyō Keizai Shinpōsha (*Kigyō Keiretsu Sōran,* various years). Indeed, that analysis indicates that the cross-shareholding ratio among group members peaked in 1993 and fell gradually over the next five years, but that—by 1998, the last year of data collection—the average ratio among the groups (16.2%) was still relatively high and only slightly lower than it had been (18%) in the 1980s.[44]

41. In 1998, as Japan dipped into its second recession in the 1990s, some companies plagued with sharply falling profits sought to rally investor confidence by publicly announcing they would have to *consider* trimming cross-held shares, especially unproductive holdings in financial institutions. Some media outlets overstated the significance of these announcements. Thus, a headline in the *Daily Yomiuri* (October 3, 1998) stated that Matsushita "plans to end cross-ownership." The story itself was far less spectacular, quoting a company official who said only that "over the mid-term, we will need to review cross-shareholding."

42. See NLI Research Institute, "*Kabunushi Mochiai Jōkyō Chōsa: 97 nendo*" (Survey on Cross-shareholding: Fiscal Year 1997), published in 1998 and available at http://www.nli-research .co.jp/mochi/mochi/htm; also see Kuroki Fumiaki, "The Present Status of Unwinding of Cross-Shareholding: The Fiscal 2000 Survey of Cross-shareholding," published by NLI Research Institute in 2001 as "NLI Research" (31).

43. Kuroki Fumiaki 2002, "Cross-Shareholdings Decline for the 11th Straight Year (FY 2001 Survey)," NLI Research, October 2001.

44. Tōyō Keizai obtains a cross-shareholding ratio for each of the six keiretsu by calculating the average percentage of shares of each presidents' council member firm held in a given year by other members of the council. To get the overall average, it sums up the ratios for each keiretsu and divides by six.

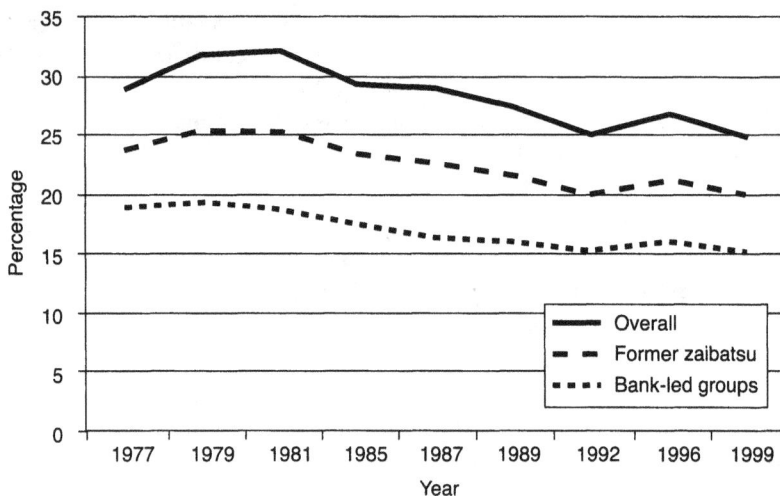

Figure 4.2. Cross-shareholding in keiretsu
Source: Japan Fair Trade Commission 2001. *Kigyō shūdan no jittai ni tsuite: dai-7-ji chōsa hōkokusho* (The State of Horizontal Business Groups: A report on the 7th survey).

These findings lead, in turn, to the following conclusion: firms may sell shares, including cross-held shares, to bolster their position under extremely adverse conditions, but firms with close relational ties are less likely to abandon such mutual holdings. Indeed, a study by Suzuki (1997) supports this conclusion. He found a reduction in one-sided shareholdings for firms listed on the Tokyo Stock Exchange between 1990 and 1997, but no change in the volume of cross-shareholdings. "These findings," Suzuki states (12) "suggest that, in choosing whether to maintain existing shareholdings, a company chooses to sell the stocks of companies with whom they have a less close relationship." His regression analysis provides still further support. In liquidating its holdings, the fact that a company has mutual holdings in a possible target firm makes it significantly less likely to sell those shares.[45]

Makihara Minoru, chairman of Mitsubishi Corp., the giant trading company, and head of the "presidents' club" representing all twenty-nine members of the Mitsubishi group, reinforces this finding by boldly vowing to

45. Suzuki attempts to explain why a firm might sell (or hold) the stock of another firm in which it owns at least 1 percent of all outstanding shares. Among the independent (explanatory) variables he tested was a condition in which the firms own mutual shares in one another. The coefficients for this variable were negative, and statistically significant at the 5 percent level, over each of the two-year test periods (1988–90; 1990–92; 1992–94; 1994–96), and over the entire period (1988–96). In total, Suzuki's logistic regression relied on more than thirty-seven thousand observations.

strengthen—not loosen—ties among members of that horizontal keiretsu (*Economist,* October 23, 1999, 71–72). The group, he says, will work together to support member activities in new growth fields such as e-commerce. "We want to be part of the new Japan as well as the old."

A careful reading of the evidence suggests that the unwinding of cross-held shares in the 1990s might have been temporary, or epiphenomenal. Indeed, the Keidanren called for the establishment of a public repository that would buy up economically unproductive but socially valuable shares from companies, and then sell them back after financial conditions improve.[46] Overall, one newspaper lamented that "companies generally appear reluctant to sell [mutually held] shares. In the midst of the persistent economic slump, cross-shareholding has become a lifeline to link corporations with banks, a notion that runs counter to the ideal of healthy business activity" (*Nikkei Weekly,* January 11, 1999, 11).

Management and Labor

To whom does the corporation belong: stockholders or employees? The answer to this question varies markedly from place to place. Under the Japanese model of corporate governance, managers control the firm for the benefit of numerous stakeholders, especially lifetime employees like themselves; by contrast, under the Anglo-American model, stockholders own and therefore should control the firm. During the 1990s, the latter approach emerged as a kind of "global standard," promoted by economists and business consultants throughout the world, but especially in the United States. In Japan, however, managers dug in their heels. In a 1999 survey of executives at 731 large firms listed on the Tokyo Stock Exchange, only 8.5 percent of respondents agreed with this statement: "A firm is owned by its shareholders, with employees constituting but one of the factors of production" (Inagami 2000).

Many Japanese began to assail the new Anglo-American orthodoxy as nothing but a betrayal of working people. For example, Kanzaki (2000, 72–3) argued in a respected economics journal that "there is no future for a firm that places its first priority on increasing share value to please stockholders." This approach, he wrote, would "neglect Japan's most valuable resource—it employees."

It is important to point out that Japanese labor unions were conspicuously quiet in the debate over corporate governance. One labor leader told me he was "not very interested" in the issue.[47] "It's too abstract. We are focusing our

---

46. After floating the plan, Keidanren let it drop as it proved hugely controversial.
47. Interview, Tokyo, October 1, 1998.

attention on concrete problems like job security, wages, and working conditions."

By contrast, managers cared a great deal about the issue. This is because they had the most to lose from a change in the system that had, for years, kept them in the center of a web of social ties between different stakeholders in the firm—without public accountability and transparency. Individual investors, who remained relatively weak in the 1990s (continuing to control less than 20 percent of market value on the Tokyo Stock Exchange),[48] were welcome to buy stock, but not to try to run the show. In the late 1990s, media outlets in Japan reported that corporate executives were continuing to make payments to *sōkaiya* to help them maintain order (i.e., quiescence) at annual shareholder meetings, despite a 1982 law strictly prohibiting such payments to "specific shareholders" (*tokushū kabunushi*). Even the managers of otherwise reputable firms—from MMC to Nomura Securities, from Toyota to Japan Airlines—earned scandalous headlines for allegedly engaging in such illegal behavior (*Nikkei Weekly,* October 25, 1997; *Daily Yomiuri,* December 25, 1997, and August 18, 1998). The National Police Agency finally intervened, encouraging firms to schedule their annual meetings on the same day. Management generally complied. In 1998, twenty-five hundred firms—including about 90 percent of those listed on the Tokyo Stock Exchange—held their annual meetings on June 26. This did indeed make it more difficult for *sōkaiya* to extort money from firms by threatening to disrupt their meetings; but it also made it virtually impossible for individual stockholders to ask pesky questions or exercise legitimate voting privileges at more than one meeting that year.

If the Japanese model of corporate governance resisted change during the 1990s, one might assume that relational ties between labor and management also survived intact. In fact, this is my contention. But Japanese and Western media outlets painted a rather different picture. From their perspective, global market forces hammered the Japanese economy at the end of the twentieth century and significantly eroded the cooperative ties between labor and management. Change, they suggested, was dramatic and ubiquitous. Even more often than they did in the mid-1970s and mid-1980s, reporters offered a steady diet of sensational stories describing the "collapse," the "end," or the "demise" of this system.[49] Some firms, we were told, introduced mar-

---

48. In terms of trading volume, individual investors lost even more ground in the 1990s. They accounted for nearly a quarter of all trading on the Tokyo, Osaka, and Nagoya stock exchanges in 1990; by 1998, however, they accounted for less than 9 percent of the trading in those markets.

49. For example: "Lifetime-Employment System Unravels as Downsizing Fever Grips Corporate Japan," *Nikkei Weekly,* June 7, 1999, 1; "Dai-jitsugyō Jidai wa Kore Kara" (The Age of Mass Unemployment Has Begun), *Aera,* June 22, 1998, 10–15; and "Japan's Worry about Work," *Economist,* January 23, 1999, 23–24.

ket incentives such as merit pay to reward employees for their unique skills and not merely their loyalty.[50] And we heard that others went much further, implementing *risutora* (corporate restructuring) or even *dai-risutora* (massive restructuring).[51] That is, they reportedly trimmed, and even slashed, their payrolls in a frantic quest for leaner, more efficient operations.

In general, though, press reports missed the mark—by quite a lot. My favorite example is an *Asahi* report (November 8, 2001, 13) that came under this headline: "The Collapse of the Japanese-Style Employment System" (Kuzureru Nihon-gata Koyō). It revealed the results of a survey of one hundred large Japanese firms coping with hard economic times by using a variety of schemes to reduce employment. The most commonly used method was "natural attrition," followed in order by "early retirement," "increased use of temporary workers," and, finally, "expansion of *shukkō* and *tenseki*" or the dispatch of employees to related firms. How many of the surveyed firms had resorted to layoffs as a way to reduce employment? Exactly zero.[52]

Or consider the reports about "major restructuring" at NTT, which set up a new holding company with more than 150 affiliated firms employing 220,000 workers. Read the fine print and you learn that, in the process of restructuring, the former government-owned telecommunications conglomerate managed to run up huge personnel and equipment costs. By 1999, those costs accounted for 60 percent of its total expenses—compared to 40 percent in 1985, when NTT was privatized.[53] And NTT's case, while extreme, was not untypical. During a decade and a half of alleged restructur-

50. As we discuss below, Japanese firms have been using merit pay—in moderation—for quite some time. Many of the news articles of the late 1990s were based on press releases from corporations announcing proposals to revise or bolster already established systems of merit pay. *Yomiuri Shinbun* carried several such articles in 1998, referring to plans by Toyota and Matsushita (February 11), NEC and Hitachi (March 14), and Fujitsu (April 2) to tinker with their compensation systems. A different article (October 17) told how Daiwa Securities Co. was considering a plan to abolish lump-sum payments to employees who retire and instead offer them higher monthly salaries.

51. Among countless examples of such stories, see Emily Thornton, "More Cracks in the Social Contract," in *Business Week*, October 13, 1997, 18; Kurihara Takako, "'Musabetsu Dairisutora' to iu Genjitsu" (The Reality Known as Indiscriminate and Massive Restructuring), *Spa*, August 11–18, 1999, 26–31.

52. This pattern was still evident in the last quarter of 2000. In a survey, the Japan Labor Institute ("Working Conditions and the Labor Market," in *Japan Labor Bulletin*, May 1, 2001, 3) found that employers were using the following methods, in order of preference, to trim payroll expenses: restricting overtime, reassigning or transferring employees, reducing midyear hires, increasing holiday leave and days off, encouraging voluntary retirement, and cutting temps. It concluded: "Since the preference for these various methods of employment adjustment is more-or-less the same as that which emerged during the oil crisis some time ago, it would seem that the termination of employment contracts with regular employees is still regarded as a last resort for Japanese firms. Even when the need to terminate employment contracts becomes obvious, they still tend to avoid dismissal and instead will call for voluntary retirement for which various incentives are offered."

53. See "Japan Restructures Gradually," *Economist*, February 6, 1999, 65–66.

ing, Japanese manufacturers reported that their personnel costs—relative to their sales—actually increased from less than 14 percent in 1980 to 18 percent in 1996.[54]

In reality, as Kato (2001, 1) notes, "large firms in Japan have been doing everything they can to avoid laying off their workers." Instead, when they had to restructure, they relied heavily on two mechanisms. One, which has been utilized for years, was the transfer (*shukkō*, if the transfer is temporary; *tenseki*, if permanent) of surplus employees to other firms affiliated through equity and/or transactional (keiretsu) ties.[55] To cite only one example, Nippon Steel established 180 subsidiaries in the 1990s to absorb, via *shukkō* or *tenseki*, about one-third of the parent firm's otherwise bloated labor force.[56] The other mechanism, which became increasingly popular over the decade, was the hiring of nonregular employees of all ages in place of regular employees straight out of high school or college. Nonregular employees include part-time workers (*arubaito*) and temporary workers (many of whom are dispatched to the jobsite by employment agencies),[57] who do not receive the package of benefits received by regular or "core" workers, even though they may work for a single employer for a long time. By 1999, nonregular workers accounted for 25 percent of all workers in Japan, about twice the share of the total labor force they occupied in the late 1970s and early 1980s (Management and Coordination Agency 1999).

These mechanisms usually produce significant distributional effects.[58] Specifically, in the case of employee transfers, large firms tend to transfer

54. To be explicit, the numerator in the ratio is actually "administrative expenses"—not personnel expenses. In fact, however, administrative expenses are driven almost entirely by personnel costs. Nissei Life Insurance (NLI) Research Institute, "Koyō Iyokukantai no naka de Takamaru Senmon Jinzai Niizu" (The Growing Need for Specialists amid Waning Employment Demand), *NLI Research Report* No. 3 (November 1998), section 3. These data were collected originally by the Ministry of Finance.

55. In a survey focusing on the practice of *shukkō*, Sato, Nagano, and Oki (1996) found that sending and receiving firms were linked through equity ties in 80.3 percent of all cases and through transactional ties in 90.3 percent of all cases.

56. Interview, November 14, 1997. In its consolidated statement of income, which was provided to the author, Nippon Steel identifies rather large losses in 1995 (106 billion yen), 1996 (70 billion yen), and 1997 (80 billion yen) that are attributable to early retirement allowances paid to employees, many of whom went to work for its subsidiaries. Hitachi also used *shukkō* aggressively in the 1990s, trimming its own payroll by ten thousand employees. See Steffensen (1998).

57. For years, dispatched workers ("temps") were only allowed to perform a small number of duties requiring specialized skills. A 1999 revision to the employment law lifted that restriction for all industries except defense, longshoring, construction, medical care, and manufacturing. Another revision, approved by the Diet in 2003, ended the restriction on "temps" in manufacturing and extended the allowable period of dispatch from one to three years.

58. In some cases, however, *tenseki* and *shukkō* are the only options short of laying off workers. This is especially true in the case of intrafirm transfers. Mazda saved hundreds of jobs in the late 1970s when it moved shop floor employees into its sales division after the oil crisis rendered its gas-guzzling rotary engine vehicles too expensive to operate. Two decades later, Isuzu did the

workers and small firms tend to receive them. From their survey of 248 *shukkō* employees and 580 *tenseki* employees (all males between the ages of fifty and sixty) who were transferred between 1992 and 1994, Sato, Nagano, and Oki (1996) found that 89.5 percent of the firms sending employees on a temporary basis (*shukkō*) and 85.5 percent of the firms sending employees on a permanent basis (*tenseki*) were rather large—with at least one thousand workers on their payroll. Of firms receiving transferees, 64.3 percent were relatively small—with fewer than three hundred employees already on their payroll. This means that transfers are likely to result in wage and benefit reductions, to say nothing of diminished prestige, for those who are transferred. In a different survey, the Ministry of Labor (now the Ministry of Health, Labor and Welfare) found that the majority of transferees are middle-aged or older workers (forty-five to fifty-nine) approaching retirement.[59]

In addition, young job seekers found it increasingly difficult to find full-time, permanent employment as firms recruited less and less from the ranks of high school and college graduates and instead filled openings with non-regular employees. As of August 2000, when Japan counted 3.1 million people as "wholly unemployed," 20 percent of the jobless were between the ages of fifteen and twenty-four while another 28 percent were between twenty-five and thirty-four. Thus, even in a rapidly "graying" society, young people made up nearly half of the unemployment rolls. Genda (2001) was right to complain that journalists, and even many academics, focused excess attention on the employment problems of middle-aged Japanese workers, but completely ignored the bigger crisis among younger workers.

Likewise, nonregular jobs became filled increasingly by women, not men. During the 1990s, the number of women in part-time and temporary employment increased much faster than the number of men in such jobs; indeed, they accounted for 75 percent of the growth in such employment.[60] This meant that, by 1999, 37.4 percent of female workers toiled in nonregular jobs, while 11.2 percent of male workers did.[61] These trends are shown

same, on a smaller scale, when it resolved to quit producing automobiles with gasoline engines and specialize in diesel. Rather than laying them off, it transferred one thousand engineers from the defunct project to the live project. See *Nihon Keizai Shinbun*, April 17, 1998, 1.

59. The MOL survey is cited in Sato (1996, 6).

60. See Japan Labor Institute, "The 2000 White Paper on Working Women," in *Japan Labor Bulletin*, June 2001, 1.

61. Management and Coordination Agency, "Rōdōryoku Chōsa Tokubetsu Chōsa Hōkokusho" (Report on the Special Survey of the Labor Force Survey), various years. In 1997, the Japanese government finally acknowledged that women are put at a disadvantage in Japan's seniority-based employment system. At the same time, however, it expressed concern about a declining birthrate, and thus could not bring itself to advocate the hiring of women to fill expected job vacancies in the future, when Japan's aging work force begins to contract more sharply. See EPA 1997. For comments on the report, see *Daily Yomiuri*, November 5, 1997.

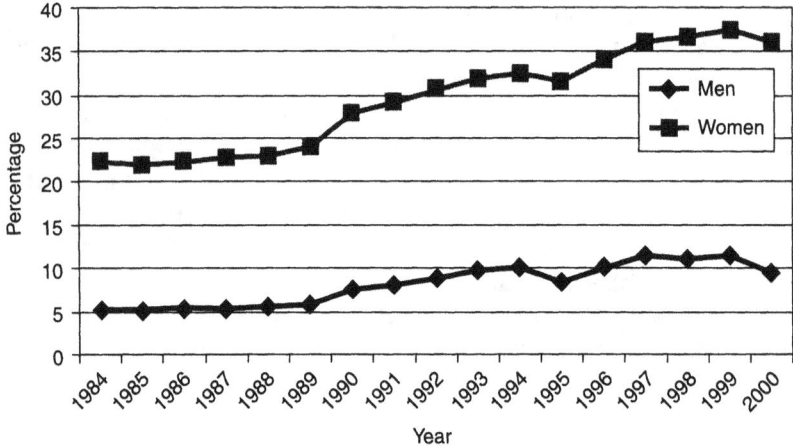

Figure 4.3. Change in "Nonregular" employment by gender, 1984–2000
Source: Ministry of Labor, *Rōdō Hakusho*, 1998, 166. *Sōmu-sho, Rōdōryoku chōsa,* various years.
Note: "Nonregular" employment equals temporary or part-time work. Years 1984, 1986, 1987, and 1989 are estimated data.

in figure 4.3. Consider, again, the example of NTT. In a cost-cutting move, it decided to hire only part-timers to handle directory assistance calls (Thornton 1997). One can safely assume that all, or virtually all, of these 14,500 part-time operators were women. In an interview (Gottfried and Hayashi-Kato 1998, 30), an executive for Manpower Japan, the Tokyo-based affiliate of the U.S. dispatching agency, said he benefits from a glut of mature, experienced, and professional women with outstanding skills who cannot find regular employment in the Japanese labor market, and are thus willing to accept nonregular jobs. "We can just go out and scoop up these people as temporary workers, and they're terrific workers."

The evidence, then, clearly points to distributional change in Japan's employment system during the 1990s, but just as clearly points to a *lack* of structural change.[62] Indeed, as in the previous subcase of business-business relations, these two phenomena (distributional change and structural continuity) are closely correlated. The use of *shukkô* and *tenseki* transfers, as well as the use of nonregular employment, introduced flexibility into an otherwise rigid labor market, making it possible for Japanese firms to maintain long-term, relational ties between management and labor—but only for a smaller group of elite employees. In other words, these mechanisms helped preserve or consolidate the status quo through a process of polarization, cre-

---

62. In its survey of the Japanese economy, the Economic Planning Agency (1996, 353) concluded that, "in general, there have been no major changes" in the Japanese employment system, particularly in the manufacturing sector.

ating what Miura (2001, 1) accurately calls a "sharp cleavage between insiders and outsiders" in the Japanese employment system.

Dirks (1997, 47) makes this point in discussing the impact of interfirm personnel transfers on the Japanese labor market. The increasing use of such transfers, he argues, allows Japanese firms to achieve "flexibility through the back door" rather than through the "classic fashion" of fluidly hiring and firing workers. Likewise, Ueda Muneaki, executive vice-president of Pasona Inc., uses similar language to describe the impact of his and other employment services agencies on the Japanese labor market. "The use of temps in Japan now is, in a sense, protecting and making possible the continuation of the existence of a core of lifetime employees" (*Daily Yomiuri*, June 10, 1998). Ueda's view has been adopted formally by Japan's big business associations. In a 1995 report, Nikkeiren, the Japan Federation of Employers Associations, called for a two-tiered system offering stable, long-term employment for "core" workers and flexible employment for part-time or temporary workers. Keidanren (1994) had earlier proposed a similar system.

Let us consider change or continuity in the best-known institutions of the Japanese employment system, beginning with lifetime employment (or *shūshin koyō*). Official statistics, displayed in figure 4.4, show little change in overall job mobility during the 1990s: the turnover rate for regular employees stood at nearly 3 percent in 1984, rose slightly during the "bubble" period of the late 1980s, and remained at that level through the 1990s. By 1999, the turnover rate for regular employees was only 3.7 percent—about one-third the level for nonregular workers. Indeed, some Japanese workers were staying even *longer* at their jobs in the 1990s than in earlier decades. In large manufacturing firms (with at least one thousand employees), the average number of years of continuous service by male managers and technicians aged 45–49 was, in 1973, 21.4 and 23.1 years (for college and high school graduates, respectively); by 1993, these numbers had risen to 23.0 and 27.3 years (Sato Hiroki 1997, 117). This trend is confirmed by Okazaki (1996, 105), who concludes that "contrary to a widespread view, the retention rate of employees from ages 50–54 to ages 55–59 has been generally increasing in both large and medium-sized firms." Higuchi (1997, 49) highlights the theme of distributional change and structural continuity by noting that fewer workers, especially female workers, enjoyed the benefits of this system of long-term employment in the 1990s. Japan's intrafirm labor market, he remarks, "shows greater long-term job tenure than before, but—on the other hand—the number of workers in such a labor market is decreasing."

Japanese firms thus continued to foster an internal labor market, rotating workers from one position to another within the company and using on-the-job training that produces firm-specific skills rather than off-the-job training

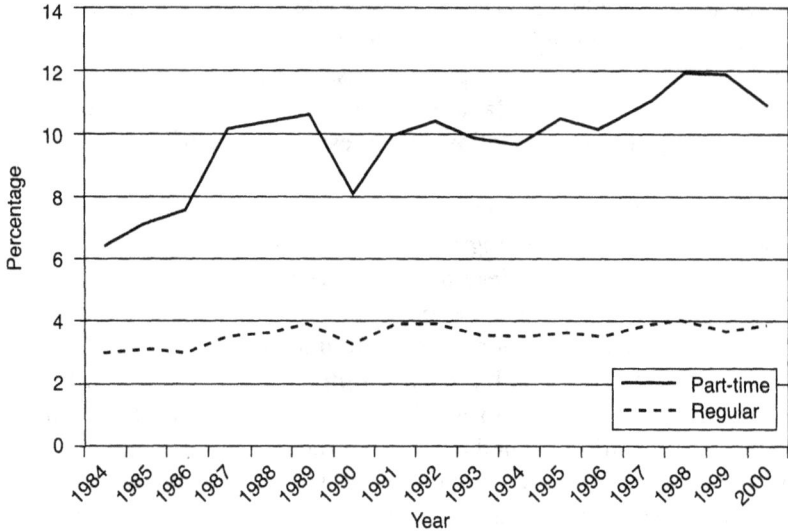

Figure 4.4. Job turnover rate, 1984–2000
Source: Ministry of Labor, *Rōdō Hakusho,* 1998, 123. Nippon Rōdō Kenkyu Kikō, "Useful Rōdō Tōkei" (2003).
Note: "Turnover rate" = number of employees who changed jobs / total employees x 100.

that yields more general knowledge.[63] Indeed, both ends of the management-labor network want to maintain the status quo. In a survey of 657 company employees conducted by the Japan Research Institute, 71 percent indicated they supported the practice of lifetime employment. And white-collar workers in Tokyo and Osaka told Morishima (1997, 7) that they strongly preferred the traditional practice of in-house training over all other methods of motivating them to work hard. On the other side, in a 1993 survey by the Japan Productivity Center, 89.3 percent of personnel managers at 304 large firms voiced support for the principle of lifetime or long-term employment.[64]

These preferences are revealed in the recruiting, hiring, and firing practices of Japanese firms. The Economic Planning Agency (1996, 353) concludes that firms in the 1990s "strived to maintain their existing workforces and made conscious efforts to limit mid-career hiring." Indeed, in 1999 the Ministry of Labor reported that only 22 percent of Japanese firms engaged in recruitment would consider hiring those who had been employed earlier at other companies (*Yomiuri Shinbun,* July 31, 1999).

63. A government study (*Rōdō Daijin Kanbō* 1996, 132) found that formal training in established facilities for vocational education was still quite uncommon in Japan in the mid-1990s. Instead, off-the-job training consisted of more informal information exchange through industry associations and personal networks.

64. The Productivity Center and JRI surveys are all discussed in Sugeno and Suwa (1997, 75).

It would appear, then, that long-term employment survived as a well-established norm in Japan—despite the economic costs imposed by global market forces in the 1990s. Kettler and Tackney (1997, 37) argue that this norm became firmly enshrined in Japanese case law, which has—since a landmark ruling in 1987 by the Yokohama regional court—assumed that employers have a social obligation to do whatever they can to avoid dismissing longtime employees. This principle was reaffirmed in a 1999 court ruling that Sega, the video game producer, had failed to uphold its social obligation when it fired a thirty-five-year employee.

Even Nikkeiren, the employers' federation, showed no interest in challenging this norm. In 1994, only 7.7 percent of 354 firms polled by the group thought they would not be able to preserve the lifetime employment system.[65] In fact, Okuda Hiroshi (1999), then chairman of both Nikkeiren and Toyota, wrote a passionate defense of the system, telling fellow executives they should "slash their own bellies before axing their employees."

And in interviews with me, executives routinely pledged their commitment to this widespread norm of job security. "Laying people off is taboo," said a Sony official.[66] "We do everything we can to avoid that." Tamura Koshiro, chief spokesman for electronics giant Sanyo, added: "Our system is very different from yours in America. We have an obligation to conserve employment. Things are changing but only very gradually. We still have to maintain social stability."[67]

What, then, about seniority pay, the second pillar of the Japanese employment system? To begin, we should note that neither tenure (years of service) nor age has ever been the *sole* factor determining wages in Japan. In the 1960s, Japanese corporations began to incorporate merit—or at least management's evaluation of an employee's merit—into their compensation systems.[68] Although this new practice became increasingly widespread, it did not displace the traditional method of wage setting in the 1990s—despite headlines suggesting otherwise. A survey by Nikkeiren (1996, 17) found that fewer than 25 percent of all firms used a personnel system that gave as much weight to individual merit as to seniority.

Rather than abandoning seniority wages for performance-based wages, some Japanese manufacturers—especially high-tech firms—began to introduce an additional layer of "capability-based wages" for employees with advanced or special skills. Workers preferred this system to merit pay because it applied to groups of workers, not individuals, and was thus viewed as more

---

65. The survey (by Nikkeiren) is also discussed in Sugeno and Suwa (1997, 75).
66. Interview, Tokyo, February 25, 1999.
67. Interview, Tokyo, April 8, 1999. Sanyo was acquired by Panasonic in 2009.
68. See Kumazawa 1997 and Nikkeiren 1969.

Table 4.2. Seniority pay: Wage Index for "core" employees by age cohort

Year	20–24	25–29	30–34	35–39	40–44	45–49	50–54	55–59
1983	100	124	171	213	268	315	352	341
1988	100	122	158	203	245	297	335	325
1992	100	120	153	188	234	270	306	312
1993	100	120	153	188	232	268	304	315
1994	100	120	155	187	230	267	305	313
1995	100	122	156	188	231	268	302	305
1996	100	122	157	191	228	267	305	311
1997	100	123	158	191	225	266	293	301
1998	100	122	156	191	225	264	292	303
1999	100	119	153	186	212	242	269	271
2000	100	117	152	186	213	237	266	260

Source: Ministry of Labor, *Chingin Kōzō no Kiban Tōkei Chōsa.*
Notes: (1) "Core" employees here are (a) male; (b) have immediately joined the firm after graduating from college; and (c) have maintained continuous employment at that firm. (2) Wage indices here are based on regular monthly payments, and thus exclude bonus payments.

egalitarian. Management liked it because it helped them retain a pool of highly skilled workers, especially younger technicians or engineers who otherwise might have been tempted to jump ship. In this respect, change in the seniority wage structure was not unlike change in the use of long-term employment system: it served to preserve the existing system by narrowing its scope of application. As Thelen and Kume (1999, 32–33) note:

> Recent company initiatives to revise traditional arrangements (seniority wages and lifetime employment) often represent efforts to selectively apply these arrangements (i.e., to single out certain workers to be covered), and modifications in traditional practices frequently represent efforts to give particular (usually skilled) workers more benefits (not fewer) than under traditional arrangements. . . . The overall trend, then, seems to be toward a (shrinking) core of (mostly skilled) workers within individual firms who continue to enjoy lifetime employment guarantees combined with an even more generous wage system.

Even with this kind of adjustment, however, the seniority pay structure proved remarkably durable. This is clearly seen in an examination of the slope of the average wage scale. As table 4.2 shows, the wage gradient for "core" employees (defined here as males who graduated from a university) changed very little during the 1990s. If seniority were becoming significantly less important in wage setting, one would expect the wage gradient to become much flatter over time. In fact, however, the curve remains quite stable. My findings are confirmed by the Economic Planning Agency (1996, 348), which reports that the wage gradient "flattened only slightly" between

1984 and 1994, and in some industries, such as automobile assembly, "hardly changed at all."

One might attribute this remarkable durability in the wage structure to demography; that is, Japan's population is "graying," and thus older workers—who can be expected to oppose a flattening of the wage gradient—are becoming an increasingly large proportion of the labor force.[69] Indeed, Dentsu (2001, 21) finds that younger Japanese workers are more inclined than their elders to agree that "salary should be based on one's ability and results"—but not by very much. In fact, only 52.6 percent of Japanese in their thirties agreed with the pro–merit pay statement, compared with 47 percent in their forties and 46 percent in their fifties. Overall, fewer than half of the Japanese surveyed by Dentsu in 2000 agreed with the statement.[70]

The third pillar of Japan's employment system is the enterprise union, an institution that governs the largely informal ties between labor and management. Here, too, the evidence points to distributional change but not structural change in the 1990s. Since 1985, the elasticity of union membership (the percentage change in the number of employees over the percentage change in the number of unionized employees) has turned negative in small firms, but has remained positive (although less than 1.0) in large firms. Nearly 60 percent of workers at large firms (those employing at least one thousand people) belonged to an enterprise union (Fujimura 1997, 303).

Even in many nonunion firms, labor and management—sharing a common interest in the firm's growth and thus in its ability to continue paying reasonable wages—continued to engage in joint consultations over investment and disinvestment decisions, employee welfare, and other issues. In the mid-1990s, administrative councils (*keiei kyōgikai*) remained in operation at more than 70 percent of firms having at least 5,000 employees, at 68 percent of those with 1,000–4,999 employees, and at 62 percent of those with 300–999 employees (Ministry of Labor 1995). Cooperation between labor and management remained strong. In the 1990s, workers moderated wage demands in exchange for job protection; as a result, the number of working days lost as a result of labor disputes fell steadily throughout the decade.[71]

The bottom line is that, by the end of the twentieth century, all the talk

69. Older workers might view a move from seniority to merit-based pay as a violation of the norm of relationalism in labor–management relations. This issue is discussed in Seike 1995.

70. Preference for seniority pay is obviously not an "Asian value." Dentsu surveyed citizens throughout Asia, not just in Japan, and found strong support for its proposition that "salary should be based on one's ability and results"—for example, 73.9 percent in China and 64.2 percent in South Korea.

71. It is typical, however, for labor strife to decline as unemployment rises. Thus, labor's quiescence may be as much a function of the hard economic times of the 1990s as the durability of relational ties between management and labor.

about corporate restructuring and the demise of the Japanese employment system amounted to little more than that. Dirks (1997, 48) puts this delicately when he says "the gap between that which is (publicly) regarded as important or desirable by Japanese management and the empirical evidence for new practices is most conspicuous." Sugeno and Suwa (1997, 56) are a bit more forceful: "Both labor and management maintain a deep attachment to the long-term employment system with its merits in stable employment and efficient human resource development. The system will therefore remain intact for quite a while."

As if to prove my point, the Ministry of Labor (1999, 12) reported that a brief uptick in economic activity in mid-1999 led Japanese manufacturers to immediately abandon or slow down their restructuring efforts. Its survey of 2,807 companies found that, after a wave of restructuring initiatives in the mid-1990s, the percentage of firms engaged in this activity (35 percent) had fallen below the previous high of 38 percent in 1993. And respondents said they expected these initiatives to taper off as the decade came to an end.

Finally, it is worth noting what firms said they resorted to when they went about restructuring. The most common method used by survey respondents was simply to scrimp on the use of overtime (19 percent). And the least utilized method? Yes, you guessed it: laying off workers (3 percent).

Staying the Course

In the 1990s, a decade in which the forces of globalization buffeted all political economies in the international system, Japan stayed the course. Although it experienced massive distributional change, it underwent remarkably little structural change. To be sure, the status quo didn't last forever. In part three (chapters 7 and 8), I document a significant relaxation of relational networks that occurred, finally, in the first decade of the new millennium. But in the final decade of the old millennium, a period of mounting political and market pressure for change, the fundamental networks of selective relationalism—government-business cooperation, interfirm cooperation, and labor–management cooperation—survived largely intact even though they became more selective and less inclusive.

Indeed, the *durability* of Japanese-style network capitalism surprised a number of informed observers. For example, the Japan Research Institute (1997, 14) concluded that, "at a time of major historic changes when, all around the world, the old political, economic, and social orders are being replaced by new ones, Japan is failing to adapt."

As it turned out, Japanese elites rallied to the defense of relational networks under stress. Government officials, for example, channeled low-cost credit to manufacturing subcontractors, and pushed them—in the words of

MITI (ZSKSK 1997b, 76) to "build even closer ties with their parent companies." In addition, they paid record subsidies to struggling firms that transferred employees to affiliates rather than lay them off.[72] And finally, they and business elites promoted the regionalization of core networks as a way to cut themselves slack in the face of globalization.

72. See the *Daily Yomiuri:* "Government Aid to Failed Firms at Record High," May 11, 1999; "Appliance Makers Seek Wage Subsidies," March 19, 1998; and "Truck Manufacturers to Get Subsidies for Cuts," July 27, 1998. In 1998, the Diet expanded the law authorizing government wage support for workers transferred to affiliates for cost-cutting reasons. But even this was not enough for Ota Hiroshi, a columnist for *Yomiuri.* In his column (*Daily Yomiuri,* November 18, 1998), he said government should get further involved because employment is too serious an issue to leave to "the mercy of markets."

5 Elite Regionalization and the Protective Buffer

The institutions of cooperation informed by selective relationalism survived largely intact during the 1990s. In the previous chapter, I documented massive distributional change, but only very limited structural change in the political economy of Japan at the end of the twentieth century. In this chapter, I explain that surprising result by using what Gourevitch (1979) calls "the second image reversed"—a perspective that examines the effect of external factors on the domestic environment.[1] In a nutshell, I find that the process of elite regionalization served as a protective buffer, checking the forces of globalization—at least for a while. In other words, by regionalizing the otherwise endangered networks of selective relationalism, Japanese elites bought themselves some breathing room, cut themselves some slack. This is because, as I discussed in chapter 1, relationalism works reasonably well in the context of development, a context in which known technology is being adopted by and diffused throughout an industrializing economy. Although relationalism appeared doomed in Japan, a fully developed economy, it enjoyed new life after being regionalized or extended into developing Asia.

For regionalization to trump globalization, the elites attempting to regionalize their homegrown networks must enjoy positional power not only in the domestic political economy but also in the regional political economy. This was certainly true for Japanese elites in the early and mid-1990s. But as I will explain in chapter 7, it became less and less true in the late

1. Gourevitch was using Kenneth Waltz's three-tiered classification of actors in the study of international relations. The first image is of individuals, and the way in which they constitute the state. The second image is of states, and the way in which they make up the international system. By reversing the second image, Gourevitch looks at the way in which states are shaped by the international system.

1990s, when the hierarchical, "flying geese" pattern of development began to break down, creating resentment among local elites, and when a fast-growing China began to emerge as a rival hegemon in East Asia.

Let us begin by recalling some basic facts. Japan has been an influential actor in Asia for many years. Even in the 1975–85 period, it was the leading provider of foreign aid to several countries in the region, a major source of capital and technology, and an important trading partner. But Japan did not then enjoy what I call "positional power" in the region because Asia was not yet an integrated economic unit, or a web of networks; it was not, in a word, "regionalized."

The process of regionalization accelerated in the 1990s, and was driven— first and foremost—by the economic interests of Japanese industry. In 1991, the bubble that had defined Japan's economy for five years finally popped, prompting cost-conscious manufacturers to run for cover. Many of them ran to Asia, which by 1995 received as much as 79 percent of the projects and 42 percent of the money invested by Japanese manufacturers in overseas production.[2]

Japanese MNCs, led by automobile and electronics producers, began to locate factories at different sites in the region based on the operating costs and, more important, the technological level of each host country. In time, the capitalist economies of East Asia began to grow together in a "flying geese" pattern, a vertical division of labor or a "techno-complementarity" that promoted trade between countries within the region, between those countries and Japan, and between those countries and Western markets. Many Japanese MNCs were able to use their new Asian production bases as export platforms to continue supplying U.S. and European markets; in some industries, such as electronics, they managed to do so far more cheaply, and with fewer political repercussions, than they could have done from home.

Asia turned out to be a safe haven for Japanese manufacturers—at least until 1997, when the region underwent a massive financial crisis. Between 1990 and 1996, Japanese producers enjoyed a profit rate of 4 percent to 5 percent in Asia—double or triple what their counterparts earned in North America and Europe, and significantly more than what they earned in Japan.[3] During the 1990s, Matsushita, for example, earned more than half of its overseas profits from its affiliates in Asia. Even as late as 2001, when the electronics giant was running a net loss of 211.8 billion yen throughout the world, including North America, Europe, and even the domestic mar-

---

2. See Ministry of Finance, annual reports. Small and medium-sized firms drove this trend, concentrating 92 percent of their overall FDI in Asia that year. See chapter 3 (and especially figures 3.1 and 3.2) for more complete data and sources.

3. METI 2003, *Kaigai Jigyō Katsudō Kihon Chōsa: Dai 31* (Basic Survey of Overseas Business Activities, Number 31).

ket of Japan, it was earning a profit (45 billion yen) in Asia.[4] "Without those profits, I wonder if we could have kept going the way we did for so long at home," confides Asaka Toshimasa, an executive in Matsushita's global strategic planning division.[5] In other words, Asia helped preserve the status quo in Japan.

Domestic elites, coordinating their regional activities from the homeland, occupied the central, most critical positions in the increasingly integrated, criss-crossing pattern of Asian trade and investment. In this way, they came to dominate the region; that is, they came to enjoy positional power. Imagine, first, a regional production network set up by a manufacturer in, say, Osaka or Nagoya. It closely supervised the activities of multiple affiliates in, say, Dalian, Penang, Bangkok, and Singapore, encouraged its most trusted Japanese subcontractors to invest in host countries and produce parts at nearby plants, forged new ties with host country firms, and replicated fundamental elements of its homegrown employment system. Then imagine a regional administrative network set up by a bureaucracy in Tokyo. It established local branches in capitals throughout the region, providing funding and guidance to both host states in Asia and to the Asian affiliates of Japanese MNCs. By the mid-1990s, Asia began to look like an extension of Japan's highly relational political economy—a web of interlocking production and administrative networks.

Indeed, Japanese political and business elites came to view the entire region, including the home base, as one organic unit, or what MITI began to call "a soft cooperation network."[6] Elite regionalization thus reinforced selective relationalism in a moment of extreme vulnerability. Although it encouraged ongoing distributional change in Japan, this expansion of productive and administrative space actually slowed down the pace of structural change in Japan. Let us examine the evidence across the three nexuses of cooperation we have considered already.

State and Industry

With the start of a new decade in 1990, Japanese bureaucrats began to find themselves more and more on the defensive. The bursting of the bubble tarnished a public image burnished by years of relative success in managing the economy. Newspaper columnists savaged them; politicians began to question their judgment. And deregulation proposals fell like giant hail-

4. Matsushita Electronics Corporation, internal document.
5. Telephone interview, December 17, 2003.
6. In this same manner, a Japanese academic argues that Japanese capital and technology have transformed Asia into what he calls a "core strategic network." For more on the bold concepts used to describe economic regional integration in Asia, see Hatch and Yamamura (1996, 5).

stones on Kasumigaseki, the district in Tokyo where most of Japan's ministries have their headquarters.

Facing an apparently inevitable decline in their jurisdictional authority at home, Japanese bureaucrats began to eagerly promote the expansion and regionalization of Japan-centered production networks.[7] In an interview, one official confided that his agency had seized on this concept as a way of protecting its otherwise threatened "turf" (*nawabari*). MITI (now METI), he said, is "searching for a new identity, a new purpose in life."[8] MOF was no less enthusiastic.

By the mid-1990s, both ministries had convened high-level deliberation councils (*shingikai*) to advise them on economic policies the Japanese government should pursue in its dealings with Asia. Over at MITI, the question was industrial policy; that is, how to build a stronger regional division of labor by meshing Japan's industrial structure even more tightly with the industrial structures of newly developed and still developing economies in the region.[9] Over at MOF, the question was monetary policy; that is, how to regionalize the use of the yen—especially for the benefit of Japanese firms operating in Asia. But according to a member of both *shingikai,* a more fundamental question may have initially propelled the two ministries into action: Could they revitalize themselves (that is, expand their authority or extend their jurisdictional reach) by pursuing regional, rather than purely national, economic policies?

"Asia is the new end zone," says Sakurai Makoto, director of the Mitsui Marine Research Institute, "and MOF and MITI are competing fiercely over who will get there first."[10]

On the broad field of ideas, of course, both ministries have been playing this game for a long time. In the 1980s, MOF created its own think tank, the Foundation for Advanced Information and Research (FAIR), to stimulate interest throughout Asia in greater regional economic cooperation. MITI,

7. Regionalization not only gave Japanese bureaucrats a new set of markets in which to intervene; it also may have relieved some of the pressure for regulatory relief at home. To the extent that Japanese firms setting up production facilities in Asia manage to escape burdensome regulations at home, they become less dedicated to the political goal of regulatory reform in Japan. Using the terminology of Hirschman (1970), they exercise the "exit" option (literally) rather than the "voice" option. And, surprisingly, some of the new regulations adopted in the 1990s have had to do with notification requirements for small and medium-sized enterprises receiving government assistance to undertake foreign direct investment. Thus, notwithstanding the conventional wisdom that views Japanese multinationals as the locomotives pulling deregulation, the evidence suggests instead that Japanese "multinationalization," or at least regionalization, has actually helped impede that process.

8. Interview, Tokyo, August 20, 1997.

9. The staff for this group produced a comprehensive report on its activities. See Kokusai Bōeki Tōshi Kenkyūjo, *Ajiadai no Sangyō Kōzō Seisaku ni kansuru Chōsa Kenkyū* (Research Report on Industrial Structure Policies for Greater Asia), March 1998.

10. Interview, June 23, 1999, Tokyo.

meanwhile, tapped its established brain trust, Ajiken (the Ajia Keizai Ken-kyūjo, which despite its official name in English—Institute on Developing Economies—is best translated as the Research Institute on Asian Economies). The studies that emerged from these and other Japanese research teams invariably invoked the concept of "flying geese," the pattern of unitary but vertically layered economic development of Asia—with Japan at the head of the flock.

MITI moved first to try to put this concept into action. In a 1987 visit to Bangkok, trade and industry minister Tamura Hajime unveiled the New Asian Industries Development (New AID) plan, an ambitious scheme to co-ordinate Japan's aid, investment, and trade policies toward the region. The plan was designed to stimulate export-oriented manufacturing throughout Asia, and to help Japanese firms upgrade their domestic operations by trans-ferring labor-intensive production to new offshore facilities. MITI vowed to implement the program in three phases: (1) collaboration with their coun-terparts in host countries to identify specific industries that, with some nur-turing, might become internationally competitive; (2) the drafting of proposals to promote those targeted industries, usually relying on a mixture of "hard infrastructure" (such as roads and electrical transmission lines) and "soft infrastructure" (such as new Japanese-style organizations reflecting co-operation between government and business); and (3) issuing yen loans and dispatching experts to implement these programs.

What made the New AID plan new was the Japanese government's effort to draft and implement industrial policies to lure both public and private capital to specific locations in Asia, rather than simply funding ODA requests from an individual host country. This is also what made it controversial. Crit-ics outside Japan viewed it as a presumptuous, intrusive, top-down approach to development, while Japanese critics outside MITI called it a power grab by the agency.

MITI bowed to critics and shelved the plan, but never abandoned the vi-sion behind it. That vision, spelled out in its annual statement of policy pri-orities, continued to be "the creation of open industrial networks" and "the support of Japanese business activities in Asia."[11] In the mid-1990s, MITI rolled out a new initiative to export industrial policies to Asia—the Cambo-dia-Laos-Myanmar Working Group (CLM-WG), which sought to promote the industrialization of those transitional economies. MITI proudly noted that this new policy group was based in Bangkok, not Tokyo, and insisted that it reflected an equal partnership between ASEAN (represented by the ASEAN Economic Ministers, or AEM) and Japan (represented by MITI). In fact, however, the CLM-WG was financed and staffed exclusively by

---

11. See MITI 1995c, 25.

MITI.[12] The organization soon evolved into the AEM-MITI Economic and Industrial Cooperation Committee (AMEICC), and broadened its coverage to include all of Southeast Asia. It also expanded its mission by, for example, pushing for stronger industrial linkages and more liberal investment policies throughout the region.

AMEICC became the umbrella organization for Japan's administrative guidance to host governments and local firms in the region. But other Japanese organizations also dispensed advice on everything from broad macroeconomic policies to sector-specific microeconomic policies. As noted in chapter 3, the Japan International Cooperation Agency (JICA) had hundreds of "experts" scattered throughout Southeast Asia during the 1990s. In the fiscal year ending in March 1999, it dispatched 645 of these advisers to Indonesia, 357 to Thailand, 336 to the Philippines, and 188 to Malaysia.[13]

In the mid-1990s, as Japanese assemblers sought to replicate their domestic keiretsu networks in Asia, policy advice often centered on how to develop supporting industries, particularly in the consumer electronics and automobile industries. For example, a JICA team in Thailand produced a detailed study that led, in 1995, to the Thai Ministry of Industry's "Master Plan for Supporting Industries."[14] In addition, a former director-general of MITI's Consumer Goods Bureau began advising the Thai government in 1998 on how to set up a public finance corporation for small and medium-sized enterprises (SMEs).[15] More generally, MITI created a regional council, including government and industry officials from ASEAN countries, as well as government and industry officials from Japan, to propose policies designed to foster the growth of SMEs in Southeast Asia.[16]

MITI also mobilized Japanese business groups to help their Asian counterparts build up not only nationally based trade associations but also, for the first time, regionwide industrial associations that directly reflected Japanese business interests. Thus, the Japan Automobile Manufacturers Association (JAMA) encouraged automakers in Southeast Asia to reorganize and revitalize their flagging ASEAN Automobile Federation (AAF); the Japan Electrical Manufacturers Association (JEMA) and Electronic Industries Association of Japan (EIAJ) joined forces with Asian manufacturers to establish a new regional grouping, Business Dialogue; and the Communications Industry Association of Japan (CIAJ) launched the Asian Telecommunications Industry

12. Interview, Koike Osamu, deputy representative, Japan Overseas Development Corporation, Bangkok, September 8, 1997.
13. Internal memo, produced by JICA planning department and released to the author on July 23, 1999.
14. Suehiro Akira, ed., *Kuni jōhō: Tai* (Country Information: Thailand) (Tokyo: Nihon-Tai Kyōkai, March 1998), 160.
15. *Nihon Keizai Shinbun*, November 11, 1998.
16. *Yomiuri Shinbun*, March 2, 1997.

Exchange.[17] A major purpose of the new regional organizations was to harmonize product and safety standards as well as certification procedures among members. MITI noted that, although U.S. standards often become de facto global standards, the European Union has moved to establish its own regional standards. "There is an urgent need to create standards based on the particular requirements of the Asia-Pacific region," the ministry asserted.[18]

Japanese government officials advised not only host governments and industries in Asia but also Japanese firms seeking to invest in the region, as well as Japanese firms that already had begun operating there. When conducted in Japan, much of this guidance takes the form of business counseling, and is directed at SMEs looking for tips on suitable industrial sites and possible joint venture partners. Indeed, in 1996 the government began preparing and distributing a manual describing all the programs available to smaller firms contemplating a move overseas. The manual (*Chūshōkigyō Kokusaika Shien Manyuaru*) was only sixty-three pages when it was first published by MITI's SME Agency. Two years later, in 1998, it had ballooned to 116 pages.

Sometimes, however, administrative guidance is directed at large firms, and—much like the *gyōsei shidō* of an earlier era—appears to encourage collusive or cartel-like behavior. That was the case in 1992, when MITI called together representatives of the consumer electronics industry and tried to reach a loose agreement on which companies would invest how much money to manufacture what products in which countries.[19]

Outside Japan, MITI used another one of its arms, JETRO (Japan External Trade Organization), which in the late 1990s operated ten "support centers" throughout Asia, to guide Japanese firms that had already built factories. In 1990, it announced a plan to create public-private councils in major cities throughout the region to provide what it called "local guidance" to those affiliates.[20] Later, in 1996, it set up the Asian Industrial Network Program to pool information on suppliers and joint venture partners.[21] JETRO provided an important coordinating function for Japanese affiliates in Asia; for example, in 1991 it helped broker an informal agreement among Japanese electronic manufacturers in Malaysia that led to a wage cartel that curbed competition for the scarce supply of electrical engineers in that country.[22]

17. Interviews with MITI officials, 1997–99.
18. *Nikkan Kōgyō*, September 20, 1996.
19. "MITI Urges Electronics Firms to Produce Abroad," *Nikkei Weekly,* June 13, 1992, 1.
20. "Ajia Shokoku ni Sangyō Ricchi Shidō" (Industrial Siting Guidance in Different Countries across Asia), *Nihon Keizai Shinbun,* September 20, 1990, 5.
21. *Nikkan Kōgyō*, October 12, 1996.
22. JETRO intervened on behalf of Japanese producers in Malaysia who complained when Sony upset the cooperative status quo by luring skilled technicians to its new factory there with wages that were 30 percent higher than the wages offered by its competitors. See "Gathering of the Clan," *Far Eastern Economic Review,* March 28, 1991, 52.

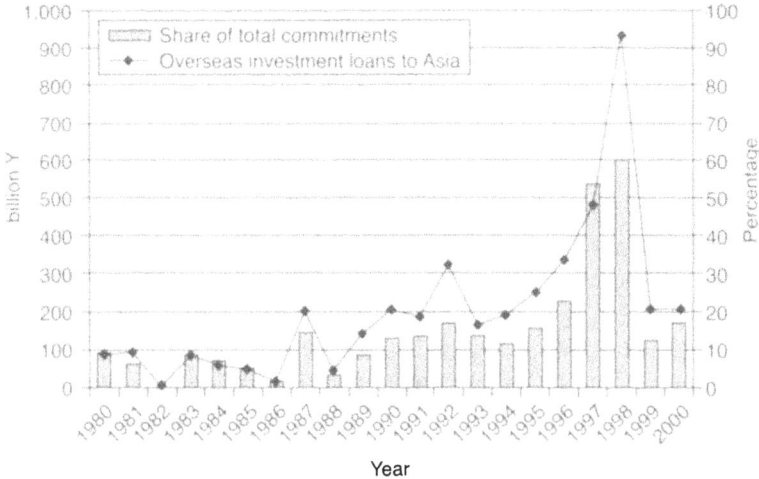

Figure 5.1. Export-Import Bank loans for JFDI to Asia
Source: Export-Import Bank of Japan, Annual Report, various years. Since 2000, Japan Bank for International Cooperation has taken over the business.

The Japanese government routinely defended its role in brokering such overseas agreements by citing the threat presented by "excess competition" between Japanese MNCs in host economies.[23]

Yet another form of guidance was financial rather than administrative. Unlike its Western counterparts, the Japanese government actively subsidizes private overseas investment, particularly FDI to Asia. (Indeed, the Japan Export-Import Bank notes proudly that "the use of public funds to finance private overseas investment is relatively unique to Japan, with almost no parallel in other countries."[24]) While the government's share of FDI financing began to diminish in the bubble period as firms drew more heavily on their own resources and on commercial banks (particularly Japanese banks that set up branches in Asia), its absolute contributions nonetheless grew substantially in the 1990s. In addition, the relative weight of FDI financing in total government lending activity also increased markedly. Beginning in the mid-1980s, the Export-Import Bank began to shift its focus from export credits to overseas investment loans—especially to Japanese firms setting up shop in Asia. By 1998, the peak year of bank activity, it was lending 939 billion yen to support private investment in the region—twenty-two times what it lent a decade earlier in 1988. As figure 5.1 shows, loans for

23. For example, JETRO (1997d, 4) fretted openly that competition between Japanese producers in Thailand was becoming "an extremely serious problem."

24. Japan Export-Import Bank, *Sanjūnen no Ayumi* (The Past Thirty Years), 1983, 40.

regionalization amounted to nearly 60 percent of the public financial institution's total business by that time.

Besides the Export-Import Bank, which in those days was accountable only to MOF, three government-affiliated financial institutions that fell under both MOF and MITI's supervision used public funds (postal savings) from the Fiscal Investment and Loan Program, a key vehicle of industrial policy during the 1950s and '60s, to guide small and medium-sized enterprises into Asia.[25] As discussed in chapter 4, those banks (Shōkō Chūkin; the Japan Finance Corporation for Small Business; and the People's Finance Corporation) were given new or expanded responsibilities in the 1990s—in large part due to the credit squeeze facing SMEs during the long economic recession in Japan, but also in part due to the new emphasis on promoting regionalization.

In 1995, for example, the Diet authorized these government banks to subsidize efforts by small firms to enter new fields—including, literally, foreign fields. This program was intended to help SMEs cope with what the government came to call "hollowing out," a process of deindustrialization that, for smaller firms, meant the loss of domestic markets as their Japanese customers (often assemblers of automobiles or electronic goods) moved overseas. Ironically, though, the new law included a remedy that contributed directly to the larger problem of "hollowing out." The Japan Finance Corporation for Small Business (JFS) was the most aggressive lender, using nearly 70 billion yen to finance 844 overseas investment projects between 1987 and 1996. And 90 percent of those projects were in Asia.[26]

JFS recognized the irony. "If we help too much, we may contribute to the loss of production facilities and jobs in Japan. But our primary mission is to assist small and medium-sized firms so they can compete in an increasingly global marketplace. If firms believe they must expand overseas to remain competitive, we must do our best to help them."[27]

25. FILP, which was tapped by the Japan Development Bank and other government-affiliated banks in the rapid growth period (1950–73) to finance loans for strategic industries, used to be known as Japan's "second budget" (because it included so much money from postal savings) and Japan's "hidden budget" (because it was beyond the deliberative reach of the Diet). The program, which later helped finance special appropriations such as public works projects and ODA loans—remained well endowed throughout the 1990s—a function of the public's preference for postal savings, which in turn was a function of the growing concern over the solvency of private banks. In 1998, a peak year, FILP was funded to the tune of 54 trillion yen. And the program remained firmly under the control of the Ministry of Finance, which merely reported income and expenses to the Diet.

26. These data come from annual reports of the Japan Finance Corporation for Small Business (JFS).

27. Interview with Ishikawa Kokuo, senior assistant manager, international section, JFS, July 5, 1999.

Business and Business

This much is obvious: some Japanese manufacturers benefited, while others suffered, from the expansion of domestic production networks into Asia during the 1990s. A report by the Kikai Shinkō Kyōkai Keizai Kenkyūjo (Economic Research Institute of the Machinery Industries Promotional Association 1995, 92) concludes that "assemblers, along with first tier suppliers, avoid problems in the domestic economy such as *endaka* [yen appreciation] by expanding overseas . . . while second, third, and fourth tier suppliers simply struggle to survive." In general, smaller firms, lacking the financial and information resources of bigger firms, were not nearly as adept at capitalizing on the economies of networking yielded by elite regionalization.[28] In addition, smaller subcontractors left behind in Japan witnessed a slow but steady erosion in the scale of markets for their goods.[29]

Seki (1999, 14–17) claims that Japanese assemblers of electrical and electronic machinery used to follow a "20 percent rule" in their relations with parts suppliers.[30] The rule was two-sided: (1) if it were at least 20 percent cheaper to buy electronic components in Asia, assemblers would begin sourcing more parts from suppliers (including Japanese suppliers) in the region rather than from suppliers in Japan; (2) on the other hand, even if parts manufactured in Asia were much cheaper, assemblers would continue to buy at least 20 percent of their supplies from parts makers in Japan. This side of the rule was apparently designed to preserve production capacity and employment in the domestic market.

But as the yen appreciated in the mid-1990s, electronics assemblers scrambled for ways to reduce production costs. The "20 percent rule" collapsed, according to Seki. And so did weaker suppliers who could not afford to reduce their prices, or who could not afford to move into Asia.

Bankruptcy statistics tell this story in simple, if depressing, terms. In the mid-1990s, a rapidly growing number of small manufacturers were unable to sustain operations as their major customers moved to set up production facilities in Asia. Only two firms went bankrupt in 1993 due to the "hollowing

28. The Economic Planning Agency (1996, 61) reports that SMEs in Japanese manufacturing industries traditionally lead by about two quarters in the cyclical recovery of corporate profits. This pattern, however, failed to hold in the mid-1990s, a fact that EPA pinned on the slower pace with which SMEs pursued regionalization strategies such as the purchase of parts and materials from suppliers in Asia.

29. A survey by the SME Agency (1998, 93) confirms that, as they transfer more and more production overseas, Japanese assemblers place fewer and fewer orders with domestic subcontracting firms.

30. Although I interviewed several representatives of Japanese firms in the electronics industry, none of them ever mentioned a "20 percent rule." They all indicated, however, that assemblers had tried—and, indeed, continued to try—to maintain a solid parts supply base in Japan.

out" of domestic industry; but by 1996, the peak of Japanese manufacturing investment in Asia, sixty-four firms suffered this fate.[31] Manufacturers that have gone out of business for this reason have been, in almost all cases, subcontractors who occupy low and often highly dependent positions near the bottom of the supply chain.

Consider the following three examples. To safeguard their anonymity, I refer to these firms only as "A," "B," and "C."[32]

A, based in Toyama Prefecture (along the Sea of Japan), was a producer of parts for printed circuit boards. In 1993, its main customer—a first-tier subcontractor for Sony, JVC, Matsushita, and other major consumer electronic firms—moved some of its domestic operations to Indonesia. This setback was compounded in 1996, when the same first-tier subcontractor moved a key production line to China. In the scramble to survive by developing alternative markets, A's owner became ill. "I lost my will to run the business," he told me. By the time it collapsed in December 1996, A had run up a debt of 240 million yen.

B, based in Miyazaki Prefecture (Kyushu), was a producer of electrical parts for automobile ignition systems. Its primary customer, a first-tier supplier of switches for Honda, moved to Thailand in 1989, and B was never able to recover. By the time it declared bankruptcy in November 1996, B's gross sales had dropped steadily from 180 million yen to 20 million yen a year.

C was a Kyoto-based producer of pressed metal parts. Sales fell steadily in the 1990s as its main customer, a first-tier supplier of automobile seats, began to shift its attention to technology tie-ups in Indonesia and Malaysia. In December 1996, when it found itself 63 million yen in debt, C finally gave up.

As these case studies indicate, small subcontractors in Japan were badly shaken by the regionalization of the Japanese economy in the 1990s. Even when they were able to find new markets for the products they used to sell to customers who subsequently set up shop in Asia, they often had to match or beat the low prices ("Asian prices") charged by rivals in Taiwan or Malaysia. "Some parent firms talk this way just to threaten their subcontractors, to tell them, 'We'll buy from suppliers in Asia if you don't cut your prices'," says one government official.[33] "Others don't just talk this way. They go ahead and source parts from Asia."

Not only the smallest subcontractors, but also those located in some of

31. Teikoku Data Bank, *Teikoku Nyūsu,* various years.
32. Data on these firms were obtained through files maintained by Teikoku Data Bank and by follow-up interviews.
33. Interview with Sora Yoshitada, director of international affairs for Zenkoku Shitauke Kigyō Shinkō Kyōkai (National Association for the Promotion of Subcontracting), an arm of MITI, November 20, 1997, Tokyo.

Japan's most rural areas, were hit especially hard by elite regionalization. One survey conducted in 1994 found that 40 percent of electrical parts producers in rural prefectures had experienced sharp reductions in orders. Why? A large majority (60 percent) of these subcontractors put the blame on overseas expansion by longtime customers (Kikai Shinkō Kyōkai 1994, 75–6).[34] To a significant degree, the history of spatial relocation of Japanese manufacturing is repeating itself—only on a regional scale. In the 1960s, assembly firms moved their large plants from increasingly high-cost urban areas to less congested locations in rural Japan. Key supply firms soon followed. Beginning in the late 1980s, Japanese assemblers moved again, replacing many of their rural factories in Japan with factories in Southeast Asia, Taiwan, and China. Seki (1993) writes that Japan's "full-set industrial structure" began to crumble in the 1990s as a new "tripolar industrial structure" began to take shape across Asia. This new regionwide structure consists of Tokyo and other major cities in Japan, which serve as the region's locus for "prototype manufacturing," and Japan's rural areas and Asian cities, which compete with one another to serve as the region's mass production sites. "Within this tripolar structure, it is Japan's hinterlands whose problems are most severe."

But not all Japanese suppliers were hurt by regionalization; indeed, those with the capital resources—and the right network connections—were able to participate actively in the game. This is, again, why I call the process "elite regionalization." Yamamoto (1996, 24) notes that 91 percent of the overseas investment by Japanese parts producers in the 1990s was undertaken by leading (first-tier) subcontractors.

Nisshin, a Honda brake parts supplier, is one example. In the 1990s, it completely reorganized its operations, shutting down a number of its smaller parts production facilities in outlying provinces and dividing its remaining, higher-tech production capacity between Japan and Asian countries in which Honda established assembly plants. In the process, it became an important member of Honda's emerging production network in Asia.[35]

As a regional supplier, Nisshin was in good company. In the early 1990s, Kume (1992, 4) found that as much as two-thirds of Japanese manufactur-

---

34. It is true, of course, that some larger urban centers—and even some areas within Tokyo (particularly those in which SMEs are concentrated)—also suffered heavy losses in employment and sales as a result of the regionalization of Japanese production. A survey by the local government of Osaka (Institute for Advanced Industrial Development [Osaka] 1996, 161), for example, found that a significant number of subcontracting firms in that city (42.2 percent of respondents) had experienced a reduction in orders following a main customer's decision to relocate certain operations to Asia. Likewise, a survey of suppliers in Ōta-ku (Jichirōrento Shokurō Keizaishibu 1997, 7–8) reveals the deep and widespread impact of so-called Asian prices.

35. Author interviews.

ing FDI in Asia was carried out by small and medium-sized enterprises—and presumably, many of these SME investors were suppliers of parts and materials. In one study, JETRO (1997b, 52) found that more than half of the Japanese SMEs operating factories in Asia in the mid-1990s were subcontractors. In another study, JETRO (1997a, 190) reported that 56 percent of all Japanese FDI to Thailand in 1995 was concentrated in supporting industries such as automobile and electronic parts.

Interestingly, though, the motives of such investors varied dramatically according to their actual size. Although all suppliers indicated that they hoped to utilize cheap labor when they established overseas operations, the larger ones were far more likely than the smaller ones to indicate that they also were responding to a specific request—perhaps even a demand—from a parent firm or major customer that, having built an offshore plant, had concluded, unhappily, that it could not procure parts of sufficient quality on a predictable, reliable schedule from existing—"purely local"—suppliers.[36] These concerns were often voiced about such basic industries as sheet metal, welding, pressed parts, metalworks, and plastics, according to the Bank of Tokyo (1995, 4): "It has become extremely difficult for assemblers to find local suppliers in these industries that can continually meet their high standards for quality and delivery time. As a result, Japanese subcontractors are moving aggressively into Asia in response to requests from their parent firms."

Consider the case of Nippon Electronics, a relatively large producer of printed circuit boards for Japanese electronics manufacturers such as Sony, Matsushita, and Sanyo. In the short run, it figured it might end up losing money if it built a factory in Malaysia, but it decided to do so anyway. The company was under steady pressure from longtime customers, and felt it had a "responsibility" (*sekinin*) to them, according to Takano Tatsuo, managing director of the subsidiary outside Kuala Lumpur: "For several years, our [Japanese] customers in Southeast Asia asked us to come and support them. They asked and asked, and finally we came. We had no choice really."[37]

Another example is Porite, a supplier of bearings for Japanese machine manufacturers. It built plants in Taiwan, China, Malaysia, and Singapore—all in response to pleas from its customers. Company president Kikuchi Isamu explained matter-of-factly why the firm moved into the region, and why such investments by a medium-sized manufacturer were not as risky as they otherwise might have appeared: "When our longtime clients started setting up plants in Southeast Asia, they asked us to make our products there instead of shipping them from Japan."[38]

---

36. See Small and Medium Enterprise Agency 1996, 208.
37. Interview, April 24, 1993, Shah Alam, Malaysia.
38. Miyai Yumiko, "Overseas Production Pioneer Porite Relies on Innovation, Client Loyalty," *Daily Yomiuri*, April 30, 1997, 17.

Or, finally, one could consider the case of Ezaki Industrial, a supplier of oil, water, air, and fuel pipes—mostly for Isuzu Motors. In the 1990s, Ezaki sold 80 percent of its output to Isuzu; its chief engineer used to work for Isuzu; and it opted to change its weekly work schedule, closing on Wednesdays, after Isuzu did the same. So Ezaki paid attention when its major customer, which started operating in Thailand in the 1960s, announced its intent to boost the local content of the trucks it assembled there, and—to achieve that goal—called on its key suppliers to set up factories in Southeast Asia. Ezaki Toshiharu, grandson of the founder, said his firm, which in 1998 was exporting ten thousand pipe units a month to the Isuzu plant in Thailand, could no longer afford to stay home. "If we want to survive, we have to grow with them," he told me.[39]

Thus, while elite regionalization clearly had a distributional effect, contributing to the bifurcation of the Japanese subcontracting system discussed in chapter 4, it did not necessarily have a structural effect. That is, it did not contribute to the dissolution of keiretsu networks in Japan—as some scholars and journalists (such as Hirsh and Henry 1997, 13) have alleged. Quite the contrary. Indeed, I argue that this process helped cement relations between assemblers and "core" suppliers in Japan.

This was in fact a stated goal of the METI agency that oversees relations between manufacturing assemblers and subcontractors in Japan. In one report, the agency (Zenkoku Shitauke Kigyō Shinkō Kyōkai 1997b, 58)[40] encouraged suppliers to "become part of the supply architecture of globally based parent companies" and thereby maintain or perhaps even strengthen ties with their customers or "parents."

Mindful of such linkages, Adachi (1996, 182) referred to Japanese manufacturing investment in Asia during the 1990s as "convoy-style" (*sendan-gata*) FDI because it typically was carried out by an assembler followed closely by his most trusted (first- and perhaps second-tier) suppliers.[41] This was especially true in the automobile industry, where subcontracting linkages traditionally have been strongest. One survey found that more than half of the Japanese affiliates operating in Asia's automobile industry were drawn to the region by the prior investments of their customers.[42] It is important, how-

39. Interview, Tokyo, June 9, 1998.
40. The agency has since changed its name to Zenkoku Chūshō Kigyō Shinkō Kyōkai. This shows just how much words matter: "shitauke kigyō," or subcontracting firm, has become an unfavorable term in Japan, because it highlights the hierarchical structure of Japanese industry, while the generic "chūshō kigyō" (small and medium-sized firm) has emerged as the preferred alternative.
41. This term (*sendan-gata*) was also used to describe the way MOF compelled stronger banks to work together to save failing institutions in the early and mid-1990s.
42. The survey, conducted in 1991 by the Nikkei Research Institute of Industry and Marketing, garnered 133 reliable responses from Japanese manufacturing affiliates operating in Asia. Thirty of these came from automakers and auto parts producers. The survey is cited by Urata (1996a, 11), who was a member of the team.

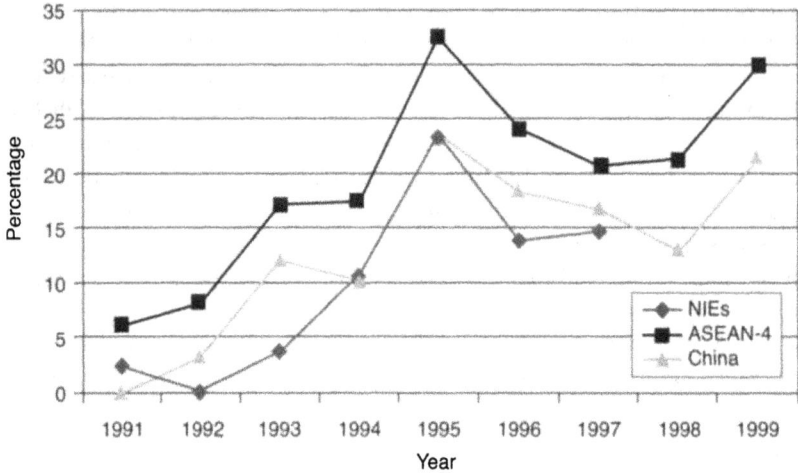

Figure 5.2. Japanese subcontractors moving into Asia
Source: Annual surveys, Research Institute on Overseas Investment (Export-Import Bank of Japan, JBIC Institute).
Note: The Institute asked respondents each year to identify the motivation behind their decision to invest in a particular location. One option was "to supply parts to an assembly manufacturer." Multiple responses were allowed.

ever, to recognize that this was a relatively new, but increasingly important, phenomenon in the 1990s. By the end of the decade, nearly 30 percent of all Japanese firms investing in the ASEAN-4 and 21.6 percent of those investing in China indicated they had decided to make the move to "supply parts to an assembly manufacturer," meaning—in nearly all cases—a Japanese transplant.[43] As figure 5.2 demonstrates, this marked a dramatic increase over previous years.

In interviews, Japanese assemblers operating in Asia often proudly claimed that they managed to boost their local procurement levels in the 1990s—a claim that, in the aggregate, was not actually borne out by the numbers.[44] Furthermore, even when they *did* successfully raise their local content, they did so largely by relying on the services of subcontractors who followed them from the home country. MITI (1998b, 244) stated this matter-of-factly: "Japanese parts manufacturers in Asia are the main suppliers for Japanese affiliates in Asia." This is confirmed by numerous studies.

43. Export-Import Bank of Japan, 1995 survey. See also Small and Medium Enterprise Agency (1997, 204), which shows the results of its own survey of SMEs. The reason most often mentioned for investing in the ASEAN-4 was "to follow one's parent firm, or main customer."
44. In 1989 and 1992, Japanese manufacturers in Asia used local suppliers in the host country for 49.8 percent and 48.5 percent of their procurements, respectively. That rate actually *fell* to 40.3 percent in 1995 and 40.9 percent in 1996. See MITI, *Wagakuni Kigyō no Kaigai Jigyō Katsudō,* various years.

JETRO (1999a) reported that 47 percent of the nearly nine hundred Japanese manufacturing affiliates it surveyed in Southeast Asia in 1998 were relying on Japanese transplants for the lion's share of their locally purchased parts and materials.[45] And in certain industries, this figure was much higher. For example, 100 percent of Japanese automakers in Thailand and 88 percent of Japanese electronics manufacturers in Indonesia reported that they relied on Japanese suppliers for at least half of their local inputs.

Focusing again on the electronics industry, Sunada, Kiji, and Chigira (1993, 64) found that 70 percent of the "local" suppliers used by Japanese assemblers in Asia were actually Japanese parts producers operating in the region. These Japanese firms completely dominated the supply base for parts such as large and small motors, magnetic heads, capacitors, and modulators. In his study of Japanese multinationals producing consumer electronics goods in Asia, Paprzycki (2005) writes that "the participation of non-Japanese [suppliers] was limited to plastic molding and metal stamping parts." Thus, if we consider the total value of parts supplied, rather than simply the number of firms supplying such parts, we can get a better picture of the dominant role of Japanese subcontractors in the electronics industries of Asia in the 1990s. Capannelli (1997, 172) found that Japanese suppliers made up 60 percent of the firms supplying Japanese electronics assemblers in Malaysia, but accounted for 82.7 percent of the value of the parts used by those same nine assemblers. This is because indigenous firms were called on most often to supply only those items with very low-value-added.[46]

In his findings, Capannelli does not disaggregate parts production based on location. In other words, the Japanese suppliers he identifies are operating in Japan, Singapore, and other countries, as well as in Malaysia. However, if one goes back to his data and restricts the analysis to "local" parts, the conclusion does not change: Japanese subcontractors dominate. Specifically, parts produced by Japanese firms in Malaysia accounted for 28.2 percent of the value of inputs used by the nine assemblers; parts produced by *all* firms in Malaysia—regardless of nationality—accounted for 36.5 percent. Kiba and Kodama (1991, 30) confirmed this result in their own study of parts used in TVs manufactured by Japanese firms in South Korea, Taiwan, Singapore, Hong Kong, Thailand, and Malaysia. They concluded that "there was an overwhelming tendency for parts to be procured from Japanese companies. The move toward procuring parts from the local area has progressed only in the form of Japanese parts manufacturers establishing local production bases."

45. JETRO does not actually "report" any such figure. But one can calculate it rather quickly by using the raw data for five countries (Thailand, Malaysia, Singapore, Indonesia, and the Philippines) on five different pages (63, 108, 151, 198, 242).
46. Watanabe (1996, 13) comes to the same conclusion.

According to a different study conducted by the Foreign Investment Advisory Service (FIAS) (1991, 41) for the government of Thailand, Japanese affiliates in Asia's electronics industry "tend to bring their own subcontractors from Japan or create their own satellite subcontractors, neither of which generates significant backward linkages with domestic firms." Likewise, Okamoto (1996, 20) expressed concern that export-oriented production by Japanese electronic firms in Southeast Asia was being carried out in "enclaves" that were well connected to Japanese subcontractors in the region, but rather poorly connected to truly local firms.

The automobile industry presents the same picture. Kumon (1997, 161) visited dozens of Japanese car and truck manufacturers in Asia and found that, in parts purchasing, they had a "high dependency on Japanese or J-affiliated suppliers." Ueno (1997, 27–38) reported that up to 70 percent of the "local" suppliers used by Japanese assemblers in the ASEAN-4 were, in reality, Japanese transplants. But this, again, actually understated the dominant position of such transplanted subcontractors. Measured in terms of the value of parts rather than in terms of the number of suppliers, these Japanese suppliers played even more significant roles in Southeast Asia during the 1990s. Consider two studies:

- JETRO (1999b, 10) found that Japanese suppliers in the region accounted for 90 percent of the value of parts purchased locally by Japanese auto manufacturing affiliates in Southeast Asia.
- Looking at this equation from the other side, Kasahara (1997, 9) found that only 11.5 percent of the value of "locally supplied" parts in the Thai auto industry came from Thai suppliers; the rest came from Japanese suppliers in Thailand.

The pattern resurfaced even when Japanese automakers set out consciously to build "Asian cars" with a preponderance of locally manufactured parts. In the case of the "City," Honda's "Asian car," which it began manufacturing in Thailand in the 1990s, the assembler used ninety-three local suppliers, sixty-seven of which (72 percent of the total) were affiliates of Japanese subcontractors. Truly local suppliers produced only very simple pressed parts.[47]

47. Interview, Tokyo, Japan, October 13, 1998, and Nishioka 1998 (18). Honda was not alone in its attempt to manufacture an "Asian car"; Nissan and Toyota launched similar projects in the 1990s. Toyota's project, the "Soluna," was the subject of an NHK documentary in February 1997 (*Ajia Senryakusha wa Kōshite Tsukurareta* or "This Is How the Asian Car Was Built"). The lengthy documentary included several interviews with the head of Toyota's parts procurement division in Thailand, a Japanese engineer who openly expressed concern about the ability of local suppliers to meet Toyota's quality standards. However, the documentary failed to report that Japanese subcontractors in Thailand were producing the lion's share of the complicated components for this "Asian Car."

FIAS (1991, 62) argued that Japanese automakers in that country deliberately avoided Thai suppliers: "One local producer claims he was excluded from the OEM market by a Japanese assembler until he could prove, by using a Japanese testing company, that his components were of higher quality than those Japanese components being used by the assembler at that time." This is reminiscent of the story, recounted in chapter 3, about the local auto parts producer who had supplied flywheels to a Japanese automobile assembler in Indonesia for several years—until early 1996, when the assembler's Japanese supplier set up a rival plant in that country.

How, then, should we characterize what was happening in the 1990s? Were Japanese manufacturers actually replicating their domestic keiretsu in Asia? The evidence suggests they were. Consider the example of MMT Engineering, a Thai affiliate of Mitsubishi Electric of Japan. Since the late 1980s, it has produced floppy disk drives for computers with parts purchased from its keiretsu suppliers in Japan, Thailand, Singapore, and the Philippines. In 1997, when I visited the manufacturing facility in Thailand, independent suppliers accounted for less than 0.7 percent of the value of those parts.[48]

Or consider the example of Siam Nissan, the Thai affiliate of the prominent Japanese automaker. All of its leading keiretsu suppliers in Japan have either established parts manufacturing facilities in Thailand or have forged technology licensing agreements with local Thai firms. In 1997, when I visited the facility, the only part that it bought from a completely unaffiliated firm was the muffler and tailpipe unit, a rather low-tech piece of equipment.[49]

Likewise, news reports show how Toyota moved into the Chinese port city of Tianjin with fourteen of its most important Japanese suppliers to manufacture passenger vehicles. The giant automaker, according to one report, "rebuilt its keiretsu supply system" in Tianjin.[50]

Others have unearthed equally compelling evidence that in the 1990s Japanese automakers attempted to bring core members of their domestic supply networks with them as they expanded into Asia. Nishioka (1998, 66), focusing on ASEAN, concluded that, "with the exception of those cases in which an established supplier has stayed home, we find very few examples of Japanese automakers [in Southeast Asia] engaging in transactions outside their established keiretsu groups." Likewise, Kasahara (1997, 22) argues that

48. Interview and survey data, Samutprakarn, Thailand, September 9, 1997.

49. Interviews, Atsugi, Japan, July 8, 1997, and Bangkok, Thailand, September 23, 1997; and company data.

50. *Asahi Shinbun*, "Chūgoku de Toyota Seisan Byōyomi" (The Countdown for Toyota in China), January 28, 2000, 13. We should note here that the Chinese government, eager to receive investment in parts manufacturing, encouraged Toyota to replicate its keiretsu network in Tianjin.

Table 5.1. Japanese members of Toyota Supply Club in Thailand

Name of Thai affiliate	Parts produced	Year established in Thailand	Name of Japanese parent	Does parent belong to Kyōhō-kai in Japan?
Aoyoma Thai	metal fasteners	1965	Aoyama	Y
Bangkok Foam	interior trim	1971	Inoac Corporation	Y
Thai Bridgestone	tires, tubes	1969	Bridgestone	Y
CI-Hayashi	carpeting	1993	Hayashi	Y
Denso Thailand	alternators, regulators	1974	Denso	Y
Enkei Thai	aluminum wheels	1987	Enkei	N
Siam GS Battery	batteries	1970	Nihon Denchi	Y
Inoue Rubber Thailand	industrial rubber parts	1970	Inoac Corporation	Y
Kallawis Autoparts	wheels	1973	Chuo Hatsujo	Y
NHK Spring Thailand	seats, springs	1963	Nihon Hatsujo	Y
Nippon Paint Thailand	paint	1968	Nippon Paint	Y
National Thai Co.	car radios	1961	Matsushita	Y
Ogihara Thailand	pressed parts	1990	Ogihara	N
Pioneer Electronics Thailand	car stereos	1991	Pioneer	Y
Sunstar Chemical Thailand	pressed parts	1989	Sunstar Engineering	N
Siam Aishin	brake drums	1996	Aishin	Y
Siam Furukawa	battery	1992	Furukawa Denchi	Y
Siam Kayaba	shock absorbers	1996	Kayaba	Y
SNC Soundproof	soundproofing	1994	Nihon Tokushu Toryo	Y
Thai Auto Works	auto body parts	1988	Toyota Autobody	Y
Thai Arrow Products	wire harness	1963	Yazaki	Y
TCH Suminoe	upholstery	1995	Suminoe Orimono	Y
TG Pongpara	steering wheels	1995	Toyoda Gosei	Y
Thai Koito	headlamps	1986	Koito	Y
Thai Kansai Paint	paint	1970	Kansai Paint	Y
Thai Parkerizing	metal coating	1979	Nihon Parkerizing	N
Thai Seat Belt	seat belts	1994	Tokai Rika Denki	Y
Thai Steel Cable	control cables	1981	Nihon Cable Systems	Y
Thai Stanley Electric	signal lamps	1981	Stanley	Y
Thai Safety Glass	windshield, windows	1988	Asahi	Y

Japanese automakers in Thailand were seeking to capture "relational rents" by conducting almost all of their business with Japanese subcontractors who belonged to their parent firm's keiretsu network.

As they did at home, Japanese automakers established cohesive supply groups in each Asian country in which they operate. These groups, which ostensibly were managed by representatives of key suppliers, but which met regularly under the auspices of the assembler, even carried the same name as the vertical keiretsu in Japan after which they were patterned. Thus, in Thailand, Nissan had its Thai Takara-kai, dominated by the local affiliates of its most trusted Japanese subcontractors; MMC had its Thai Kashiwa-kai; Toyota had its Thai Kyōhō-kai; and so on. Table 5.1 is a comprehensive list, provided by Toyota in 1997, of the thirty-two Japanese members of the automaker's supply club in Thailand. It includes the affiliates of many of Toyota's major subcontractors in Japan—from Denso to Aishin, from Kallawis to Kayaba, from Koito to NHK Spring. In fact, the parents of all but four of these Thai affiliates belong to Toyota's supply club in Japan.

Some observers have countered by noting that Japanese supply networks in Thailand, Indonesia, and Malaysia were actually more "open" and less exclusionary than parts supply networks in Japan.[51] This observation is correct but misleading because it ignores the fact that automobile markets in Asia in the 1990s were still tiny compared to the Japanese market and that parts suppliers, as a result, were unable to achieve economies of scale—and thus unable to operate at maximum efficiency—without selling to a wider circle of customers. Indeed, representatives of Japanese automakers in Asia told me that, when their keiretsu suppliers first followed them into the region, they encouraged those suppliers to sell parts to other automakers as well. In the words of one such representative: "We wanted them to get to the point where they could be really efficient and produce parts cheaply. They couldn't get there by relying solely on us."[52]

If this successfully explains the difference between Japanese keiretsu in Asia and Japanese keiretsu in Japan, one would expect such variation to decline gradually as automobile markets in host countries throughout the region get larger and larger. That is, the need to engage in extra-keiretsu transactions would lessen as suppliers begin to achieve economies of scale when they sell only to their primary customers. Higashi (1995, 46–7) states this most simply: "As the market grows, the emphasis on *group-ka* [tighter ties inside the group] also grows."

Table 5.1 supports this logic. It shows that none of the four "independent" affiliates in Toyota's supply club in Thailand moved into that country in the 1992–97 period, when the Thai auto market was growing most rapidly. On the other hand, three of the four came in a period of steady but less dramatic growth: Ogihara (1990), Sunstar (1989), and Enkei (1987). The data in table 5.1 are suggestive, but not conclusive.

To test the hypothesis that Japanese automobile manufacturers moved more aggressively in the mid-1990s to replicate their keiretsu networks in Asia as automobile markets in that region grew, I carried out an ordinary least squares (OLS) multiple regression analysis using company-level data on three Japanese assemblers (Toyota, Nissan, and MMC) and scores of subcontractors identified by each assembler as a member of its supply club in Thailand and Indonesia. I found a positive and statistically significant

51. See, for example, Dobson 1997 (246), Kamo 1997 (77), Tejima 1997 (87–88) and Guiheux and Lecler 2000 (13–16).
52. Interview, Bangkok, Thailand, September 2, 1997.

correlation between the regionalization of production by assemblers and the regionalization of production by their subcontractors. And while this correlation disappeared when I restricted the analysis to an earlier period (1989–91), it reappeared quite clearly in a later period (1995–97). I encourage readers who enjoy statistical analysis to view the results in Hatch (2005).

Although they examine different aspects of this issue, several other statistical studies come to the same general conclusion: far from jettisoning their homegrown keiretsu, Japanese manufacturers replicated them in the 1990s, and used them strategically as they expanded into Asia. For example:

- Miller, Reed, and Talerngsri (2006) use a probit analysis to study the effect of interindustry linkages on Japanese FDI in Thailand during the 1990s. They confirm that vertical keiretsu ties encourage additional investment, particularly by suppliers hoping to take advantage of the agglomeration of manufacturing in the host country.
- Belderbos, Capannelli, and Fukao (1998) use a tobit model to explain the variation in local content ratios (measured both by local value added and the procurement of inputs from local suppliers) of 157 Japanese electronics manufacturers operating in Asia in 1992. They find that membership in a vertical keiretsu, especially one with strong intragroup ties, led to increased local content, particularly for Japanese affiliates operating in Southeast Asia and China, where the indigenous supply base was then still weak.[53] This, they conclude (12), reflects the fact that Japanese MNCs replicated their supply networks "mostly . . . through the establishment of overseas manufacturing plants by existing Japanese manufacturers of parts and components, in which the latter were often assisted by the 'core' firm of the keiretsu."
- Sazanami and Wong (1996) use a multiple regression analysis to try to understand why Japanese MNCs engage in intrafirm (or intragroup) trade; that is, trade between a parent company and an overseas affiliate in which the parent owns some equity. One possible explanation they test is that MNCs hoped to exploit established keiretsu ties. The results, using 1992 data on trade in twenty-two manufacturing industries, show that keiretsu ties (reflected in subcontracting or "production consignment" arrangements) did not—in general—explain this trading behavior. But this finding lands on its head when they introduce a dummy variable for location; thus, for Japanese MNCs operating in Asia, it turns out that keiretsu ties *did* matter a great deal.

---

53. Capannelli (1997, 196) obtained similar results using a larger sample (618 firms).

What about horizontal keiretsu, the ties between nominally independent firms in a variety of different industries? As it turns out, this domestic institution, too, was re-created on a regional basis in the 1990s. Many firms advancing into Asia relied on keiretsu members for help. For example, manufacturers planning to invest there routinely leaned on their group's main bank to supply funding for new plant and equipment, and leaned on their group's general trading company to pave the way by forging political connections with host country leaders, finding industrial real estate, and handling overseas logistics. A Mitsui Corp. official told me that his firm did most of what he called "preparation" (*junbi*) for keiretsu members investing in China and Southeast Asia.[54]

The important role of horizontal keiretsu in Asia is confirmed by Belderbos (1997), who uses a multinomial logit model to study the factors that caused 204 Japanese electronics and precision machinery manufacturers to invest (or not invest) in different regions of the world. The results indicate that firm-specific assets, such as R&D capability and marketing expertise, drove firms to invest in North America and Europe, but horizontal keiretsu ties drove them to invest in Southeast Asia. "A striking finding," Belderbos concludes (217), "is that, while the possession of *firm-specific* intangible assets is in general a prerequisite for investment in Western industrialized countries, it is *inter-firm* linkages that are the major determinants of the decision to invest in Southeast Asia."

Although I have, until now, focused exclusively on keiretsu, I should not limit my analysis of the regionalization of interfirm ties to this particular institution alone. It is best to treat "keiretsu" as a metaphor for industrial cooperation, which in the 1990s tended to be more intensive and more durable in Japan than elsewhere. With this in mind, it is useful to note that Japanese manufacturing affiliates in Asia operated much like first-tier subcontractors for their parents in Japan. They were tightly controlled by the home office, which—as noted in chapter 3—coordinated the swapping of parts among various regional operations. For example, in 1996 Toyota affiliates in Southeast Asia traded $200 million in parts with one another; before the Asian financial crisis erupted, the parent company in Japan was planning to quadruple the volume of this intraregional, intrafirm trade by 2000.[55] Thus, we can conclude that Japanese manufacturers formed not only interfirm but also intrafirm networks across the region.

In the 1990s, then, elite regionalization fostered both the reorganization and the consolidation of business ties in Japan.

---

54. Interview, July 15, 1997, Tokyo.

55. See Matsuoka Katsunori, "Accord Drives Change to Asian Car-making," *Nikkei Weekly*, April 7, 1997.

Management and Labor

In the 1990s, many in Japan began to voice concern that domestic industry was being "hollowed out" by the shift of factories and manufacturing jobs to Asia. This shift was clearly dramatic in some sectors and for some jobs. In the electrical machinery industry, for example, Japanese manufacturers expanded their payroll at plants across Asia by 180,000 between 1990 and 1995, while—at the same time—eliminating 150,000 jobs at plants in Japan.[56]

But the impact of this "hollowing out" was not felt equally by all; women suffered far more than men. While the number of male Japanese workers in the industry grew by 100,000 over those five years, the number of female workers fell by 250,000. As a result, women—who had accounted for 46 percent of Japan's electrical machinery workers in 1990—accounted for only 38 percent in 1995.[57]

These numbers present no mystery.[58] During this period, Japanese electronics manufacturers reassigned to Asian women a large proportion of the assembly line work traditionally performed by Japanese women. By contrast, they continued to employ men in the higher-paying management and technical positions at prototype plants in Japan and in mass production facilities in Asia.

Thus, the regionalization of Japanese production contributed to the kind of distributional change described in chapter 4. At the same time, however, it served to block or inhibit structural change in the Japanese employment system during the 1990s, thereby helping to maintain the strong relational ties that bind longtime employees to their employers. Japanese manufacturers, in particular, incorporated their Asian operations into regionwide personnel systems that allowed them to better protect the job security of their typically male, middle-aged workers with firm-specific or insider skills.

During the hard economic times of the 1990s, managers at those manufacturing firms scrambled to cut production costs, particularly labor costs. As we have seen, however, they were not inclined to lay off "core" workers (regular employees). Instead, they relied on less drastic means such as *shukkō* ("seconding," or the temporary transfer of employees), including what I call "cross-border *shukkō*," to trim their payrolls. Asia, home to an expanding list

56. Data on employment in Asia come from MITI, *Wagakuni Kigyō no Kaigai Jigyō Katsudō*, various years. Data on domestic employment come from Management and Coordination Agency, *Rōdōryoku Chōsa Tokubetsu Chōsa* (Special Survey on the Labor Force), various years.

57. Although this trend is most pronounced among medium-size firms, it is quite evident at some large firms as well. At Sanyo, for example, women made up 33.1 percent of the workforce in 1985, but only 21.9 percent in 1995. See Toyonaga 1998 (4).

58. Indeed, Toyonaga (1998, 5–10) performs a simple regression analysis that confirms the correlation between the regionalization of production and the loss of jobs for women in Japan's electronics industry.

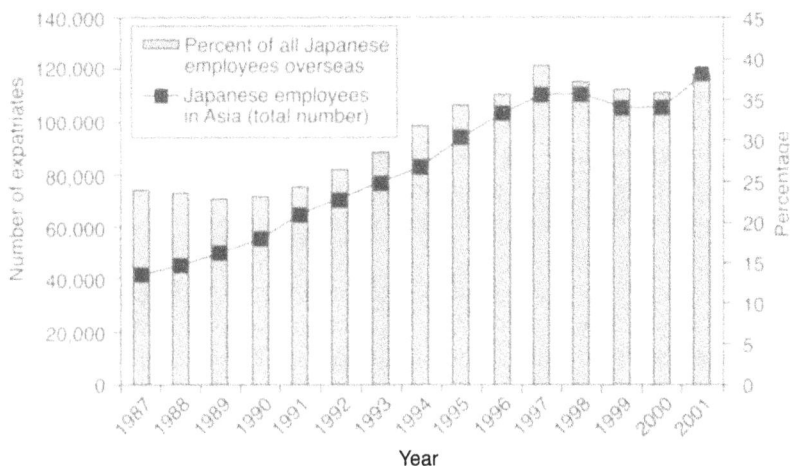

Figure 5.3. Japanese expatriates in private firms in Asia
Source: Ministry of Foreign Affairs, *Kaigai Zairyū Hōjinsū Chōsa Tōkei*, various years.

of Japanese manufacturing affiliates, functioned as a "parking place" to store surplus white-collar workers from Japan.

Compared to Japan, Asia was booming in those days. So Honda transferred a large number of supervisors from home-based operations to affiliates in the region, especially in Thailand. According to a Honda spokesman, this eased some of the growing pressure in Japan, where payroll was growing faster than sales. "Our network of operations [in Asia] provides more flexibility in personnel management."[59]

The same was true for Nissan. "We have too many managers at Nissan Motors in Japan," confided an executive for the automaker. "Our overseas operations give us a convenient way to relieve this excess supply of management staff."[60]

When Hitachi ran into trouble in the early 1990s, it set a goal of reducing domestic employment by ten thousand workers, relying most heavily on natural attrition, an early retirement program, and temporary transfers, including cross-border *shukkō*.[61] In 1991, the electronics giant had 450 Japanese managers stationed overseas, including Asia; by 1996, that number had nearly doubled to 830. Hitachi's experience is not extraordinary. As figure 5.3 shows, the total number of Japanese employees at private firms in Asia increased almost twofold over that period, reaching 103,688 by 1996.[62]

59. Interview, October 13, 1998, Tokyo.
60. Interview, July 24, 1992, Tokyo.
61. Interview, July 29–30, 1998, Hitachi City.
62. Ministry of Foreign Affairs, *Kaigai Zairyū Hōjinsu Chōsa Tōkei,* various years.

Cross-border *shukkō* is an expensive practice, both financially and politically. Japanese MNCs must pay much higher salaries and benefits to their expatriate managers than to their local managers at overseas affiliates—in some cases, as much as ten times more. Furthermore, they receive heated, often blistering, criticism from host government officials for using Japanese rather than local staff at their operations in Asia. Given these two constraints, one would expect to find a steady reduction in the share of these expatriate managers.

In fact, however, there was remarkably little progress on this front during the 1990s, despite repeated pledges by Japanese parent companies to "localize" (*genchika*) their Asian operations. This stubborn commitment to a relationship-based personnel policy was evident not only in wholly owned subsidiaries but also in joint ventures in which the Japanese partner owned less than 50 percent of the stock. "In places like Indonesia and the Philippines, where we do not have a majority of the equity," said Yokoi Akira, vice-president for international affairs at Toyota, "we are still able to aggressively send in our own management team and maintain control."[63] Even in those rare instances in which an Asian manager ended up in charge of production, finance, or some other important division in a Japanese subsidiary or joint venture, he often was paired with an expatriate manager, who served as a "big brother" or adviser.[64]

As figure 5.4 shows, the percentage of expatriate (Japanese) supervisors (directors) at Japanese manufacturing affiliates in Asia remained relatively high throughout the 1990s, and even increased slightly to more than 40 percent by 1998. Indeed, Kitajima (1997, 55) found that nearly 60 percent of Japanese machinery manufacturers in Thailand, Malaysia, and Singapore planned to maintain or increase the number of expatriate technicians and managers they employed at those overseas affiliates. Even more surprisingly, Kitajima (1997, 57) found that 96.2 percent of those firms planned to maintain or increase the number of Japanese directors supervising their operations.

Official statistics grossly understate the scale of the expatriate staff at Japanese manufacturing affiliates in Asia. This is because most of these staffers are engineers and technicians who rotate into such jobs for relatively short periods of time, thereby avoiding host country tax obligations and circumventing host country restrictions on the supply of work permits for foreigners.[65]

63. See Asahi Shinbun, "Ajia no Jidōsha Sangyō: Zadankai," November 27, 1996, 15.
64. Interviews, Bangkok, Beijing, Jakarta, Kuala Lumpur, Seoul, Singapore, Taipei, 1992–99. See also Nakamura and Padang (1999, 22).
65. Interviews, Bangkok, Beijing, Jakarta, Kuala Lumpur, Seoul, Singapore, Taipei, 1992–97. See also Kumon 1997 (165) and Lin 1995 (67).

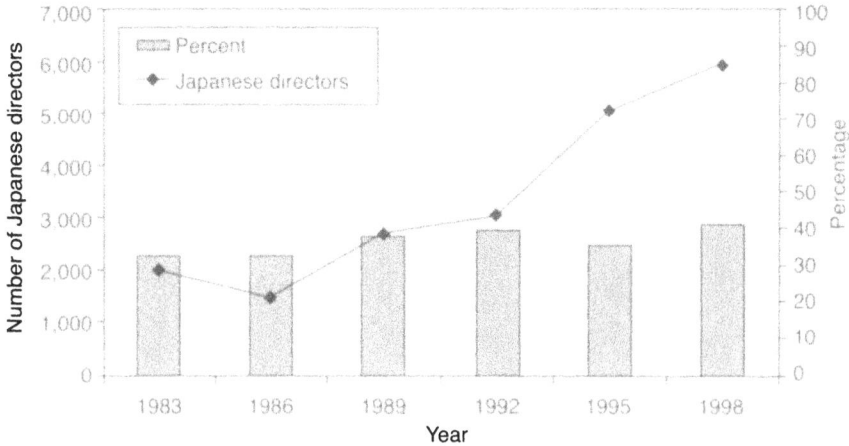

Figure 5.4. Japanese directors at Japanese manufacturing affiliates in Asia
Source: MITI, *Kaigai Jigyō Katsudō Kihon Chōsa* (Basic Survey on Overseas Business Activities), various years.
Note: "Asia" equals China, Asian NIEs, ASEAN-4.

In chapter 3, I pondered various explanations for the slow pace of localization, and found that the most plausible one had to do with the desire of
Japanese employers to preserve the relational ties they had nurtured so carefully in Japan over the years. This explanation is supported by evidence that,
in transferring technology, Japanese parent firms in the 1990s continued to
prefer to dispatch technicians from home rather than rely on experts in the
host country who could be armed with technical manuals or even trained in
Japan via on-the-job training.[66] And the Japanese state often supported this
bias. At a 1997 seminar in Bangkok on strategies to cope with the region's
unfolding currency crisis, JETRO officials encouraged Japanese assemblers
in Thailand to consider importing an even larger number of technicians
from Japan to work directly with their Thai (and Thailand-based) subcontractors on a long-run project to increase the quality of locally produced
parts. JETRO offered the services of its own Japan Overseas Development
Corporation, which traditionally has dispatched Japanese technicians who
are unemployed or who have retired from their jobs at home.[67]

It should be noted here that cross-border *shukkō* can move in either direction. Parent companies in Japan, using what they call "on-the-job training
programs," routinely imported less-skilled Asian workers from their regional

66. In addition to the numerous works on technology transfer by large manufacturing firms,
which have been cited in chapter 3, please see Kawai et al. (1997, 51) and Yahata (1996, 6). They
examine technology transfer by Japanese SMEs and come up with similar findings.
67. JETRO, "Seminaa Rejime: Kawase Hendō ni Taeru Shizai Chōtatsu ni Tsuite" (Sum-
mary of a Seminar on Procuring Inputs in the Midst of Exchange Rate Fluctuations), JETRO
Bangkok office, September 5, 1997, 3.

affiliates and put them to work on home-based assembly lines, and particularly in "3 K" jobs (that is, *kiken, kitsui, kitanai;* or in English, dangerous, difficult, and dirty jobs). This happened either when the supply of Japanese workers willing to perform such labor in Japan was low, or when the supply of Asian workers at overseas affiliates became overabundant. For example, in 1992, Toyota sent about two hundred workers from its assembly plant in Indonesia to its plants in Japan to receive on-the-job training. This was double the number of "trainees" sent in an average year. Why? Nakamura and Padang (1999, 93) provide a succinct explanation: the parent company in Japan "was experiencing a boom and faced a shortage of manpower . . . [while its affiliate in Indonesia] did not have favorable market conditions and suffered from excessive manpower."[68] In addition, parent companies in Japan moved export-oriented assembly lines—and thus jobs—back to Japan when relative costs shifted in response to exchange rate adjustments. For example, in 1997, when the yen weakened against the dollar, Matsushita moved its production of sixteen-inch and twenty-five-inch color TV sets back to Japan from Malaysia—even though it anticipated having to run its Japanese plants at a loss for at least a short time. It did so because it wanted to protect domestic jobs, according to Shirafuji Hiroyuki, managing director of Matsushita TV (Ishibashi 1997, 19). Or, in less altruistic language, it wanted to avoid the sociopolitical cost of losing its investment in relational ties at home.[69]

Thanks to this ongoing concern about domestic employment, leading Japanese labor organizations were able to express qualified support for business plans to "rationalize" production activities through regionalization. In one report, Denki Rengō (1998, 169)—the Electrical Workers Union, a subset of Rengō (Japan Trade Union Confederation)—argued that Japanese manufacturing investment in Asia, carried out as part of a regional division of labor, actually protected the jobs of skilled "core employees" in Japan. The union welcomed regionalization that would promote the upgrading of Japan's domestic industrial structure. This position is quite different from the one taken by Rengō's U.S. counterpart, the AFL-CIO, in the debate over the North American Free Trade Agreement. In an October 9, 2003, interview, Nakajima Shigeru, executive director of international affairs for Rengō, defended his organization's unique position:

68. In interviews, host government officials often complained to me that training programs set up by Japanese manufacturers were nothing more than a scheme to supply their domestic factories with cheap labor from their Asian factories. And the Japanese government has all but acknowledged as much. In a 1999 report, the Ministry of Justice alleged that some Japanese manufacturers had forced their Asian "trainees" to work extra hours without extra pay, often on tasks that had nothing to do with their training program (*Daily Yomiuri*, August 11, 1999).

69. As noted in chapter 3, this motivation of protecting domestic employment also helps explain Japan's relatively low level of reverse imports from manufacturing affiliates in Asia.

Japan is a small country with limited raw materials. So our response to globalization is, naturally, quite different from unions in the United States and Europe. We have to work with companies to help them preserve their international
competitiveness. Manufacturing is the key. We must protect our industrial structure and keep it strong. Because we have to import food and raw materials,
unions must cooperate with employers in manufacturing to safeguard the health
of industry.

The point here is not that Rengō is wildly different from the AFL-CIO, or
that it has been somehow "co-opted" by the Japanese business community
while its American counterpart has remained a vigilant opponent of "rationalization" through regionalization. The point is that Japanese FDI into Asia,
motivated in part by the desire to maintain network ties, has produced a
wholly different outcome than U.S. FDI into Mexico. Elite regionalization
was carried out in a way that earned the support of Japan's labor elites.

Coping with Crisis

In this chapter, I demonstrated that elite regionalization in the 1990s helped
preserve if not strengthen network ties under stress in the political economy
of Japan, while at the same time narrowing the distribution of gains from selective relationalism. All three nexuses of cooperation—that is, the ties between state and industry, between otherwise independent firms, and
between labor and management—were fortified by the regional expansion
of Japanese institutions.

Although one might have expected the Asian financial crisis of 1997–98
to immediately overturn the status quo, it did not. The crisis did, as I will
argue in chapter 7, create new economic and political conditions that eventually helped to disrupt elite regionalization and thus undermine selective
relationalism. But its short-term impact was surprisingly subtle. This is because Japanese business and bureaucratic elites used extraordinary measures to cope with the collapse of markets in Asia and, in the process,
managed to cling to positional power in the region for a little while longer.

For Japan's business elites, the challenge was to stabilize production networks that were experiencing a massive shock. Parent firms jumped into action, pumping money into Asian affiliates. For example, 244 joint ventures
in Thailand received emergency capital transfusions from foreign parents
between November 1997 and January 1999—and nearly two-thirds of that
money came from Japan.[70]

---

70. See Uehara 1999, 20. The *Far Eastern Economic Review* (July 29, 1999, 52) reported that
the Japanese government—through the Export-Import Bank—helped finance a number of
these capital injections.

Japanese assemblers worried most about key subcontractors whose fortunes suddenly sagged in the failing economies of Asia. In the automobile industry, they pursued a three-pronged strategy based on regionalized relationalism to prop them up. First, they provided emergency financial assistance to members of their local supply groups. Toyota, for example, agreed to make advance payments to its parts producers throughout Asia, and financed critical but short-run expenses such as the lease of equipment.[71] Nissan also came to the defense of its beleaguered parts suppliers in Thailand, subsidizing up to $26 million in production there.[72] Second, to breathe some life into an otherwise flat market, the parent companies temporarily assigned to their affiliates in Asia some of the production chores that had, until then, been done entirely in Japan. Toyota, for example, gave its Thai affiliate the responsibility of manufacturing—and then exporting—a line of pickup trucks. Stanley Electric transferred a share of the production of headlights to its affiliate in Thailand.[73] Mitsuba, meanwhile, turned over all production of integrated circuit flasher relays to its Thai affiliate, which then exported the goods back to Japan.[74] Third, parent firms dramatically boosted the import of parts from struggling suppliers in Asia. In 1997, when the regional crisis first struck, Toyota in Japan was buying only 2.5 billion yen worth of auto parts from its subcontractors in Asia; a year later, it announced that it would raise the value of such imports to 14 billion yen by 2000—a nearly sixfold increase.[75] Honda, meanwhile, increased its import of auto parts manufactured in Thailand by 150 percent in 1998.[76] And MMC began importing parts from Japanese suppliers in Thailand for use in the Galant, produced in the United States, and the Lancer, produced in Japan (Mori 1999, 23).

Of course, Japanese assemblers hoping to ride out the economic storm in Asia had to do more than just shore up their supply base; they also had to hang onto their labor force. Here, too, regionalized relationalism came in handy. To cite just one example from the auto industry, Toyota officials boasted that they did not lay off regular employees in Southeast Asia during the early months of the crisis—even though they had to suspend production at several factories.[77] One reason they were able to fulfill their pledge of

---

71. See *Nikkei Weekly*, October 19, 1998, 18; and December 21, 1998.
72. See *Nikkei Weekly*, May 11, 1998, 19.
73. See *Nihon Keizai Shinbun*, February 5, 1998.
74. See *Nikkei Sangyō Shinbun*, April 6, 1998.
75. See *Nikkei Weekly*, October 5, 1998, 18. Aishin Seiki, one of Toyota's most trusted suppliers in Japan, also got into the act by importing door locks from its affiliates in Thailand and Indonesia (*Nikkei Weekly*, October 26, 1998, 18). Asahi Glass did the same, importing auto glass for as many as fifty thousand vehicles a year from its affiliate in Thailand (see *Nikkei Weekly*, January 11, 1999, 18).
76. See *Nikkei Weekly*, September 21, 1998, 22.
77. Interview, Tokyo, November 27, 1997.

protecting jobs was that they dramatically expanded their program of sending overseas employees to Japan for training. In 1998, at the peak of the crisis, Toyota doubled the number of Southeast Asians in its training program (from 250 to 500), and doubled the amount of time spent in Japan (from an average of three months to an average of six months) (Fourin 1998b, 6). We should not be surprised to learn that the Japanese state helped finance this and other training programs through the Association for Overseas Technical Scholarships, an arm of MITI.

For Japan's political elites, the Asian crisis created an opportunity to flex their muscles. "There were a lot of needs, and we tried to fill them," one official told me.[78] This time, MOF moved first. In September 1997, it called for an Asian Monetary Fund (AMF) that would use local currencies, primarily the yen, to rescue any regional economy facing a balance of payments crisis. The chief architect, Sakakibara Eisuke, head of MOF's international finance division, traveled throughout the region touting the plan. With one exception, the countries of Asia warmly embraced it. They had just witnessed the debacle in Thailand, where the International Monetary Fund (IMF) had offered only limited help—and then, with strings tightly attached. But China, now growing rapidly and beginning to acquire its own regional clout, was reluctant to give Japan greater authority in Asia. So it complained to U.S. officials, who blew the whistle on the AMF, calling it a dangerous scheme that would undermine the IMF's authority and create too much "moral hazard." To the great disappointment of political leaders in Southeast Asia, Japan, nestled squarely beneath a U.S. nuclear umbrella, sheepishly withdrew its proposal.[79]

MITI had more success. It used the crisis as a pretext to aggressively pursue its controversial scheme of implementing a regionwide industrial policy. It began by convening "joint public-private sector dialogues" under the auspices of AMEICC in Bangkok to consider how it might collaborate with state officials in each country to help "guide" investments that would contribute to the development of the entire region. When it discussed its vision for AMEICC, MITI deployed virtually the same logic (and rhetoric) it had trumpeted in the 1960s when it was defending the use of industrial policies at home. The Asian economic crisis, the ministry argued, reflected the failure of government officials in the region to cooperate with one another and with firms in their own countries—a dual oversight that led to uncoordinated production and excess competition, which unduly lowered the price of manufacturing goods (*Nihon Keizai Shinbun*, November 23, 1998, 3). AMEICC was designed, on paper at least, to overcome this failure of industrial policy.

---

78. Interview, Tokyo, July 23, 1999.
79. This account draws heavily on Terry (2002, 245–55).

To spur economic recovery, the Japanese government announced in 1998 that it would dramatically increase the flow of ODA loans and grants, as well as technical assistance, to its hardest-hit neighbors in Asia. On its face, the emergency plan to spend $80 billion over ten years seemed undeniably generous. But upon closer inspection, one quickly realized that it included a number of items designed to strengthen relational ties between the Japanese state and Japanese industry, as well as to help maintain interfirm and labor–management ties.

First, the aid package renewed the controversial practice of "tying"; that is, providing financing for a project only on the condition that it is carried out by home country firms. Asian countries hit by the crisis were to receive a total of $6 billion in "special loans" over three years for equipment purchased from Japanese suppliers or for public works performed by Japanese contractors.[80]

Second, the package made it possible to dispatch an unprecedented number of JICA experts to Asia, providing advice to host country officials on everything from industrial structure reform to trade finance.[81] This advice, as noted earlier, tended to favor the interests of Japanese MNCs operating in those countries. And in the case of a new program proposed by the head of Nikkeiren (Japan Federation of Employers Associations), it also served the interests of firms remaining in Japan. For the first time ever, the government recruited "white collar experts" from Japan's private sector—particularly its financial institutions—to provide guidance to Asian governments on such matters as accounting and auditing. All of the volunteers—an estimated one thousand each year—were between the ages of forty and sixty-nine; many, it turned out, had been rendered superfluous by the hard economic times in Japan. For this reason, a JICA official told me, the program was able to help Japanese firms as well as Asian governments. "In most of these Asian countries, there is a serious shortage of administrators trained in fields such as financial management. On the other hand, in Japan, we now have an excess number of such people."[82]

Finally, the massive aid package included a significant amount of financing for Japanese firms in Asia, particularly the SMEs that in the late 1990s made up the all-important supply base for machinery assemblers and that were then threatening to abandon the region, where markets had dried up, and return home. Some of this money went to host governments, which in turn loaned it to private interests. In 1999, Malaysia, for example, received $160 million as a "two-step loan" targeted at SMEs, especially Japanese suppliers, suffering from the credit crunch in that country. Much of the money,

80. *OECF Newsletter*, No. 73, April–May 1999.
81. JICA handout, "Activities for ASEAN Financial Crisis in Fiscal 1998," undated.
82. Interview with Shukunobe Masami, July 23, 1999, Tokyo.

however, was channeled to Japanese firms through government-affiliated banks in Tokyo. For example, as of July 1999, the Export-Import Bank of Japan had agreed to provide $900 million in additional assistance to Japanese affiliates in Indonesia through what it called "investment financing."[83]

Furthermore, these government-affiliated banks were authorized, for the first time, to provide operating funds for Japanese SMEs in jeopardy of closing down existing facilities in Asia—not just to subsidize new overseas investments for plant and equipment. Under this new program, public funds were loaned to the parent company in Japan, which was then expected to inject capital into its affiliate in Asia. In just the first three months of 1999, JFS loaned nearly $10 million to keep fourteen affiliates afloat.[84]

In addition, MITI tried to maintain investment in Asia by expanding its already generous program insuring foreign bank loans for the overseas activities of Japanese affiliates. In March 1998, the government announced it would begin to cover ordinary credit risks, such as the bankruptcy of an overseas affiliate that had borrowed money.[85] Then, a few months later, it announced it would relax the insurance program further by eliminating the requirement that Japanese parent firms participate in providing up-front guarantees for overseas loans made to their affiliates.[86]

The Japanese state did not try very hard to disguise the fact that its massive bailout plan for Asia was also designed to help Japanese industry. Indeed, when he announced his $30 billion piece of the package in 1998, Finance Minister Miyazawa Kiichi noted candidly that a substantial sum would go to Japanese SMEs. OECF (1999, 7) justified the expenditures in these terms:

> Japanese companies, which have contributed greatly to the economies of these countries, are also facing difficulties due to the economic crisis. If this situation continues, it would be difficult to invigorate these economies with new economic activity, with the strong possibility that many companies might have to pull out of the region. This would be damaging to the local economies, and could possibly have damaging effects on the bilateral relationships of these countries with Japan.

Host governments throughout Asia were grateful. Compared to the United States, which they viewed as unhelpful and obnoxious (paradoxically triumphant and nagging at the same time), they regarded Japan as gener-

83. JICA handout, "JICA and Japan's Support to Cope with Asian Financial Crisis," July 22, 1999.

84. Interview with Ishikawa Kokuo, senior assistant manager, international section, JFS, July 5, 1999.

85. *Nikkei Weekly*, March 9, 1998.

86. *Yomiuri Shinbun*, July 11, 1998.

ous and quiet.[87] But they weren't naïve; they understood Japan's self-interest in the region's economic revitalization. They knew that Japanese efforts to shore up the region's tottering production networks were also designed to strengthen Japan's own networks. They realized that the Asian crisis was jeopardizing Japan's positional power in the region, and they feared the consequences. In September 1998, Singapore's ambassador-at-large Tommy Koh greeted visiting MITI minister Yosano Kaoru by invoking the agency's favorite metaphor: "We need the Japanese goose to grow strong so that it can lead the other geese in the region to fly again."[88]

Koh, however, may not have recognized the underlying paradox: The longer Japanese elites used desperate measures to rescue the flying geese pattern of regionalization and thereby preserve the solid ties of relationalism at home, the longer it would take for Japan to rediscover its own wings.

87. A headline in one of Bangkok's English-language daily newspapers (*The Nation,* September 1, 1997) captured the resentment felt toward not only the Washington D.C.-based International Monetary Fund, which had imposed stiff requirements on Asian borrowers, but also toward the United States in general: "West Rides on Asian Money Crisis." The article, written by Thanong Khathong and Vatchara Charoonsantikul, begins with these words: "The United States is reaping the economic and geo-political benefits of the foreign exchange crises in Thailand and the rest of East Asia, although its ultimate objective is to slow growth in China and preempt Japan from becoming its global economic rival." The article went on to refer to the economic crisis as a massive "transfer of wealth" from Asia to the United States.

88. *Straits Times* (Singapore), September 24, 1998.

6 The Costs of Continuity

What was so wrong about Japanese bureaucrats and corporate executives working feverishly in 1998 to rescue the flying geese pattern of regionalization led by Japan? After all, the Asian financial crisis was still spreading and, in some countries, getting deeper. Was it not threatening to ground the entire flock? The problem was this: the bird came home to roost. That is, elite regionalization in Asia extended the shelf life of selective relationalism in Japan, which had already lived well beyond its expiration date. For Japan, the consequences were increasingly dire. By the late 1990s, relationalism had become highly selective, organizing the Japanese political economy into close-knit networks that tended to privilege insiders and exclude outsiders. And it had become characterized, more than ever, by institutional rigidity, with the insiders who hoarded network resources unable to recognize new opportunities and the outsiders who might have recognized those opportunities unable to access the existing resources necessary to seize them.

In this chapter I seek to calculate the actual costs of maintaining the relational status quo. These came in two forms: distributional costs, which are borne by outsiders and which, in the Japan of the late 1990s, were reflected in, for example, the widening income gap; and general welfare costs, which are borne by the political economy as a whole and which, in the Japanese case, were reflected in low levels of entrepreneurial activity and declining innovative capacity. I spend more time discussing the latter, because these welfare effects have been understudied, and because they are impossible to grasp with a conventional perspective that treats government bureaucrats as proxies for a power-maximizing "state" and corporate managers as proxies for a profit-maximizing "firm." Such a utilitarian approach cannot explain the sociopolitical motives of public and private actors who work to maintain a web of relationships that provides them with positional power but, in the long run, undermines the capacity of the state and the profitability of the firm.

As I argued in chapter 1, strong ties always come with both benefits and costs. On the one hand, they provide what Yamagishi (1998 and 1999) calls "reassurance" (which, as he pointedly notes, is quite different from "trust"). Actors who forge strong ties with (and thereby make long-term, credible commitments to) one another are reassured that they will not be subjected to opportunistic behavior (cheating). The result is a set of institutions that reduce transaction costs, a stable structure that allows resources such as capital, labor, and information to circulate rapidly inside that (confined) social space. On the other hand, a relatively dense network structure characterized by strong ties will constrict the free flow of resources, including information. It will, as Granovetter (1973 and 1974) and Burt (1992) argue, and as I discussed in chapter 1, serve as a barrier to new ideas and new projects.

In a developing economy, one in which firms can continue to adopt technology from the global reservoir of revealed technical knowledge, the benefits of this dense pattern of social organization outweigh the costs. This is because the chief obstacle facing such an economy is the shortage of institutions to cope with the collective action problems that impede firms from making productive investments, or the collective action problems that later lead to overinvestment. Firms in a developing economy, an economy that is playing follow the leader, can generally see the technological path ahead. What they cannot so easily detect are the landmines placed along the way by fellow travelers.

In a developed economy, however, the costs of strong ties ultimately outweigh the benefits. This is because firms no longer can simply adopt existing technology and transfer it to related firms; they now must pursue radical innovations. That is, they must acquire and develop new ideas and new information in an environment of technological uncertainty. But firms in a highly relational political economy are unable to do this; they are bound by strong ties and thus cut off from such sources of new ideas and information.

In the 1990s, Japan sat on the cutting edge of the global technology frontier. It was a fully developed economy whose manufacturing firms, to compete effectively, had to introduce new products and develop new production techniques. But they were not always able to take such bold steps, in large part because they were paying excessively high opportunity costs under a system of selective relationalism, a system that has degenerated into "institutional collusion."

In Japan, elites who occupy pivotal positions in relational networks have colluded by monopolizing or hoarding the resources tucked inside those networks. In this way, collusion has had a distributional effect. By definition, outsiders—those who do not enjoy positional power in the Japanese political economy—have been handicapped by this uneven distribution of resources.

Consider, for example, the rather specific impact on Japanese consumers, who—collectively—have constituted the largest group of outsiders in the political economy of Japan. Due to barriers created by relational networks encompassing the Japanese state and private industry, as well as barriers created by interfirm ties, they have been forced to pay prices well above the global market price for everything from fruit to furniture. In the 1990s, this distributional effect became quite pronounced. In an analysis of changes in import and domestic producer price differentials between February 1985 and February 1995, Kimura, Kawai, and Tanaka (1996) document a steadily growing gap for a large number of the 139 commodities under study and conclude that Japan's nontariff trade barriers actually expanded over that decade (1985–95).[1] This conclusion is confirmed in a follow-up analysis by Sazanami, Kimura, and Kawai (1997, 3), which traces the gap to "government regulations and restrictive private business practices that may not necessarily be designed to discriminate against imports, but in fact limit their market penetration."

More generally, selective relationalism has contributed to the growing income gap between rich and poor in Japan. This gap first became apparent in the "bubble years," when asset prices soared to unprecedented levels.[2] But it kept on widening through the "lost decade," when the economy stagnated and those trying to survive outside relational networks ended up with less and less. According to the OECD (2006, 98), Japan was the only advanced industrialized democracy in the world to experience an increase (5%) in the number of its citizens living in absolute poverty[3] between the mid-1980s and 2000. During the same period, the proportion of its population living in relative poverty[4] climbed sharply to more than 15 percent —the fifth highest in the OECD and well above the organization's average of 10 percent. Driven by this expansion in the number of poor people, the most commonly used indicator of market income distribution (the Gini coefficient, which ranges between zero, or complete equality, and one, or complete inequality) jumped in Japan from 0.31 in the mid-1980s to 0.41

1. They actually considered two indicators: import pass-through rates and domestic-import price differentials (DID). The latter, which is more relevant to the discussion here, measures change in prices at the "second layer," and thus may reveal the presence of trade barriers. DID can be defined mathematically as PDI(yen)—PM(yen)] / E, where PDI(yen) is the proportional change in the domestic input price index (on a yen basis), and PM(yen) is a proportional change in the import price index (on a yen basis), and E is the rate of yen appreciation (in terms of the nominal effective exchange rate).

2. To cite just one indicator, the Nikkei average of prices on the Tokyo Stock Exchange climbed to 38,915 yen in 1989. This represented a quadrupling of stock prices in just six years.

3. The OECD defines "absolute poverty" here as an income that is less than one half of the median disposable income in 1985 and adjusted for price increases in subsequent years.

4. The OECD defines "relative poverty" as less than one half of the median household disposable income.

in 2000—a growth rate that was more than double the OECD average.[5] The Gini coefficient for Japan's distribution of disposable income also grew much faster than average—from 0.27 to 0.31.[6] By 2000, economists such as Tachibanaki (2000, 76) were bemoaning the growing "polarization" of Japanese society.

There is a fierce debate within Japan over the actual cause of this widening income gap.[7] Although some, such as Ohtake (2006), blame the "graying" of Japan's population, many others, including Higuchi and MOF's Policy Research Institute (2003), point instead to the growing wage differential between regular employees, Japan's labor elite, and nonregular employees, whose ranks increased dramatically in the 1990s. Yashiro (2007, 285) puts it this way:

> Japanese employment practices lie at the heart of the inequality. Specifically, I mean the way in which companies have tended to divide their employees between those on the inside and those on the outside, providing insiders with lavish benefits while forcing outsiders to bear the costs. Inequality between regular and nonregular employees is symbolic of this.

I side with Yashiro, whose analysis helps explain the dramatically wide pay gap that emerged in the 1990s between male workers (who tend to be regular employees) and female workers (who tend to be nonregular employees). But he could have gone even further: other kinds of outsiders also found themselves increasingly on the short end of the stick in Japan. For example, in the late 1990s, when the jobless rate reached a record high (for the postwar period) of about 5 percent, foreign workers accounted for a disproportionate share of those unemployed. In Hamamatsu, Shizuoka, an area filled with automobile parts production facilities that in the past had served as a magnet for Brazilian immigrants of Japanese ancestry, an estimated two thousand of the community's ten thousand Japanese-Brazilian residents were jobless (*Yomiuri Shinbun*, October 4, 1998).

Likewise, small manufacturers and their workers suffered disproportionately as sales volumes, profit rates, and wages began, in the mid-1990s, to lag

---

5. Even after this remarkable growth in market income inequality, however, the OECD notes that its 2000 estimate for Japan (0.41) is still below the OECD average (0.44). Economists with other groups have produced different numbers. Rengō (2006), for example, estimates that Japan in 2000 had a Gini coefficient of 0.48.

6. Unlike its estimate of market income inequality, the OECD's estimate of disposable income inequality in Japan for 2000 is above the group average (0.30). This lends weight to those who believe Japan's widening income gap is caused primarily by the growing wage differential between regular and nonregular employees.

7. The opening bell of the increasingly contested public debate on income (in)equality in Japan might have rung on May 2000. That is when two of Japan's most respected monthly magazines—*Chūō Kōron* and *Bungei Shunjū*—carried special reports on this problem. The former devoted forty pages to the issue.

further and further behind those of large manufacturers and their employees (*Nihon Keizai Shinbun*, July 9, 1997, and March 12, 1998; SME Agency 1998, 23). By 1998, 47.1 percent of the manufacturing firms filing for bankruptcy were extremely small (capitalized at less than ten million yen) and another 48.2 percent were small or medium-sized (capitalized at between ten million and fifty million yen); only 4.6 percent of the failed manufacturers that year were reasonably large (capitalized at more than fifty million yen) (Teikoku Data Bank, *Teikoku Nyuusu*, January 19, 1999, p. 12).

In the 1990s, this sharp division between haves and have-nots was relatively new—and thus as unwelcome as it was unfamiliar. For nearly a half century, Japanese had prided themselves on living in the industrialized world's only "classless" society, one in which virtually everyone is "middle class" or "middle stream" (*chūryū*). Although this claim had always been exaggerated, it now was patently unsupportable. "People are losing the perception that society offers the chance for equal development," says Uchida Shinji of the Nomura Research Institute (*Yomiuri Shinbun*, August 6, 1998). Satō (2000, 73), after analyzing data on social mobility, offers this equally bold conclusion: "The dream of becoming middle class is eroding."[8]

Until the 1990s, Japanese elites had been able to cover a large share of the distributional costs associated with selective relationalism. Profits were high enough; wages were good enough; jobs were abundant enough. In other words, Japan's relation-based economy had yielded sufficient gains to allow insiders to make side payments to excluded outsiders handicapped by their marginal positions in exchange networks. Consumers, for example, received side payments in the form of generous after-market service.

Over time, however, the system became increasingly outmoded and the costs of those strong ties of cooperation (between state and industry, between firms, and between management and labor) began to swamp the gains. Even insiders began to suffer economic losses as Japanese capitalism matured. Specifically, they paid an increasingly stiff price for what I refer to as their own "information impactedness," an inability to receive clear signals (such as price signals) outside their own network structures. In sum, elite actors—from bureaucrats to company managers to lifetime employees —began to miss opportunities because they could not recognize and act

---

8. Satō's study is intriguing. Using the results of the government's survey on social mobility (SSM), which has been conducted every ten years since 1955, he identifies five distinct social strata in Japan, including upper-level white-collar employees (UWE) who occupy the top professional or managerial positions offering the greatest security, pay, and prestige. He finds that forty-year-old members of the baby-boom generation (born between 1936 and 1955) were far less likely to break into the UWE strata than forty-year-old members of the previous generation (born between 1926 and 1945). They even faced significantly higher obstacles than their distant peers born between 1916 and 1935.

upon them. As a result, the Japanese economy began to lose its ability to generate profits, create new industries, and sustain employment.

In chapter 2, I provided an overview of these opportunity costs. Here I offer two more concrete examples of how an outmoded system of relationalism led in the 1990s to information impactedness, which in turn took its toll on the Japanese economy:

- Close ties between government regulators and bank executives contributed to the crisis that began with the collapse of mortgage lending companies (*jūsen*), spread to regional banks such as Hokkaido Takushoku, and eventually touched the entire financial services industry in Japan. In March 1998, Japanese banks estimated they were carrying up to $300 billion in nonperforming loans.[9] According to Horiuchi (1998, 150–62), they ended up in this deep hole because financial regulators hoping to retire into amakudari positions at banks under their supervision were induced to authorize high-risk banking practices. Using a simple statistical test, Horiuchi found that banks accepting amakudari officials from MOF and the BOJ had a bad loan ratio almost double that of banks declining to accept amakudari officials. This assertion is supported by strong anecdotal evidence. Until the mid-1990s, when they acknowledged their financial woes, the *jūsen* had been run by twenty-six executives. More than a third of those twenty-six executives (ten) had "descended" from MOF.[10]
- Interfirm ties hurt the Nissan Motor Co., which accumulated $20 billion in interest-bearing debts on its way to a grave financial crisis in the late 1990s. Nissan, Japan's number-two automobile manufacturer before running into so much trouble that it had to be bailed out by France's Renault, expanded capacity without paying attention to its bottom line. When it came time to reduce output and streamline operations, the firm was unable to move quickly—in large part because of longtime business alliances. As it turns out, all three of Nissan's leading suppliers (Calsonic, Kansei, and Unisia-jecs) were run by former Nissan directors, and half of its distributors were directly supervised by the automaker. (By contrast, Toyota maintained strict control over only 7% of its dealers.) As the *Asahi Shinbun* concluded, "One reason for the sharp drop in [Nissan's] sales is said to be this bureaucratic (*sarariman-teki*) management."[11]

9. The figure was revised upward (from about $200 billion) after Japanese banks were pressured to use the more inclusive definition of nonperforming loans. See Horiuchi (1999, 26).

10. *Nihon Keizai Shinbun,* January 27, 1996.

11. *Asahi Shinbun,* "Nissan Dai-risutora: 'Keieijin no Sekinin' Doko ni" (Nissan's Major Restructuring: Where Does the Responsibility of Management Lie?), October 20, 1999, 13.

Reforming (or Not Reforming) Relationalism

For Japanese elites, the regionalization of domestic networks in the 1990s was a double-edged sword. With one blade, they cut themselves slack, preserving a system of selective relationalism that—at least in the short run—afforded them positional power in Japan. With the other blade, however, they weakened the Japanese economy and thus jeopardized their own economic interests. Some unusually enlightened members of the Japanese establishment recognized what was happening, and issued desperate calls for structural reform to (a) broaden participation in policy networks, and (b) allow information to flow more freely in the Japanese political economy.

Gyōten Toyō, former vice minister of international affairs for the Ministry of Finance, was one of these reformers. He blamed the economic stagnation of the 1990s on what he called the "troika" of Japanese politicians, bureaucrats, and business leaders who "cooperate behind closed doors in formulating policy." Once upon a time, he wrote,

> the troika demonstrated a tremendous ability to lead and help bring about a dynamic economy. However, there have been dramatic changes in the world economy over the past twenty years. . . . Unfortunately, the troika has not been able to keep up. Efforts by different groups to maintain their vested interests have given rise to inertia. Attempts to break the logjam and create a new system of governing have not borne fruit.[12]

Nukazawa Kazuo (1998), former managing director of the Keidanren, was another reformer. He complained that Japan's political economy lacked transparency, and that information was too often locked inside exclusionary networks of human relationships. "Information is money," he noted, "and it is difficult to prevent the select group of people who are close to the authorities, and who thus have access to information, from gaining advantage in the market."

Even within the Japanese bureaucracy, reformers tried to mobilize. For example, a report commissioned by the Economic Planning Agency (1998a, 23) noted that the political and economic institutions of Japan were well suited to an era of "catch-up economic growth," but not to the present era. "As the need to explore the frontiers of technology has grown, we now find it imperative to uphold the principle of competition on the basis of efficiency. The current system based on long-term ties of cooperation is outdated." MITI (1998b, 155) went even further, stating that "Japan, as it enters the twenty-first century, must carry out a dramatic reform of its industrial structure if it hopes to maintain its competitiveness."

12. *Yomiuri Shinbun,* May 10, 1998, 1.

In building a new policy framework, however, bureaucrats often fell back on the tried and the true. For example, Matsushima Shigeru, director of MITI's policy planning office, tilted his head in confusion when I asked if his agency would curtail its routine use of administrative guidance. Of course not, he answered. But it certainly would try to "devise new policies that are more appropriate for Japan's current stage of development."[13]

And Japanese politicians repeatedly failed to carry out structural reform—at least until the first decade of the new century. The Products Liability Act, approved by the Diet in 1994, was one example of continuity disguised as change. On paper, the new act brought Japan into line with other industrialized democracies that use rules of strict liability in tort cases. In fact, however, the act was implemented in such a way that it continued to rely heavily on alternative dispute resolution procedures, discussed in chapter 1, that block the disclosure of information about defective products. These procedures include face-to-face negotiations between consumers and manufacturers (*aitai kōshō*), as well as mediation services provided by organizations such as the Product Safety Association (Shōhin Anzen Kyōkai) and the Electric Home Appliances Association (Kaden Seihin Kyōkai), which are affiliated with METI and thus likely to be biased in favor of the manufacturer.[14]

Relationalism and Innovation

For better and for worse, selective relationalism directly affects the ability of firms to innovate. In the rapid growth period (1950–73), it stabilized an otherwise volatile market for Japanese manufacturers, allowing them to vigorously absorb and diffuse existing technology from the global reservoir of existing know-how. In the 1990s, however, it presented an obstacle to mature, entrenched firms hoping to develop basic or breakthrough technology.[15] Japan's ICT (information and communication technology) industries hit a wall during the "lost decade," when radical change in the global environment—such as the development of cross-border software standards—called for new business strategies. For years, Japanese high-tech firms were "catching up, just copying what America already had made," Nishi Kazuhiko, president of ASCII Corp., a Japanese software manufacturer, told a reporter in 1993. "Now there's not much left uncopied, and we are all facing the much tougher question of what to do next."[16]

13. Interview, Tokyo, June 4, 1998. Matsushima said, for example, that his agency had begun to promote "industrial clusters" (*sangyō shūseki*) that are more open and less centralized than keiretsu networks. I return to this new industrial policy later in the chapter.

14. See Maclachlan (1999, 260–62).

15. For two very different views, see Gerlach (1995) and Kodama (1991).

16. Brenton Schlender, "Japan: Hard Times for High Tech," *Fortune*, March 22, 1993, 19.

Was such pessimism really warranted?[17] Some observers believe Japanese manufacturers never lost their technological prowess, and that the economic woes of the 1990s were caused only by the massive buildup of unproductive assets in the financial sector. The real economy, according to these observers, was alive and well; Japan's big manufacturers would return to their world-beating ways as soon as the banking system found its feet.[18] Others, such as Katz (1998), believe innovating firms had been dragged down by the heavy weight of highly protected, highly regulated "deadwood" sectors such as food processing that produced largely for the domestic market. Large export-oriented firms in machine manufacturing remained highly competitive, according to this view, and would help Japan rise from the ashes —once the state carried out regulatory reform and eliminated the deadwood.

The evidence, however, supports Nishi's concern about Japan's innovative capacity in the 1990s. First, the nation did in fact fall behind other industrialized nations, especially the United States, in private sector spending on R&D over the decade. In fact, its spending grew at about the same rate (9% a year in the late 1980s) as U.S. spending until 1991, but then all but flattened out (1% a year) at around ten trillion yen per year through the rest of the decade (Science and Technology Agency 2000).[19] U.S. spending, by contrast, continued to rise sharply, and by the end of the decade it was nearly three times higher than Japan's. This analysis is supported by survey data indicating that Japanese manufacturers chiefly marshaled their R&D resources for the development of new applications with old technology. In one study, Kikai Shinkō Kyōkai (1998, 10) found that most firms were content to continue to use existing know-how; fewer than 27 percent of firms were planning to innovate.

One could argue, of course, that this slowdown in R&D spending reflects nothing more than a slowdown in the Japanese economy as a whole. Firms, according to the view, were earning less, and thus investing less. But Japan's technology troubles in the 1990s become even more obvious if one looks at R&D output rather than input. Worldwide patent applications by Japanese inventors were completely flat in the first half of the decade, and then increased less than 10 percent in the second half. By contrast, worldwide

17. Suzuki (1996) answers that question with a defiant "no."

18. This view is associated with unrepentant "revisionists" such as Fingleton (2000) who express both admiration for—and fear of—Japan's (latent) economic power, as well as macroeconomists such as Posen (1998) who believe Japan simply pursued the wrong mix of policies.

19. By fiscal year 2000, the amount had climbed to 10.86 trillion yen. See also Watanabe and Hemmert (1998, 51–55). In their study, Japanese investment in R&D as a share of total investment fell from 13.2 percent in 1987 to 8.9 percent in 1994, and R&D intensity (research expenditures as a share of total sales) also dropped—in real terms—during the 1990s.

patent applications by U.S. inventors jumped 66 percent during the 1990s, while those by German inventors actually doubled.[20] And Japan began to lag further and further behind other industrialized countries in the publication of scientific articles. By 2001, Japan ranked seventeenth in the OECD (2006, 131) in the number of articles per population; it was the only G-7 country below the OECD average.[21]

The Japanese state attempted to jump-start the nation's innovation system in the late 1990s by dramatically increasing what had been extraordinarily low levels of public spending on basic research[22] and by encouraging greater collaboration between private firms and universities, which had been highly regulated.[23] But the results were disappointing. During the 1990s, the number of scientists and engineers leaving Japan to pursue research elsewhere constantly exceeded the number of scientists and engineers coming to Japan. "We lost a lot of dynamic people, and didn't let enough smart immigrants come here," lamented Yakushiji Taizo, a technology policy adviser to the prime minister.[24] The numbers tell the story: in 1995 alone, this "brain drain" was equivalent to a net loss of 110,000 people.[25]

For Japanese firms, the bottom line was reduced competitiveness. In the late 1980s and as recently as 1991, those firms were judged the world's most competitive by the International Institute for Management Development (IMD), a leading business school in Switzerland.[26] In 1997, Japan was number 17 in the IMD rankings. By 2001, it had fallen even further to number 26.[27]

A better way to measure industrial competitiveness may be to look at the value added by manufacturers. In the first half of the 1990s, value added by Japanese manufacturers of general machinery and precision instruments

20. Science and Technology Agency, *Kagaku Gijutsu Yōran* (Science and Technology Handbook), various years.

21. See also Boyer (2003, 157), who conducts similar research and finds that Japan in the mid-1990s produced fewer than half as many research articles—on a per capita basis—as Germany, and only a little more than one-third as many as France.

22. See Inose (1997, 22).

23. See Pechter and Kakinuma (1999).

24. Interview, Tokyo, July 5, 2007.

25. See Science and Technology Agency (1996, 61–62). Of the scientists and engineers leaving Japan, most are headed to the United States or Europe. And most of those coming to Japan hail from Asia.

26. IMD uses 323 different criteria, from GDP growth to high school graduation rates, to measure competitiveness.

27. In a survey of 670 firms conducted by the Tokyo Chamber of Commerce (1996, 3), 65 percent said they thought Japanese manufacturing had lost some of its competitive edge in the 1990s. The chamber explained this pessimism by noting that, in the past, Japanese manufacturers had managed to climb out an economic hole by holding the line on wages for workers and parts prices for subcontractors. "But even though they have tried again to squeeze water from a virtually dry towel, manufacturers continue to face hard times."

fell 20 percent; value added by manufacturers of transportation equipment fell 13 percent.[28] Of the four major machinery industries, only electronics managed to achieve growth. But this was due primarily to a temporary surge in domestic demand for computer and telecommunication equipment in the early 1990s; indeed, the industry's fortunes turned sour in the second half of the 1990s as demand collapsed. Profits in these machinery industries plummeted nearly 60 percent in the first half of the decade, then recovered a little in 1996—only to fall sharply again.

For Japan as a whole, the bottom line was sluggish economic growth as firms moved too slowly to upgrade their technological capabilities. From 1991 through 1999, Japan's economy managed to grow (on average) by only 1.3 percent a year—less than any other industrialized economy in the world. And at the end of the "lost decade," it just barely avoided the dubious distinction of being the only economy since the global depression of the 1930s to experience three consecutive years of contraction. (Japan's GDP grew by 0.2 percent in 1999. And this "achievement" was made possible only with the help of statistical sleight of hand by the Economic Planning Agency.[29])

In the past, Japan had relied on exports to sail through hard economic times. But in the 1990s exports were concentrated in sectors with low-growth intensity, and thus failed to do the trick. Legewie (1997, 24–25) reports that, in 1992, only 5 percent of Japanese exports belonged to product groups that had enjoyed high performance. Rather than exports, it was extraordinary government spending on public works—enough to push the budget deficit up to 9.4 percent of GDP in fiscal year 2000—that kept the economy afloat. By the end of the century, the construction industry, which received more cash than any other industry targeted in the stimulus packages of the 1990s, employed close to seven million people, or 10.4 percent of Japan's workforce.[30]

Public spending on construction is a poor substitute for private investment in new information and communication technologies. In the 1990s, Japanese firms failed to invest heavily (or steadily) in ICT. The Japan Research Institute (1998, 17–18) reports that ICT investment reached its peak in 1996, ac-

28. MITI, *Kōkōgyō Shisū Nenpō* (Annual Report on Manufacturing and Mining Indices), various years.

29. In calculating growth for October–December 1999, the EPA omitted data showing extraordinarily weak capital investment by Japanese financial institutions. These data have been included in previous government studies of economic growth. But if it had followed its standard practice and included these data in its calculation, EPA would have had to report an even gloomier (and more politically damaging) GDP figure than it ultimately did. See Stephanie Strom, "Japan Assailed for Omitting Data in Growth Calculations," *New York Times*, May 24, 2000.

30. *Nihon Keizai Shinbun,* May 3, 1998, 9. Employment in some rural prefectures was sustained by public works spending. In Hokkaido, for example, the construction industry accounted for 52 percent of new job offers in the summer of 1997 (*Daily Yomiuri,* July 20, 1997, 3).

counting for as much as 9.4 percent of all spending on machinery, but then quickly plummeted. Just a year later, at the end of 1997, it accounted for as little as 3 percent of spending on machinery. U.S. investment in ICT was much more aggressive.[31] A comparative study by the Japan Economic Research Center (1998) found that the total value of Japanese goods and services incorporating ICT (both "hard" technology such as computer machinery and "soft" technology such as computer programs) was only 7 percent of Japan's GDP in 1996, a relatively good year; by contrast, the value of U.S. goods and services incorporating ICT was 9.9 percent of U.S. GDP in 1996.

In the race to develop cutting-edge technologies, why did Japan, which looked like a sure winner just a decade earlier, slip so far behind in the 1990s? Some blame the Japanese system of higher education, which they say fails to promote independent scholarly research at a sufficiently advanced level.[32] Others, including the Japanese government, blame Japanese culture in general, saying it is conformist and thus stifles creativity.[33] But these explanations fall short because they cannot tell us why success in Japan's case so quickly turned to failure. The answer, I argue, has more to do with the institutions—or, more precisely, the underlying network structures—that came together to form selective relationalism in Japan.

In the 1990s, state-industry cooperation, which had worked so well when public and private technocrats could see the technological road ahead, impeded the important signaling function of the market, which provides "bottom-up" information on consumer needs and wants to producers. Interfirm linkages, which had facilitated the diffusion of already developed technology through established networks, limited opportunities for acquiring new ideas for product, process, and organizational innovation. At the same time, intrafirm linkages between labor and management, which had promoted teamwork and thus served to protect the firm's investment in human capital, inhibited risk-taking in an environment of technological uncertainty.

In the aggregate, these relational ties informed a national system of innovation that was ill-equipped to cope with such uncertainty. The system was founded on what Rtischev and Cole (1998, 3) call "organizational continuity"; that is, it works well when the status quo is stable, but "less well when

---

31. One study estimates that, in the mid-1990s, ICT accounted for less than 20 percent of total business investment in Japan, compared with 40 percent in the United States. It also concludes that only 2 percent of Japan's GDP was invested in ICT, compared with 3 percent for the United Kingdom and 4 percent for the United States. These results are cited in Irene M. Kunii, "Will Technology Leave Japan Behind?" *Business Week*, August 31, 1998.

32. See, for example, Karthaus (1997), who laments the comparatively low quality of chemistry training in general, and polymer science in particular, in Japan.

33. See the Ministry of Labor (1996, 90–91), which assails Japan's "risk-averse institutional culture." Also see Ikawa Yojiro, "'Village Mentality' Makes Winning Nobel Prize Even Harder for Japanese," *Daily Yomiuri*, October 22, 1997; and Ikeda (1997).

there are fundamental and frequent changes in industry standards and dominant designs."[34] Steffensen (1998, 519), for his part, suggests that business networks in Japan have constructed "complex, costly, proprietary, and customized information systems" that tend to be exclusionary and thus inward-looking. Okimoto and Nishi (1996, 203) use different words to make virtually the same argument. Japan's system of innovation, they argue,

> is not designed to encourage bold new conceptualizing, radical departures from the prevailing orthodoxy, and freewheeling exploration of territories unmapped by known theories. Instead, Japanese organization is geared to operate on the basis of caution, conservatism, and incremental change. It filters out bold new ideas if those ideas cannot be readily proved. It can be accommodating in such areas as hardware, because hardware is predictable and susceptible to design proof; but radical, new concepts seldom pass through the intricate mechanism of consensual deliberation.

Although rich with insight, these descriptions do not tell the whole story. What they leave out is the sociopolitical motivation that drives it: elite actors who had occupied central positions in Japanese exchange networks were disinclined to promote or pursue radical innovations because such innovations, by definition, threatened established relationships, and thus threatened their own positional power.

Small Is Beautiful

A burgeoning body of literature suggests that, for many countries, small and medium-sized enterprises (SMEs) represent a vital source of new technology, especially "breakthrough" innovations.[35] In the United States, for example, Okimoto and Saxonhouse (1987, 399) found that SMEs produce a relatively large number of patents with a relatively small amount of investment in R&D; in Japan, however, they found that SMEs are not as productive in generating new technology. Of thirty-four major technological innovations achieved over a twenty-year period in postwar Japan, SMEs accounted for

34. This is similar to Yamamura (2003), who offers a long view of the relationship between the institutional design of an economy and the underlying "technological paradigm." Japan's economic stagnation in the 1990s, he argues, resulted from a mismatch between its "cooperation-based capitalism" and the "breakthrough phase" of the twenty-first-century technology paradigm based on digitization. When the current paradigm matures and stabilizes (in, say, 2020), he argues, Japan will regain its economic dynamism and the Anglo-American system of market-oriented capitalism—which does better during a breakthrough phase than during a maturation phase—will fall behind, just as it did in the 1970s and '80s.

35. Bonin (1991, 276) puts it this way: "When the process of innovation is broken down into phases, it appears that small firms have an advantage in the initial stages of invention, as well as an advantage for less expensive, but much more 'radical,' inventions." Also see Freeman (1982); Dasgupta and Stiglitz (1980); and Kamien and Schwartz (1982).

only two. This finding is confirmed by the Small and Medium Enterprise Agency (1996), which reports that 70.6 percent of manufacturing subcontractors in Japan have never filed a patent. It concludes that "technical development activity in the small manufacturing sector has fallen to a low ebb."

In the 1950s and 1960s, Japanese SMEs tended to depend heavily on large keiretsu sponsors for not only capital and markets but also technology. In spite of this, some small enterprises—perhaps even many—prospered, growing into large, independent, innovative firms with names such as Canon and Kyocera. But when Japan's economy matured and growth began to slow, such powerful upstarts became few and far between. Indeed, small manufacturing firms in Japan were, in the 1990s, more likely to *shrink* than to grow in size.[36] As Tokuhisa (1997, 75) argues, "a new generation of SMEs has yet to step forward and continue the progress that others have made." In 1997, Kiyonari Tadao, the president of Hosei University, noted that microenterprises (tiny start-up ventures) are popping up virtually everywhere in the industrialized world—with the exception of Japan, where such small firms were "rapidly declining in number."[37]

The Global Entrepreneurship Monitor evaluates countries on their respective ability to launch and sustain new business activities. In 2000, it ranked Japan dead last among the twenty-one industrialized nations it surveyed.

Figure 6.1 paints this picture in sharp contrast. The rate at which Japanese entrepreneurs launch new firms fell steadily from the early 1970s, when 7 percent of all firms were start-ups. In the early 1990s, the start-up rate fell below the closure rate for the first time in the postwar period; this means, of course, that Japanese firms were unable to hold their own and are, in the aggregate, declining in number. By the end of the decade, the start-up rate was about 3 percent (but only 2% in manufacturing)—well below the U.S. start-up rate of about 14 percent.

Who were these brave souls who bucked the tide in the 1990s by opening their own businesses? Journalists painted an uplifting picture of young, restless, highly educated, and computer-savvy entrepreneurs forming a "venture vanguard" in Japan—much like in the United States.[38] But the reality was

36. See Small and Medium Enterprise Agency (1996). In the 1988–90 period, 7 percent of SMEs shrank substantially in size (as measured by number of employees) and nearly 8 percent grew substantially. But in the 1991–93 period, almost 9 percent of SMEs shrank and only 6 percent grew.

37. Kiyonari Tadao, "Japan's Small Businesses Need Bigger Hand," *Nikkei Weekly*, July 14, 1997.

38. See, for example, Peter Landers, "Venture Vanguard: Small Firms Aim to Re-ignite Japan's Entrepreneurial Spirit," in *Far Eastern Economic Review*, July 31, 1997; Kazunari Yokota, "Start-ups Find Ways to Vault into Mainstream Economy," in *Nikkei Weekly*, November 8, 1999; and Chisaki Watanabe (Associated Press), "Young Japanese Venture Online for Better Jobs," in *Seattle Times*, June 15, 2000.

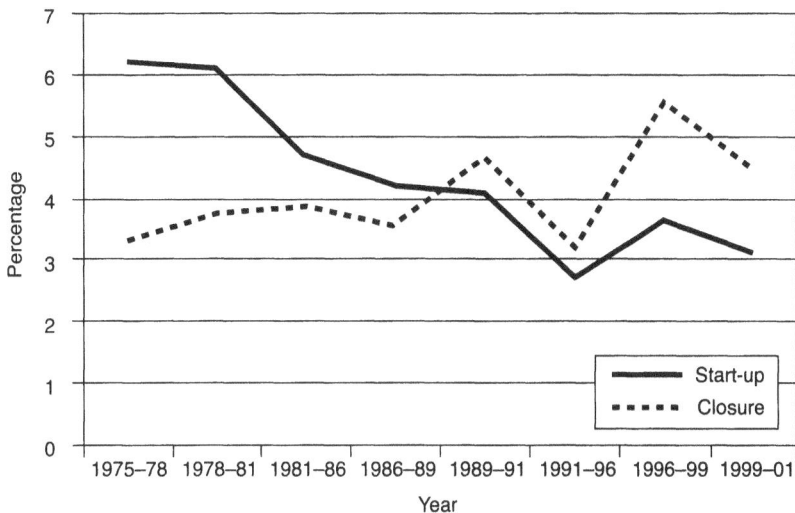

Figure 6.1. Business start-up and closure rates
Source: Small and Medium Enterprise Agency, *Chūshō Kigyō Hakusho,* 2003.
Note: All industries, yearly average.

quite different.[39] According to the government's Research Group on New Business Creation (1999), which conducted a survey of more than one thousand microenterprises identified in 1998 by the *Nihon Keizai Shinbun* as new, fast-paced, and innovating, the typical venture businessman at the end of the twentieth century was fifty-five; did not have a technical background in science or engineering (64 percent of the presidents of these venture firms did not); and, in a surprising number of cases (36 percent), had not even graduated from a four-year college.[40] Only 12.5 percent of these microenterprises were involved in information technology.[41]

39. In critiquing the journalistic view of Japanese entrepreneurs, Genda (2001) focuses on age. In 1987, 25.2 percent of those aged 25–34 were self-employed; by 1997, only 19.4 percent were. Likewise, in 1987, 21.6 percent of those aged 35–44 were self-employed; by 1997, only 20.9 percent were. He concludes: "The reason young people have no desire to be entrepreneurs is that, in today's difficult economic climate, it is becoming harder than ever before to run a business."

40. Respondents to this survey came from a directory of twenty-four hundred venture firms listed in Nihon Keizai Shinbunsha, *1998-nenban Nikkei Benchaabijinesu Nenkan* (The 1998 Nikkei Venture Business Yearbook), which focused on firms that (a) possess their own technology or know-how; (b) have enjoyed high growth; and (c) are relatively young. The National Institute of Science and Technology, the sponsor of the "Research Group on New Business Creation," followed up this survey with two policy reports—Sakakibara (1999) and Maeda (1999)—containing recommendations on how to promote high-tech venture firms.

41. A different study by the Nikko Research Center (1991, 32–1) found that eight of the top ten firms engaged in information processing and information services were established by large manufacturers of information hardware (such as Hitachi) or large users of information software

☐ Independent ■ Spin-off ☐ "Affiliates" (*norenwake*) ■ "Directed Affiliates" (*bunsha*)

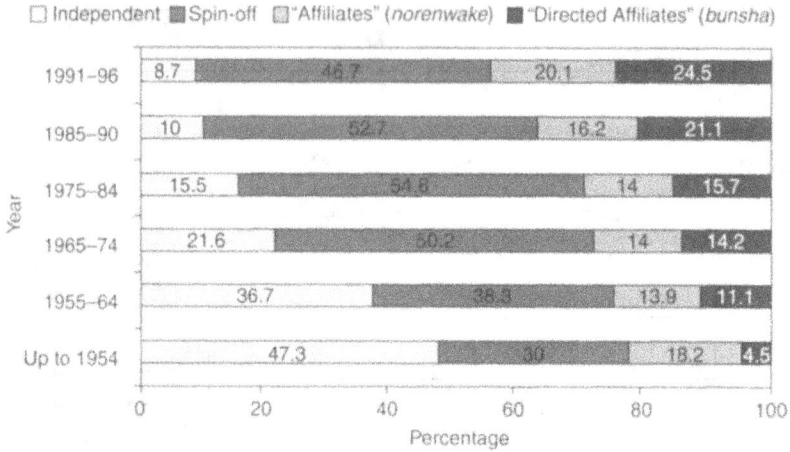

Figure 6.2. Character of start-ups in different periods
Source: Small and Medium Enterprise Agency, *Chūshō Kigyō Hakusho*, 1997, 320, and 2002.

Perhaps the most telling fact about the start-ups is that they increasingly tended to be affiliated in some way with a large firm. Figure 6.2 documents this trend over time. Among start-ups created between 1991 and 1996, only 8.7 percent could be classified as truly independent (by contrast, nearly half of the start-ups founded in the early 1950s were independent). All of the other firms created in the 1990s were tied to a parent firm: 46.7 percent were classified as "spin-offs" (in which an employee retires from an existing firm to start his own); 20.1 percent were "affiliates" (or, in Japanese, "*norenwake,*" a pattern in which an employee retires from a firm but intends to maintain a business relationship with his former employer); and 24.5 percent were "directed affiliates" (or, in Japanese, *bunsha,* a pattern in which an employee sets up a new firm under the direction of his old employer). Although the government slightly revised its classification scheme, the trend continued through the decade: in 2001, only 6 percent of Japanese start-ups were truly independent.

A program created in 1995 by mega-computer maker Fujitsu is an example of what can only be called "sponsored entrepreneurship." The company agreed to provide matching investment funds to employees who decided to launch their own technology firms. This, according to Katayama (1996, 242), provided a tremendous opportunity for "people who are unable to make full use of their abilities within the confines of a large organization." One should note, however, that the program came with one

---

(such as Nomura Securities). The two independent firms in this key industry were established in the 1960s.

important stipulation: if the start-up proved successful, Fujitsu retained the right to gobble it up.

There are least two problems with sponsored entrepreneurship. One is that large firms tend to be risk-averse, and their tethered offspring are likely to share this trait. Nishizawa Jun'ichi (1988), the inventor of the semiconductor laser, recalls how he first tried to sell his idea to NTT, the Japanese telecommunications giant. They told him they were unwilling to invest in such an "uncertain proposition." So he had the technology commercialized in the United States. The other problem with sponsored entrepreneurship is that large firms launching start-ups may be motivated more by a desire to trim expenses via personnel transfers (*shukkô* or *tenseki*) than by any authentic hunger for innovation. In other words, they may be trying to relieve employment pressures jeopardizing core workers, not trying to promote new ideas.

Relationalism and Start-ups

My analysis thus far has begged the question: Why was the business start-up rate in Japan so low? In 1998, the Japanese government asked entrepreneurs to help them solve this puzzle.[42] Respondents identified three main obstacles they faced in launching their firms: obtaining capital; developing suppliers, distributors, and customers (*torihikisaki*); and securing employees. Let us consider each of these problems separately.

In the 1990s, financing for new Japanese ventures was woefully underdeveloped and, as a result, many independent microenterprises were asphyxiated at birth. Banks and securities firms continued to dominate the venture capital market in Japan, which had only about 150 funds dedicated to high-growth, high-risk investments.[43] This paled in comparison with the United States, which in 1995 had about one thousand venture capital funds that pumped about $5 billion into infant firms. U.S. funds invested early, usually before a new venture became one year old. Japanese funds were far more cautious; they invested much later—usually after a firm already had proved it could fly.[44] A microenterprise in Japan generally had to struggle to stay afloat for at least five to ten years before it could dream of going public via an initial public offering (IPO).

In the United States, venture capital funds typically provide a lot more than capital; in most cases, the managers of these funds have acquired tech-

42. SME Agency, "Chūshō Kigyō Sōzōteki Katsudō Jittai Chōsa," December 1998. The results are also contained in SME Policy Research Group (1999, 84).
43. In Japan, even the venture capital funds tended to be affiliated with big banks and securities firms.
44. See, for example, Hata (1997, 64) and Ueda (1996, 205–6).

nical expertise in a particular field—whether biotechnology or e-commerce —and will provide valuable market information to new ventures. Even today, Japanese funds tend to view themselves, by contrast, as mere financiers. As Hata (1997, 64) argues, "Unlike their counterparts in the U.S., Japanese venture capitalists do not provide management assistance."

This brings us to the second obstacle mentioned by Japanese entrepreneurs: the cultivation of customers, suppliers, and distributors (*torihikisaki*). In a different survey, the Japan Productivity Research Institute (1997, 3) asked 335 venture firms to list the sources of information they found most useful in running their firms.[45] Venture capital funds, mentioned by only 1.5 percent of respondents, showed up at the very bottom of the list of eleven possible sources. Respondents also gave low marks to management consultants, government agencies, and other venture firms. Ironically, they gave the highest marks by far to "customers, suppliers, and distributors" (*torihikisaki*), which were mentioned by 83 percent of respondents. This reflects a catch-22. By definition, venture firms desperately need information about the market, especially about potential customers, suppliers, and distributors. In Japan, however, they tend to have difficulty obtaining such information unless they are already affiliated with customers, suppliers, or distributors. This is because that information traditionally is locked inside established business networks. A basic principle, formulated a bit differently in chapter 1, tells us that the stronger the ties in any exchange network, the harder any core member will work to safeguard his investment in "social capital," or in the long-standing, mutually reinforcing relationships that hold the network together.

Finally, entrepreneurs indicated they often were stymied by difficulties in securing skilled personnel. This should come as no surprise to anyone who knows anything about the Japanese labor market of the 1990s, which remained quite rigid. The top graduates of Japan's leading engineering and business schools continued to be snatched up by the largest firms, and employed there for years. A survey carried out in 1999 by the Japan Institute of Institute of Labor found that Japanese software engineers in Japan remained with their employer, on average, for seven years and two months; their counterparts in California's Silicon Valley stayed, on average, one year and two months.[46] A follow-up survey in 2000 confirmed that seniority-based pay continued to retard job mobility in the Japanese software industry.[47] What this meant for Japanese start-ups in the 1990s was obvious: unless one was a sponsored entrepreneur (an affiliate), one faced an uphill battle in recruiting

---

45. The respondents were drawn from the same registry of venture firms (*Nikkei Benchaa Kigyō Nenkan*) used by the Research Group on New Business Creation.

46. See Tatsumichi (2001, 13).

47. Ibid.

the best and brightest technicians and managers. Here, too, relationalism shifted transaction costs from insiders to outsiders.

Independence as a Virtue

In a fully developed economy, a high level of selective relationalism serves to curb the growth of venture business. It cannot, however, smother it altogether. Even in the 1990s, Japanese entrepreneurs undoubtedly defied the odds and launched their own independent start-ups. And when they did, one might guess that they performed relatively well—primarily because, as untethered operators, they tended to be less risk averse and more dynamic. That is, they were more willing—and more able—to quickly seize market opportunities than firms locked into established business relationships. I tested this hunch by examining data on small manufacturers in machinery and metalworking industries in two very different locations in Japan: Hitachi City, where SMEs are tightly linked to one megamanufacturer; and Gifu Province, where SMEs tend to be much more independent. To the maximum extent possible, I tried to compare firms that were similar in all respects but location (and thus, by extension, level of independence). In each area, I examined data for the early and mid-1990s, when machinery/metalworking manufacturers throughout Japan faced roughly the same set of adverse conditions in the macroeconomy.

Hitachi City, located in Ibaraki Prefecture, northeast of Tokyo, is a classic company town (*jōkamachi*).[48] Its namesake, a huge conglomerate that produces everything from rice cookers for homes to turbines for nuclear reactors, is not only the largest employer in the area; it also serves as the customer of last resort for a small army of manufacturing subcontractors, many of them engaged in casting, welding, or other forms of metalworking and many others engaged in parts production. In 1991, those firms in Hitachi City employed 9,841 workers and generated sales of 469 billion yen. Five years later, metalworking and machine manufacturing SMEs in Hitachi City employed only 1.5 percent fewer workers (9,736 altogether), but they generated 12.2 percent less in sales (418 billion yen altogether). In other words, sales fell much more sharply than employment in that area.

Gifu Prefecture is located in the middle of Japan, nearly two hundred miles from Tokyo and 125 miles from Osaka. It is well known for its cutlery, paper, and plastics industries, but—unlike Ibaraki—does not have any large-scale assembly plants operated by world-class machine manufacturers.[49]

---

48. The Japanese term, *jōkamachi,* literally means "town under the castle," suggesting a feudal relationship of domination and deference.

49. Gifu Prefecture has an average of only twenty employees per business, making it 41st out of Japan's forty-seven prefectures in terms of size of establishment.

Thus, SMEs in Gifu tend to supply a variety of assemblers; they are generally not sole subcontractors. During the 1990s, the number of employees in metalworking and parts production fell by about 6 percent in that prefecture—a steeper fall than in Hitachi City. Despite this, however, sales by those SMEs in Gifu held their own during the same period—whereas they fell precipitously in Hitachi City.

One could argue that these two cases are extreme, and that I selected them merely because I knew they would support my hunch. Or one might argue that data for Hitachi City are skewed by the idiosyncratic performance of that area's leading manufacturer (Hitachi). To try to settle the matter, I visited a third location: Ōta Ward located in the Keihin industrial belt of southwest Tokyo. By the 1990s, this ward, which emerged as a center of military arms production in the 1930s and early 1940s, had perhaps the densest concentration of machinery subcontractors in all of Japan. Although it is populated by a number of large assemblers, its industrial structure is otherwise rather similar to Hitachi City. In the automobile and industrial machinery industries, Nakano (2004, 24) found that the typical Ōta supplier had a long-standing relationship with only one assembler. Subcontracting networks, he wrote, were "rather hierarchically vertical structures." Based on his survey of 167 metalworking and machinery manufacturing SMES in Ōta Ward, Fukushima (1998, 96) found that 43 percent consider themselves first-tier subcontractors, 32 percent consider themselves second-tier subcontractors, and nearly 10 percent view themselves as third-tier subcontractors.

Like Hitachi City and Gifu Prefecture, the number of employees in Ōta Ward fell during the first half of the 1990s. But like they did in Hitachi City, and unlike Gifu Prefecture, sales at these manufacturing plants fell even more sharply—by as much as 22 percent between 1990 and 1995.

Although my findings are merely suggestive, they are confirmed by other studies. Hashimoto (1997, 154–55) compares the Japanese model of industrial agglomeration, characterized by network cohesion and centralization, with more open networks in Silicon Valley and northern Italy. The former, he argues, stifled entrepreneurship, while the latter fostered it. And while Ibata-Arens (2005, 149) limits her analysis to Japan, she comes up with a similar conclusion by comparing Ōta Ward unfavorably with the Kyoto region. In the latter, she argues, SMEs had to learn to survive on their own creative energies—without the help of keiretsu networks. Out of necessity, they forged horizontal ties, looked outside Japan for new markets, and—over time—turned the Kyoto region into a "model of entrepreneurship and innovation."

Pressed by such arguments, the government appeared ready to change its position on the best industrial structure for Japan. MITI even established a commission to advise it on policies to nurture innovating, risk-taking small and medium-sized enterprises. The commission's final report (*Chūshō Kigyō Seisaku Kenkyūkai Saishū Hōkoku*), produced in May 1999, included a lengthy critique of existing government policies, but very few recommendations of its own.

For the most part, government strategy boiled down to finding new ways to increase public assistance for small business. For example, the commission proposed a relaxation of eligibility requirements for government programs, thereby allowing an additional sixteen thousand companies to call themselves "SMEs" and, if they so desired, to receive aid.[50] In addition, MITI offered to loan up to 5.5 million yen to unemployed or retired individuals who wished to start their own ventures.[51] The agency also proposed an expansion of its credit guarantee program for small business. Finally, it worked with local governments to help set up "venture foundations" to finance start-ups and "industrial clusters" to facilitate entrepreneurial activity.[52]

The results were underwhelming. In the case of local venture financing, eleven of the forty-seven foundations made no investments at all in fiscal 1998, and many others made fewer investments than they did the previous year. In the case of "industrial clusters," Ibata-Arens (2005, 213) called the central government's involvement "the kiss of death" for too many otherwise promising local initiatives. And while representatives of venture business groups praised the government's new commitment to entrepreneurship, they didn't seem impressed with the actual program. Ito Masaaki, founder of Smart Valley Japan, called it "more of the same":

> Government officials, business leaders, and even many academics keep talking about how to incorporate the new entrepreneur into Japan's industrial base. They are counting on the existing set-up, the organizations and systems already in place, to carry out some kind of revolution. This is the point I do not understand. The existing set-up is the problem.[53]

Indeed, this was one of those moments where the state might have done more by doing less. That is, instead of increasing public assistance to SMEs, Japanese government officials might have considered simply enforcing the Anti-Monopoly Act more vigorously, reducing regulatory barriers to entry, and, in the process, introducing stronger market incentives into the economy.

---

50. See the press release issued by JETRO on October 29, 1999, and posted on the web at http://www.jetro.org/newyork/focusnewsletter/focus8.html.
51. *Daily Yomiuri*, "MITI to Fund Small Business Start-ups," September 13, 1998.
52. *Nikkei Weekly*, "Economic Debate Focuses on Small Firms," November 8, 1999.
53. Interview, Tokyo, October 1, 1998.

Hollowing Out

Just as "deindustrialization" entered the vocabulary of Americans in the late 1970s and early 1980s, *kūdōka* (or "hollowing out") found its way into the Japanese lexicon in the 1990s. It was a confusing term that engendered controversy—primarily because it meant different things to different people.

To factory workers, it had everything to do with the number of manufacturing jobs in Japan. In the first half of the 1990s, Japanese manufacturers reduced their domestic labor force by more than one million employees—even as they hired an additional 520,000 workers for their overseas operations, including 436,000 in Asia.[54] But as I mentioned in chapter 5, labor leaders did not complain because manufacturers mitigated the effect on regular (chiefly male) employees in home-based prototype plants. Indeed, they worked overtime to hang on to those longtime employees. Ernst (2006, 172) describes it this way:

> To sustain jobs, especially for expensive knowledge workers, large Japanese firms attempt to sustain an unequal division of labor with Asia. They attempt to keep basic and applied research at home, plus "design work which promotes added value, and basic programming development," while product and system customization plus process adaptation are developed in major overseas markets such as the Asian NIES and China.

To business executives, *kūdōka* had to do with the quantity and quality of industrial linkages. As I mentioned in chapter 5, smaller manufacturers that were unable to secure the capital to join larger producers in the overseas exodus suddenly faced shrinking demand along with persistently high costs in the domestic market. The SME Agency (1996, 109) put it this way: "By encouraging the transfer of large corporate operations overseas, the high cost structure of the Japanese economy will at the same time deal a heavy body blow to small manufacturers in general and to those involved in the subcontract system in particular." Bigger, better-connected subcontractors, however, did not complain because they were able to follow their "parents" (major assemblers/customers) as they expanded into Asia.

To local governments, *kūdōka* had to do with the size of the tax base. Japan's rural areas were hit hard. In twelve of the smallest prefectures across Japan, the number of factories dropped by more than 5 percent between 1991 and 1997.[55] Tottori prefecture lost 11.1 percent of its manufacturing base during that time; Saga lost 10.7 percent; Fukui lost 9.6 percent.

---

54. Domestic employment statistics come from Management and Coordination Agency, *Rōdōryoku Chōsa Tokubetsu Chōsa* (Special Survey on the Labor Force); overseas employment figures come from MITI, *Wagakuni Kigyō no Kaigai Jigyō Katsudō.*

55. *Nihon Keizai Shinbun*, "Chihō Eigyō Kyoten Genshō ga Kasoku," August 4, 1997, 1.

Kikai Shinkō Kyōkai (1994, 68–71) reported that two-thirds of Japanese automakers and nearly half of electrical machine manufacturers were planning to reduce domestic capacity and expand overseas production. This shift was most pronounced in rural Japan, where 77 percent of firms in the automobile industry and 51 percent of firms in the electronics industry planned to replace domestic production capacity with new or expanded manufacturing overseas. Unsurprisingly, Asia was the favorite destination. Two-thirds of the surveyed manufacturers (and a whopping 80 percent of electrical machine manufacturers based in rural prefectures) were expanding operations in that region. In the first half of the 1990s, Japanese manufacturing investment in Asia increased dramatically while manufacturing investment in new plant and equipment in rural Japan dropped sharply.[56]

To the central government, *kūdōka* seemed to have a lot to do with the nation's trade balance. In the 1990s, MITI (1998a, 71–74) developed a complex metric to evaluate the impact of Japanese FDI on exports and imports (and, to be fair, on Japan's domestic production and employment as well). In making these calculations, it began with the assumption that Japanese investment in Asia (and, indeed, in the world at large) yields three direct effects on the domestic economy of Japan. One of these, which is positive, is an "export stimulation effect," an increase in Japanese exports, particularly capital and intermediate goods used by overseas affiliates. The other two are negative: an "import effect," an increase in reverse imports from overseas affiliates, and an "export displacement effect," a decrease in the volume of Japanese exports that now are produced by overseas affiliates.[57]

MITI (1998a, 68) found that Japanese FDI had a net positive effect on Japan's trade balance in the 1991–93 period, but a negative and worsening effect in 1994 and 1995. It attributed this deterioration to a trend on the part of overseas affiliates to purchase more parts from local suppliers (including other Japanese affiliates) in the host country, as well as a growing volume of reverse imports from overseas affiliates. (As expected, Asia is the leading source for those imports. In a separate study, JETRO (1998, 18) asked parent companies in Japan to identify the region they rely on most

56. Economic Planning Agency (1995, 291), and Industrial Bank of Japan (1995, 3).

57. The "export stimulation effect" is equivalent to the volume of investment in plant and equipment by overseas affiliates x the share of capital goods they import from Japan, plus the volume of parts procurement by overseas affiliates x the share of such components they import from Japan. The "import effect" equals the volume of sales by overseas affiliates x the share of their sales to Japan. The "export displacement effect," the most controversial measure, is the volume of sales by overseas affiliates x (1—ratio of sales to Japan) x Japan's share of world exports. Legewie (1997) does a good job of critiquing the methodology used in MITI (1995b, 33–41) to calculate direct effects. In particular, he notes that trade barriers erected by foreign governments make it unlikely that FDI is displacing as many exports as the model predicts. MITI revised its methodology in 1998 based on the impressive econometric analysis of Fukao and Amano (1998), who concluded that Japan was indeed hollowing.

for reverse imports; 81 percent said Asia.) The direct impact on domestic production and employment, according to MITI (1998a, 69–70), turned negative even sooner. Thus, by the central government's definition, FDI did indeed contribute to the hollowing out of Japan in the 1990s.[58]

Despite this finding, MITI (1996, 78) joined business and labor elites in pushing for the continued regionalization of Japan's domestic political economy: "To maintain their international competitiveness, Japanese corporations have no choice but to invest overseas, setting up and expanding production, distribution, development, and supply networks in those markets."

In reality, of course, hollowing out—like globalization—can be both "good" *and* "bad." That is, it can hurt real people, especially the weak; but it also can foster positive economic change, creating new opportunities for investment through a reallocation of resources. Japan in the 1990s probably experienced too much "bad" hollowing out (with its distributional effects on women, small business, rural prefectures, and so on) and too little "good" hollowing out (because Japanese FDI reflected elite regionalization).[59] Let me explain.

Neoclassical economists believe that FDI tends to generate indirect effects on the home economy that will more than compensate for any negative direct effects. For example, Legewie (1997, 21) notes that "FDI can lead to a strengthening of the global competitiveness of companies investing abroad," and this, in turn, should lead to increased production and employment in the multinational firm's home country. And Kwan (1997), using modern trade theory, argues that FDI typically brings about a more efficient allocation of production factors in the investing country, thereby raising real income.

If we apply this logic to the case of Japan, we should expect to find, among other things, a positive and significant correlation between a Japanese firm's overseas production ratio and the efficiency (and thus profitability) of its domestic operations. That is, parent firms (or industries) that produce a larger amount of their total output in overseas factories (relative to firms that concentrate more on domestic production) should also enjoy higher

58. We should acknowledge, however, that MITI was internally divided over *kūdōka* and what kind of threat it actually represented. MITI researchers (Nakamura and Shibuya 1995, 31–33) represented the mainstream. They downplayed the threat, saying Japanese manufacturers were retaining R&D facilities and prototype production plants in Japan even as they expanded mass production overseas. On the other hand, the MITI Industrial Policy Bureau (1996, 100) warned that, without countermeasures to stimulate domestic investment, Japan would lose 1.24 million jobs domestic jobs in the second half of the 1990s. The alarmists within MITI were proven wrong—thanks to the nature of elite regionalization (as well as the depreciation of the yen and the Asian financial crisis, both of which slowed down the otherwise torrid pace of FDI).

59. These very real distributional effects make me unwilling to agree with Ishiyama (1996), who boldly argues that Japan did not experience *enough* hollowing out in the 1990s.

profit margins relative to firms that concentrate more on producing at home. The Economic Planning Agency (1995, 282–83) conducted its own statistical test, fully expecting to confirm this standard assumption of neoclassical economic theory. But it could not. The analysis showed that the relative earnings-to-sales ratio of Japanese parent firms in 1992 was only very weakly correlated with the overseas production ratio. More interestingly, when it confined its analysis to FDI in Asia, it found that the relative profitability of Japanese parents actually *fell* as their overseas production ratio rose (relative to other firms that stayed home).[60] (Of course, parent firms are able to repatriate a large share of the profits earned by their Asian affiliates; thus, they still can achieve a net gain from FDI in spite of losses incurred at domestic operations.)

If we again apply the standard assumptions of neoclassical economic theory to the case of Japanese FDI in Asia, we should find that *kūdōka* comes with new opportunities for more productive investment in the home country. Indeed, this is what happened in the United States in the 1980s. Deindustrialization was associated with industrial upgrading as labor-intensive manufacturing steadily yielded to more technology-intensive activities.[61] But this virtuous cycle did not occur in Japan in the 1990s. New high-tech industries did not take root. Okina and Kōsaka (1996, 46) note one important difference: "Japan's industrial hollowing out derives from not only an exodus of manufacturing industry, but also the inability of foreign companies to set up operations in Japan," and thereby replace lost capital. In 1997, the ratio of outward investment by Japanese manufacturers to inward investment by foreign manufacturers was 9:1, which reflects the costs of relationalism manifested in exclusionary and inflexible capital and labor markets. Here, the "outsiders" are literally just that: foreign firms who find it difficult to enter a Japanese market characterized by strong relational ties.

This, finally, moves us closer to understanding why observed results diverge from neoclassical assumptions. The answer is this: relational ties—not unfettered market forces—drove the Japanese political economy for many years, even through the 1990s. In other words, the hollowing out of the Jap-

---

60. The EPA study actually measured industries, not firms. That is, it tested the impact of the overseas (or regional) production ratio (X) of a given industry on its domestic earning/sales ratio (Y). For both tests (overseas and regional production ratios), the profitability of the automobile and electronics industries fell below the regression line. In the case of overseas production in total, the coefficient for X was +0.22; in the case of overseas production in Asia, the coefficient was –0.48. The EPA test relied on data from MITI's comprehensive 1992 survey of firms with overseas operations.

61. Although employment in the U.S. manufacturing sector has fallen steadily since the 1940s, output in that sector has remained remarkably stable—even during the decade of the 1980s. This is a function of the high rate of productivity growth in manufacturing relative to other sectors of the U.S. economy, particularly services. See, for example, Clarida and Hickok (1993) and Rowthorn and Ramaswamy (1997).

anese economy was not accompanied by any significant reallocation of the factors of production because those factors (capital, labor, technology) were dedicated to particular relationships, and were thus "sticky." As recently as 2002, Japanese manufacturers with overseas operations were confiding to government officials that they were trying very hard to retain their domestic operations and employment by moving into higher-value-added production at home, but they were experiencing a variety of problems in doing so. Among other things, they said they found it difficult to relocate and retrain domestic workers to face new challenges. Based on interviews with nearly one hundred firms, the JBIC Institute (2003, 26) concluded that "this [desired] shift in domestic operations is not simple."

As noted earlier, investments in relational ties are equivalent to sunk costs, and central members of established networks will not blithely walk away from such investments. Instead of fostering a reallocation of production factors and structural adjustment in Japan, the regionalization of the domestic political economy merely eased the short-term costs of "sticky" relationalism. By expanding their operations into Asia, Japanese firms helped preserve relational ties at home while extending them across a wider geographical space.

PART THREE
The New Millennium

7 Grounding Asia's Flying Geese

In the early and mid-1990s, elite regionalization protected Japan's political economy from the "creative destruction" of globalization. This was a fine thing for Japan's well-positioned and thus powerful insiders: the bureaucrats who held top posts in the leading economic ministries, the managers who ran Japan's largest multinational corporations, and the regular employees who enjoyed long-term employment in those corporations. They all welcomed this outcome. But this unlikely prolongation of the status quo imposed perverse consequences on almost everyone else in Japan, especially younger and female workers, and on the Japanese economy as a whole. These outsiders longed for structural change in a system that had turned them into uncompensated losers.

Change, though limited in character and scope, finally came to Japan in the very late 1990s, when the destructive forces of globalization began to outweigh the protective forces of elite regionalization, when Japanese government and business elites steadily lost positional power in Asia, and when the flying geese pattern, with Japan positioned as the lead goose, fell apart. In the next chapter, I show how Japan's political economy slowly began to adopt a new form; in this chapter, meanwhile, I pinpoint the source of that change in the external environment.

By the new millennium, Japanese capital and technology no longer dominated the region: FDI flows from Japan in the 1998–2000 period thinned to half what they had been in the gung-ho period of 1995–97, while flows from the United States expanded.[1] Indeed, U.S. manufacturers hungry for mergers and acquisitions pumped more than $21 billion into the region

1. United Nations Conference on Trade and Development, *World Investment Report*, 2000 and 2002.

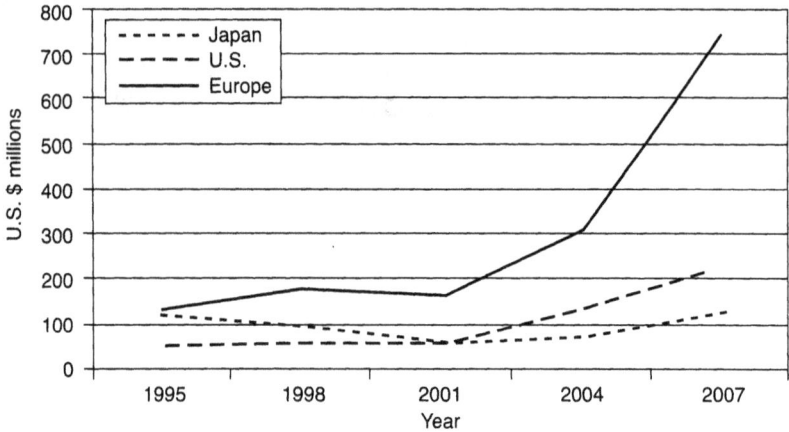

Figure 7.1. Bank claims on Asia
Source: Calculated by author from Bank of International Settlements, table 9B (consolidated banking statements, time series).

during those three years, while Japanese manufacturers invested less than $14 billion.[2] And Japanese banks, longtime leaders in commercial financing in Asia, were eclipsed by their European rivals; by 2002, they held $99.8 billion in outstanding loans, while European banks held $376 billion—nearly four times more.[3] Since then, as figure 7.1 shows, the gap has widened much further. In addition, the Japanese state no longer exerted unrivaled influence in Asia, even in what had seemed to be quasi-imperial outposts such as Bangkok or Kuala Lumpur.

"We used to think of Southeast Asia as our exclusive playground, but we can't anymore," a METI official said wistfully in an October 2003 interview. "There are too many other important players there now."

Four related events conspired to undermine the positional power of Japanese elites in Asia and ground the flying geese. One was the Japanese innovation crisis of the mid-1990s, which prompted Japanese MNCs to increasingly restrict the flow of technology to non-Japanese partners in the region, which in turn caused host country business and political elites to protest what they called self-serving policies and practices. Another was the Asian financial crisis of the late 1990s, which ultimately helped to dislodge Japanese corporate interests from their central positions in the region's network structure. The third event was the rise of China, which used its position

2. U.S. data come from the Bureau of Economic Analysis, while Japanese data come from Ministry of Finance. Both U.S. and Japanese authorities define "Asia" to include South Asia, but the U.S. definition also includes Australia and New Zealand.

3. Bank for International Settlements, "BIS Consolidated Banking Statements," table 9.

as a seemingly endless supplier of cheap labor to attract capital and technology from multiple sources and emerge as a fast-flying rival to the lead goose in Asia's economic development pattern. The fourth and final event was a gradual but steady decline in Japan's official development assistance to Asia, undermining support for Japanese economic interests in the region. I will consider each of these events individually.

Regional Backlash

In chapter 3, I identified a paradox that became painfully obvious in the early 1990s: while Asian elites, especially government officials and academics, complained loudly about the restrictions placed on the use of Japanese technology, evidence showed that local manufacturers often preferred to do business with Japanese rather than Western MNCs. I explained this by noting that host country business executives generally sought profits rather than autonomy: the strings that came attached to Japanese technology were equivalent to network ties that linked them profitably to Japanese banks, suppliers, and distributors, and to the Japanese government. As long as they continued to gain a large share of the benefits of those network ties, local manufacturers were also willing to bear the costs.

By the mid-1990s, however, the costs often seemed to outweigh the benefits. Japanese technological innovation began to slow dramatically in the 1990s, a consequence of continuing to rely on an outmoded model of political economy (selective relationalism) to drive production. The result was that Japanese firms ultimately found themselves with less and less technology to transfer. Although they continued to shift manufacturing to sites in South Korea, Southeast Asia, and Greater China (the mainland, Hong Kong, and Taiwan), they tried to hold on ever tighter to their production know-how. This fact is starkly evident in figures on the transfer of technology from Japan to Asia.

In the 1990s, the Asian affiliates of Japanese firms secured a large share of Japan's technology licenses to the region. In fact, the transfer of technical knowledge from Japanese parent firms to their own subsidiaries and affiliates in Asia came to account for half of all the nation's technology exports to the region. The trend was particularly pronounced in the case of China, where such intrafirm deals accounted for only 21.4 percent of all technology exports in 1992 but 71.9 percent in 1995.[4]

As Japanese MNCs tightened their grip on the technology they transferred to Asia, host country elites began to resist more and more often, and more and more dramatically. Here are just two examples of how government officials in Asia finally began to act on such complaints.

4. Science and Technology Agency, computer printouts.

In the mid-1990s, Mahathir bin Mohamad, then the prime minister of Malaysia, traveled to France and signed an agreement with Citroën to collaborate on the production of a small passenger car, the Tiara. This represented a complete about-face for Mahathir, who in the 1980s had launched a "Look East" policy designed to emulate Japan's model of development and who had invited MMC, the Japanese automaker, to get behind the wheel of his national car project, the Proton. As the experienced partner in the joint venture, MMC supplied both capital and technology for Proton's early models: the Saga, the Wira, and the Perdana. But Mahathir began to openly grumble that MMC was refusing to allow Malaysian firms to play an important role in manufacturing the engine, transmission, and other critical components. So he did what had been unthinkable: he bypassed Malaysia's longtime mentor and reached out to Europe. "We want to learn from the French, for instance, in design, sophistication, and so on. We don't want to remain bound to one source" (*International Herald Tribune,* August 11, 1994).

About the same time, the U.S. auto giant General Motors was trying to set up a massive plant to assemble the Opel Zafira in Thailand, but immediately ran into a wall. Japanese MNCs completely dominated the market, not only for vehicle assembly but also for parts production. One after another, Thai-based suppliers refused to sign contracts with GM. "A number of them said they could not do business with us," recalled a GM executive.[5] Frustrated, the giant manufacturer asked the Thai government to waive a stringent (54%) requirement for domestic content, thereby allowing GM to source components from around the world. The Thai government, which had, until then, seemed beholden to Japanese interests, surprised nearly everyone by agreeing. Indeed, its Board of Investment soon went even further by issuing a formal invitation to American and European automakers to set up additional plants in Thailand. With evident pique, it complained that "the Japanese have never been keen on transferring design and engineering expertise to their Thai counterparts" and encouraged Western firms to enter the host country market "through joint ventures with wholly owned Thai firms with minimal keiretsu ties."[6]

From Market Domination to Competition

In June 1997, the Thai baht collapsed and a financial crisis spread quickly, like a contagious disease, throughout much of Asia. As markets dried up and credit tightened, Japanese economic and political elites faced a radical

5. Telephone interview, September 23, 1997.
6. Thai Board of Investment, "Investment Opportunities Study," 1995.

new challenge: How could they manage to hold on to the positional power they had come to enjoy in the region?

Japanese parent firms tried to stabilize their tottering production bases by investing additional capital in affiliates and providing special support for subcontractors. The Japanese state, fearing the worst, offered a massive new commitment of foreign aid, including the $30 billion Miyazawa Initiative, a portion of which targeted home-based firms operating in Asia. These extraordinary measures kept the patient alive in the short run, but proved insufficient in the long run. Japanese assemblers such as Matsushita and Toyota had to curtail production, and in turn many of the smallest and most vulnerable subcontractors—who had supplied parts to those assemblers—ultimately had to close their Asian facilities. The regional web of production and administrative networks became badly frayed.

It is true, of course, that crises typically create opportunities as well as challenges; and this crisis was, at least for outsiders, no exception. Distressed firms in cities such as Jakarta and Seoul became available for purchase at fire-sale prices, host countries relaxed restrictions on foreign investment, and exports from those economies with depreciated currencies suddenly became cheaper, and thus more competitive. But Japanese MNCs proved far less nimble than their Western counterparts in moving to seize those opportunities. In particular, U.S. firms, such as Proctor & Gamble, Hewlett-Packard, and Seagram, used mergers and acquisitions to dramatically increase their presence in the region. In 1999 alone, they invested $5.8 billion in such deals, which accounted for 23 percent of all merger and acquisition (M&A) purchases in Asia that year (Hamilton-Hart 2004, 139). In the automobile industry, completely dominated until then by Japan, Western firms finally gained an Asian foothold by buying shares in Japanese firms burdened with debt: Renault in Nissan, Ford in Mazda, Daimler-Chrysler in MMC.

With the exception of consumer goods such as appliances and audio-video systems, Western MNCs already had won a significant market share in Asia's (and especially China's) electrical and electronics industry. Now, responding swiftly to new opportunities, they were managing to claim turf, even in Southeast Asia, that once had been controlled exclusively by Japanese MNCs. By 2003, the Japanese government was fretting openly. In its white paper on trade and investment, JETRO (2003, 49) acknowledged the new reality: "The ASEAN region is becoming a major battleground for the countries of Europe, North America, and elsewhere, which are seeking to reap the benefits of strengthened cooperation within the region."

In addition, indigenous Asian firms became increasingly competitive in high-tech industries such as semiconductors, computers, DVD players, liquid crystal displays (LCDs), and plasma display panels (PDPs). Taiwanese and

Chinese firms came out of the crisis relatively unscathed, able to invest heavily in new technology, while Korean firms emerged smaller but smarter and stronger than ever. By 2004, for example, two such Korean manufacturers —Samsung and LG Electronics—came close to cornering half of the global market for PDPs. Although some Japanese authors, reminiscent of Western writers in the 1980s, have blamed this development on technology piracy, including rather flagrant violations of intellectual property rights,[7] a more likely explanation is that Asian nations in the late 1990s, much like Japan in an earlier period, found ways to channel relatively cheap financial capital and relatively strong human capital into dynamic, emerging industries. Asia was no longer a largely Japanese game.

Chinese Leapfrog

In 1992, Deng Xiaoping toured the special economic zones of southern China and committed the Communist Party to further market reforms to accelerate the pace of development. As China became markedly more open to foreign investment and imports, its economy grew faster and its political leaders grew more assertive in the region. In the process, it challenged the flying geese structure in which China, once a technological laggard, had brought up the rear of the flock.

With its abundant supply of cheap and disciplined labor, China emerged in the late 1990s as one of the most attractive investment sites in the world —and certainly the most attractive in Asia. In the automobile industry, Western firms such as Volkswagen rushed in to capture a first-mover's advantage. In the electronics industry, Beijing and local governments encouraged foreign firms to establish export-oriented facilities, but also required them to compete against one another for coveted licenses and contracts.[8] The race was on. While the Middle Kingdom received only 36 percent of FDI flows to China and ASEAN in the period between 1988 and 1992, it was, by the end of the decade, receiving about 72 percent (MacIntyre and Naughton 2005, 87). Global manufacturers began to concentrate on China, often shifting

---

7. See, for example, *Shūkan Tōyō Keizai*, "Kan-tai-chū '10-nen sensō'ni hangeki kaishi: Soshi se yo! Nihon no gijutsu ryūshutsu" (Launching a Counterattack in the "10-Year War" with Korea, Taiwan, and China: Block the Outflow of Japanese Technology!), August 28, 2004, 28–39.

8. By welcoming foreign investors, China behaved quite differently from Japan (circa 1950–80). But it actually adopted a very similar position on technology transfer. In the electronics industry, in particular, Beijing restricted entry into final assembly and key components production, and often awarded licenses and contracts to MNCs that agreed to share technology with local manufacturers. For more on this, see Marukawa Tomoo, "Towards a Strategic Realignment of Production Networks: Japanese Electronics Companies in China," http://www.iss .u-tokyo.ac.jp/~marukawa/towardastrategic.pdf.

operations from other locations, especially other locations in Southeast Asia. Although Japanese MNCs had built entrenched and often protected positions in the markets of ASEAN, they, too, felt the tug.

In January 2004 I visited a Matsushita affiliate in Malaysia that had once prospered by manufacturing air conditioners and exporting them to 120 different countries, including dozens in Asia and Europe. Now, however, the plant was barely able to hold its own, according to Yasuda Shuji, the general manager of MAICO Malaysia. "We are struggling to keep up with low price competition in China," he told me. It turned out that MAICO's chief competitor was a plant in Guangzhou, China—owned by none other than Matsushita, which by that time had fifty-eight subsidiaries in the Middle Kingdom. "I am not sure how we can survive," Yasuda confided.

China has emerged as an important nexus in a restructured web of production networks in East Asia. Known as "the factory to the world," an export superpower, Greater China began to account for the largest share of Asia's extraregional exports in 2000—surpassing even Japan's share (35% to 33%) (MacIntyre and Naughton, 89–90). And it began to heavily import capital goods and parts, especially through intraindustry and intrafirm ties, from ethnic Chinese capitalists in Southeast Asia, as well as from Korea and Japan. In 2003, China replaced the United States as South Korea's leading trade partner; a year later, it replaced the United States as Japan's leading partner.

On the political front, China emerged in the new millennium as a leader in the new game of regional integration, a game increasingly played as much by formal rules as by informal networks. In 2001, it began negotiating with Southeast Asian states to form a China-ASEAN free trade agreement that would dramatically reduce tariffs on trade between the two parties. About the same time, China proposed an "early harvest program" to speed up the liberalization of trade in seven thousand commodities. ASEAN elites welcomed the Chinese initiative. Supachai Panitchpakdi, the former deputy prime minister of Thailand who became director-general of the World Trade Organization (WTO) and then secretary-general of UNCTAD (United Nations Conference on Trade and Development), predicted that Southeast Asia would enjoy a new but longer-lasting period of economic growth by tying itself more closely with China: "This growth would be more sustainable than previous periods of rapid expansion because intra-Asian trade will be enhanced so much that it will override any fluctuations or vicissitudes coming from the rest of the world."[9]

Thailand was the first member of ASEAN to take advantage of the offer; in October 2003, it forged a bilateral agreement with China to liberalize

9. See Michael Richardson, "ASEAN Is Ready to Embrace Market: Southeast Asia Sees China as Export Market," *International Herald Tribune*, April 27, 2002.

trade in 188 agricultural commodities, excluding rice. Trade between the two countries is now dominated by the China Certification and Inspection Company (CCIC), a joint venture between a Chinese state-owned enterprise, Chinese MNCs in Thailand, and some of Thailand's largest conglomerates. The CCIC, which not only handles trade logistics but also conducts research on Thailand's agricultural industry, is doing the kind of work that used to be done by general trading companies from Japan, such as Mitsui and Mitsubishi.[10]

Perhaps most important, China is slowly but surely emerging as a technological power with strong local firms such as Haier, Konka, and TCL. Party-state elites, guided by the same techno-nationalism that informed Japanese bureaucrats during and after World War II, invited foreign manufacturers to operate in China, but did far more than bureaucrats in ASEAN to help wrest control of production know-how. They refused to allow any one supplier of foreign capital and technology to dominate the Chinese market, and instead encouraged vigorous competition between U.S., European, Japanese, Korean, and Taiwanese MNCs.[11] They required foreign firms to forge joint ventures with local firms, many of them state-owned enterprises, and strategically failed to enforce rules designed to protect intellectual property rights.

History—specifically, what the Chinese refer to as "a century of humiliation" at the hands of foreign powers—has shaped this policy approach. During the first half of the twentieth century, China suffered bitterly under Japanese occupation and regional hegemony. As a consequence, its elites are almost obsessively wary of any regionalization scheme promoted by their Japanese counterparts. This skepticism is expressed cogently by Ding Xinghao of the Shanghai Institute of International Studies: "Japan's view is always a flying geese formation with Japan as the head goose. Our memories are long, so we aren't about to fly in Japan's formation."[12]

From the very beginning, this posed an obvious challenge for Japanese government and business elites. Across the rest of the region, they had made deep inroads by inviting their Asian counterparts to join administrative and

---

10. Suehiro Akira, "The Creation of an 'East Asian Community,' or Odd Japan Out," in *Social Science Japan* 28 (March 2004): 5.

11. China has what Myrdal (1968) might consider a "hard" state, or what Migdal (1988) would call a "strong" state. That is, the Chinese state is at least semiautonomous; it is not captured by powerful social interests. Political elites are thus able to develop long-term policy objectives based on their interpretation of the national interest, which largely has to do with protecting the integrity and sovereignty of the nation-state. This is evident in the way they deal with foreign investors; they oppose technology agreements that subordinate the state's long-term strategic interests to short-run commercial interests.

12. Quoted in Chalmers Johnson, "The Problem of Japan in an Era of Structural Change," Research Report 89–04, Graduate School of International Relations and Pacific Studies, University of California at San Diego, June 1989, p. 19.

production networks that they created and dominated. Although Japanese elites had managed to re-create such networks in a few places in China, such as in the port city of Dalian (located in what used to be Japan's puppet state of Manchukuo), they generally were unable to acquire the kind of positional power they enjoyed in the rest of Asia. Now, with China flexing its economic and political muscles throughout the region, Japanese elites find they are unable to hold onto the pivotal positions in networks they constructed during the 1990s.[13]

Less ODA for Asia

In the 1990s, Tokyo used its official development assistance (ODA, or foreign aid) to help Japanese MNCs, as well as Japanese bureaucrats, maintain their positional power in Asia. The Miyazawa Initiative, discussed in chapters 3 and 5, was simply the most recent and dramatic example of this effort. But as Japan's economic woes continued into the new millennium, and as multilateral lending organizations, led by the United States and the United Kingdom, placed new pressures on Japan, Tokyo found that it could sustain neither the high volume nor the commercial nature of its aid to developing Asia.

Most simply, a cash-strapped Japanese government began trimming its overall ODA budget in FY 1998. Three years later (FY 2001), Japan lost its much ballyhooed standing, one that it had enjoyed for a decade, as the world's leading aid donor, and nine years later (FY 2007), its aid budget had fallen to just 62 percent of its peak level.

In the immediate aftermath of the Asian financial crisis, these cuts did not dramatically affect Japan's aid to the region in which it operated as "lead goose." This is because the share of Japanese ODA to Asia actually increased during those years. In fact, as recently as 2002, the region continued to receive a traditionally large share (60.7%) of Japan's total bilateral ODA. But by 2006, the region's share had fallen to only 26.8 percent (see figure 7.2). Other areas of the world, particularly war-torn Afghanistan and a variety of desperately poor nations in Africa, began to receive far greater attention.

In addition, Japanese ODA began to lose its unabashedly commercial orientation. As noted in chapter 3, Japan was unique among international donors

13. In the past, Japanese elites fared best in China by working closely with local governments rather than with Beijing. Interprovincial competition for foreign capital and technology allowed them to mediate China's incorporation into the emerging regional economy. Breslin (1996, 485) makes a similar point, arguing that Japanese corporate interests "have done much to shape the pattern of China's integration into the regional economy." In the new millennium, however, China finds itself less and less dependent on Japanese elites for access to resources in the regional economy.

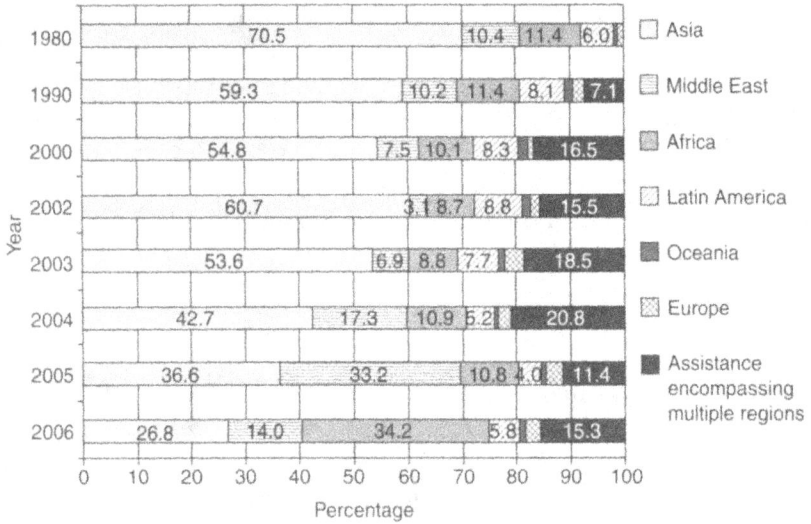

Figure 7.2. Japanese bilateral ODA by region
Source: Ministry of Foreign Affairs, *Japan's ODA White Paper,* 2007.

of aid for prioritizing economic growth ahead of humanitarian relief; specifi-cally, it emphasized yen loans for infrastructure projects rather than grants for social services, and its aid was often "tied"—explicitly or implicitly—to the use of Japanese contractors. But in the new millennium, Japan returned to its ear-lier commitment to "untie" its aid;[14] Kawai and Takagi (2004, 265) found that Japanese contractors were, by 2004, on the receiving end of only 15 percent of their government's "soft" loans to foreign countries. And while Japanese ODA retained a distinctive emphasis on loans, the share of new development lend-ing in its overall aid budget fell steadily in the new millennium. One way to measure this is to look at the amount of aid set aside for social infrastructure, economic infrastructure, and production sectors, as opposed to, say, human services. That amount, as recorded by the Development Assistance Commit-tee (DAC) of the OECD, was 87 percent of Japanese ODA in 1990 (23% for so-cial infrastructure, 32% for economic infrastructure, and 17% for production sectors) and 74 percent in 2000 (27%, 37%, and 10%); but by 2004, it had de-clined to 59 percent (22%, 30%, and 7%).[15]

14. As noted in chapter 5, the process of "untying" yen loans, which began in the 1970s, came to an abrupt halt in the 1990s, when the government decided to target Japanese MNCs in its program to promote the reconstruction of Asia. This was spelled out most explicitly in the Special Yen Loans Facility, a part of the 1998 Miyazawa Initiative. As Hook and Zhang (1998, 1066) state, "Japanese foreign economic interests were again openly acknowledged as the pri-mary concern guiding the government's aid policy."

15. Data from DAC, "International Development Statistics," http://oecd.org/dataoecd/50/17/5037721.htm.

This did not happen without a struggle. In response to pressure from the OECD and the World Bank, which encouraged donors to focus on poverty alleviation in very poor states in Africa and elsewhere, the Japanese government engaged in a bitter policy dispute. On one side, the Ministry of Foreign Affairs (MOFA) convened various committees—such as the Enshakkan Kondankai (Advisory Committee on Yen Loans), which completed its deliberations in August 2000, and the Dainiji ODA Kaikaku Kondankai (Second Advisory Committee on ODA Reform), which published its interim report in August 2001—that appeared to support the international consensus. On the other side, METI set up its own research group that strongly opposed that consensus. In a policy brief prepared for METI, Kimura (2001) called for a two-pronged approach to ODA: humanitarian aid for desperately poor countries and a development program for Asia based on a regionwide industrial policy. In a separate and even more defiant brief, Ohno (2001) encouraged METI to reject the "Western way" of ODA and continue to pursue Japan's long-standing agenda of promoting "Asian dynamism" by strengthening the existing regional production network. MOFA ultimately won the policy war. The Koizumi cabinet, which assumed control of the government in 2001, showed more and more interest in reorganizing and centralizing the complex ODA bureaucracy in a manner that would eventually give greater authority to the Ministry of Foreign Affairs (MOFA), thereby diminishing the influence of MOF, METI, and—consequently—Japan's business interests.[16] He appointed Ogata Sadako, formerly the UN High Commissioner for Refugees, as head of JICA, and began talking about aid in language more familiar to his Western allies. More specifically, the prime minister began to describe aid as a tool to promote "human security," environmental protection, and poverty alleviation, rather than as a tool to promote dynamic technological growth or a "flying geese" pattern of economic development in Asia. At the same time, he floated the idea of giving nongovernmental organizations (NGOs), then subordinate to the ODA bureaucracy, a greater and more independent role in the delivery of aid (Hirata 2002). In 2003, this new discourse was enshrined in Japan's revised ODA charter. Five years later, in 2008, JICA, still under the thumb of MOFA, became the lead aid implementing agency as it absorbed the

---

16. Obviously, this transition did not occur overnight. Even as recently as 2003, METI was exercising considerable influence over Japan's ODA policy. The ministry announced in April of that year that it planned to use aid to China and Southeast Asian nations as a means of bolstering domestic business interests. It even threatened to cut ODA to specific countries that failed to take actions designed to help Japanese MNCs in the region. *Asahi Shinbun* (April 8, 2003) quoted a METI official: "If the investment climate for Japanese firms doesn't improve, it's possible aid payments may fall, since we couldn't justify such assistance to the Japanese public."

"soft loan" functions of JBIC.[17] As one might imagine, JBIC viewed this as a palace coup; on the eve of the takeover, one bank executive told me bluntly, "We're being castrated" (*uchi wa kyosei sarete iru*).[18]

As a result of all these changes, Japanese ODA no longer serves to buttress embattled networks in the domestic political economy by promoting elite regionalization in Asia. Business executives based in the region certainly notice the difference, and have begun to complain that that they no longer get any significant help from Tokyo. "Japanese leaders should be doing more," gripes Harashima Nobuyoshi, a vice president in Hitachi's Beijing office. "Every other country is gung-ho now in trying to be the top salesman in China."[19]

A New Pattern: Horizontal Integration

As noted in chapter 3, Japanese production networks in East Asia were organized during the 1990s into vertical hierarchies engaged predominantly in a triangular trade pattern, where Japanese parents supplied high-tech components for assembly at overseas plants, which then exported finished goods to markets in the United States and Europe. That pattern, elite regionalization of Japanese networks, brought about the worst kind of "hollowing out" or deindustrialization for Japan because it kept domestic resources from being reallocated and thus locked in the status quo. Thanks to the confluence of events described earlier in this chapter, that pattern is now becoming obsolete. By 2001, these Japanese networks were increasingly producing goods for local consumption in Asia, or for the Japanese market ("reverse imports"), and they were increasingly securing parts from suppliers in the host country. In addition, they increasingly relied on local capital and technology, thereby moving from a vertical to a horizontal division of labor within the region.

One can certainly overstate the nature of these developments. As I noted in chapter 3, one of Japan's best-known economists has found that Japanese MNCs continue to be slow in localizing their Asian operations. Compared to U.S. and European firms in the region, Fukao (2006) reports that Japanese multinationals are still relying heavily on Japanese-affiliated parts suppliers, and continue to lean heavily on Japanese expatriate managers. And in a 2006 survey of more than one thousand Japanese affiliates in Asia, the JBIC

17. MOFA denied a newspaper's report that, despite the ODA reorganization plan scheduled to take effect in 2008, it had struck a secret deal with MOF to allow the finance ministry to maintain its role in providing "soft loans" to foreign governments. See *Japan Times*, "Secret Deal on ODA Authority," February 23, 2006.

18. Interview, Tokyo, July 4, 2007.

19. *Business Yahoo*, "Japanese Companies in China Want More Support from Japanese Government," April 11, 2002.

Institute (2007, 56–57) found that 44 percent were continuing to complain about a shortage of indigenous Asian suppliers with sufficient technological skills, while 43 percent of affiliates were still bemoaning the lack of local Asian managers who were both qualified and not too expensive to hire. Consequently, as recently as 2006, 72 percent of Japanese SMEs operating overseas were in Asia, and 59.4 percent of expatriate managers dispatched to Japanese affiliates around the world were in Asia.[20]

The Japanese government continues to use the region as a laboratory for new industrial policies. In 2004, for example, METI launched a new program to help credit-hungry Japanese MNCs secure funding for their local operations in Asia. Smaller firms, in particular, had complained that many Japanese banks have withdrawn from the region or curtailed lending, and that they do not have sufficiently close ties with host country banks to secure credit. Under the new policy, an expansion of the ministry's trade insurance system (Nippon Export and Investment Insurance or NEXI), the government guarantees bonds issued in the local currency.

Overall, however, the evidence points to a gradual but significant change in the pattern of regionalization, a change that was eagerly anticipated by Seki Mitsuhiro in 1997, when he wrote that, if Japan embedded itself more thoroughly and less defensively in Asia, the region would eventually evolve "from a 'flying geese pattern of development' to a 'single plane of development'" (247). Japanese MNCs, he wrote, would learn to fly alongside their Asian counterparts, forging more equal partnerships and transferring technology more freely. Likewise, this change was highlighted by Ernst (2006, 186), when he wrote that the Japanese electronics industry "now critically depends on the region, not only as a global export production base, but also as a major and increasingly sophisticated market for its products, services and technology, and as a source of lower-cost knowledge workers."

Consider, first of all, the change in the direction of sales by Japanese MNCs in Asia. In the mid-1990s, those manufacturing affiliates, especially electronics firms, sold a relatively large share of their production in Western markets, but relatively little in the Japanese home market or in the local market. In 1990, exports to Japan (also known as reverse imports) accounted for only 12 percent of total sales by Japanese manufacturing affiliates in Asia; by the end of the decade, they accounted for nearly 25 percent of total sales.[21] Even vehicle makers got into the act; in 2002, Honda and Yamaha

20. Data on SMEs come from JBIC Institute (2007, 69), which surveyed 1,071 Japanese SMEs operating overseas, including 774 in Asia. Data on expatriate managers come from *Kaigai Shinshutsu Kigyō Sōran* (Directory of Japanese MNCs), published annually by Tōyō Keizai Shinpōsha. In its 2006 survey, the researchers found that Japanese MNCs dispatched 46,057 people to overseas affiliates, including 27,354 who landed in Asia.

21. METI, *Kaigai Jigyō Katsudō Kihon Chōsa,* various years.

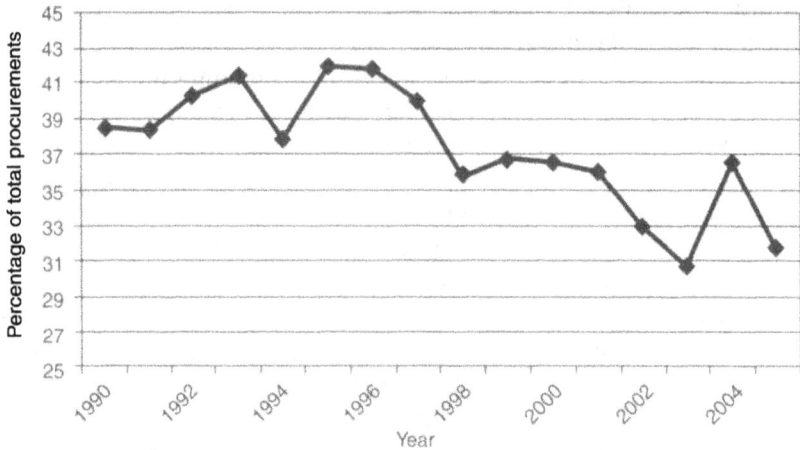

Figure 7.3. Imports from Japan by Japanese manufacturers in Asia
Source: METI, *Kaigai Jigyō Katsudō Kihon Chōsa*, various years.

began importing motorcycles from their China and Taiwan affiliates, while Isuzu and Fuji Heavy Industries began importing trucks and minivans from their operations in China and Thailand, respectively.[22] At the same time, Japanese manufacturers in Asia have managed to increase their sales activity in local and regional markets, rather than merely exporting their output to the West. In particular, Japanese MNCs in China began to treat the host country as a viable market rather than merely an export platform—boosting their share of local sales from one-third of total sales in the early 1990s to about one half of total sales in 2005.[23]

Japanese manufacturing affiliates in Asia also have decreased their reliance on their home country as a source of parts for offshore assembly. In 1990, they relied on Japan for nearly 40 percent of all procurements; by 2005, they had cut that share to 31 percent (see figure 7.3). As early as 2000, Toyota's assembly operation in Thailand began making plans to procure all its parts locally.[24] Even though many of these local suppliers are Japanese affiliates themselves, government data point to a marginal decrease in reliance on Japanese parts suppliers in host countries. In 2002, 42.5 percent of Japanese affiliates in Southeast Asia indicated they received more than half of

22. Aoki Takuo, "Asia-Made Scooter Imports Blaze Trail into Japanese Markets," *Nikkei Weekly*, October 1, 2001; and James Brooke, "Japan's Export Power Drifts across the China Sea," *New York Times*, April 7, 2002.
23. See METI, *Kaigai Jigyō Katsudō Kihon Chōsa*, various years, including 2007 (for 2005 data).
24. Uehara Masashi, "Auto Giant in Thailand to Procure Parts Locally," *Nikkei Weekly*, June 28, 2000.

their supplies from Japanese affiliates—down from 47 percent in 1998.[25] And even those Japanese assemblers who rely heavily on Japanese suppliers in the host country are beginning to purchase parts from members of rival keiretsu[26] or from completely independent Japanese manufacturers. China, in particular, has attracted a large number of Japanese suppliers with no keiretsu ties.[27]

In Southeast Asia, as well as in China, local manufacturers have managed to dramatically boost their technological abilities, and are no longer valued merely for their low costs and low prices. In 2000, the *Nikkei* reported that Japan's leading electronics firms, "scrambling over one another in a search for electronics parts," flocked to an industrial exhibition in Shenzen to examine offerings from Chinese, Hong Kong, and Taiwanese firms with factories in that area.[28] Taking advantage of increased capabilities in the local market, Japanese MNCs are now producing new models and high-end products in Asia, especially in China. Sanyo, for example, opted to manufacture a new multicolor printer at a joint venture in Guangzhou, while Toyota built a new truck at its Samrong plant in Thailand and signed a pact with First Automotive Works, China's leading automaker, to produce luxury cars and sport utility vehicles (SUVs) for China's nouveau riche.[29] Other Japanese MNCs, anxious to hang on to market share, have taken the extraordinary step of licensing their technology to Chinese competitors. For example, Hitachi moved quickly to contract with a local firm to produce projection TVs in China, while Matsushita did the same to produce digital TVs.

Although many Japanese MNCs continue to jealously hang on to their domestic R&D facilities, a few have begun to turn over such work to Asian affiliates.[30] Inevitably, this has created a situation that was, in the 1990s anyway, almost unthinkable: Japanese firms now are relying heavily on Asian engineers. Toyo Engineering, which designs chemical factories, employs more technical staff abroad (mostly in India, Thailand, and Malaysia) than in Japan; as of May 2008, it had three thousand foreign workers and twenty-

25. JETRO, "Shinshutsu kigyō jittai chōsa (Ajia-hen): Nikkei seizōgyo no katsudō jōkyō," 2002 and 1998.

26. One example: Zhengzhou Nissan, a Chinese affiliate of the Japanese/French assembler, manufactures a pickup truck with a transmission made by Aisin Seiki, a member of the Toyota group. See *Nikkei Weekly,* "Japanese Firms Rethink Strategies in China," September 11, 2000.

27. *Nikkei Weekly,* "Small Firms Join Exodus to China, Seeking Lower Costs, Local Markets," April 29, 2002.

28. *Nikkei Weekly,* "Region's Top Manufacturers Match Quality, Cost, Sparking Buyer Scramble," September 18, 2000.

29. *Nikkei Weekly,* "China Skims Cream of Corporate Crop," November 5, 2001; *Nikkei Weekly,* "Japanese Firms Entering New Globalization Era," December 27, 2004, and January 3, 2005; and *Nikkei Weekly,* "Japan Auto Firms Rush to Ink Joint Venture Deals in China," June 10, 2007.

30. *Nikkei Weekly,* "Electronics Firms' Overseas Operations Evolve," September 11, 2000.

five hundred Japanese workers doing R&D work.[31] This situation has been created in large part by the dwindling number of Japanese youth graduating from engineering schools and the increasing number of older Japanese engineers, many of whom took advantage of an early retirement option in the 1990s, leaving the home country to take positions in Asian firms.[32] So employment agencies such as Altech have set up training centers in Chinese universities to recruit engineering students and train them in the Japanese language and business culture. Even the government has gotten involved: METI set up an "Asian Talent Fund" to help Asian students find work in Japan, and it pushed the Justice Ministry to let foreign visitors stay in Japan if they can meet standards used to certify Japanese technology workers.[33]

NEC Soft, a software developer, is just one of the many high-tech firms to turn to overseas markets to fill critical research positions in Japan. It successfully blazed this trail in 2001, when it hired nine recent graduates of Chinese engineering schools. The newcomers from China "have already mastered the software development language used at their universities," crowed an NEC Soft executive. "With new Japanese graduates, we usually have to give them one to two years to master the language."[34]

Further evidence of the collapse of the region's "flying geese" pattern comes in the form of capital flows—this time, from Asia to Japan. I must not overstate the case: these flows do not, in the aggregate, constitute a roaring river. Although Japan's relational networks have begun to open up, especially in the financial sector, they remain a barrier to foreign investment. But given the long history of elite regionalization, it is remarkable to find that capital is now flowing in the "opposite" direction. Shanghai Electric, a state-owned enterprise headquartered in China, has acquired two venerable Japanese firms: Ikegai, a machine tool maker, and Akiyama Machinery Manufacturing, a printing press maker. Many individual investors from Asia, able to move quickly and take risks, also have set up shop in Japan. One such pioneer is Yan Hao, the Chinese founder of Tokyo-based EPS, which con-

31. Martin Fackler, "High-Tech Japan Running Out of Engineers," *New York Times*, May 17, 2008.

32. One might argue that this is the same as—or quite similar to—the situation in the 1990s, when Japanese MNCs used *shukkō* to dispatch surplus managers and technicians to their affiliates in Asia. But it is as different from that situation, described in chapter 5, as horizontal, arm's-length integration is different from vertical, intranetwork integration. These engineers are going to work for Asian firms, not Japanese MNCs, and they often are being dispatched to Asia by temporary employment firms, not by their own employers or by the Japanese government. See *Asahi Shinbun*, "Asian Firms Seek Japanese Workers," September 8, 2001; *Japan Times*, "Asia Beckons for Some Skilled Retirees," January 3, 2007; and *New York Times*, "A Japanese Export: Talent," May 24, 2007.

33. Ibid., and *Nikkei Weekly*, "Japan to Promote Testing for IT Engineers in Asia," October 9, 2000.

34. *Nikkei Weekly*, "Skilled Chinese Add to Foreign Firms' Might," November 12, 2001.

ducts clinical tests for Japanese drug companies. EPS has been listed on the Jasdaq stock market since 2001.[35]

Even if they don't operate in Japan, many Asian firms have begun to secure funds there, either through brokerage houses or stock exchanges. Indeed, they have filled a gap left by Western firms that retreated from Japanese capital markets in the lean years after 9/11. Daiwa Securities reports that it served as broker for seven foreign firms in 2003, helping them raise a total of eighty-eight billion yen in Japan. All seven firms were from Asia: China, Hong Kong, Taiwan, and Singapore.[36]

None of these developments should be interpreted to mean that Japanese MNCs have been entirely eclipsed by Asian firms, or that they and the Japanese government no longer play a significant role in the integration of Asian economies. Rather, the evidence suggests that elite regionalization has given way to a more open, formal, and reciprocal process. To understand this, one need look no further than the plethora of regional pacts forged in the first decade of the new millennium.

In 2003, Japan joined forces with other states in the region to create the Asia Broadband Program, jointly exploring the use of satellites, fiber-optic cables, and other technologies to develop a more integrated infrastructure for Internet access.[37] A year later, three of those states—Japan, China, and South Korea—agreed to collaborate on the development of new technologies for fourth-generation cell phones, digital broadcasting, and open-source software.[38] Also in 2004, industry groups in Japan and China pledged to work together on a project to standardize codes used in Web-based transactions.[39] None of these agreements reflects the positional power of Japanese government or business interests; instead, each is a defensive measure, reflecting nothing more than a shared ambition to acquire greater autonomy from U.S. (or, more precisely, Microsoft and Google) technology.

It is true, of course, that Japan has shown strong and creative leadership in advancing the cause of financial regionalism. But, again, its efforts to regionalize the yen do not reflect positional power; Japanese MNCs would not benefit any more than Thai or Taiwanese business interests. After withdrawing its 1997 proposal for an Asian Monetary Fund in the face of harsh criticism from Japan's most important ally, the United States, the Ministry of Finance quickly got behind an alternative approach that allows central banks in Asia to dig themselves out of financial holes by engaging in bilateral cur-

35. Ibid.
36. *Asahi Shinbun*, "Asian Companies Target Japanese Investors," April 9, 2004.
37. See Aso Taro, "Toward a Ubiquitous Network Society," *New Breeze* (Winter 2005).
38. *Japan Times*, "Asia Trio Embark on Quest to Lead in Cutting-Edge Tech," April 6, 2004. Tilton (2007) offers an intriguing analysis of this agreement.
39. *Japan Times*, "Groups Agree on E-commerce Standardization," April 20, 2004.

rency swaps. Unlike the AMF, the Chiang Mai Initiative would not supplant (and thus, according to the United States, undermine the role of) the International Monetary Fund. Likewise, MOF and METI are leading a long-term effort to establish a regional bond market. The Asian Bond Market Initiative is designed to tap into the region's substantial pool of savings, rather than relying on fickle capital markets outside the region, and make such savings available for domestic investment.

Compared with its leadership in promoting financial regionalism, Japan has proved to be a follower in efforts to enhance regional integration through trade liberalization. It has lagged far behind China on this front. After Beijing launched its plan for a China-ASEAN Free Trade Agreement, Tokyo responded with a call for its own "Comprehensive Economic Partnership"—a call that, to many, seemed too little, too late.[40] In Southeast Asia, government and business elites did not try to disguise their disappointment. "In contrast with the ASEAN-China agreement, the ASEAN-Japan proposal is at the initial stage and lacks details and a program of implementation," remarked Hank Lim, research director at the Singapore Institute of International Affairs, at an April 2003 symposium in Tokyo.[41] Even the Japanese press covering Prime Minister Koizumi's visit to Southeast Asia in January 2002 sounded underwhelmed. An *Asahi* reporter described the prime minister's speech outlining his proposal as a "departure from his usual straight talk," one that drifted "into the realm of diplomatic platitude."[42]

Pushed by METI, the Japanese government did finally forge bilateral "economic partnership agreements" (which are broader and less formal than free trade agreements) with important members of ASEAN. And in August 2006 it began pushing for a comprehensive trade and investment liberalization scheme encompassing sixteen members of Asia (the ten ASEAN states, Japan, China, South Korea, Australia, New Zealand, and India)—a fact that has restored some of its diminished reputation as a leader in the region. But the more important fact is that Japan no longer can sew the region together through informal network ties that it dominates; instead, it must content itself with formal-legal agreements. The era of elite regionalization has ended.

Good News or Bad News?

How should we evaluate these trends? For many observers, the answer is obvious: Japan is losing. A reporter for *Asahi* notes that China, which used to

40. "The China-ASEAN FTA proposal changed everything," according to a METI official I interviewed in Tokyo on October 7, 2003. "We realized we really had to get busy."

41. *Japan Times*, "Tokyo Under Pressure to Do More to Upgrade ASEAN State Economies," April 25, 2003.

42. *Asahi Shinbun*, "Asian Initiative Empty without Free Trade," January 16, 2002.

trail even the ASEAN-4 in technological capacity, is now achieving "high-tech catch-up" as it consolidates its position as the world's leading producer of steel, cement, chemicals, and TVs.[43] And Yoshitomi (2005) notes that China, not Japan, now sits at the center of a "grand production and distribution network" that is integrating Asia. "China is importing technologically sophisticated intermediate goods and parts from many Asian neighbors, including Japan, South Korea, Taiwan, and ASEAN members, and it is processing them and turning out final goods, which are then exported."

It is true, of course, that Japanese firms now must compete far more aggressively with Asian rivals. Consider the experience of Toshiba: although it cut costs by shifting some of its production to China, it also ended up in an ever tighter competition at home, thanks in large part to competing imports from China. In FY 2003, it had to reduce prices for household electronics by an average of 9.4 percent, and ended up losing 587 billion yen—an amount that exceeded its cost savings in China.[44] Toshiba's experience is dramatic, but not unique. In a 2002 survey, Japan's Employment Information Center asked hundreds of large manufacturers if they were facing severe price competition from imports. More than half answered yes. Asked to identify the source of competing imports, they overwhelmingly named China, then South Korea (though only one quarter as often as China), and then the United States.[45] Likewise, the prime minister's Economic and Social Research Institute found that three out of four Japanese firms claimed they were losing profits due to rapidly falling prices. And they were resorting to what, in the past, would have been viewed as desperate measures; for example, 70 percent of those firms struggling to stay afloat reported that they planned to change suppliers.[46]

It also is true that Japanese bureaucrats now must share the regional stage with their Chinese, Korean, and even ASEAN counterparts. With increasing humility, they seem to recognize this fact. Consider, for example, a report by MITI (1999b: 55–6) on "industrial policies for the 21st century." The authors suggest that Japan and Asia are now wholly interdependent; neither can survive without the cooperation of the other. "Japan must be more than a bridge between Asia and the West; it must move beyond the 'flying geese' model and participate in the search for a new approach to development." Al-

43. *Asahi Shinbun,* "Ajia no 'Gankōgata' hatten ni ihen" (The Collapse of the Asia "Flying Geese" Pattern of Development), January 9, 2001, 7.

44. *Yomiuri Shinbun,* "'China Effect' Generates Profits for Some," May 30, 2003.

45. Employment Information Center, "Kokusai bungyō no shinten to koyō ni taisuru eikyō ni kansuru hōkokusho" (A Report on the Progress toward an International Division of Labor and Its Effect on Employment); cited in Watanabe Hiroaki, "Globalization of Production Activities, Changes in Production Technology, Technological Innovation and Employment," *Japan Labor Bulletin,* August 1, 2003.

46. *Yomiuri Shinbun,* "'China Effect' Generates Profits for Some," May 30, 2003.

though Japanese bureaucrats continue to use industrial policies to influence investment in Asia, they have lost much of their financial muscle and thus their leverage. Japanese ODA to Asia, as noted earlier, is a trickle of what it used to be.

Undeniably, then, these trends amount to a loss for Japanese bureaucrats, as well as for the executives and regular employees of Japanese multinational corporations. But we must not confuse Japanese elites with "Japan." The end of elite regionalization has had, I argue, a net positive effect on Japan. Exposed more fully to the strong winds of globalization, Japan is finally undergoing structural change in the domestic institutions of its political economy. And in the end, those who have been outsiders in an exclusionary system of selective relationalism are beginning to enjoy the benefits of this change.

8 Some Change . . . at Last

In the red dawn of this millennium, Japan's political economy began to acquire a new shape—but only at the margins. The ancien régime did not crumble completely; political and business elites who had come to enjoy the positional power afforded by selective relationalism continued to resist change.

Vogel (2006, 3) is certainly correct: "As government officials and industry leaders scrutinized their options, they selected reforms to modify or reinforce existing institutions rather than to abandon them." And yet the Japanese government *did* enact laws and rules to promote greater market liberalization, while industry *did* adopt policies and practices that allowed for greater flexibility. The net effect was gradual and minimal change—a looser and less exclusionary relationalism.

In the previous chapter, I described a disjuncture in the external environment—more precisely, the collapse of the "flying geese" pattern of regional development—that made possible even such limited change in Japan. In this chapter, I document that change, mapping out the still shifting shape, the still evolving network ties, of the domestic political economy.

One man's story seems to symbolize both the new opportunities for outsiders, and the continued resistance from insiders in Japan. Horie Takafumi, a thirty-something entrepreneur, exploded onto the stage in the early days of the new millennium, attracting hopes and fears about revolutionary change in the political economy of Japan. Just about everyone agreed that the president of Internet start-up Livedoor represented something new, but they disagreed about what that meant. To some, especially a younger generation, Horie was a delightfully independent actor, a hyperkinetic human dynamo in an otherwise stale system characterized by relational rigidity. But to long-standing elites, he was a dangerous force, a cowboy capitalist who wasn't just "shaking things up"—he was leaving chaos everywhere in his wake. In his single-minded pursuit of Nippon Broadcasting, Horie generated deep resentment from those who enjoyed positional power in Japan. Comparing him to Tanaka Kakuei, the populist prime minister who in the 1970s was implicated in a bribery scandal, one critic warned ominously that "as with Kaku-san, it is not impossible that those who worship the god of money could one day find themselves the subject of its vengeance."[1]

Within a year, Horie landed in a Tokyo courtroom, defending himself against charges of securities fraud. He was eventually convicted and sent to prison for two and a half years. Did the empire of selective relationalism strike back? Was a revolution revoked? Probably not: I suspect that Horie's own hubris, not the resentment of others, was responsible for this man's fall from grace. But the fact that critics who could not possibly know the details of his financial dealings were willing to so boldly predict his demise speaks volumes about the resilience of the status quo.

Saeki Keishi, an economist at Kyoto University, has emerged as a kind of spokesman for Japanese elites waging war against creeping change, which he sometimes describes as globalization but more often, in a rather stern voice, calls "Americanization"—a trend toward "individual freedom, market competition, meritocracy, pursuit of profits, a gamelike spirit of competitive rivalry, and bold entrepreneurship." A political economy with such characteristics may work well enough in the United States, because it reflects American values; but it will certainly fail in Japan, a group-oriented society with radically different values. Saeki (2000, 38), who must have felt sickeningly vindicated by the global financial crisis that began in the United States in 2008, extols the virtues of the status quo. To survive, he writes, Japan must recognize its fundamental strength, "the ability to build organizations and tie them together":

> What our country requires is the strengthening of its comparative advantage as a Japanese-style society based on the formation of organizations at various levels and the establishment of an order centered on collective activities and personal relationships. The areas in which the Japanese economy has an advantage are in manufacturing with local ties rather than in global finance, in the technology of the artisan rather than in the management of information as data, in local coexistence rather than in global competition, in the human economy rather than in the cyber-economy.

A more fantastic version of this antichange message is embedded in a recent film, *Baburu e Go* (Back to the Bubble Period). The time is March 2007; Japan faces an eight hundred trillion yen debt, which is growing at the rate

1. Funabashi Haruo, "The Perils of Money Worship," *Japan Journal,* June 2005, 16.

of ninety billion yen a day. Unless something rather extraordinary is done, the country will experience the worst kind of death in less than two years: "The big banks will fail, triggering a domino effect. The gap between rich and poor will widen. Twenty million people will lose their jobs. Crime will spread. Japan will implode!"

To avoid this catastrophe, a "good" MOF official sends Mayumi, a teenage girl (played by the archetypally innocent, and thus "cute," Hiruse Ryoko), back in time, back to 1990, the last and most bubbly moment of the bubble. Her mission is to find her mother, a Hitachi researcher who had invented a washing machine that, it turns out, doubled as a time machine. Mother already had traveled back to 1990 to persuade a "bad" MOF official not to push a measure that would unleash a series of events leading inexorably to Japan's demise. Along the way, however, mother has gone missing—and the rescue plan needs an infusion of youthful vigor.

Mayumi arrives, full of curiosity, horror, and soapsuds, in a Wonderland of neon lights, fancy new buildings, and "too much money." Japan has turned into an American funhouse of overconsumption. At a noisy disco, she asks a reveler, "How can you be so frivolous?" And, it seems, so hopelessly ignorant—a condition that is revealed when he parries her prescient thrust: "What's wrong with enjoying life?"

In the movie's climactic scene, Mayumi manages to find her mother and the family duo saves the day by thwarting the plans of the venal bureaucrat, who—it turns out—is secretly doing the bidding of U.S. financial interests. Mission accomplished, Mayumi and Mom send themselves into the future, where Tokyo is a booming but orderly metropolis, and where the "good" MOF official is now prime minister and the high-tech Hitachi researcher (Mom) is first lady. Good government and smart but maternal industry are wedded, again, for the benefit of a wholesome Japan, which is once again enjoying "continued prosperity." In this film, the invisible hero is relationalism.

I hope my point is generally clear: those who occupy powerful positions in the Japanese political economy have actively resisted efforts to open up its relational networks. But while they have been able to minimize the scope and depth of change, they have not been able to block it altogether. Those dissatisfied with the status quo, those I have described here as outsiders, have begun to score some critical victories.

One example is the information disclosure law that took effect in April 2001. This was the culmination of a twenty-year battle by a coalition of citizen groups, Information Clearinghouse Japan, which became increasingly fed up with the government's ability to hoard information, thereby shielding itself and its favored interests, especially big business interests. The law is flawed, and already has been badly abused by the government, but it nonetheless reflects an important breakthrough in that it upholds a basic right of Japanese citizens to know why and how public officials act as they do. The Japanese government, which now responds more swiftly—and more often affirmatively—to requests for public information, and which has even taken to preemptively disclosing information by posting it on the Internet, is far more transparent in this new millennium than it was in the 1990s.[2]

Another victory of frustrated outsiders over entrenched insiders came in the 2002 local election in Nagano, which I discussed briefly in chapter 2. As governor of that prefecture, Tanaka Yasuo imposed a moratorium on dam building—a policy that infuriated development interests, government officials, and journalists belonging to the local press club (*kisha-kai*). Conservative members of the Nagano prefectural assembly used a no-confidence vote in 2002 to force the pro-environment governor to step down. But Tanaka immediately ran again, and local voters overwhelmingly reelected him.[3]

In chapter 4, I evaluated the extent of continuity versus change in the political economy of 1990s Japan by carefully examining each leg in the three-legged stool of selective relationalism. To be consistent, I reuse that methodology below to evaluate the extent of continuity versus change in today's political economy, one that is buffeted more and more by the winds of globalization, and protected less and less by the shield of regionalization. This methodology serves as a kind of scorecard, allowing us to keep track of the ongoing battle between insiders and outsiders, between the forces representing the relational status quo and the forces representing a break. You already know what I think the evidence reveals: buoyed by a shift in the external environment, the forces of change are finally winning—but not yet decisively.

State and Industry

In the first decade of the new millennium, the mutually reinforcing ties between state and industry in Japan did weaken somewhat, narrowing the range of opportunity for "administrative guidance" and other forms of government intervention. But one should not overstate the extent of such change. Japan's economic ministries, led by METI and MOF, continued to use their still relatively close ties with corporate interests to regulate economic activity both formally and informally. This is rather unsurprising: given the chance, bureaucrats will wield whatever tools they have at their

2. There are, of course, glaring exceptions to this rule. In 2002, Tokyo Electric Power Co. acknowledged that it had falsified reports submitted to the government in order to disguise safety problems at its nuclear reactors. Although a whistleblower had informed METI about the cover-up, the ministry sat on the information for two years before taking any action. *Reuters*, August 2, 2002.

3. "Nagano's Champion of Change," *Japan Times*, September 4, 2005.

disposal. Continuity is perhaps most evident in the bureaucracy's use of industrial policies. In June 2002, the *Asahi* newspaper published a series of articles about METI's effort to return to its traditional position in the "driver's seat of the Japanese economy."[4] Ministry officials told the paper they had placed too much faith in the unfettered market, fiddling while Japan stagnated and China, by comparison, boomed. Using a new organization based on public-private partnership, METI now would promote pathbreaking R&D and new business creation through "industrial realignment." Toyoda Masakazu, head of the ministry's Industrial Competitiveness Strategy Council, told the newspaper the council would try to "make strong companies stronger to spawn the next Microsoft or Intel."

In addition to ongoing and rather targeted efforts to promote the development of a small rocket (the GX) and a Concorde-like supersonic jet (the NEXST), the ministry has been focusing on three broad themes:

- *Promoting and protecting domestic technology.* For example, METI spent 31.5 billion yen to promote a joint research project by five Japanese chip makers hoping to standardize manufacturing techniques for next-generation semiconductors.[5] In addition, the ministry leaned on NEC to sell its plasma display operation to domestic rival Pioneer rather to a foreign investor, and intervened in at least ten other cases involving unwelcome technology transfer.[6]
- *Fostering new industries.* METI has identified seven strategic "service-related" industries that it intends to nurture: digital home appliances, robots, health and welfare, environment and energy, business support services, fuel cells, and entertainment software. But the ministry appears firmly wedded to established players; among the first firms approved for support under the government's Industrial Revitalization Law were Sumitomo Metal, Fuji Heavy Industry, Tokyo Motor, and Mitsubishi Corporation—those Ibata-Arens (2005, 100) calls "the usual suspects," or what I call "insiders."
- *Strengthening industrial networks.* For example, METI serves as the coordinator of the "industrial cluster program," a set of nineteen projects to bring together large firms, SMEs, universities, and other institutions in region-specific "human networks" to develop new products and services based on cutting-edge technology.

4. Kanamitsu Takashi and Kimijima Hiroshi, "Sangyō saihen hikikane yaku ni: Tsūsan kara keisan e mosaku suru seisaku kanchō" (Striving to Be the Catalyst in Industrial Reorganization: A Policy Agency Struggles to Make the Transition from MITI to METI), *Asahi Shinbun*, May 30, 2002, 9.

5. Ibid.

6. *Economist*, "(Still) Made in Japan," April 10, 2004.

Compared to METI, MOF has been more modest in its pursuit of new industrial policies. This, too, is unsurprising; MOF's bureaucratic capacity has been reduced by Japan's financial woes, for which the ministry was widely blamed. Nonetheless, in the first part of the new millennium, MOF continued to use its authority over government-affiliated financial institutions, such as the Japan Development Bank (JDB), to promote investment. Here is just one example of MOF intervention, which caught the eye—and the criticism —of some in the media: in FY 2000, JDB provided nearly two hundred billion yen in new loans to electric power companies that probably did not need concessionary or below-market credit.[7]

At the same time, however, outsiders began to openly challenge the status quo. For example, they raised a ruckus in July 2000, when the government announced a plan to use $2 billion in public funds to help rescue the ailing Sogo Co., a giant retailer that had—through its own mismanagement —accumulated as much as $18 billion in debt. Among the many vocal critics was Takagi Masaru, an economics professor at Meiji University (and a former banker). "The spirit of capitalism is nowhere to be seen in this nation right now," he railed in one newspaper article (*Mainichi Shinbun,* July 7, 2000). "It is a desperate situation." Japanese citizens apparently felt the same way; in opinion polls, they overwhelmingly opposed the government's bailout plan. Government officials took heed. They abandoned the bailout proposal, leaving Sogo no alternative but to file for bankruptcy.[8]

Then came "Lionheart," named for his big hair and feisty spirit. For proponents of change in state—industry ties in Japan, the tenure of Koizumi Jun'ichiro was a pivotal moment.[9] The telegenic politician breezed into the prime minister's office in April 2001, calling for "structural reform without

7. See, for example, *Asahi Shinbun,* "Public Financial Institutions Must Be Put under Microscope," December 20, 2001.

8. It should be noted, however, that Sogo approached the government for help only after it failed to persuade a Japanese bank now controlled by U.S. investors to write off some of the retailer's debt. Seventy-two other banks had endorsed Sogo's plan, but Shinsei Bank balked. That bank is owned by Ripplewood Holdings, a U.S. partnership, which purchased the assets of the failed Long Term Credit Bank of Japan from the Japanese government in 1999 and thus became Sogo's second largest creditor.

9. Readers may wonder why I use the term "change" more often than the term "reform," which appears to be preferred by many Western, especially American, commentators. My reason is that "reform" implies a correction, the transformation of something "bad" into something "good"—or at least "better." Although I happen to agree with liberals who believe the Japanese political economy today is still not sufficiently responsive to market forces, I do not believe this was always true (or that it will *always* be true in the future). Japanese relationalism was suited to economic conditions until the mid-1970s, when Japan reached the global technological frontier. In the same way, China's local state-led development model seems well suited to economic conditions today. Neoliberal policy prescriptions, cast as "reforms," are not always "best" or even "better."

sacred cows," and stepped down in September 2006, a year after leading his Liberal Democratic Party to a stunning electoral victory. What happened in between?

Koizumi did not initially meet high expectations.[10] For example, his campaign to promote further deregulation faltered at first as it faced ongoing opposition not only from many bureaucrats but also from many business groups, according to Suzuki Yoshio, a member of the prime minister's Council for Regulatory Reform.[11] By 2003, the number of regulations on the books (11,007) remained higher than the number in 1990 (10,581), and a METI survey found that Japanese firms continued to pay much more than their counterparts in other countries for basic services such as transportation— more than double the cost in Germany and nearly triple the cost in the United States.[12] And the cost of living in Tokyo remained relatively high until 2005, when it finally lost its dubious distinction as the world's most expensive city, at least according to the Economist Intelligence Unit.[13] One newspaper, noting that Koizumi was "battered, bruised, and looking wobbly," asked ominously: "Is he washed up, or will deregulation get him off the ropes?"[14]

In time, Koizumi seemed to find his feet. His deregulation campaign finally gained some traction as it targeted such important areas as the electrical and natural gas retail markets, and as his cabinet authorized dozens of "special zones for structural reform" proposed by local government.[15] And after an equally slow start, his cabinet finally did push commercial banks to begin writing off the nonperforming loans that were weighing down the Japanese economy like a giant anvil. In addition, the prime minister oversaw a dramatic reduction (50%) in the size of Japan's "second" or "hidden" budget, the Fiscal Investment and Loan Program (FILP), which increasingly served as the source of funds for pork-barrel projects, including yen loans for infrastructure projects in Asia (as part of the government's ODA program). Related to this, Koizumi pushed through a measure closing, privatizing, or consolidating the eight government-affiliated financial institutions that had spent FILP funds. And before leaving office, the prime minister finally persuaded the Diet to approve his pet project—privatization of the postal savings and insurance system.

10. See, for example, George Mulgan (2002) and Sakakibara (2005).

11. *Nikkei Weekly*, "Past Performance Dogs Deregulation Efforts," September 17, 2001.

12. Ishida Mamoru, "Regulation Remains a Problem," *Japan Times*, April 22, 2003.

13. EIU, *Worldwide Cost of Living Survey*.

14. Asahi Shinbun, "Kieta? Koizumi jintsūriki: iryōhi sanbai futan mondai" (Koizumi's Supernatural Power: Has It Vanished? The Case of the Tripling of Medical Expenses), February 19, 2003, 4.

15. See, for example, *Asahi*, "Start-ups Lighting Up Deregulated Electricity Market," July 21, 2004.

Sakaiya Taichi, who was an elite bureaucrat in the Ministry of International Trade and Industry before becoming a political commentator, has argued that Koizumi failed to curb bureaucratic authority. Indeed, he writes, Japan's bureaucracy became stronger, not weaker, during "Lionheart's" time in office.[16] In a similar vein, a bureaucrat turned academic, Ko Mishima (2005, 14), has argued that the prime minister "completely failed to impose meaningful change on the bureaucracy." Although these rather similar perspectives provide a useful antidote against exaggerated claims of a "Koizumi revolution," they overlook significant change in two areas.

First, the eccentric executive dramatically increased the centralized power of the prime minister, relative to the bureaucracy, by entrusting the job of policy formulation to the newly created Cabinet Office (*kantei*). The Cabinet Office is made up of "ministers of state" who report directly to the prime minister and who draw on their own independent staff, thus insulating them from the interests of the established ministries. For example, in formulating policies to respond to Japan's banking crisis, Koizumi relied on the Council on Economic and Fiscal Policy, which then was headed up by Takenaka Heizo, a Keio University economist with no previous experience in government. MOF was not entirely removed from the process, but it had to go through Takenaka and CEFP to influence policy.[17] Likewise, MITI found that it had to go through the Cabinet Office to secure support for new policies to promote innovative new industries.[18] For example, the Cabinet Office, not METI, was responsible for the 2001 "e-Japan" strategy (which fostered the remarkably fast diffusion of broadband technology throughout the country) and the 2004 "u-Japan" strategy (to build a "ubiquitous network society" by 2010).

"The bureaucracy had become rather hidebound, very stodgy," a member of the Cabinet Office explained to me.[19] "We represented fresh air, a chance to shake things up by advancing some provocative policies."

The second significant change brought about by Koizumi was the narrowing of opportunities for amakudari, the practice of "descending from heaven" (the bureaucracy) into the private sector, the practice that most concretely reflects the mutually reinforcing ties between state and industry. One cannot deny that progress was agonizingly slow:

16. See Sakaiya and Noguchi (2005, 141).

17. For an intriguing analysis of the council's battle with what the newspaper calls the "Old Guard," see *Nikkei Weekly*, "CEFP Hits Ruling Party Road Blocks," July 25, 2005.

18. Kanamitsu Takashi and Kimijima Hiroshi, "Yakuwari usure, seijiryoku teika: Tsūsan kara keisan e mosaku suru seisaku kanchō" (Its Role Has Weakened and Its Political Power Has Declined: A Policy Agency Struggles to Make the Transition from MITI to METI), *Asahi Shinbun*, May 31, 2002, 11.

19. Interview, Tokyo, July 5, 2007.

- In 2001, Kansai International Airport Co. came to be known, derisively, as "mini-Kasumigaseki" because six of its nine directors were ex-bureaucrats who had "descended" from the central government.[20]
- In 2002, the *Asahi* newspaper concluded that "cozy business-bureaucrat relations are as tight as ever."[21] Ministries continue to actively recruit postretirement jobs for career-track civil servants, the paper reported. It used the new information disclosure law to determine that 36 percent of the 2,418 civil servants who had retired from the central government since 2000 were now working for companies that had won contracts with the employees' former ministries.
- In March of 2003, Transport Minister Ogi Chikage demanded the resignation of all board members of the companies affiliated with four public highway corporations who had assumed their positions after retiring from the public corporations. Four months later, most of the former bureaucrats remained in their positions.[22]

But despite fierce resistance from insiders enjoying positional power,[23] Koizumi's efforts to change the rules of the game did ultimately pay off. By privatizing, closing, or consolidating a number of quasi-public corporations, he dramatically reduced the number of amakudari transfers. And just as important, his frequent statements condemning the practice generated not only news articles but also critical statements and positions by other political parties and leaders. For example, the Democratic Party of Japan felt so much pressure on this issue that, in 2003, it promised—if given a majority in the Diet—to take steps to curtail the practice.[24] And Koizumi's successor in 2006, Abe Shinzo, pushed legislation to end the use of contracts to secure amakudari posts.[25]

In the end, one wonders, what really enabled Koizumi to make this kind of progress toward relaxing the otherwise tight, even exclusionary ties between bureaucrats and business interests in Japan? Some political scientists, such as Noble (2006) and Tiberghien (2007), attribute Koizumi's success to the fact that, during his five years in office, he acted as a "political entre-

---

20. *Yomiuri Shinbun,* "Bureaucrats Sapping Vitality of Privatized Airport," July 4, 2001.

21. *Asahi Shinbun,* "Ministries Give Farewell Gifts to Bureaucrats—Amakudari Jobs," October 22, 2002.

22. *Asahi Shinbun,* "Amakudari Execs Defy Minister," July 2, 2003.

23. We should not be surprised to learn that that resistance has continued. *Japan Times* has reported that 34 percent of senior bureaucrats who retired in FY 2005 ended up with jobs in quasi-public corporations (January 6, 2007), and that the practice of amakudari has been taken up by universities, which apparently are hiring more and more retired government officials (October 9, 2007).

24. *Japan Times,* "DPJ to Pledge Ban on Amakudari," August 5, 2003.

25. *Japan Times,* "Watanabe Vows Bill to Fight Amakudari," December 30, 2006.

preneur," seizing opportunities in the domestic environment to advance his "reform" agenda. But they ignore the more important factor, a dramatic change in the external environment: with the decline of elite regionalization, Japan was, at last, more fully exposed to the forces of globalization.

Business and Business

Unlike state–industry ties or labor–management ties, relations between nominally independent Japanese businesses do not appear, on the surface at least, to have changed very much during the first decade of the new millennium. For example, rivals in high-technology fields continue to engage in strategic cooperation—as happened when Matsushita and Toshiba integrated their LCD operations, and when NEC and Hitachi forged a joint venture to manufacture memory chips. "This growing web of collaboration among IT companies," mused *Nikkei* in an October 29, 2001 editorial, "makes it increasingly difficult to tell allies from competitors in the industry." Those inclined to view such things in terms of culture might conclude that social norms penetrate the business world even more thoroughly than they do elsewhere in the political economy of Japan. I am inclined to think differently. Peek below the surface and you will find significant change, along with powerful resistance to such change, in this leg of selective relationalism.

Let us start, as before, with an examination of collusive practices between firms that, in a free market economy, should compete. Bid-rigging scandals continued to roil Japan's political economy in the first decade of the twenty-first century. Although the most serious scandals emerged in 1993 and 1994, when thirty-two representatives of private firms and public agencies were arrested for either giving or taking bribes on government contracts, that wasn't the end of this sordid story. In 2004, the Japan Highway Public Corporation (JHPC) authorized collusion by about fifty companies bidding on projects to construct steel bridges, going so far as to create a "bid winner allocation chart." A year later, a citizens group estimated that, thanks to *dangō*, local governments overpaid construction companies by as much as 1.16 trillion yen for public works in FY 2005 alone.[26] The Japan Fair Trade Commission (JFTC) found criminal violations of the Anti-Monopoly Act (AMA) in 2006, when eleven companies rigged the bids for construction of sewage treatment facilities throughout Japan, and in 2007, when five construction companies rigged the bids for a project to extend the subway line in Nagoya.

When the JHPC scandal broke in 2005, Okuda Hiroshi, then chairman of Nippon Keidanren (Japan's big business group), sounded surprisingly tolerant about the practice of *dangō*. "It's a custom you find just about every-

---

26. Reiji Yoshida, "Bid-rigging? Hey, It's Just Your Taxes," *Japan Times*, July 3, 2007.

where (*tsutsu uraura*) in Japan," he told reporters at a press conference.[27] Given this statement, as well as the new series of incidents, one could be excused for assuming that nothing has changed in this aspect of interfirm relations. In fact, however, much has changed.

For one, the law against such behavior is finally more in line with existing provisions in other advanced capitalist nations. In 2005, the Diet approved an amendment to the Anti-Monopoly Act that raised the penalty for bid-rigging from 6 percent to 10 percent of revenues earned by colluding firms. In 2009, it boosted the penalty again—this time to 15 percent—and jacked up the maximum prison term for individuals convicted of bid-rigging from three to five years. Even the American Chamber of Commerce in Tokyo, which had complained for years about lax antitrust enforcement, was now complaining that proposed penalties were too strong.

Another change is that the JFTC itself has become more aggressive in its enforcement of the AMA. Its staff expanded from 520 officers in 1995 to 765 in 2007, while its budget has risen from less than six billion yen in 1995 to more than eight billion yen in 2007.[28] These increases in personnel and funding have allowed the commission, which in the past had been called a "paper tiger," to investigate more cases—and to investigate them more carefully.

This tougher legal and administrative environment has resulted in less collusion, according to research by the Japan Citizen's Ombudsman Association.[29] In a 2002 study of public works contracting throughout Japan, the association found that the average ratio of winning price to government-established maximum price was 95.3 percent—a sign of likely collusion. But the ratio has fallen every year since then, and reached 91 percent in 2005—a sign of increased competition.

What about keiretsu, the sometimes controversial but generally legal groupings of complementary firms? Let me start by considering the vertical ties that bind machinery assemblers and parts suppliers. In some industries, especially automobiles, subcontracting endures as an important institution; indeed, Toyota and Honda—the most "Japanese" of Japan's automakers—never abandoned their keiretsu. In fact, in 2004, Okuda Hiroshi, chairman of Toyota, declared that close relations with subcontractors, especially those producing high-tech parts, determined the "life or death" of his company: "We have to hold on [to them] tightly."[30] And Honda strengthened ties with favored subcontractors such as Sanoh, Kikuchi, and Daido Steel, purchasing an even larger share of their outstanding stock.[31] Meanwhile, three "mixed

27. *Asahi Shinbun*, "Bid-rigging Lexicon Speaks Loudly about Japan," July 13, 2005.
28. JFTC annual reports.
29. Reiji Yoshida, "Bid-rigging? Hey, It's Just Your Taxes," *Japan Times*, July 3, 2007.
30. *Japan Times*, "Okuda Ups Sales Forecast by 1 Million," November 2, 2004.
31. Mitsubishi Economic Research Institute, *MERI Monthly Circular*, No. 932, August 2007.

breed" automakers (those with large amounts of foreign equity) moved in the second half of this past decade to strengthen ties with their suppliers after allowing those ties to weaken or even break in the first half.[32]

Nissan had been the first to dismantle its vertical keiretsu. In 2000, after falling into debt and being acquired by Renault, it cut its supply base in half, releasing as many as six hundred longtime subcontractors. Mazda quickly followed suit, shifting to U.S.-style competitive bidding after Ford bought up one-third of its shares. MMC was the last to act, shutting down its supply club in 2002 after Daimler-Chrysler acquired a controlling stake in the firm.

More recently, however, each of these "mixed breed" automakers has had a change of heart. Mazda has returned to Japanese-style subcontracting, while MMC has created a new keiretsu including many of the subcontractors that had belonged to the old Kashiwa-kai. Even Nissan, led in 2007 by "Le Cost Killer" Carlos Ghosn, told stockholders he would do his best to repair frayed ties with suppliers,[33] while a Nissan executive told me the firm would begin to invest more heavily in its most competitive subcontractors.[34] To that end, the automaker dramatically increased its shareholdings in Calsonic Kansei Corp., a major supplier of modular systems such as dashboards and instrument panels.[35]

Although it seems clear that automobile assemblers and suppliers are resisting change in keiretsu relations, that industry is unique. In all other manufacturing sectors, parts suppliers appear to be reducing their dependence on a small coterie of long-standing customers (assemblers of finished goods), according to a study by Mitsubishi UFJ Research and Consulting.[36] In the consumer appliances industry, for example, only one-third of suppliers indicated in 2005 that they relied on three or fewer leading customers for at least 61 percent of their sales. That is a big change from 1995, when 70 percent of suppliers in that sector indicated that they relied on such a small number of customers for at least 61 percent of their sales. What this means is that suppliers are casting a wider net and trying to avoid exclusionary relationships that compromise their autonomy. A more recent study indicates machinery assemblers are starting to do the same, although not as aggressively and for different (cost-cutting) rea-

32. *Asahi Shinbun*, "Jidōsha 'keiretsu' kaiki: Mitsubishi kyōryokukai, Nissan wa shusshizō chōkiteki ni wa yūri" (The Return of the Automobile Keiretsu: The Mitsubishi Group and Nissan See a Long-term Benefit in Deepening Their Investments), June 26, 2005.

33. Nikkei Weekly, "Ghosn Hint at New Management Style," June 25, 2007.

34. Interview, Tokyo, October 5, 2003.

35. *Asahi Shinbun*, "Cost-Conscious Automakers Rediscover Value of Keiretsu," July 2, 2005.

36. Mitsubishi UFJ Research and Consulting, "A Questionnaire Survey of Recent Changes in Business Relations in Manufacturing," November 2005; referenced in METI, *White Paper on Small and Medium-Sized Business*, 2006, 110.

sons.[37] METI suggests that subcontracting relations today are beginning to look more like a "mesh" of relatively loose and complex ties rather than a rigidly hierarchical pyramid.[38] Some have attributed this change in subcontracting to the "IT revolution," which they believe mandates more flexible relations between assemblers and suppliers.[39] But METI, like me, highlights a broader change: Japanese MNCs, including assemblers and suppliers, are now participating in a new international division of labor based on "global optimal location strategies," rather than a regional division of labor based primarily on longstanding business ties.[40]

The other form of complementary network organization, horizontal keiretsu, came under severe stress in the late 1990s as Japanese lenders and borrowers struggled to cope with the credit squeeze created by the massive volume of nonperforming loans. As we saw in chapter 4, companies tried to raise money and bolster their financial position by selling off shares in weak or underperforming firms, including affiliated firms in which they had invested for many years. In addition, and even more remarkably, banks that served as the heart of Japan's horizontal keiretsu crossed over boundaries and merged with banks serving rival groups. In chapter 4, I predicted that, once the crisis in Japanese financial markets began to subside, firms would return to the practice of stable and even cross-shareholding, albeit less enthusiastically than they did earlier. I also suggested that the six bank-centered groups were likely to reconsolidate into four looser groups. Both predictions came true in the first decade of the new millennium.

Regrouping began instantly. For example, as Sumitomo Bank and Sakura Bank, center of the Mitsui group, made plans to merge, members of what had been two rival keiretsu prepared to do the same. Sumitomo Chemical and Mitsui Chemical joined forces to create the largest chemicals manufacturer in Japan, while Sumitomo Construction and Mitsui Construction merged to create a new giant contractor. Likewise, the merger of Fuji Bank, center of the Fuyo Group, and Dai-Ichi Kangyo, center of the DKB Group, prompted consolidation in the steel industry as NKK (Fuyo group) and Kawasaki Steel (DKB) forged an alliance.[41] In other groups, long-standing ties still tug hard. For example, after it ran into financial trouble in 2005, automaker MMC received a bailout of 540 billion yen—half of which came from three loyal members of its keiretsu (Mitsubishi Heavy Industries, Bank

37. Fujitsu Research Institute, "Survey of Changes in Transaction Relationships between Enterprises," December 2006; referenced in METI, *White Paper on Small and Medium-sized Business,* 2007.

38. METI, *White Paper on Small and Medium-sized Business,* 2006, 111.

39. See, for example, Noguchi (2002). For a contrarian view about the impact of technological innovation, see Morita and Nakahara (2004).

40. METI, *White Paper on SMEs,* 2006, 107.

41. *Economist,* "Japan's Keiretsu: Regrouping," November 25, 2000.

of Tokyo Mitsubishi, and Mitsubishi Corp., which collectively became the automaker's leading shareholder).[42] Generally, though, a new pattern of interindustry ties, what Shimotani (2004) calls the "big four regime," is now emerging in Japan.

Far from disappearing like the dinosaur, the practice of cross-shareholding also continued into the new millennium. It is true that mutually held or "stable" shares have, for the most part, continued to decline as a percentage of outstanding shares among listed firms. But the trend has been neither constant nor overwhelming. Nomura Securities reported that the percentage of such stable shares actually *rose* in fiscal year 2006—for the first time since that company began gathering data in 1990.[43] Some observers, including Iwai (2007), have called this a short-term blip, primarily a function of 2007 legislation that would authorize triangular mergers and that could therefore fuel takeover bids. For example, Nippon Steel, Sumitomo Metal, and Kobe Steel exchanged notes promising to sell shares to one another in the event that any one of the companies became the target of a takeover attempt. But it turned out that other firms were interested in boosting their cross-shareholdings to reinforce synergies embedded in their relationship. For example, Toyota recently invested about $325 million in Matsushita, while Matsushita has increased its stake in Toyota.[44] By exchanging hostages in the form of stock, Toyota has signaled its interest in drawing on its partner's strength in environmental and safety technologies, while Matsushita has signaled its interest in the increasingly high-tech, electronics-dependent automobile market.

But this discussion overlooks an important change in shareholdings. As table 8.1 shows, foreigners have dramatically increased their presence in the Tokyo Stock Exchange—from 8.1 percent of market value in 1995 to 28 percent in 2007. This increase has been particularly dramatic in the new millennium. It has definitely *not* come at the expense of Japanese individuals, who continue to hold less than 20 percent of market value—down slightly from the percentage they held in 1990 (23.1%), and down dramatically from what they held in 1960 (46.3%). Rather, it has come at the expense of domestic financial institutions and corporations.

Unlike stable shareholders, foreign investors have been neither passive nor quiet. They have challenged management positions, often calling for deeper restructuring and greater dividend payments. For example, in 2001 alone, the California Public Employees Retirement System (CalPERS), which is now in-

42. *Japan Times,* "MMC Execs Resign as Automaker Gets ¥540 Billion Bailout," January 29, 2005.

43. *Nikkei Weekly,* "Cross-shareholdings on the Rise," July 2, 2007.

44. *Nikkei Weekly,* "Toyota, Matsushita Get Cozy," July 2, 2007.

Table 8.1. Foreigners in the Tokyo Stock Exchange

Year	Government	Financial institutions	Business corporations	Security companies	Individuals	Foreigners (corporations and individuals)
1960	0.2	30.6	17.8	3.7	46.3	1.3
1970	0.2	32.3	23.1	1.2	39.9	3.2
1980	0.2	38.8	26.0	1.7	29.2	4.0
1990	0.6	45.2	25.2	1.7	23.1	4.2
1995	0.3	42.8	27.7	1.2	19.9	8.1
1996	0.3	41.1	27.2	1.4	19.5	10.5
1997	0.2	41.9	25.6	1.0	19.4	11.9
1998	0.2	42.1	24.6	0.7	19.0	13.4
1999	0.2	41.0	25.2	0.6	18.9	14.1
2000	0.1	36.5	26.0	0.8	18.0	18.6
2001	0.2	39.1	21.8	0.7	19.4	18.8
2002	0.2	39.4	21.8	0.7	19.7	18.3
2003	0.2	39.1	21.5	0.9	20.6	17.7
2004	0.2	34.5	21.8	1.2	20.5	21.8
2005	0.2	32.7	21.9	1.2	20.3	23.7
2006	0.2	31.6	21.1	1.4	19.1	26.7
2007	0.3	31.1	20.7	1.8	18.1	28.0

Source: Tokyo Stock Exchange (www.tse.or.jp).
Notes: Number of shares has been calculated on the basis of "unit share" since 1985; figures represent percentages and do not always add up to 100 due to rounding.

vesting heavily in Japanese corporations, began to flex its muscles by voting against management proposals at sixty shareholders' meetings in Japan. In 2007, as well, foreign investors pushed rival proposals at the annual meetings of thirty companies.[45] For the most part, outsiders have been outvoted, and thus defeated—but they have made waves. "The growing number of overseas shareholders is putting pressure on corporate Japan to reform its outdated and murky way of conducting business," one newspaper reported.[46]

In a momentous development, the activism of foreign shareholders has begun to rub off on domestic investors, albeit slowly. Institutional investors, notoriously docile in the past, have begun to speak up, as evidenced by the first-ever proxy fight at the June 2002 annual meeting of Tokyo Style, a clothing manufacturer. Even the Government Pension Investment Fund has begun to urge other institutional investors to use their voting rights to bring about corporate change.[47] Institutional Shareholder Services, a U.S. con-

45. *Nikkei Weekly,* "Shareholders Reject Record Number of Activist Motions," July 2, 2007.
46. Makoto Sato, "Making Waves," *Nikkei Weekly,* November 5, 2001.
47. *Asahi Shinbun,* "Investors Finally Find Their Voice, Get Tough on Companies," June 5, 2002.

sulting firm, established a Tokyo office in 2001; by the end of 2006, it was serving fifty clients in Japan.[48]

We should be careful not overstate the significance of such developments. Although the "barbarians"—foreign and domestic—may be "at the gate," as a headline in the *Economist* (April 3, 1999) suggested, they still remain, for the most part, on the outside. The managers of Japanese corporations have been able to rely on insiders, such as stable shareholders (including fellow keiretsu members), to resist the forces of change far more effectively than many observers anticipated. But recent developments suggest that this resistance is increasingly futile. As Japanese capital markets become less regulated and more globalized, change becomes inevitable. The process is yielding a gradual but ineluctable movement toward looser interfirm ties. One development, which seemed unimaginable in the mid-1990s, symbolizes this trend: since 2000, Japanese entrepreneurs have been able to search the Web for new sources of financing as well as new markets for their goods and services.[49] This seems a far cry from the close, reciprocal ties between main banks and corporate borrowers, and between parent firms and subcontractors, that sewed together the Japanese business world for so many years.

Labor and Management

Cooperation between labor and management, a hallmark of the ideal-typical Japanese firm, came under even sharper scrutiny in the first decade of the new millennium. Critics, especially Western economists and management consultants, became more adamant, arguing that the Japanese economy would not regain its vitality as long as firms remained saddled with the fixed costs of lifetime or longtime employees earning wages based on seniority. More often than not, they called for sweeping changes in corporate governance. As shown in chapters 2 and 4, the ideal-typical Japanese firm has been "governed" quite differently from its counterpart in the West, or at least the United States and the United Kingdom. Instead of prioritizing the profit-making interests of stockholders, management in Japan has had greater freedom to prioritize the growth-sustaining interests of employees— a distinctive orientation made possible by the system of stable shareholding.

One critic, David Marra (2007), a principal in the Tokyo office of A. T. Kearney, a business consulting firm, complained that Japanese firms tend to hoard cash rather than use it to improve earnings and reward shareholders.

48. See *Japan Times,* "Murakami's Influence Will Linger," December 28, 2006.
49. On new sources of financing, see *Yomiuri Shinbun,* "Entrepreneurs, Lenders to Connect Online," February 2, 1999. On new markets, see *Asahi Shinbun,* "Oyajitachi no dokuritsu sengen" (A Declaration of Independence by Parent Firms), November 19, 2000.

"The large amount of cash held by Japanese firms," he wrote, "suggests a huge loss to the nation's economy in the form of reduced operating performance, not to mention the effect of value destruction on shareholders." Another critic, Yonekura Seiichiro (2000, 65), argued that the Japanese model of corporate governance worked well in an earlier era of steady growth, but has become outdated. Employees today need to be able to move freely from stagnant to more dynamic industries, or from poorly managed to well-managed firms. Corporations, he argued, "should employ a form of corporate governance that prioritizes shareholders in order to effect more dynamic changes—even if it means temporary losses of jobs—based on the recognition that we are in the midst of great upheaval."

But analysts supporting the status quo, such as Sato (2000) and Tsutagawa (2004), noted that Japanese firms using the traditional model of governance, most notably Toyota, remain relatively strong. And entrenched executives of such firms clung fiercely to their primary objective: to retain positional power and avoid yielding control to outsiders, including shareholders. In doing so, they presented themselves as the guardians of job security. Katayama (2002, 57) quotes Canon president Mitarai Fujio to this effect: "Lifetime employment nurtures loyalty, which is the backbone of Japanese capitalism."

In the end, the forces of change appear to have won this contest—but not by very much. Let me explain this conclusion by first examining legislation championed by the prime minister's Cabinet Office but resisted by Keidanren, the big business lobby, and by the Ministry of Justice. In 2002, the Diet amended Japan's Commercial Code to allow large firms to choose between two models: an American-style structure with a CEO supervised and audited by a smaller, independent board of directors, or a Japanese-style structure (*kansayaku*), dominated by management, but one that has at least three auditors, a majority of whom must be outsiders.[50]

The measure was hailed as a major reform of Japanese corporate governance, a shift to "global standards." However, due to resistance from those enjoying positional power in corporate Japan, from the managers charged with carrying out the new law, it ultimately proved less consequential than many had expected. By June 2004, Seki (2005) found that fewer than 3 percent of the largest firms listed on the Tokyo stock exchange had decided to adopt the new system. Further analysis showed that many firms retaining the *kansayaku* tradition were conforming to the law by defining "outsiders" rather loosely. For example, *Asahi* evaluated compliance at member firms in the Toyota supply club, and found that twenty-one of the twenty-three "outside" au-

50. For an expanded discussion of this issue, see Ahmadjian (2003).

ditors were actually current or former executives of other group companies.[51] For example, honorary chairman Toyoda Shoichiro served as "outside" auditor at Aisin Seiki, while chairman Okuda served as "outside" auditor at Denso Corp. Both firms are first-tier parts suppliers in the Toyota keiretsu.

As they did in the 1990s, Japanese firms engaged in *risutora* (restructuring) —but often without really shaking things up. Yes, they cut costs and restored profits, but they were reluctant to change long-standing practices and, in particular, to sever long-standing ties. As Katz (2007) argues, corporate executives "learned to do things more cheaply but not necessarily differently." For example, while some giant conglomerates moved aggressively to shed operations outside their main area of business expertise, concentrating instead on core operations, many other megafirms balked. This was due to the fact that corporate managers continued to enjoy their position at the center of a web of social relationships—with employees as well as suppliers.[52] For example, Hitachi, which produces everything from washing machines to nuclear plants, announced in 2003 that it would try to boost profits by shedding 20 percent of its operations. But a year later, it dramatically scaled back its restructuring plan, choosing to shed only 10 percent of its operations.[53] "In many cases, we couldn't find good buyers" for underperforming operations, a Hitachi executive explained to me. "We realized we would have to close too many plants, jeopardizing too many workers."[54]

After a decade of wrangling over corporate governance, a decade of sparring over corporate organization, what, then, is the state of labor–management relations? I answer this by focusing on what have been the two key institutions in this leg of selective relationalism: lifetime or long-time employment, and seniority-based pay.

For most regular employees, Japan's labor elite, the institution of lifetime employment survived the political and business wars. Corporations reduced payroll by shifting redundant workers to affiliated firms via *shukkō* or *tenseki*, encouraging older workers to retire early, and filling occasional vacancies with part-time or temporary workers. Laying off regular employees was a last

---

51. *Asahi Shinbun*, "Shagai kansayaku 9 wari 'miuchi' Toyota Grūpu 11-sha" (90 Percent of the Outside Auditors at 11 Toyota Group Firms Turn Out to Be Family Members), May 28, 2003. This, of course, was not a new development. When the Diet revised the commercial code in 1993 to create the *kansayaku* system, companies "moved quickly to appoint executives from affiliated (keiretsu) firms to the new position of statutory auditor."

52. Yamamoto Takatoshi (2002, 120), director of securities research for Morgan Stanley Japan, predicts the demise of Japanese conglomerates that are unable to focus on core operations and shed the rest. Managers resist this kind of restructuring, he writes, "because they have attached greater importance to the benefits of workers and the local governments where plans are located than they have to stockholders."

53. *Asahi Shinbun*, "Hitachi Applies Brakes to Bold Reform Drive," February 6, 2004.

54. Interview, Hitachi City, August 5, 2005.

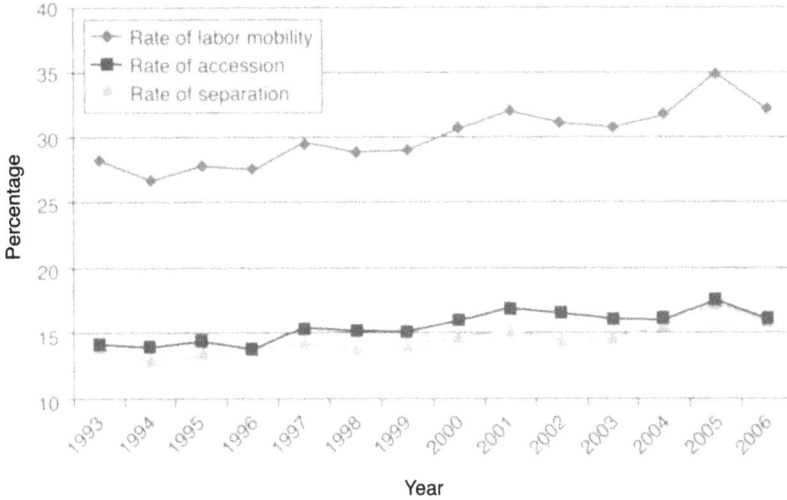

Figure 8.1. Trends in labor mobility
Source: Ministry of Health, Labour and Welfare, *Chingin Kōzō Kihon Tōkei Chōsa* (*Basic Survey of Wage Structure*), 2004.
Notes: (1) Rate of accessions = Number of hired employees / Number of regular employees (A) (as of July 1); Rate of separation = Number of separated employees / Number of regular employees (B) (as of July 1); Rate of labor mobility = (A) + (B); (2) From 1991, construction is included. 3) As industries covered have been partially increased since 2004, figures do not connect to those before 2003.

resort, and rarely used—even in the most desperate circumstances.[55] As a result, most regular employees managed to hold on to lifetime or longtime employment. A survey by the Policy Research Institute of MOF (2003) found that 84.1 percent of firms maintained the practice of lifetime employment —a small drop from 1999, when 90.3 percent did so. And a survey of 1,066 firms by the Ministry of Health, Labor and Welfare (2004) found that more than 75 percent intended to maintain long-term employment for their "core" workers.[56] Most remarkably, the average job tenure for regular workers actually *climbed* from 10.9 years in 1990 to 12.1 years in 2004.[57] Figure 8.1 shows that, when one includes nonregular employees in the equation, labor mobility has increased in Japan—but even then, only at the margin.

Although the institution of lifetime employment remained alive and well, the number of workers able to access it declined markedly. That is, distrib-

55. See Japan Institute of Labor, "Working Conditions and the Labor Market," *Japan Labor Bulletin,* May 1, 2001, 3.

56. This finding is supported by a survey ("Corporate Human Resource Strategies and Workers' Attitude towards Work") conducted in 2003 by the Japan Institute of Labor. Only 15 percent of responding companies agreed that a "fundamental review [of the practice of lifetime employment] is necessary."

57. Ministry of Health, Labor and Welfare, 2004, "Chingin kōzō kihon tōkei chōsa" (Basic Survey of Wage Structure).

utional change in this area of Japan's political economy accelerated during the first decade of the new millennium. Even as Japan's economy has improved, firms have continued to control the number of regular employees on their payrolls. By 2007, the share of "nonregular" (part-time and temporary) employees in the overall labor force had grown to an unprecedented level of 35.5 percent. And women, always exploited in the Japanese labor market, but perhaps more so today than ever before, accounted for most of that growth. While fewer than 20 percent of men in the workforce were part-time or temporary employees, more than 55 percent of women were.[58] And young people, who make up a disproportionate share of the unemployed in Japan, found it harder and harder to find regular employment after graduating from high school or even college—a problem documented by scholars such as Genda (2001) and Kawamoto (2003). While the jobless rate for middle-aged workers (45–54) inched up to 4 percent by 2004, the rate for youth (under twenty-five) climbed above 10 percent.

Unlike lifetime employment, the seniority-based wage system appears, at least according to some sources, to be on the way out. In 2003, the Japan Productivity Center for Socio-Economic Development reported that nearly 40 percent of companies responding to a survey indicated they already had adopted a system of performance-based pay.[59] This was a sharp increase from 1996, when fewer than 10 percent indicated they had done so. Companies adopted the new approach not only to motivate workers but to trim payroll costs; the combination of a "graying" workforce and seniority-based pay had been driving up operating costs for many years. Most companies indicated they had adopted such a system for professional staff, but others—such as Toyota—announced they would use the new system for rank-and-file employees as well.[60]

Upon closer inspection, however, the actual scale of this new trend is uncertain. Many companies reporting a switch from seniority to merit pay systems acknowledge they calculate new wage rates based on group performance, not individual performance. For example, they might use the performance of a product line, a division, or even an entire plant to determine the annual wages of workers in that particular group.[61] In other cases, firms have instituted merit-pay systems, but then withdrawn them or watered them down under protest from employees and their unions. A Fujitsu executive

58. Ministry of Internal Affairs and Communication, October 2007.

59. See *Japan Times*, "Nearly 41% of Firms Have Adopted Merit-Based Annual Pay," March 5, 2003.

60. *Japan Times*, "Toyota to Make Full Shift to Performance-Based Pay," February 18, 2004.

61. The number of companies using such group-based performance evaluations is "conspicuous," according to *Yomiuri Shinbun* ("Performance-Based Pay Systems Catching on Fast," March 7, 2003).

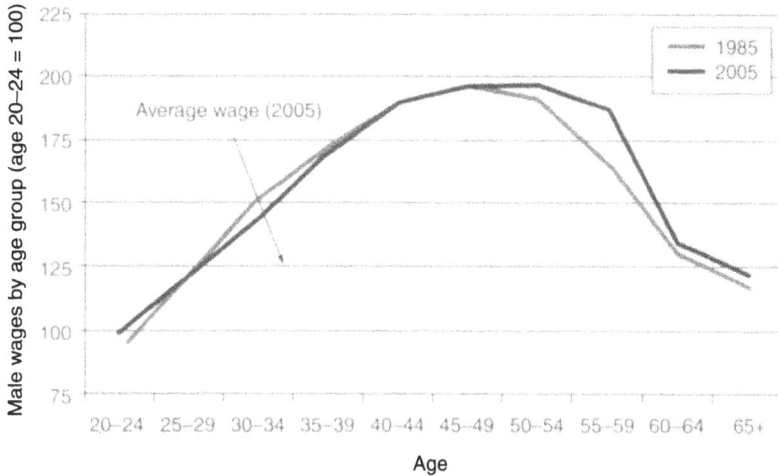

Figure 8.2. Seniority pay
Source: HSBC Tokyo, Ministry of Health, Labor and Welfare, *Oriental Economist,* June 2007.

told me his company determined that merit pay for its employees was creating more costs than benefits: "It just wasn't working out."[62]

One management consultant has argued that managers, just as much as rank-and-file workers, "cling tenaciously" to the old system. The new pay schemes they have adopted in recent years are, "with very few exceptions," retooled seniority wage schemes, according to Jo Shigeyuki (2006):

> Each year's recruits start out with the same entry-level pay [the lowest wage level], which has hardly changed over the last twenty years after inflation is factored in, and they all receive gradual pay increases year by year and become eligible for promotion into management posts around the edge of forty. In other words, there has been no change in the practice of requiring new employees to slave away at the bottom of the corporate hierarchy for a considerable period of time. About the only modification is that some employees now advance somewhat more quickly than others.

The view that the institution of seniority-based wages, like lifetime employment, remains alive and well for the "labor elite" is supported by new research conducted for the Ministry of Health, Labor and Welfare, and documented in figure 8.2. It shows that age/wage curves for 1985 and 2005 virtually overlap, except that wages now plunge after age 60 instead of after 55. Workers aged 40–60 earn 75 percent more than 20–24 year olds, and 30 percent more than 30–34 year olds.

62. Interview, July 2007, Tokyo.

We shouldn't be surprised to discover that managers are quite reluctant to break the strong ties that bind them to core employees in the firm. Not only do those ties sustain long-standing practices; they also provide a source of positional power. But what intrigues me is the fact that labor—management ties have loosened at all, that employees and employers are finding more open-ended ways to connect. To take just one example, in 2004, a headhunting firm (Recruit) collaborated with Yahoo! Japan to build a website for job-seekers—one that is not sponsored by the government or geared for the lifetime job "market." Those seeking part-time employment post their qualifications and experience, and also the days and locations they wish to work.[63] This kind of development suggests that resistance to change is finally being overcome, at the margins, by the crushing weight of globalization—a force that once was kept at bay by elite regionalization. Japanese corporations, desperate to cut costs, now have little choice but to relax intrafirm relational networks.

Implications for Japan

In chapter 6, I argued that selective relationalism had helped to slow down the rate of dynamic technological growth in Japan. By extension, I argue here that the loosening of such relational networks has contributed to Japan's economic recovery. It reflects a structural change that should help the nation meet the requirements of a domestic economy that is postindustrial, and the demands of a global economy that is increasingly open.

Others point to trends in the Japanese political economy and find bad news. They note, for example, that the number of manufacturing workers in Japan shrank by 9.2 percent from 2001 to 2004—much faster than the rate of decline in total employment (5.2%).[64] In my view, however, this is probably good news. Japan is finally "hollowing out" in a positive way, restructuring its economy to make room for new industries and new firms that can compete in the twenty-first century. The slowly accumulating evidence is anecdotal, but nearly ubiquitous:

- Newspapers report that more and more Japanese white collar workers are acquiring new skills outside work by taking graduate classes in the evening. Some are leaving solid but dull jobs to start up their own firms. "I grew tired of the old rules," one such *sarariman* (salaryman) told *Asahi*.[65]
- New ventures now have easier access to capital, including two stock mar-

63. The new joint venture is called Indival Inc. See *Japan Times*, "Firms Set Up Net-Based Job Scheme," February 27, 2004.
64. See Kikkawa Takeo, "Kamaishi: Where the Galaxy Express Meets the Sanriku Coast," *Social Science Japan Newsletter*, March 2007.
65. *Asahi Shinbun*, "Jibun wa jibun de migaku shika . . ." (If I Want to Improve Myself, I Must Improve by Myself), October 22, 2000.

kets—MOTHERS in Tokyo and HERCULES in Osaka—that did not exist in 1999. The combined capitalization of these two markets has expanded rapidly to twenty trillion yen by 2005 (OECD 2006, 144). Both allow firms to list before they have begun to show a profit. In response, JASDAQ also has relaxed its listing requirements.

- Academics are actively promoting entrepreneurship. One of them, Tsukio Yoshio, a professor in the Graduate School of Frontier Sciences at the University of Tokyo, has called on Japan to decentralize and downsize its business community: "We must abandon our belief that bigger is better."[66]
- METI announced in 2004 that Japan was experiencing a miniboom in new business ventures in service industries that, in the past, had experienced little growth. It noted that younger entrepreneurs had launched many of the successful companies.[67]
- Tokyo's Shibuya, a glitzy neighborhood of offices and shops, now is home to a number of small Internet start-ups. Many are staffed by young people who could not find regular employment or who choose to forego it—people who, in the past, were derisively called "*freetas*" (under-employed).
- Small firms are collaborating in larger numbers with one another, and with universities, on important R&D projects. Motohashi (2004) suggests this new trend is transforming Japan's national innovation system for the better.

It adds up to this: Japan is changing, slowly but surely. And the pace of change may even accelerate in the wake of the Democratic Party of Japan's victory in the lower house elections of August 2009.

Time will tell. What is already clear, though, is that many today welcome structural change in the political economy of Japan. Even a government panel, commissioned by former prime minister Koizumi's Council on Economic and Fiscal Policy, has called for the creation of "a diverse, multi-talented society in which individuals can realize their dreams."[68] This sounds rather different from government reports of the past, with their talk of new industrial policies and manufacturing investment. It suggests that globalization has finally begun to trump elite regionalization—for better or worse. We now must wait to learn if this breakthrough, achieved just as Japan was engulfed by the financial firestorm that began on Wall Street in 2008, proves to be more than a Pyrrhic victory. The domestic economy, as it turned out, was burned very badly in 2009—just as it opened itself to global pressures for change.

66. See Tsukio Yoshio, "Come the Revolution," *Look Japan,* March 2001, 13.
67. *Japan Times,* "Small Firms Said Creating New Business," April 28, 2004.
68. Special board of inquiry for examining Japan's 21st Century Vision, "A New Era of Dynamism: Closer Ties and a Wide Range of Opportunities," April 2005.

Conclusion

Beyond Asia

The case study outlined in this book demonstrates clearly that, during the 1990s, Japanese government and business elites managed to preserve the administrative and production networks that made up the highly relational political economy of Japan by extending those networks into developing Asia, where they were able to generate net gains. This is because strong relational ties work best in the context of development, when firms are still adopting technology from the global reservoir of existing know-how. Thus, by going regional, Japanese elites bought themselves precious time in the face of pressures associated with globalization: (a) growing demands from political and business leaders in other industrialized countries to abandon selective relationalism and instead adopt what have been called "best practices" or "global standards" for organizing economic activity; (b) increasingly stiff competition brought on by liberalization; and (c) market volatility created by rising levels of capital mobility. In other words, Japanese elites temporarily sidestepped the onerous task of making structural changes to the highly relational political economy of Japan. However, with the collapse of the flying geese pattern of development in Asia, the jig appears to be up: Japan is now undergoing some of the changes that had been avoided for such a surprisingly long time.

Although my argument about regionalization and globalization is novel, it is not entirely new. Katzenstein and Shiraishi (1997, 344) touch on it in their comparative analysis of Japan in Asia and Germany in Europe when they suggest that states suffering a loss of economic sovereignty due to globalization may try to "compensate" by pursuing regional integration schemes over which they have some control. And it is even foreshadowed in a roundabout way by Moravcsik (1994), who argues that state executives in Europe have used regional institutions (and more specifically, the supranational institutions of the European Community/European Union) to "cut slack" for themselves at home, where myriad domestic actors otherwise impose constraints on their policy authority. This approach sets him apart from Putnam (1988), who believes state executives want to "tie their hands," or encourage domestic actors to impose constraints on them, so as to increase their leverage in negotiations with other state executives. To the contrary, Moravcsik (64) writes that, when bargaining at the supranational level (and specifically here, at a regional level above the nation-state), the heads of state in Europe

> have a strong incentive to create intergovernmental cartels, perpetuating traditional foreign policy prerogatives. The result: They have enhanced their institutional, informational, and ideological control over EC policy to the point where they dominate domestic agendas. Effective opposition is costly and, as a result, generally incoherent, almost always taking the form of scattered negative criticism.[1]

This book, then, does not break completely new ground in showing that regionalization can boost the power of domestic actors who control or guide that process. Unlike previous efforts, however, it does offer an integrated, comprehensive framework for understanding how and why this is possible. In building this framework, I have relied heavily on the "embeddedness" or "network" literature in economic sociology, and have sought to incorporate it, for the first time, into a model of political economy.

In this conclusion, I briefly retrace my steps before highlighting two issues—causation and motivation—that merit further analytical inquiry and empirical research. In addition, and most importantly, I use the theoretical model presented in chapter 1, as well as the lessons learned inductively through the case study presented in chapters 2 through 8, to spell out the conditions under which elites might be able to utilize regionalization to trump globalization. I then consider other possible cases that might satisfy those conditions.

Once around Lightly

Chapter 1 noted an underappreciated fact: economic and political exchange is almost always embedded, to a greater or lesser degree, in a structure of social relations. In simple terms, we may occasionally get a haircut from someone we have never met, but rarely from someone who has not been

---

1. One implication of Moravcsik's controversial argument is that the EU's often noted "democratic deficit" is not an accident, but rather an intended result of state executives seeking leverage over domestic interests.

recommended to us by a valued source of information. Most transactions occur within a network of human relationships, not in a faceless spot market. In some places, such as Japan, exchange networks are, on the whole, rather cohesive; that is, relational ties between network members are rather strong. In a political economy sewn together by such strong ties, and thus a political economy characterized by a high level of what I call "selective relationalism," well-positioned actors—those who occupy central positions inside those exchange networks—will be able to control access to resources, particularly information, embedded in those networks. The stronger the network ties, the greater the opportunity for the exercise of such positional power.

In chapter 2, I examined the domestic political economy of Japan, charting the rise of selective relationalism in the postwar period and probing the exchange networks that defined this system of network capitalism. The exercise helped establish a baseline to use later in measuring the amount of change or continuity in the "three-legged stool" of cooperation between state and industry, between otherwise independent firms, and between labor and management inside the firm. It was found that valuable resources such as information were locked inside the relatively closed and exclusionary networks of the Japanese political economy. In chapter 3, I shifted the analysis to the international (or, more precisely, the regional) level and documented the efforts of Japanese government and business elites in the 1990s to regionalize this system of selective relationalism through such means as official development assistance and foreign direct investment. These elites, it was learned, acted as agents of economic integration who enjoyed positional power in the region—much as they had at home.

I returned to the domestic level in chapter 4, looking for evidence of change or continuity in key indicators of relationalism in Japan at the end of the twentieth century. This analysis suggested that Japan experienced massive distributional change in the 1990s, but very little structural change in its political economy. Chapter 5 attempted to explain this result by looking at Japan from the outside in. It showed how elite regionalization—the export of Japanese administrative and production networks to Asia—helped to rescue Japanese relationalism in the 1990s, a time of crisis at home. Although this process has contributed further to the marginalization of already peripheral players in the political economy of Japan, it has at the same time consolidated and tightened existing ties between "core" members of administrative and production networks. In chapter 6, I considered the implications of this process and suggested that rescuing relationalism was precisely the wrong medicine for the Japanese economy. This is because strong relational ties, which provided important benefits when Japan was still developing, began to impose heavy costs after that economy had become fully developed or mature. The problem, then, was not networks in the abstract; Saxenian (1994) demonstrates this brilliantly in her comparison of business practices in Silicon Valley in northern California, where networks are open and flexible, and Route 128 in the Boston area, where firms are more often organized into vertical hierarchies. The problem was the inward-looking ("locked in") and exclusionary ("locked out") character of exchange networks in Japan. Indeed, Saxenian's description of Route 128 applies nicely to Japan: "Corporations that invested in dedicated equipment and specialized worker skills find themselves locked in to obsolete technologies and markets, while hierarchical structures limit their ability to adapt quickly as conditions change. Their inward focus and vertical integration also limit the development of a sophisticated infrastructure, leaving the entire region vulnerable when large firms falter" (9).

Chapter 7 showed that several factors, from the stagnation in Japan's innovation system to the Asian financial crisis, from the emergence of rival sources of capital and technology to the rise of Chinese economic power, conspired to undermine the flying geese pattern of development. Japanese elites, who had come to dominate the region's vertically structured administrative and production networks, lost their positional power in Asia. In the process, elite regionalization cracked and then crumbled. It no longer served as a break or buffer against the powerful forces of globalization. Chapter 8 returned to the domestic level, documenting the slow but steady transformation of the Japanese political economy. Although institutions such as administrative guidance, keiretsu, and lifetime employment have not disappeared, they are changing. Social networks in Japan have opened up, become less exclusionary.

Causation

This book has adopted what Gourevitch (1978) calls a "second image reversed" perspective; that is, it has examined the international political economy's "feedback effects" on the domestic political economy of a single country. I concede that globalization may be the awesome, punishing force it is so often said to be, but I also assert that the domestic actors trying to cope with its impact may not always be the flotsam and jetsam they are so often said to be. Under admittedly restrictive conditions, those public and private actors may even be able to utilize a countervailing force—that is, regionalization— to trump globalization and thwart its power to compel institutional convergence among different nation-states in the international system.

Some may find it frustrating that my analysis does not specify the precise mechanism through which external forces such as globalization and regionalization shape domestic actors, or through which domestic actors may use those forces. To do so, however, is impossible; the transmission belt is not fixed in space or time. Instead, it is best to think about such forces as imposing undetermined constraints and creating indefinite opportunities, the extent of which depends not only on the size and scope of the forces but also on the vulnerabilities and capabilities of domestic actors. As I demonstrated here, Japanese elites had, by the early 1990s, become deeply exposed to globalization as they liberalized domestic markets and participated in global institutions. But they also had come to occupy a powerful position, or set of positions, in an increasingly integrated or networked Asia from which they could use regionalization as a hedge, a kind of protective shield.

Motivation

Of all the questions addressed in this book, perhaps the most vexing one has been this: How can we explain the behavior of Japanese political and business elites in the 1990s, when they moved to preserve the institutional status quo—despite the fact that the costs of selective relationalism, measured in rent-seeking behavior, organizational rigidity, inefficient investment, and high consumer prices, had clearly come to outweigh the benefits?

Economistic assumptions of "rational choice" will not carry us very far, unless we use a highly plastic definition of "utility" (the preferences that rational actors are out to maximize). It seems rather unlikely that business elites, in particular, would rationally choose to undermine the health of the economy, and thus jeopardize their own economic well-being. What could be the "utility" in that?

At the same time, however, we need not resort to ungrounded cultural arguments that amount to generalizations about the way "the Japanese" or even "Japan" traditionally behaves. And we should be able to offer a stronger explanation for institutional continuity than "path dependence," which simply suggests that established institutions narrow the options available to actors, and thus fundamentally shape if not preemptively dictate the next move to be taken by those actors. I believe this book does indeed offer a stronger explanation.

Japanese political and business elites were not motivated solely or perhaps even primarily by economic interests such as high salaries or profit rates, and they were not passive subjects driven to repeat the past. I have argued here that Japanese elites, operating within a given structure of human relationships, were motivated by a desire to maintain the positional power they had come to enjoy in a system of selective relationalism. This power, derived from occupying central nodes in an exchange network, meant that elites were less dependent on other actors for access to information and other nominally shared resources tucked inside that network. Conversely, it meant that other actors in the exchange network were *more* dependent on elites for access to those resources. Thus, for elites, positional power carried with it much more than just a material advantage to be used in political or economic competition. It also carried a certain amount of prestige and status.[2]

Is the Japan/Asia Case Sui Generis?

The theoretical model used in this thesis seems to neatly cover the Japanese case; so neatly, in fact, that a skeptic might be justified in wondering whether it is merely a post hoc, idiographic explanation for a single, nonportable case. To properly address such skepticism, we first must define the conditions under which the model "works"; that is, the conditions under which elites could possibly regionalize domestic institutions under stress and thereby protect themselves against the forces of globalization. Following the model's logic, I have assembled the following "recipe" of necessary ingredients:

1. An advanced, capitalist state whose political economy is held together by relatively strong relational ties.
2. A nearby region comprised entirely or largely of developing economies.
3. Elites from the developed country who occupy pivotal positions in the flow of private and public capital, as well as merchandise trade, within the surrounding region; in other words, elites who enjoy at least a modest level of positional power in the region.

The case of the United States in Latin America (Central and South America) would seem to satisfy the second and third conditions. The U.S. government is the leading provider of bilateral aid to most Central and South American states, and despite friction with Venezuela, it still dominates policy networks in the region. U.S. MNCs account for nearly half of all the FDI flowing into the region every year. In Mexico, the power of the United States is especially pronounced; it accounts for 65 percent of all FDI inflows. At the end of the 1990s, eight of Mexico's top ten firms (in terms of sales) were affiliates of U.S.-based multinationals: General Motors, Chrysler, Ford, Cifra (Wal-Mart), Femsa (Coca-Cola), IBM, Sabritas (Pepsi), and General Electric.[3]

But this case fails to meet condition number one. The United States, as I pointed out in chapter 1, used to have a political economy characterized by

2. In her analysis of the "tea pourers' rebellion" in a Kyoto city office, Pharr (1984) notes that status continues to play an important function in ordering Japanese society.
3. Data come from United Nations, *Foreign Investment in Latin America and the Caribbean, 1998 Report*. Santiago, Chile: Unit on Investment and Corporate Strategies, Division of Production, Productivity and Management, December 1998.

strong relational ties—but not anymore. Relationalism in the United States long ago gave way to a more atomistic system of spot market exchange, as well as mutual suspicion between government and business, and between management and labor. In fact, compared to Japan, the United States today is probably at the opposite end of any spectrum of relationalism.

The case of Germany in central and eastern Europe seems a much better fit. In the 1990s, the German state was providing more than half of the bilateral ODA to central and eastern European states making the transition from socialism to capitalism.[4] Perhaps more important, it was paving the way for many of these countries hoping to join the European Union, championing their proposals for accession and helping them secure regional funds for economic adjustment. In 1989, Germany persuaded the EU to create two programs: PHARE (Poland and Hungary: Assistance for Restructuring their Economies), which has funded rural development and infrastructure projects; and INTERREG (Interregional Cooperation), which has promoted cross-border ties between member countries and candidate countries. More than any other EU member, Germany stood to prosper from such programs. Davis and Dombrowski (1997, 15) note that, in the mid-1990s, Poland and the Czech Republic, Germany's immediate neighbors to the east, received over half of INTERREG funds.

Like Japan in Asia and the United States in Central America, Germany has come to dominate FDI flows into central Europe, supplying about 30 percent of the foreign direct investment received each year by the Czech Republic, about 25 percent received by Hungary, about 21 percent by Slovakia, and 20 percent by Poland.[5]

The factors motivating German multinationals to invest in central Europe sound rather like those that motivated Japanese multinationals to invest in Asia. According to Lemoine (1998, 4) German MNCs "were faced with high domestic production costs and [so] they intensified the transfer of production to low wage countries." While Katzenstein (2005, 125) notes that those firms "have been slow to build cross-regional production networks" by transferring technology, others suggest that German MNCs eventually will serve to link the economies of central and eastern Europe with those, especially Germany's, in the west. To some degree, this may already be happening. For example, Linden (1998, 7) notes that Siemens has built factories in Hungary, Poland, and the Czech Republic, and is swapping parts among them. Aniol et al. (1997, 232) notes that Volkswagen, after forging an agreement with the Czech Republic in 1990 to rescue that country's leading automobile

---

4. See Kraus (1996, 124–25).

5. Estimates come from the individual countries. My thanks to Gunter Heiduk, professor of economics at the University of Duisburg, for help in collecting these data.

manufacturer, has created a German-dominated network of parts suppliers. More than half of its subcontractors were German.

Many scholars have suggested that Germany's model of capitalism, a corporatist model in which the state provides a high level of social welfare and oversees cooperation, or "co-determination," between management and labor, faced a severe crisis in the 1990s. At the critical moment of unification, Streeck (1998, 86) suggests that

> German capitalism may have met its limits with respect to the size of its product markets, its capacity to maintain product leadership, its ability to manage its labor supply, or more than one of these at the same time. Indications were that, in response, it had begun slowly to deteriorate into a pattern where socially instituted markets, negotiated management, structurally conservative politics, quasi-public associational governance, and cultural traditionalism resulted no longer in industrial upgrading, but in an ever-expanding number of people being relegated to an ever more expensive and, ultimately, unsustainable social safety net in the widest sense, being kept out of employment at public or in employment at private expense.

But like Japan, Germany apparently "muddled through" this crisis in the 1990s, without undergoing any major transformation of its political economy. Vitols (2004, 20) notes that, despite enormous market pressure as well as national legislation in response to that pressure, Germany's bank-based financial system "remains quite strong, and is the primary source of external finance for most types of firms." Streeck and Trampusch (2005, 190) find that, "after eight years of sometimes dramatic political conflict over welfare state reform, by 2003 non-wage labor costs, far from having come down, had risen further by two percentage points, with no end in sight." And Schmidt (2002, 73) concludes that "the country was largely stymied in reform efforts throughout the decade."

As they did in trying to explain Japan's stubborn resistance to change, scholars have struggled to understand why a failed status quo managed to prevail in Germany. Streeck and Trampusch (2005, 190) ask the question most bluntly: "What prevents a fundamental restructuring—and nothing else would probably do—of a welfare state that is now widely recognized as strangling the labor market?" In answering their own question, they toss out a variety of factors—from vested interests to social norms—but ultimately shrug their shoulders: "Resistance to change has assumed traits that an outside observer might easily be tempted to consider nothing short of irrational" (191).

In addressing this puzzle, a surprisingly small number of scholars have adopted a "second-image reversed" perspective that considers the effect of external forces on domestic actors in Germany. And those who have done so have tended to look only at "Europeanization," the rapidly accelerating and deepening integration of markets that was, until May 2004, confined—at least legally and formally—to western Europe. For example, Schmidt (2002, 48) argues that Europeanization, defined as the process of building a common market and monetary union, "rather than intensifying global forces of competition, may very well have attenuated them," especially for Germany. This has been especially true in the field of interest rate, budget, tax, and exchange rate policy. In this field, Schmidt writes (90), Europeanization "has been little more than an extension to Europe and its member states of Germany's own traditional macroeconomic patterns and prejudices."

Perhaps it is only a matter of time before scholars begin to expand their definition of "Europeanization" to include the incorporation of central and eastern Europe into the broader regional project. Although Schmidt does not fully explore the implications of her own analysis, she seems to understand that this new, expanded process of regionalization may have an especially powerful impact on the domestic political economy of Germany. Unlike the proliferation of mergers and acquisitions in western Europe that began in the late 1980s in anticipation of the common market, she recognizes that "the move of production facilities to eastern Europe is directly related to the search for lower costs as well as for geographically contiguous and culturally related countries where the German model can be transplanted easily but the costs are lower" (172).

Obviously, much more research must be done to determine whether German elites have, like their Japanese counterparts, tried to preserve the status quo by regionalizing their relational ties. But the preliminary evidence is at least suggestive.

Bringing Society Back in to Social Science

The headline over the essay in the June 1997 issue of the *Journal of Economic History* asked, rather sheepishly, "Is it Kosher to Talk about Culture?" Peter Temin, the author of that essay, was not at all shy in answering, "yes." Academics may not know exactly how to use such an "elusive concept," he wrote (268), but they certainly ought to try.

I am decidedly ambivalent about such an agenda. On the one hand, the field of political science today is increasingly populated by "collective identities" and "epistemic communities" that sometimes seem to pop out of nowhere and float in space, like ghosts in a Halloween fun house. On the other hand, it cannot be denied that ideologies, norms, values, and beliefs matter, and that they often matter a great deal. In the end, we do not have to choose between thought and practice. Our goal should be to resurrect Gramsci's mission of finding a way (or ways) to trace the links between the material and the nonmaterial, to ground the otherwise high-flying concepts of intersubjective meaning and shared images in the concrete world of social structure. We must examine the ways in which ideas and institutions inform one another, and create opportunities for—and impose constraints upon—individual action.

Economic sociologists—from Mark Granovetter to David Knoke, Richard Emerson to Ronald Burt, Gary Hamilton to Yamagishi Toshio—have made an extremely valuable contribution in this regard. An underlying objective in this book has been to introduce their contributions to those working in the field of political economy, and thereby increase the flow of information across the disciplinary divide separating scholarly networks.

The Social Foundation of Political Economies

Coming to the end, some readers may conclude that I am nothing more than a secret agent of globalization, an American ideologue promoting a neo-liberal agenda. After all, my analysis suggests that Japan's economic recovery was long delayed in the 1990s by the illiberal reality of strong network ties.

But my ideological biases are not so simple. I recognize the short-term efficiency, but also the long-term violence, of unfettered markets. Indeed, if we can learn anything from the global financial crisis that began in 2008, it is that the Anglo-American model of capitalism is highly unstable and thus may carry unacceptable risk. Japan, linked more tightly than ever before to the rest of the world economy through commodity, service and financial markets, suffered enormous costs from dramatically tightening credit and declining exports. Advocates of relationalism (which had become a Japanese and—less coherently—an Asian way of doing business) suddenly had very good reason to sound triumphant.

Or did they? Just as Japan recovered more slowly in the late 1990s than other Asian economies facing financial distress, so too did it recover more slowly in 2009 than its neighbors, especially China. It began to grow again in the second quarter of that year, but somewhat anemically. Even with all the domestic change that came with the collapse of the "flying geese" pattern in Asia and the erosion of rearguard regionalization, Japan's political economy remained more institutionally stable than many others.

In the end, my sympathies lie with critics of globalization—but more for political than economic reasons. Local communities should be allowed to exercise some discretion in how they mesh with the global economy. What neo-liberals describe as "best practices" are only better if one favors economic efficiency over other values such as political autonomy and social harmony. In choosing regionalization over globalization in the 1990s, Japanese elites revealed a different utility function, not necessarily a worse one. And they, or perhaps insurgent forces in Japan, were entitled to choose their own path out of the mess of 2009 as well.

References

Abe, Hitoshi. 1978. "Shingikai Seido no Suii" (Change in the Shingikai System). *Chiiki Kaihatsu* 160: 8–14.

Adachi Fumihiko. 1996. "Kyūseichō suru Ajia to Nihon Chūshō Kigyō" (A Rapidly Growing Asia and Japanese Small- and Medium-Sized Firms). In *Shin-chūshō kigyō-ron o Manabu* (Toward a New Analysis of Small- and Medium-Sized Firms), ed. Tatsumi Nobuharu and Satō Yoshio. Tokyo: Yūhikaku.

Ahmadjian, Christina L. 1997. "Japanese Autoparts Supply Networks and the Governance of Interfirm Exchange." Paper based on a PhD dissertation, Columbia University.

——. 2003. "Changing Japanese Corporate Governance." In *Japan's Managed Globalization: Adapting to the Twenty-First Century*, ed. Ulrike Schaede and William Grimes, 215–40. Armonk, N.Y.: M. E. Sharpe.

Akamatsu, Kaname. 1962. "A Historical Pattern of Economic Growth in Developing Countries." *Developing Economies* 1.

Akerlof, George A. 1970. "The Market for 'Lemons': Qualitative Uncertainty and the Market Mechanism." *Quarterly Journal of Economics* 84 (August): 488–500.

Albert, Michel. 1991. *Capitalisme Contre Capitalisme.* Paris: Editions du Seuil.

Alexander, Arthur. 1997. "U.S.-Japan Relations and the Japanese Economy." *JEI Report*, No. 25A (July 4).

Ali, Anuwar. 1994. "Japanese Industrial Investments and Technology Transfer in Malaysia." In *Japan and Malaysian Development: In the Shadow of the Rising Sun*, ed. K. S. Jomo. London: Routledge.

Allen, Nancy J. 1994. "The Cross-national Transfer and Tranformation of Managerial and Organizational Knowledge: American and Japanese Direct Investment in Indonesia." PhD dissertation, Harvard University.

Altbach, Eric. 1997. "Small and Medium-Sized Businesses in the Changing Japanese Economy." *JEI Report*, No. 31A (August 15).

Amin, Samir. 1999. "Regionalization in Response to Polarizing Globalization." In *Globalism and the New Regionalism*, ed. Björn Hettne, András Inotai, and Osvaldo Sunkel. New York: Palgrave Macmillan.

Amsden, Alice. 1989. *Asia's Next Giant: South Korea and Late Industrialization.* New York: Oxford University Press.

Amyx, Jennifer A. 2004. *Japan's Financial Crisis: Institutional Rigidity and Reluctant Change.* Princeton: Princeton University Press.

Anchordoguy, Marie. 1988. "Mastering the Market: Japanese Government Targeting of the Computer Industry." *International Organization* 42, no. 3 (Summer).

Anderson, Benedict. 1983. *Imagined Communities: Reflections on the Origin and Spread of Nationalism.* London: Verso.

Aniol, Włodek, Daneš Brzica, Timothy A. Brynes, Péter Gedeon, Hynek Jeřabek, Peter J. Katzenstein, Zuzana Poláčková, Ivo Samson, and František Zich. 1997. "Returning to Europe: Central Europe between Internationalization and Institutionalization." In *Tamed Power: Germany in Europe,* ed. Peter J. Katzenstein, 195–250. Ithaca: Cornell University Press.

Anuroj, Bonggot. 1995. "Japanese Investment in Thailand: The Nature and Extent of Backward Linkages." PhD dissertation, University of New South Wales.

Aoki, Masahiko. 1987. "The Japanese Firm in Transition." In *Political Economy of Japan,* vol. 1: *The Domestic Transformation,* ed. Kozo Yamamura and Yasukichi Yasuba. Stanford: Stanford University Press.

——. 1998. *Information, Incentives and Bargaining in the Japanese Economy.* Cambridge: Cambridge University Press.

Aoki, Masahiko, Kevin Murdoch, and Masahiro Okuno-Fujiwara. 1996. "Beyond the East Asian Miracle: Introducing the Market-Enhancing View." In *The Role of Government in East Asian Economic Development,* ed. Masahiko Aoki, Hyung-ki Kim, and Masahiro Okuno-Fujiwara. Oxford: Oxford University Press.

Aoki, Takeshi. 1992. "Japanese FDI and the Forming of Networks in the Asia-Pacific Region: Experience in Malaysia and Its Implications." In *Japan's Foreign Investment and Asian Economic Interdependence,* ed. Shojiro Tokunaga. Tokyo: University of Tokyo Press.

Asanuma, Banri. 1984. "Nihon ni okeru Buhin Torihiki no Kōzō: Jidōsha Sangyō no Jirei" (The Parts Supply Structure in Japan: A Case Study of the Automobile Industry). *Keizai Ronsō* (Kyoto University) 133, no. 3: 137–58.

Baba, Hiroji. 1986. *Fuyūka to Kin'yūshihon* (Achieving Prosperity and Finance Capital). Kyoto: Minerva Shōbo.

Baldwin, David A. 1980. "Interdependence and Power: A Conceptual Analysis." *International Organization* 34 (Autumn): 471–506.

Bank of Tokyo. 1995. "Kakudai suru Nihon no Tai-Higashi Ajia Bōeki" (Japan's Expanding Trade with East Asia). *Tōgin Chōhō* 39, no. 34 (August 24).

Bartlett, Randall. 1989. *Economics and Power: An Inquiry into Human Relations and Markets.* Cambridge: Cambridge University Press.

Bates, Robert H. 1981. *Markets and States in Tropical Africa: The Political Basis of Agricultural Policies.* Berkeley: University of California Press.

Beechler, Schon. 1992. "International Management Control in Multinational Corporations: The Case of Japanese Consumer Electronics Firms in Asia." *ASEAN Economic Bulletin* (November).

——. 1995. "Corporate Strategies of Japanese and American MNCs in Southeast Asia: Key Success Factors." Paper presented to a conference on "Managing for Success: Japanese and U.S. Corporate Strategies in Southeast Asia," Columbia University, November 9.

Belderbos, Rene A. 1997. *Japanese Electronics Multinationals and Strategic Trade Policies.* Oxford: Oxford University Press.

Belderbos, Rene, Giovanni Capannelli, and Kyoji Fukao. 1998. "Local Procurement by Japanese Electronics Firms in Asia." Paper presented at the National Bureau of Economic Research seminar, Osaka, June 25–27.

Berger, Suzanne, and Ronald Dore, eds. 1996. *National Diversity and Global Capitalism.* Ithaca: Cornell University Press.

Bernard, Mitchell, and John Ravenhill. 1995. "Beyond Product Cycles and Flying Geese: Regionalization, Hierarchy, and the Industrialization of East Asia." *World Politics* 47, no. 2 (January).

Bonin, Bernard. 1991. "Oligopoly, Innovation, and Firm Competitiveness." In *Technology and National Competitiveness: Oligopoly, Technological Innovation, and International Competition,* ed. Jorge Nosi, 267–81. Montreal: McGill-Queen's University Press.

Boyer, Robert. 2003. "The Embedded Innovation Systems of Germany and Japan: Distinctive Features and Futures." In *The End of Diversity? Prospects for German and Japanese Capitalism,* ed. Kozo Yamamura and Wolfgang Streeck. Ithaca: Cornell University Press.

Bremner, Brian. 2001. "Cleaning Up Japan's Banks—Finally." *Business Week,* December 7.

Breslin, Shaun. 1996. "China in East Asia: The Process and Implications of Regionalization." *Pacific Review* 9, no. 4: 463–87.

Broadbent, Jeffrey. 1998. *Environmental Politics in Japan: Networks of Power and Protest.* Cambridge: Cambridge University Press.

——. 2000. "The Japanese Network State in U.S. Comparison: Does Embeddedness Yield Resources and Influence?" Asia-Pacific Research Center, Stanford University, occasional paper series (July).

Burt, Ronald S. 1992. *Structural Holes: The Social Structure of Competition.* Cambridge: Harvard University Press.

Calder, Kent E. 1988. *Crisis and Compensation: Public Policy and Political Stability in Japan.* Princeton: Princeton University Press.

——. 1989. "Elites in an Equalizing Role: Ex-Bureaucrats as Coordinators and Intermediaries in the Japanese Government-Business Relationship." *Comparative Politics* (July): 379–403.

Callon, Scott. 1995. *Divided Sun: MITI and the Breakdown of Japanese High-Tech Industrial Policy, 1975–1993.* Stanford: Stanford University Press.

Cameron, Gavin. 1997. "Catch-up and Leapfrog between the USA and Japan." Unpublished paper for Nuttfield College, Oxford University (May).

Capannelli, Giovanni. 1997. "Industry-wide Relocation and Technology Transfer by Japanese Electronic Firms: A Study of Buyer-Supplier Relations in Malaysia." PhD dissertation, Hitotsubashi University.

Cerny, Philip G. 1995. "Globalization and the Changing Logic of Collective Action." *International Organization* 49, no. 4 (Autumn): 595–625.

Chen, Edward K. Y., and Teresa Y. C. Wong. 1997. "Hong Kong: Foreign Direct Investment and Trade Linkages in Manufacturing." In *Multinationals and East Asian Integration,* ed. Wendy Dobson and Chia Siow Yue. Ottawa: International Development Research Centre.

Chia, Siow Yue. 1997. "Singapore: Advanced Production Base and Smart Hub of the Electronics Industry." In *Multinationals and East Asian Integration,* ed. Wendy Dobson and Chia Siow Yue. Ottawa: International Development Research Centre.

Clarida, Richard H., and Susan Hickok. 1993. "U.S. Manufacturing and the Deindustrialization Debate." *World Economy* 16, no. 2 (March): 173–92.

Coleman, James S. 1988. "Social Capital in the Creation of Human Capital." *American Journal of Sociology* 94: S95–S120.

Colignon, Richard A., and Chikako Usui. 2003. *Amakudari: The Hidden Fabric of Japan's Economy.* Ithaca: Cornell University Press.

Collinson, Simon, and David C. Wilson. 2006. "Inertia in Japanese Organizations: Knowledge Management Routines and Failure to Innovate." *Organization Studies* 27, no. 9: 1359–87.

Cook, Karen S., Richard M. Emerson, Mary R. Gillmore, and Toshio Yamagishi. 1983. "The Distribution of Power in Exchange Networks: Theory and Experimental Results." *American Journal of Sociology* 89, no. 2 (September): 275–305.

Cooke, T. E. 1996. "The Influence of the Keiretsu on Japanese Corporate Disclosure." *Journal of International Financial Management and Accounting* 26, no. 3: 174–89.

Covrig, Vicentiu, and Buen Sin Low. 2005. "The Relevance of Analysts Earnings Forecasts in Japan." *Journal of Business Finance and Accounting* 32, nos. 7–8 (September–October): 1437–63.

Crozier, Michel. 1964. *The Bureaucratic Phenomenon.* Chicago: University of Chicago Press.

Dasgupta, Partha, and Joseph Stiglitz. 1980. "Industrial Structure and the Nature of Innovative Activity." *Economic Journal* 90, no. 358 (Spring): 266–93.

Davis, Patricia, and Peter Dombrowski. 1997. "Appetite of the Wolf: German Foreign Assistance for Central and Eastern Europe." *German Politics* 6, no. 1 (April): 1–22.

Denison, Edward, and William Chung. 1976. *How Japan's Economy Grew So Fast.* Washington, D.C.: Brookings Institution.

Denki Rengō. 1998. *Nikkei Denki Kigyō no Kaigai Shinshutsu to Kokunai Sangyō/Koyō e no Eikyō* (Foreign Direct Investment by Japanese Electronics Firms and the Impact on Domestic Production and Employment). June. Tokyo: Denki Sogo.

Dentsu Institute for Human Studies. 2001. "Value Changes with Globalization: Japan Remains Groping, Asia Takes an Opportunity—the Fifth Comparative Analysis of Human Values." Tokyo: Dentsu Institute for Human Studies.

Deutsch, Karl W. 1963. *Nerves of Government: Models of Political Communication and Control.* New York: Free Press.

———. 1981. "On Nationalism, World Regions, and the Nature of the West." In *Mobilization, Center-Periphery Structures, and Nation-Building: A Volume in Commemoration of Stein Rokkan,* ed. Per Torsvik, 51–93. Bergen: Universitetsforlaget.

Dirks, Daniel. 1997. "Employment Trends in Japanese Firms." In *The Japanese Employment System in Transition: Five Perspectives,* by Dirks, Hemmert, Legewie, Meyer-Ohle, and Waldenberger. Deutsches Institut fur Japanstudien Working Papers (No. 3).

Dobson, Wendy. 1997. "Crossing Borders: Multinationals in East Asia." In *Multinationals and East Asian Integration,* ed. Wendy Dobson and Chia Siow Yue. Ottawa: International Development Research Centre.

Dore, Ronald. 1973. *British Factory, Japanese Factory: The Origins of National Diversity in Industrial Relations.* Berkeley: University of California Press.

———. 1986. *Flexible Rigidities: Industrial Policy and Structural Adjustment in the Japanese Economy, 1970–80.* Stanford: Stanford University Press.

———. 2005. "Deviant or Different: Corporate Governance in Japan and Germany." *Corporate Governance: An International Review* 43, no. 3 (May): 437–46.

Doremus, Keller, Louis Pauly, and Simon Reich. 1998. *The Myth of the Global Corporation.* Princeton: Princeton University Press.

Dower, John. 1990. "The Useful War." In *Shōwa: The Japan of Hirohito,* a special issue of *Daedalus* 119 (Summer): 49–70.

Eckstein, Harry. 1975. "Case Study and Theory in Political Science." In *Handbook of Political Science,* ed. F. I. Greenstein and Nelson W. Polby, 79–138. Reading, Mass.: Addison-Wesley.

Economic Planning Agency (EPA). 1995. *Nihon Keizai no Genkyō: Heisei 7-nen Keizai no Kaiko to Kadai* (The Current State of the Japanese Economy: A Review of the 1995 Economy and Issues for the Future). Tokyo: EPA Printing Bureau.

——. 1996. *Keizai Hakusho, Heisei 8-nenban: Kaikaku ga Tenbō o Kirihiraku* (Economic White Paper, 1996: Reforms Open a New Outlook). Tokyo: MOF Printing Bureau.

——. 1997. *Working Women: In Search of a New Social System; The White Paper on Employment.*

——. 1998a. *Kōzō Kaikaku ni Chōsen, Keizai Shakai ni Dainamizumu o* (Recommendations for Structural Reform and Bringing Dynamism to the Economy). A report from the Keizai Shingikai (Deliberation Council on the Economy). June.

——. 1998b. *Bukka Repōto '98: Bukka Antei no haikei o saguru.* Tokyo: EPA Printing Office.

——. 1998c. *Nihon no kōporēto gabanansu: kōzō bunseki no shiten kara* (A Structural Analysis of Corporate Governance in Japan). Tokyo: MOF Printing Office.

Economist Intelligence Unit. 1998. "Worldwide Cost of Living Survey." http://www.eiu .com/4wCP5311/pressrelease/WCOLDE98.html.

Elder, Mark. 1998. "Why Buy High? The Political Economy of Protection for Intermediate Goods Industries in Japan." Paper prepared for delivery at the annual meeting of the American Political Science Association in Boston.

Emerson, Richard M. 1962. "Power-dependence Relations." *American Sociological Review* 27: 31–40.

——. 1972. "Exchange Theory, Part II: Exchange Relations and Networks." In *Sociological Theories in Progress (Volume Two)*, ed. J. Berger, M. Zelditch, and B. Anderson, 58–87. Boston: Houghton Mifflin.

Endo, Koshi. 1996. "Jinji-satei-seido no Nichibei Hikaku" (A Comparison of the U.S. and Japanese Performance Evaluation Systems). In *Ōhara Shakai Mondai Kenkyūjō Zasshi* 449: 1–29.

Ernst, Dieter. 2006. "Searching for a New Role in East Asian Regionalization: Japanese Production Networks in the Electronics Industry." In *Beyond Japan: The Dynamics of East Asian Regionalism*, ed. Peter Katzenstein and Shiraishi Takashi, 161–87. Ithaca: Cornell University Press.

Evans, Peter. 1995. *Embedded Autonomy: States and Industrial Transformation.* Princeton: Princeton University Press.

Evans, Peter, and John Stephens. 1988. "Studying Development since the Sixties: The Emergence of a New Comparative Political Economy." *Theory and Society* 17: 713–45.

Ferejohn, John. 1991. "Rationality and Interpretation: Parliamentary Elections in Early Stuart England." In *The Economic Approach to Politics: A Critical Reassessment of the Theory of Rational Action*, ed. Kriston Renwick Konioe. New York: Harper Collins.

Field, G. Lowell, and John Higley. 1980. *Elitism.* London: Routledge and Kegan Paul.

Fingleton, Eamonn. 2000. *In Praise of Hard Industries: Why Manufacturing, Not the Information Economy, Is the Key to the Future.* New York: Houghton Mifflin.

Flamm, Kenneth. 1996. *Mismanaged Trade? Strategic Policy and the Semiconductor Industry.* Washington, D.C.: Brookings Institution Press.

Fligstein, Neil. 1996. "Markets as Politics: A Political-Cultural Approach to Market Institutions." *American Sociological Review* 61 (August): 656–73.

Foreign Investment Advisory Service (FIAS). 1991. "Impediments to Backward Linkages and BUILD, Thailand's National Linkage Program." A report to Thailand's Board of Investment (September), Washington D.C.

Fourin. 1998a. *Tōnan Ajia-Taiwan-Taishū no jidōsha buhin sangyō* (The Automobile Parts Industry in Southeast Asia, Taiwan, and Oceania). Nagoya: Fourin.

——. 1998b. *Jidōsha Chōsa Geppō No. 157* (Monthly Report on the Global Automative Industry).

Freeman, Christopher. 1982. *The Economics of Industrial Innovation.* Cambridge: MIT Press.

Fujimura Hiroyuki. 1997. "New Unionism: Beyond Enterprise Unionism?" In *Japanese Labour and Management in Transition: Diversity, Flexibility and Participation*, ed. Mari Sako and Hiroki Sato, 296–314. London: Routledge.

Fukao Kyoji. 2006. "'Genchika' okureru Nihon kigyō" (Japanese MNCS: Slow on Localization). *Nihon Keizai Shinbun,* July 5, 18.

Fukao, Kiyoshi, and Amano Michifumi. 1998. "Taigai Chokusetsu Tōshi to Seizōgyō no 'Kūdōka'" (Foreign Direct Investment and Industrial Hollowing). *Keizai Kenkyū* 49, no. 3 (July): 259–76.

Fukushima, Hisakazu. 1998. "Chūshō Kigyō Shūseki to Bungyō Kōzō: Ōtaku Kikai Kinzoku Kōgyō no Jittai Chōsa" (The Agglomeration and Division of Labor among Small- and Medium-sized Enterprises: A Survey of the Machine and Metalworking Industries in Ota Ward). *Nihon Daigaku Keizaigakubu Keizai Kagaku Kenkyūjo,* No. 26.

Fukuyama, Francis. 1995. *Trust: Social Virtues and the Creation of Prosperity.* New York: Simon and Schuster.

———. 2004. *State-Building: Governance and World Order in the 21st Century.* Ithaca: Cornell University Press.

Funabashi Haruo. 2005. "Collusion Course." *Japan Journal,* September 16.

Garrett, Geoffrey. 1998. *Partisan Politics in the Global Economy.* Cambridge: Cambridge University Press.

Genda Yuji. 2001. *Shigoto no naka no aimai no fuan* (Vague Anxiety in the Workplace). Tokyo: Chūō Kōron-sha.

George Mulgan, Aurelia. 2002. *Japan's Failed Revolution: Koizumi and the Politics of Economic Reform.* Canberra: Asia Pacific Press.

Gerlach, Michael. 1992. *Alliance Capitalism: The Social Organization of Japanese Business.* Berkeley: University of California Press.

———. 1995. "Economic Organization and Innovation in Japan." Unpublished paper, University of California at Berkeley.

Gottfried, Heidi, and Nagisa Hayashi-Kato. 1998. "Gendering Work: Deconstructing the Narrative of the Japanese Economic Miracle." *Work, Employment, and Society* 12, no. 1 (March).

Gourevitch, Peter. 1978. "The Second Image Reversed: International Sources of Domestic Politics." *International Organization* 32, no. 4: 881–911.

———. 1996. "The Macropolitics of Microinstitutional Differences in the Analysis of Comparative Capitalism." In *National Diversity and Global Capitalism,* ed. Suzanne Berger and Ronald Dore. Ithaca: Cornell University Press.

Gramsci, Antonio. 1992. *Prison Notebooks.* New York: Columbia University Press.

Granovetter, Mark. 1973. "The Strength of Weak Ties." *American Journal of Sociology* 78: 1360–80.

———. 1974. *Getting a Job.* Cambridge: Harvard University Press.

———. 1985. "Economic Action and Social Structure: The Problem of Embeddedness." *American Journal of Sociology* 91: 481–510.

Gregersen Hal, and J. Stewart Black. 1999, *Daily Yomiuri,* November 6.

Guiheux, Gilles, and Yveline Lecler. 2000. "Japanese Car Manufacturers and Parts Makers in the ASEAN Region: A Case of Expatriation under Duress or a Strategy of Regionally Integrated Production?" In *Global Strategies and Local Realities: The Auto Industry in Emerging Markets,* ed. John Humphrey, Yveline Lecler, and Mario Salerno. London: Macmillan.

Guzzini, Stefano. 1993. "Structural Power: The Limits of Neorealist Power Analysis." *International Organization* 47, no. 3 (Summer): 443–78.

Håkansson, Håkan. 1987. "Product Development in Networks." In *Industrial Technological Development: A Network Approach,* ed. Håkan Håkansson. London: Croom Helm.

Haley, George T., Chin Tiong Tan, and Usha C. V. Haley. 1998. *New Asian Emperors: The*

Overseas Chinese, Their Strategies and Competitive Advantages. Oxford: Butterworth Heinemann.

Hall, Peter A., and David Soskice. 2001. *Varieties of Capitalism: The Institutional Foundations of Comparative Advantage.* New York: Oxford University Press.

Hamaguchi, Eshun. 1977. *"Nihonrashisa" no Saihaken* (Rediscovery of "Japaneseness"). Tokyo: Nihon Keizai Shinbunsha.

Hamilton-Hart, Natasha. 2004. "Capital Flows and Financial Markets in Asia: National, Regional, or Global." In *Beyond Bilateralism: U.S.-Japan Relations in the New Asia Pacific,* ed. Ellis S. Krauss and T. J. Pempel, 133–53. Stanford: Stanford University Press.

Harada, Yutaka. 1998. *1970 Nen Taisei no Shūen* (The End of the 1970s System). Tokyo: Tōyō Keizai Shinpōsha.

Harari, Ehud. 1986. "Policy Concertation in Japan." Social and Economic Research on Modern Japan, occasional papers no. 58/59. Berlin: Schiller.

——. 1998. "Creative and Reckless Adventurousness: Knowledge, Power and Governance (In) Effectiveness in Japan: The Economic Bubble and Its Aftermath." Paper F-80, Institute of Social Science, University of Tokyo, Discussion Paper Series (November).

Hashimoto, Jurō, ed. 1996. *Nihon Kigyō Shisutemu no Sengoshi* (The Postwar History of the Japanese Enterprise System). Tokyo: University of Tokyo Press.

Hashimoto Jurō. 1997. "Nihon-gata sangyō shūseki: Saisei no hōkōsei" (Japanese-Style Industrial Agglomeration: The Possibility of Revitalization). In *Nihon-gata sangyō shūseki no miraizō: jōkamachi-gata to 'ōpun komyunitī-gata* (A Future Image of Japanese-Style Industrial Agglomeration: From the 'Castle Town' Model to the 'Open Community' Model), ed. Kiyonari Tadao and Jurō Hashimoto. Tokyo: Nihon Keizai Shinbun-sha.

Hata, Nobuyuki. 1997. "Nihon no Ote VC de wa Benchaakigyō o Sodaterarenai" (Microenterprises Cannot Grow under Japan's Large-Firm-Dominated VC Market). *Ekonomisuto* (March 18).

Hatch, Walter. 1998. "Grounding Asia's Flying Geese: The Costs of Depending Heavily on Japanese Capital and Technology," *Briefing,* National Bureau of Asian Research (April).

——. 2005. "Transplanting Keiretsu: Empirical Evidence from Southeast Asia's Automobile Industry." *Japanese Economy* 33, no. 2 (Summer): 54–66.

Hatch, Walter, and Kozo Yamamura. *Asia in Japan's Embrace: Building a Regional Production Alliance.* Cambridge: Cambridge University Press.

Higashi, Shigeki. 1995. "Thai no Jidōsha Sangyō: Hogo Ikusei kara Jiyūka e" (The Thai Automobile Industry: From Protection to Liberalization). *Ajiken Waarudo Torendo* no. 4 (July).

Higuchi, Yoshio. 1997. "Trends in Japanese Labour Markets." In *Japanese Labour and Management in Transition: Diversity, Flexibility and Participation,* ed. Mari Sako and Hiroki Sato, 48–49. London: Routledge.

Higuchi Yoshio and Policy Research Institute (MOF). 2003. *Nihon no shotoku kakusa to shakai kaisō* (Income Differentials and Social Class in Japan). Tokyo: Nihon Hyōronsha.

Hirata, Keiko. 2002. *Civil Society: The Growing Role of NGOs in Japan's Aid and Development Policy.* New York: Palgrave.

Hirschman, Albert O. 1958. *The Strategy of Economic Development.* New Haven: Yale University Press.

——. 1970. *Exit, Voice, and Loyalty: Responses to Decline in Firms, Organizations, and States.* Cambridge: Harvard University Press.

Hirsh, Michael, and E. Keith Henry. 1997. "The Unraveling of Japan Inc.: Multinationals as Agents of Change." *Foreign Affairs* 76, no. 2 (March–April): 11–16.

Hirst, Paul, and Grahame Thompson. 1996. *Globalization in Question.* Cambridge: Polity Press.

Hiwatari, Nobuhiro. 1996. "Japanese Corporate Governance Reexamined: The Origins and Institutional Foundations of Enterprise Unionism." Unpublished paper for a conference at Columbia University Law School.

Hollingsworth, J. Rogers, and Robert Boyer. 1997. "Coordination of Economic Actors and Social Systems of Production." In *Contemporary Capitalism: The Embeddedness of Institutions*, ed. Hollingsworth and Boyer, 1–47. Cambridge: Cambridge University Press.

Hook, G., and S. Zhang. 1998. "Japan's Aid Policy since the Cold War." *Asian Survey* 38, no. 11: 1051–66.

Horiuchi, Akiyoshi. 1998. *Kin'yū Shisutemu no Mirai: Furyō Saiken Mondai to Biggu Ban* (The Future of the Financial System: The Problem of Non-Performing Loans and the Big Bang). Tokyo: Iwanami Shoten.

———. 1999. "Financial Fragility and Recent Developments in the Japanese Safety Net." *Social Science Japan Journal* 2, no. 1 (April): 23–43.

Hurrell, Andrew. 1995. "Explaining the Resurgence of Regionalism in World Politics." *Review of International Studies* 21: 331–58.

Ibata-Arens, Kathryn. 2005. *Innovation and Entrepreneurship in Japan*. Cambridge: Cambridge University Press.

Ichikawa, Shu. 1996. *Hazusareru Nihon: Ajia Keizai no Kōsō* (The Japan That Could Be Left Behind: A Proposal for the Asian Economy). Tokyo: NHK Books.

Ikeda, Masataka. 1996. "Henbōsuru Nihongata Shitauke Shisutemu" (The Transformation of the Japanese Subcontracting System). In *Shin Chūshō Kigyō-ron o Manabu* (Toward A New Analysis of Small- and Medium-Sized Firms), ed. Tatsumi Nobuharu and Satō Yoshio. Tokyo: Yūhikaku.

Ikeda, Masyoshi. 1999. "Kaitai: Nissan no Keiretsu Meeka wa Gaishi Keitai ni Ikinokori o Kakeru" (Dissolution: Nissan's Keiretsu Subcontractors Try to Survive by Tying Up with Foreign Firms). *Ekonomisuto* (December 14).

Ikeda, Nobuo. 1997. *Jōhōtsūshin Shinkakumei to Nihon Kigyō* (The Digital Revolution and Japanese Firms). Tokyo: NTT Publishers.

Imai, Ken'ichi, and Kaneko Ikuyo. 1988. *Nettowāku soshiki-ron* (Theory of the Network System). Tokyo: Iwanami Shoten.

Imai, Ken'ichi, and Yamazaki Akiko. 1992. "Dynamics of the Japanese Industrial System from a Schumpeterian Perspective." SJC-R Working Papers Series No. 3 (July), Stanford Japan Center.

Inagami Takeshi, ed. 2000. *Gendai Nihon no kōporēto gabanansu* (Corporate Governance in Contemporary Japan). Tokyo: Tōyō Keizai Shinpōsha.

Industrial Bank of Japan. 1995. "Hollowing-out of Japanese Industry." Unpublished paper by the industrial research department (July).

Inomatsu, Satoshi. 1998. "Japanese Direct Investment and Changes in East Asian Industrial Structure." In *Deepening Industrial Linkages among East Asian Countries*, ed. Sano Takao and Osada Hiroshi. March. Tokyo: Institute of Developing Economies.

Inose, Hiroshi. 1997. "Boosting the Basic." *Look Japan* (March): 22–23.

Inoue, Ryūichirō. 1997. "Nihon Kigyō to Ajia Nettowaaku" (Japanese Firms and Asian Networks). *Jetoro Sensaa* (May).

Institute for Advanced Industrial Development (Osaka). 1996. "Ōsaka Keizai Hakusho, Heisei 8: Endaka no Eikyō to Gurōbaru Katsudō" (1996 White Paper on the Osaka Economy: Global Activities and the Effect of Yen Appreciation).

Ishibashi, Asako. 1997. "Manufacturers Shift Strategies in Asia." *Nikkei Weekly*, July 15, 19.

Ishida, Hideto. 1983. "Anti-competitive Practices in the Distribution of Goods and Services in Japan: The Problem of Distribution Keiretsu." *Journal of Japanese Studies* 9, no. 2 (Summer).

Ishiyama, Yoshihide. 1996. "Is Japan Hollowing Out?" MIT Japan Program Working Paper 96–08.

Itagaki, Hiroshi. 1997. *The Japanese Production System: Hybrid Factories in East Asia.* Hampshire, U.K.: Macmillan Business.

Itami, Hiroyuki. 1989. "Nihon kigyō no 'jinponshugi' shisutemu" (The Employee-firstism of the Japanese Firm). In *Nihon no Kigyō* (The Japanese Firm), ed. Imai Ken'ichi and Komiya Ryutaro. Tokyo: University of Tokyo Press.

———. 1998. "The Structural Upgrading of East Asian Economies and Networks." In *Can Asia Recover Its Vitality? Globalization and the Roles of Japanese and U.S. Corporations,* ed. Institute of Developing Economic (IDE) and JETRO. Tokyo: IDE.

———. 1993. "Atarashii Sangyō Dainamizumu (The New Industrial Dynamism). *Asuteon* 29 (Summer): 88–99.

Ito, Mitsutoshi. 1995. "Administrative Reform." In *The Japanese Civil Service and Economic Development: Catalysts for Change,* ed. Hyung-Ki Kim, Micho Muramatsu, T. J. Pempel, and Kozo Yamamura. Oxford: Oxford University Press.

Iwai Katsuhito. 2007. "Kaisha wa shain o mamotte kureru ka" (Do Companies Really Protect Their Workers?). *Bungei Shunjū* (March): 94–104.

Iyori, Hiroshi. 1995. "Kokusai-teki na Nagare ni Sotta Dokkinhō no Unyō o" (Implementing the Anti-Monopoly Law in Accordance with International Trends). *Nihon Keizai Kenkyū Sentaa Kaihō* 724 (March 15).

Japan Economic Research Center, ed. 1998. *Heisoku Yaburu IT Sangyō (Information Technology Industries: Overcoming Obstacles).* Tokyo: Nihon Keizai Shinbun.

Japan Fair Trade Commission. 2001. *Kigyō shūdan no jittai ni tsuite: dai-7-ji chōsa hōkokusho* (The State of Horizontal Business Groups: A Report on the 7th Survey). Tokyo: JFTC.

Japan Finance Corp. for Small Business. 1996. "Saikin no keizai jōsei to chūshō kigyō no ugoki" (Recent Economic Developments and Trends in Small and Medium-Sized Enterprises). *Chūshōkōko Repōto no. 96–4* (November).

———. 1997. "Jidōsha, Kadenkigyō ni miru Shitauke Bungyō Kōzō no Henka: Kōzō Hendō ni Tsuyoi Shitauke Kigyō no Shutsugen" (The Division of Labor among Subcontractors in the Automobile and Consumer Electronics Industries: The Appearance of Strong Subcontracting Firms in the midst of Structural Change). *Chūshōkōko Repōto no. 97–2* (May).

Japan Machinery Exporters Association. 1994. "Wagakuni Kikai Sangyō no Ajia ni okeru Seisan Bungyō Jittai ni tsuite" (The Actual State of Productiion and Division of Labor by Japanese Machine Industries Operating in Asia). Unpublished report (June).

Japan Productivity Research Institute. 1997. "Wagakuni Benchaa Kigyō no Keiei Kadai" (Issues in the Management of Japanese Venture Firms). *Seisansei Kenkyū* 22 (July): 1–4.

Japan Research Institute. 1988. "Kokusai keizai kankyō gekihenka ni okeru sōgōteki keizai kyōryoku suishin chōsa hōkokusho: Ajia nettowaaku no kōchiku ni mukete" (Promoting Comprehensive Economic Cooperation in an International Economic Environment Undergoing Dramatic Change: Toward the Construction of an Asian Network). Tokyo: Economic Planning Agency.

———. 1997. "The Long-Term Outlook for the Japanese Economy: Revitalization for the 21st Century." *Japan Research Quarterly* 6, no. 2 (Spring).

———. 1998. "The Japanese Economy in 1998: Avoiding a Meltdown." *Japan Research Quarterly* 7, no. 1: 3–63.

Japan Small Business Corp. 1997. "Haiteku Kigyō no Kaigai Tenkai" (The Internationalization of High-Tech Firms). *Kaigai Tōshi Gaido, no. 139* (July).

Japanese Chamber of Commerce and Industry (Bangkok). 1997. *Dai-sankai, Nikkei kigyō no Kōkendo: Chōsa Hōkokusho* (The Contribution of Japanese Firms in Thailand: Report on the Third Survey). April.

JBIC Institute. 2003. "Wagakuni seizō kigyō no kaigai jigyō tenkai ni kansuru chōsa hōkoku, 2002 nendo" (A Report on the Overseas Operations of Japanese Manufacturing Firms, FY 2002). *Kaihatsu kin'yū kenkyū jōhō* 14 (January).

———. 2007. "Wagakuni seizō kigyō no kaigai jigyō tenkai ni kansuru chōsa hōkoku, 2006 nendo" (A Report on the Overseas Operations of Japanese Manufacturing Firms, FY 2006). *Kaihatsu kin'yū kenkyū jōhō* 33 (February).

JETRO 1997a. *1997 Jetro Hakusho, Tōshi Hen* (1997 White Paper on Foreign Direct Investment).

———. 1997b. "Ajia Shinshutsu Chūshō Seizō Kigyō no Jirei Kenkyū" (A Case Study of Small- and Medium-Sized Manufacturing Firms Investing in Asia). *Jetro Sensā*. June.

———. 1997c. "Ajia Seisan Nettowaaku: Nihon Kigyō no Mirai Senryaku o Tenbō suru" (Asian Manufacturing Networks: Anticipating the Future Strategies of Japanese Firms). *Jetro Sensā* (May): 48.

———. 1997d. "Zai Tai Nikkei Seizōgyō Jittai Chōsa" (A Survey of Japanese Manufacturing Affiliates in Thailand). *Tsūshō Geppō,* June 9.

———. 1998. *Gyaku Yunyū no Jittai ni kansuru Ankeeto Chōsa* (Survey Report on Reverse Imports). August. Tokyo: Kaigai Keizai Jōhō Sentaa.

———. 1999a. *Shinshutsu Kigyō Jittai Chōsa: Ajia-hen* (A Survey of Investing Firms: Asia Edition). Tokyo: JETRO.

———. 1999b. *Tsūshō Geppō* (Monthly Report of SMEs). May 31.

———. 2003. *Bōeki Tōshi Hakusho* (White Paper on International Trade and Investment). Tokyo: Bōeki Shinkō Kyōkai.

Jichirōrento Shokurō Keizaishibu. 1997. "Baburu Hōkaigo no Machikōba no Keiei Jittai" (The Management of Small Factories Following the Collapse of the Bubble). July.

Jin Shin'ichi. 1996. "Kūdōka o Kangaeru" (Thinking about Hollowing Out). *Kaigai Tōshi Kenkyūjohō.* July.

Johnson, Chalmers. 1982. *MITI and the Japanese Miracle.* Stanford: Stanford University Press.

Jo Shigeyuki. 2006. "Kowareta rēru ni wa noranai" (We Can Ride This Broken Rail No Longer). *Chūō Kōron* (August): 42–49.

Kagano, Tadao. 1999. "Crisis and Aftermath: The Prospects for Institutional Change in Japan." Roundtable discussion sponsored and published by the Asia/Pacific Research Center, Stanford University, May 3.

Kagano, Tadao, Nonaka Ikujiro, Sakakibara Kiyonori, and Okuno Akihiro. 1983. *Nichibei Kigyō no Keiei Hikaku* (A Comparison of Management Practices in Japanese and American Firms). Tokyo: Nihon Keizai Shinbunsha.

Kamien, Morton I., and Nancy L. Schwartz. 1982. *Market Structure and Innovation.* Cambridge: Cambridge University Press.

Kamo, Kineko. 1997. "Nihon Jidōsha Kigyō no Gurōbaru Senryaku to Ajia Keizai Ken" (The Global Strategies of Japanese Automobile Firms and the Asian Economic Zone). In *Ajia no Jidōsha Sangyō* (Asia's Automobile Industry), ed. Maruyama Yoshinari. Tokyo: Aki Shobō.

Kanō, Yoshikazu. 1996. "Ajia no sangyōka ga Nihon shijō o Nerau" (The Industrialization of Asia, Which Is Aimed at the Japanese Market). *Shūkan Tōyō Keizai* (September 14): 78–82.

Kanzaki, Kōzaki. 2000. "'Kabuka Chōjūshi no Keizai Shifuto de Shain o Mamoru Koto wa Furukusai'—Kore de Yoinoka?") ("In the Economic Shift toward an Economy That Emphasizes Stock Values, Protecting the Employee Is Old-Fashioned"—Is This Right?). *Ekonomisuto* (March 14): 72–73.

Kao, John. 1993. "The Worldwide Web of Chinese Business." *Harvard Business Review* (March–April).

Karthaus, Olaf. 1997. "Polymer Education in Germany." *Kōbunshi* 54, no. 10: 733.

Kasahara, Hiroyuki. 1997. "Transfer and Adaptation of Manufacturer-Supplier Relationships from Japan to Thailand: A Case of the Automobile Industry." Unpublished paper, July 28.

Katayama Osamu. 1996. *Japanese Business into the 21st Century: Strategies for Success.* London: Athlone Press.

———. 2002. "Nihon ni wa Nihon no Shihon shugi ga aru" (When in Japan, Do Capitalism as the Japanese Do). *Voice* (October): 57–60.

Kato, Takao. 1998. "Preliminary Findings on the Nature and Scope of Career Development of Managers in Japan, the U.S., and Germany: Evidence from a Cross-National Survey." In *Kokusai Hikaku: Daisotsu Howaitokaraa no Jinsai Kaihatsu/koyō Shistemu: Nichi, Bei, Doku no Daikigyō* (Personnel Development and Employment Systems for White Collar College Graduates: An International Comparison of Large Firms in Japan, the U.S., and Germany). Tokyo: Japan Institute of Labor.

———. 2001. "The End of 'Lifetime Employment' in Japan? Evidence from National Surveys and Field Research." Working paper no. 185, Columbia Business School, Center on Japanese Economy and Business.

Katz, Richard. 1998. *Japan, the System That Soured: The Rise and Fall of the Japanese Economic Miracle.* Armonk, N.Y.: M. E. Sharpe.

———. 2007. "Whither Corporate Reform? Mixed Messages." *Oriental Economist* 75, no. 5 (May): 1.

Katzenstein, Peter. 2005. *A World of Regions: Asia and Europe in the American Imperium.* Ithaca: Cornell University Press.

Katzenstein, Peter, and Takashi Shiraishi. 1997. "Regions in World Politics—Japan and Asia, Germany in Europe." In *Network Power: Japan and Asia,* ed. Katzenstein and Shiraishi. Ithaca: Cornell University Press.

Kawai, Hideo, Nishizawa Futoshi, Handa Jun'ichirō, and Ishijima Kazuhiro. 1997. "Ajia Shinshutsu Chūshō Seizō Kigyō no Jirei Kenkyū" (Case Studies of Asian Investment by Japanese SMEs in Manufacturing). *Jetoro Sensaa* (June): 50–61.

Kawai, Masahiro, and Shinji Takagi. 2004. "Japan's Official Development Assistance: Recent Issues and Future Directions." *Journal of International Development* 16 (no. 2).

Kawai, Masahiro, and Shujiro Urata. 1996. "Trade Imbalances and Japanese Foreign Direct Investment: Bilateral and Triangular Issues." Discussion paper no. F-52, APEC Study Center, Waseda University and Institute of Developing Economies, Tokyo.

Kawamoto Yuko. 2003. "Wakamono no shitsugyō o nantoka shiyō" (Doing Something for Unemployed Youth). *Ronza* (June): 114–17.

Keidanren. 1994. *Review of the Japanese Economy* (special issue). Tokyo: Keidanren.

Kester, W. Carl. 1996. "American and Japanese Corporate Governance: Convergence to Best Practice?" In *National Diversity and Global Capitalism,* ed. Suzanne Berger and Ronald Dore, 107–37. Ithaca: Cornell University Press.

Kettler, David, and Charles T. Tackney. 1997. "Light from a Dead Sun: The Japanese Lifetime Employment System and Weimar Labor Law." *Comparative Labor Law and Policy Journal* 19, no. 1 (Fall).

Kiba, Takao, and Kodama Fumio. 1991. "Measurement and Analysis of the Progress of International Technology Transfer: Case Study of Direct Investment in East Asian Countries." NISTEP Report No. 18. April. Tokyo: National Institute of Science and Technology Policy, Science and Technology Agency.

Kikai Shinkō Kyōkai. 1994. *Kikai Sangyō ni okeru Seisan Bungyō Shisutemu no Shōrai Tenbō* (Machinery Industries and Prospects for the Manufacturing Division of Labor). May.

——. 1995. "Ajia Chiiki e no Seisan Shifuto to Sono Eikyō: Ryōsan-gata kikai buhin sangyō no kūdōka no shiten kara" (The Shift of Manufacturing to Asia and Its Effect on Large-scale Machinery Parts Industries: From the Perspective of Hollowing-out). Working Paper H6–4. May.

——. 1998. *Engineering Industries of Japan: Moving toward New Operations, New Products.* No. 32.

Kim, Hicheon, Robert E. Hoskisson, and William P. Wan. 2004. "Power Dependence, Diversification Strategy and Performance in Keiretsu Member Firms." *Strategic Management Journal* 25: 613–36.

Kimura, Fukinari. 1996. "Nihon no Taigai Chokusetsu Tōshi no Tokuchō" (The Characteristics of Japanese Foreign Direct Investment). *NIRA Seisaku Kenkyū* 9, no. 10: 8–13.

——. 2001. "Keizai Seisaku to shite no Kōteki Keizai Kyōryoku no Shōrai" (The Future of Official Economic Cooperation as Economic Policy). Unpublished memo for the METI Study Group, July.

Kimura, Fukinari, Kawai Hiroki, and Tanaka Iwao. 1996. "Naigai Kakakusa to Bōeki Shōheki: Kakaku Deita o Mochiita Bunseki" (Price Differentials and Trade Barriers: Analysis of Trade Data). In *Mita Gakkai Zasshi* 89, no. 2 (July): 85–100.

Kishii Daitarō. 1999. "Historical Features of Japan's Public Utility Laws and the Limits of 'Deregulation'." *Social Science Japan Journal* 2, no. 1 (April): 45–63.

Kitajima, Mamoru. 1997. "ASEAN Shokoku no Kōgyōka to Nihongata Shisutemu no Iten: Nihonteki Keiei/Seisan Shisutemu no Kokusai Iten ni okeru Kadai" (Industrialization in ASEAN Countries and the Transfer of the Japanese System: Issues Related to the Cross-Border Transfer of Japanese Management and Production Systems). Kikai Shinkō Kyōkai Kenkyūjo Hōkokusho H8–10. March.

——. 1998. "Ibunka Shakai ni okeru Nihon-teki Monozukuri no Tokushitsu" (Japanese Production in a Different Cultural Setting: The Industrial Sociology of Japanese Manufacturing Affiliates in ASEAN). *Kikai Keizai Kenkyū*, no. 29 (October).

Kitamura, Haruo. 1992. *PL Hō Kō Kangaeyō: Seizōbutsu Sekinin wa Sekai no Jōshiki* (Let's Think This Way about a PL Law: Product Liability Makes Good Global Sense). Tokyo: Daiyamondo-sha.

Kitschelt, Herbert. 1999. "Competitive Party Democracy and Political Economic Reform in Germany and Japan." Paper prepared for the conference on "Germany and Japan: Nationally Embedded Capitalism in the World Economy," Cologne, June 24–26.

Knoke, David. 1990. *Political Networks: The Structural Perspective.* Cambridge: Cambridge University Press.

Knoke, David, Franz Urban Pappi, Jeffrey Broadbent, and Yutaka Tsujinaka. 1996. *Comparing Policy Networks: Labor Politics in the U.S., Germany, and Japan.* Cambridge: Cambridge University Press.

Kobayashi, Shigeru. 1966. *Sony wa Hito o Ikasu* (Sony Makes the Best Use of Talent). Tokyo: Nihon Keiei Shuppan-kai.

Kodama, Fumio. 1991. *Emerging Patterns of Innovation: Sources of Japan's Technological Edge.* Boston: Harvard Business School Press.

Koike, Kazuo. 1981. *Nihon no Jukuren* (Skill Formation in Japan). Tokyo: Yūhikaku.

Kojima, Kiyoshi. 1978. *Direct Foreign Investment: A Japanese Model of Multinational Business Operations.* London: Croom Helm.

Kono, Hirokazu. 1997. "Ajia ni okeru Nikkei Seisan Kigyō no Katsudō to Mondai-ten" (The Activities and Problems of Japanese Manufacturing Companies in Asia). In *Ajia no Butsuryū: Genjō to Kadai*, ed. Keio University Research Center on Regional Affairs. Tokyo: Keio University Press.

Kosai, Yutaka. 1997. "Industrial Policy in Developmentalism and in Polymorphic Liberalism: The Murakami Theses Reconsidered." In *A Vision of a New Liberalism? Critical Essays on Murakami's Anticlassical Analysis,* ed. Kozo Yamamura. Stanford: Stanford University Press.

Krasner, Stephen D. 1984. "Approaches to the State: Alternative Conceptions and Historical Dynamics." *Comparative Politics* 16, no. 2 (January): 223–46.

———. 1985. *Structural Conflict: The Third World against Global Liberalism.* Berkeley: University of California Press.

Kraus, Willy. 1996. "Economic Effects of German Reunification on West and Eastern Europe." In *Economic Transformation in Eastern Europe: A Challenge for Japan and Germany,* ed. H. Hax, W. Klemer, W. Kraus, T. Matsuda, and T. Nakamura. Heidelberg: Spinger.

Krauss, Ellis, and Robert Pekkanen. 2004. "Explaining Party Adaptation to Electoral Reform: The Discrete Charm of the LDP?" *Journal of Japanese Studies* 30, no. 1 (Winter).

Kumazawa, Makoto. 1997. *Nōryokushugi to Kigyō Shakai* (Merit-Based Management and Corporate Society). Tokyo: Iwanami Shoten.

Kume, Gorota. 1992. "Trends and Prospects of Japanese Direct Investment in Asia: Increased Contribution to Economic Development of Asian Countries." *Research Institute for Overseas Investment,* No. 1 (May).

Kume, Ikuo. 1998. *Disparaged Success: Labor Politics in Postwar Japan.* Ithaca: Cornell University Press.

Kumon, Hiroshi. 1997. "The Automotive Assembly Industry." In *The Japanese Production System: Hybrid Factories in East Asia,* ed. Itagaki Hiroshi. Hampshire, U.K.: Macmillan Business.

Kumon, Shumpei. 1982. "Some Principles Governing the Thought and Behavior of Japanists (Contextualists)." *Journal of Japanese Studies* 8, no. 1 (Winter): 5–28.

Kuroda, Masahiro. 1996. "International Competitiveness and Japanese Industries, 1960–1985." In *International Productivity Differences: Measurement and Explanations,* ed. Karin Wagner and Bart van Ark. Amsterdam: North-Holland.

Kurzer, Paulette. 1991. "Unemployment in Open Economies: The Impact of Trade, Finance, and European Integration." *Comparative Political Studies* 24, no. 1 (April): 3–30.

Kusano, Atsushi. 1995. "Shingikai wa kakuremino de aru" (The Deliberation Councils Are a Cover-up). In *Nihon no Ronsō: Kitoku Ken'eki no Kōzō* (Japan's Debate: The Structure of Vested Interests), 195–200. Tokyo: Tōyō Keizai Shinpōsha.

Kwan, C. H. 1997. "The Rise of Asia and Japan's 'Hollowing Out' Problem." *NRI Quarterly* (Spring).

LaCroix, Sumner, and James Mak. 2001. "Regulatory Reform in Japan: The Road Ahead." In *Japan's New Economy: Continuity and Change in the Twenty-first Century,* ed. Magnus Blomström, Bryon Gangnes, and Sumner LaCroix, 215–41. New York: Oxford University Press.

Laumann, Edward O., and David Knoke. 1986. "Social Network Theory." In *Approaches to Social Theory,* ed. Siegwart Lindenberg, James S. Coleman, and Stefan Nowak. New York: Russell Sage Foundation.

Lawrence, Robert Z. 1996. *Regionalism, Multilateralism and Deeper Integration.* Washington, D.C.: Brookings Institution.

Lee, Chung. "Institutional Reform in Japan and Korea: Why the Difference?" Unpublished paper, February 2005.

Legewie, Jochen. 1997. "Foreign Direct Investment, Trade, and Employment: The Role of Asia within the Discussion of Industrial Hollowing Out in Japan." Working paper 97/1, Deutsches Institut fur Japanstudien (DIJ).

———. 1998. "The Political Economy of Industrial Integration in Southeast Asia: The Role of Japanese Companies." DIJ Working Paper 98/1, Deutsches Institut fur Japanstudien.

——. 1999. "Economic Crisis and Transformation in Southeast Asia: Strategic Responses by Japanese Firms in the Area of Production." DIJ Working Paper 99/3, Deutsches Institut fur Japanstudien.

Lehmbruch, Gerhard. 1999. "The Rise and Change of Discourses on 'Embedded Capitalism' in Germany and Japan and Their Institutional Setting." Paper prepared for a conference on "German and Japanese Capitalism," Cologne, Germany.

Lemoine, Francoise. 1998. "Integrating Central and Eastern Europe in the European Trade and Production Network." Briefing Paper #9, Berkeley Roundable on the International Economy, http://brie.berkeley.edu/.

Lin, Zhuoshi. 1995. "Higashi Ajia no Gijutsu Chikuseki to Nihonteki Gijutsu Iten Shisutemu" (The Japanese System of Technology Transfer and the Accumulation of Know-how in East Asia). In *Ajia no Gijutsu Hatten to Gijutsu Iten* (Asia's Technological Development and Technology Transfer), ed. Chen Bingfu and Lin Zhuoshi. Tokyo: Bushindo.

Lincoln, Edward. 2001. *Arthritic Japan: The Slow Pace of Economic Reform.* Washington, D.C.: Brookings Institution.

Lincoln, James R., Michael L. Gerlach, and Christina L. Ahmadjian. 1996. "Keiretsu Networks and Corporate Performance in Japan." *American Sociological Review* 61 (February): 67–88.

Linden, Greg. 1998. "Building Production Networks in Central Europe: The Case of the Electronics Industry." Working Paper 126, Berkeley Roundtable on the International Economy (July).

Lockwood, William. 1965. "Japan's 'New Capitalism'." In The *State and Economic Enterprise in Japan,* ed. William Lockwood. Princeton: Princeton University Press.

Lucas, Robert E., Jr. 1988. "On the Mechanics of Economic Development." *Journal of Monetary Economics* 22: 3–42.

Mabuchi, Masaru. 1994. *Ōkurashō Tōsei no Seiji Keizaigaku* (The Political Economy of MOF Control). Tokyo: Chūō Kōronsha.

——. 1997. *Ōkurashō wa Naze Oitsumerareta no ka: Seikan Kankei no Henbō* (Why Is MOF in Such a Fix? The Transformation of Politician-Bureaucrat Relations). Tokyo: Chūō Shinsho.

Machado, Kit G. 1995. "Transnational Production, Regionalism, and National Development: The Case of the Japanese Motor Vehicle Industry in East Asia." *Waseda Journal of Asian Studies* 17: 25–41.

MacIntyre, Andrew, and Barry Naughton. 2005. "The Decline of a Japan-Led Model of the East Asian Economy." In *Remapping Asia: The Construction of a Region,* ed. T. J. Pempel. Ithaca: Cornell University Press.

Maclachlan, Patricia L. 1999. "Protecting Producers from Consumer Protection: The Politics of Product Liability Reform in Japan." *Social Science Japan Journal* 2, no. 2 (October): 249–66.

——. 2000. "Information Disclosure and the Center-Local Relationship in Japan." In *Local Voices, National Issues: The Impact of Local Initiative in National Policy-making,* ed. Sheila A. Smith. Ann Arbor: Center for Japanese Studies, University of Michigan.

——. 2002. *Consumer Politics in Postwar Japan.* New York: Columbia University Press.

Maeda, Noboru. 1999. *Shinbijinesu Moderu ni yoru Nihon Kigyō no Tsuyosa no Henkaku: "Kagaku Gijutsu Shin Sangyō Sōzō Rikkoku Jitsugen" e no Shinariō* (The Transformation of the Japanese Firm through a New Business Model: Toward the Realization of a Nation Built on Science, Technology and New Industry Creation). NISTEP Policy Study No. 3 (May), National Institute of Science and Technology Policy.

Management and Coordination Agency. 1999. "Rōdōryoku Chōsa Tokubetsu Chōsa Hōkokusho" (Report on the Special Survey of the Labor Force Survey). February.

Marra, David. 2007. "Japan Just Starting to Bask in Light of Good Governance." *Nikkei Weekly*, July 2.

Marsden, Peter V. 1983. "Restricted Access in Networks and Models of Power." *American Journal of Sociology* 88, no. 4 (January): 686–717.

Maruyama, Yoshinari, ed. 1997. *Ajia no Jidōsha Sangyō* (The Asian Automobile Industry). Tokyo: Akishōbo.

Matsuoka, Katsunori. 1997. "Accord Drives Change in Asian Car-making." *Nikkei Weekly*, April 7.

Mattli, Walter. 1999. *The Logic of Regional Integration: Europe and Beyond.* Cambridge: Cambridge University Press.

McGuire, J., and S. Dow. 2003. "The Persistence and Implications of Japanese Keiretsu Organization." *Journal of International Business Studies* 34: 374–88.

Micklethwait, John. 1997. "Silicon Valley: The Valley of Money's Delight." *Economist* (March 29).

Migdal, Joel. 1988. *Strong Societies and Weak States: State-Society Relations and State Capabilities in the Third World.* Princeton: Princeton University Press.

Miller, Chris, Geoff Reed, and Pawin Talerngsri. 2006. "Vertical Linkages and Agglomeration Effects in Japanese FDI in Thailand." *Journal of the Japanese and International Economies* 20: 193–208.

Miller, Gary J. 1992. *Managerial Dilemmas: The Political Economy of Hierarchy.* Cambridge: Cambridge University Press.

Milner, Helen V. 1988. *Resisting Protectionism: Global Industries and the Politics of International Trade.* Princeton: Princeton University Press.

——. 1997. *Interests, Institutions and Information: Domestic Politics and International Relations.* Princeton: Princeton University Press.

Mingsarn, Santikarn Kaosa-ard. 1993. "Comparative Analysis of Direct Foreign Investment in Thailand." Paper for a conference sponsored by the Hoover Institution, Stanford University, on "Japan and the Regionalization of Asia."

——. 1994. "Regional Investment and Technology Transfer in Asia: A Thai Case Study." In *Intra-Regional Investment and Technology Transfer in Asia: A Symposium Report,* ed. Asian Productivity Organization. Tokyo: APO.

Ministry of Health, Labor and Welfare (MHLW). 2004. *Rōdō Keizai Hakusho* (White Paper on Labor Economy). Tokyo.

Ministry of Labor. 1995. *Nihon no Rōshi Komunikeeshon no Genjō* (The State of Labor-Management Communication in Japan). Tokyo: MOF Printing Bureau.

——. 1996. *Chiteki Sōzōgata Rōdō to Jinji Kanri* (Knowledge-Creating Work and Personnel Management). Tokyo: Rōdō Daijin Kanbo.

——. 1998. *Rōdō Hakusho, Heisei 10 Nenban* (Small Business in Japan, 1998). Tokyo: Japan Institute of Labor.

——. 1999. "Rōdō Keizai Dōkō Chōsa, Heisei 11-nen 5-gatsu" (Labor Market Trends for May 1999). *Rōdō Daijin Kanbo Seisaku Chōsa-bu* (June).

Mishima, Ko. 2005. "The Stumbling Block." *Far Eastern Economic Review* (September).

MITI. 1995a. *Tsūshō Hakusho, Heisei 7-nenban* (White Paper on Trade and Industry for 1995). Tokyo: MOF Printing Bureau.

——. 1995b. *Wagakuni Kigyō no Kaigai Jigyō Katsudō, Dai 24-kai* (Overseas Business Activities of Japanese Firms, No. 24). Tokyo: MOF Printing Bureau.

——. 1995c. *Tsūshō Sangyō Seisaku no Jūten: Heisei 8 Nendo* (Commercial and Industrial Policy Priorities for 1996). Tokyo, internal publication.

———. 1996. *Wagakuni Kigyō no Kaigai Jigyō Katsudō, Dai 25-kai* (Overseas Business Activities of Japanese Firms, No. 25). Tokyo: MOF Printing Bureau.

———. 1997. *Tsūshō Hakusho, Heisei 9-nenban* (White Paper on Trade and Industry for 1997). Tokyo: MOF Printing Bureau.

———. 1998a. *Wagakuni Kigyō no Kaigai Jigyō Katsudō, Dai 26-Kai* (The Overseas Business Activities of Japanese Firms, Number 26). Tokyo: MOF Printing Bureau.

———. 1998b. *Tsūshō Hakusho, Heisei 10-nenban* (White Paper on Trade and Industry for 1998). Tokyo: MOF Printing Bureau.

———. 1999a. *Wagakuni Kigyō no Kaigai Jigyō Katsudō, Dai 27-Kai* (The Overseas Business Activities of Japanese Firms, Number 26). Tokyo: MOF Printing Bureau.

———. 1999b. "21 Seiki Keizai: Sangyō Seisaku no Kadai to Tenbō" (The 21st Century Economy: Issues Surrounding Industrial Policy, and Prospects for the Future). Unpublished policy report (June).

MITI Industrial Policy Bureau. 1996. "Kaigai Tenkai Senryaku ni kakaru Kigyō Chōsa Hōkoku" (Survey on Overseas Operating Strategies of Japanese Firms). November.

Mittelman, James H. 2000. *The Globalization Syndrome: Transformation and Resistance.* Princeton: Princeton University Press.

Miura, Mari. 2001. "Globalization and Reforms of Labor Market Institutions: Japan and Major OECD Countries." F-94, Institute of Social Science, Domestic Politics Project No. 4 (July).

MOFA (Ministry of Foreign Affairs). 1999. *Japan's Official Development Assistance: Annual Report 1998.* Tokyo: Association for the Promotion of International Cooperation.

Moore, Barrington, Jr. 1966. *Social Origins of Dictatorship and Democracy: Lord and Peasant in the Making of the Modern World.* Boston: Beacon Press.

Moravcsik, Andrew. 1994. "Why the European Community Strengthens the State: Domestic Politics and International Cooperation." Working Paper Series No. 52, Center for European Studies, Harvard University.

Mori, Minako. 1999. "New Trends in ASEAN Strategies of Japanese-Affiliated Automobile Parts Manufacturers." In *RIM: Pacific Business and Industries* (Sakura Institute of Research) 1, no. 43.

Morishima, Motohiro. 1997. "Changes in Japanese Human Resource Management: A Demand Side Story." *Japan Labor Bulletin* (November 1).

Morita Hodaka and Nakahara Hirohiko. 2004. "Impact of the Information Technology Revolution on Japanese Manufacturer-Supplier relationships." *Journal of the Japanese and International Economies* 18 (February): 390–415.

Morozumi, Yoshihiko. 1966. *Sangyō Seisaku no Riron* (The Theory of Industrial Policy). Tokyo: Nihon Keizai Shinbunsha.

Motohashi Kazuyuki. 2004. "Economic Analysis of University-Industry Collaborations: The Role of New Technology-Based Firms in Japanese National Innovation Reform." Working paper 04-E-001, Research Institute on Economy, Trade and Industry (RIETI).

Mukoyama, Hidehiko. 1996. "Development of Asian Small and Medium Companies and Japanese Small Business Investment in Asia." *Rim: Pacific Business and Industries* 1, no. 31.

Murakami, Yasusuke. 1992. *Han-koten no Seiji-keizaigaku* (An Anti-Classical Political-Economic Analysis). Tokyo: Chūōkōron-sha. [Translated into English and published in 1996, *An Anti-Classical Political-Economic Analysis: A Vision for the Next Century.* Stanford: Stanford University Press].

Murakami, Yasusuke, Kumon Shumpei, and Satō Seizaburō. 1979. *Bunmei to Shite no Ie Shakai* (*Ie* Society as a Pattern of Civilization). Tokyo: Chūōkōron-sha.

Muramatsu Michio, 1981. *Sengo Nihon no Kanryōsei* (Postwar Japan's Bureaucratic System). Tokyo: Tōyō keizai shinpōsha.

Myrdal, Gunnar. 1968. *Asian Drama: An Inquiry into the Poverty of Nations, Vol. 2.* New York: Twentieth Century Fund.

Nakamura, Keisuke. 1996. *Nihon no Shokuba to Seisan Shisutemu* (The Japanese Production System and the Organization of Work). Tokyo: University of Tokyo Press.

Nakamura, Keisuke, and Padang Wicaksono. 1999. *Toyota in Indonesia: A Case Study on the Transfer of the TPS.* Jakarta: Center for Japanese Studies, University of Indonesia.

Nakamura, Yoshiaki, and Minoru Shibuya. 1995. "The Hollowing Out Phenomenon in the Japanese Industry." MITI Research Institute, August.

Nakane, Chie. 1970. *Japanese Society.* Berkeley: University of California Press.

Nakano, Koichi. 1998. "Becoming a Policy Ministry: Organization and Amakudari of the Ministry of Posts and Telecommunication." *Journal of Japanese Studies* 24, no. 1 (Winter): 95–117.

Nakano Tsutomu. 2004. "Bridging Roles of SMEs in a Large-Scale Industrial District: A Structural Approach." University of Michigan—Flint School of Management, Working Paper no. 2004–02.

Nakashima, Takamasa. 1998. "Industrial Relations and Ethnicity: The Case of MSC, a Japanese-Owned Automobile Manufacturer in Thailand." Paper for the Asian Regional Conference on Industrial Relations, Tokyo.

Nakatani, Iwao. 1984. "The Economic Role of Financial Corporate Grouping." In *The Economic Analysis of the Japanese Firm,* ed. Aoki Masahiko. Amsterdam: North Holland.

Nakazawa, Takao. 1997. "Ote Meikaa Kaifuku no Kage de Torinokosareru Chūshō Seizōgyō" (Small and Medium-sized Manufacturers Have Been Abandoned in the Wake of the Recovery of Large Manufacturers). *Ekonomisuto,* April 29.

Nesadurai, Helen. 2002. "Globalisation and Economic Regionalism: A Survey and Critique of the Literature." CSGR Working Paper #108–02 (November), Centre for the Study of Globalisation and Regionalisation, University of Warwick.

Nikkeiren. 1969. *Nōryokushugi Jidai no Jinji Kōka* (Performance Evaluation in the Era of Merit-Based Management). Tokyo: Nikkeiren.

———. 1995. *Shin-Jidai no Nihonteki Keiei* (Japanese Management in a New Era). Tokyo: Nikkeiren.

———. 1996. *"Shin-jidai no Nihonteki keiei" ni tsuite no Forōappu Chōsa* (A Follow-up Study to "Japanese Management in a New Era"). Tokyo: Nikkeiren.

Nikko Research Center. 1991. *Analysis of Japanese Industries for Investors.* Tokyo: Nikko Research Center.

Nishiguchi, Toshiro, and Alexandre Beaudet. 1999. "Kaosu ni okeru Jiko Soshiki-ka: Toyota Gurūpu to Aishin Seiki Kasai" (Self-Organization in Chaos: The Toyota Group and the Aishin Fire). *Soshiki Kagaku* 32, no. 4: 58–72.

Nishihara, Shigeki. 1987. *Yoron kara Mita Dōjidaishi* (Contemporary History as Seen from Opinion Polls). Tokyo: Brain Shuppan.

Nishioka, Tadashi. 1998. "ASEAN ni okeru Jidōsha Sangyō no Dōkō to Wagakuni Chūshō Buhin Meikaa e no Eikyō ni tsuite" (The State of the Automobile Industry in ASEAN, and Its Influence on Japanese SME Parts Producers). *Chūshō Kōko Repōto No. 98–1* (April).

Nishizawa, Jun'ichi. 1988. "We Need Creativity." *Voice* (December).

Noble, Gregory. 2006. "Koizumi and Neo-liberal Economic Reform." *SSJ Newsletter* 34 (March).

Noguchi, Yukio. 1995. *1940 Taisei Ron, Saraba "Senji Keizai"* (The 1940 System: Farewell to the "Wartime Economy"). Tokyo: Tōyō Keizai Shinpōsha.

———. 2002. *Nihon kigyō no Kakumei: Daisoshiki kara shososhiki e* (A Revolution in Japanese Firms: From Large Organizations to Small Organizations). Tokyo: Nihonkeizai Shinbunsha, 2002.

North, Douglass C. 1990. "Institutions and a Transaction-Cost Theory of Exchange." In *Perspectives on Positive Political Economy*, ed. James E. Alt and Kenneth A. Shepsle. Cambridge: Cambridge University Press.

Nukazawa, Kazuo. 1998. "Nihon Keizai: Sengo kara 21 Seiki e" (The Japanese Economy: From the End of World War II to the 21st Century). *Gaikō Forum* (January): 48–57.

Odagiri, Hiroyuki. 1989. "Riekisei to Kyōsei" (Profitability and Competitiveness). In *Nihon no Kigyō (The Japanese Economy)*, ed. Imai Ken'ichi and Komiya Ryutarō. Tokyo: University of Tokyo Press.

OECD (Organisation for Economic Cooperation and Development). 2000. *OECD in Figures*. Paris: OECD.

OECD. 2006. *Economic Surveys: Japan*. Paris: OECD.

OECF (Overseas Economic Cooperation Fund). 1999. "Q&A on Asian Economic Crisis Support." *OECF Newsletter* (April–May).

Ogino, Hiroshi. 1997. "The Sōkaiya's Grip on Corporate Japan." *Japan Quarterly* (July–September): 15–22.

Ohmae, Ken'ichi. 1990. *The Borderless World: Power and Strategy in the Interlinked Economy*. New York: Harper Business.

Ohno Kenichi. 2001. "Ajia Dainamizumu no tame no tsūshō seisaku to enjo seisaku" (Trade and Aid Policies for Asian Dynamism). Memo for the METI Study Group, July.

Ohtake Fumio. 2006. "Nihon wa futatabi Ajia no shuyaku ni naru" (Japan Will Once Again Play the Leading Role in Asia). *Chūō Kōron* (April): 196–205.

Okamoto, Yumiko. 1996. "Shuyō Sangyō no Taigai Chokusetsu Tōshi no Dōkō: Denshi/Denki Sangyō" (Trends in Foreign Investment by Leading Industries: The Electronic and Electrical Industries). *NIRA Seisaku Kenkyū* 9, no. 10.

Okamuro, Hiroyuki. 1995. "Changing Subcontracting Relations and Risk-Sharing in Japan: An Econometric Analysis of the Automobile Industry." *Hitotsubashi Journal of Economics* 36 (December): 207–18.

Okazaki, Keiko. 1996. "A Measurement of the Japanese Lifetime Employment System." *Keio Business Review* 33: 105–15.

Okimoto, Daniel. 1989. *Between MITI and the Market: Japanese Industrial Policy for High Technology*. Stanford: Stanford University Press.

Okimoto, Daniel I., and Gary Saxonhouse. 1987. "Technology and the Future of the Economy." In *The Political Economy of Japan*, vol. 1, *The Domestic Transformation*, ed. Kozo Yamamura and Yasukichi Yasuba. Stanford: Stanford University Press.

Okimoto, Daniel, and Yoshio Nishi. 1996. "R&D Organization in Japanese and American Semiconductor Firms." In *The Japanese Firm: The Sources of Competitive Strength*, ed. Masahiko Aoki and Ronald Dore. Oxford: Oxford University Press.

Okina, Yuri, and Akiko Kōsaka. 1996. "Japanese Corporations and Industrial Upgrading: Beyond Industrial Hollowing Out." *Japan Research Quarterly* 5, no. 2 (Spring): 45–91.

Okita, Saburo. 1986. "Pacific Development and Its Implications for the World Economy." In *The Pacific Basin: New Challenges for the United States*, ed. James W. Morely. New York: Academy of Political Science.

Okuda Hiroshi. 1999. "Keieisha yo, kubikiri suru nara seppuku seyo" (Hey Managers, If You Lay Off Your Workers, You Might as Well Commit Ritual Suicide). *Bungei Shunjū*, October.

Okuno-Fujiwara, Masahiro. 1997. "Toward a Comparative Institutional Analysis of the Government-Business Relationship." In *The Role of Government in East Asian Economic Development: Comparative Institutional Analysis*, ed. Masahiko Aoki, Hyung-Ki Kim, and Masahiro Okuno-Fujiwara. Oxford: Oxford University Press.

Olson, Mancur. 1982. *The Rise and Decline of Nations: Economic Growth, Stagflation, and Social Rigidities*. New Haven: Yale University Press.

Oman, Charles. 1984. *New Forms of International Investment in Developing Countries*. Paris: OECD.

Ōtake, Hideo. 1997. *Seikai Saihen no Kenkyū: Shin Senkyo Seido ni yoru Sōsenkyo*. (A Study of Political Realignment: The First Election under the New Electoral System). Tokyo: Yūhikaku.

Panglaykim, J. 1983. *Japanese Direct Investment in ASEAN: The Indonesian Experience*. Singapore: Maruzen.

Paprzycki, Ralph. 2005. *Interfirm Networks in the Japanese Electronics Industry*. New York: Routledge.

Park, Woo-hee. 1992. "Japan's Role in the Structural Adjustment of the Asian-Pacific Economies." *Journal of International Economic Studies* 6 (March).

Pascale, Richard, and Thomas P. Rohlen. 1983. "The Mazda Turnaround." *Journal of Japanese Studies* 9, no. 2 (Summer): 219–63.

Pastor, Manuel, and Carol Wise. 1994. "The Origins and Sustainability of Mexico's Free Trade Policy." *International Organization* 48, no. 3 (Summer): 459–89.

Patrick, Hugh, and Henry Rosovsky, eds. 1976. *Asia's New Giant*. Washington, D.C.: Brookings Institution.

Pauly, Louis W., and Simon Reich. 1997. "National Structures and Multinational Corporate Behavior: Enduring Differences in the Age of Globalization." *International Organization* 51, no. 1 (Winter): 1–30.

Pechter, Kenneth, and Sumio Kakinuma. 1999. "Coauthorship Linkages between University Research and Japanese Industry." In *Industrializing Knowledge: University-Industry Linkages in Japan and the United States*, ed. Lewis M. Branscomb, Fumio Kodama, and Richard Florida. Cambridge: MIT Press.

Pempel, T. J. 1998. *Regime Shift: Comparative Dynamics of the Japanese Political Economy*. Ithaca: Cornell University Press.

———. 1999. "Structural Gaiatsu: International Finance and Political Change in Japan." *Comparative Political Studies* 32, no. 8: 907–32.

Pharr, Susan J. 1984. "Status Conflict: The Rebellion of the Tea Pourers." In *Conflict in Japan*, ed. Ellis S. Krauss, Thomas P. Rohlen, and Patricia G. Steinhoff. Honolulu: University of Hawaii Press.

Polanyi, Karl. 1944. *The Great Transformation: The Political and Economic Origins of Our Time*. Boston: Beacon Press.

Policy Research Institute (MOF). 2003. *Shinten suru kōporēto gabanansu* (Corporate Governance in Transition). Tokyo: Nihon Hyōronsha.

Posen, Adam. 1998. *Restoring Japan's Economic Growth*. Washington, D.C.: Institute for International Economics.

Price, John. 1997. *Japan Works: Power and Pardox in Postwar Industrial Relations*. Ithaca: Cornell University Press.

Putnam, Robert D. 1988. "Diplomacy and Domestic Politics." *International Organization* 42 (Summer): 427–61.

———. 1993. *Making Democracy Work: Civic Traditions in Modern Italy*. Princeton: Princeton University Press.

Reich, Robert B. 1991. *The Work of Nations: Preparing Ourselves for Twenty-first Century Capitalism*. New York: Knopf.

Rengō. 2006. "Rising Gaps and the Polarization of Society." Presentation by Assistant General Secretary Oumi Naoto (February 24).

Research Group on New Business Creation. 1999. *Nihon no Benchaakigyō to Kigyōsha ni kansuru Chōsa Kenkyū* (A Survey on Start-up Firms and Their Founders in Japan). NISTEP Report No. 61 (March), National Institute of Science and Technology Policy.

Rōdō Daijin Kanbō. 1996. *Chiteki Sōzō-gata Rōdō to Jinji Kanri* (Creative, Knowledge-Based

Labor and Human Resources Management). Tokyo: Rōdō Daijin Kanbō Seisaku Chōsabu.

Rohlen, Thomas. 1989. "Order in Japanese Society: Attachment, Authority and Routine." *Journal of Japanese Studies* 15, no. 1: 5–40.

Romer, Paul M. 1986. "Increasing Returns and Long-run Growth." *Journal of Political Economy* 94, no. 5: 1002–37.

Rowthorn, Robert, and Ramana Ramaswamy. 1997. "Deindustrialization: Causes and Implications." IMF Working Paper 97/42 (April).

Rtischev, Dimitry, and Robert E. Cole. 1998. "The Role of Organizational Discontinuity in High Technology: Insights from a U.S.-Japan Comparison." Paper prepared for a conference on "Business Venture Creation and New Human Resource Management in Japan, Europe and the U.S.A," sponsored by Deutsches Institut fur Japanstudien, Tokyo, October.

Rubio, Mauricio. 1997. "Perverse Social Capital: Evidence from Colombia." *Journal of Economic Issues* 31, no. 3 (September).

Saeki Keishi. 2000. "Nihon no zashō" (The Fall of Japan). *Shokun* (October): 26–38.

Sakai Kuniyasu. 1990. "The Feudal World of Japanese Manufacturing." *Harvard Business Review* (November–December): 38–49.

Sakaiya Taichi and Noguchi Yukio. 2005. "Zoku giin shi shite kanryō no kōwarai" (With the Demise of the LDP Policy Tribes, the Bureaucrats Are All Smiles). *Bungei Shunjū,* October, 138–48.

Sakakibara Eisuke. 2005. "Zaisei kōzō kaikaku wa suterareta no ka?" (Has Structural Reform of the Financial System Been Abandoned?). *Ekonomisuto* (March 22): 79–81.

Sakakibara, Kiyonori. 1999. *Benchaabijinesu: Nihon no Kadai* (Venture Business: Issues in Japan). NISTEP Policy Study No. 2 (May), National Institute of Science and Technology Policy.

Samuels, Richard. 1987. *The Business of the Japanese State: Energy Markets in Comparative and Historical Perspective.* Ithaca: Cornell University Press.

——. 1994. *Rich Nation, Strong Army: National Security and the Technological Transformation of Japan.* Ithaca: Cornell University Press.

Satō Hikaru. 1998. "Daitenhō haishi ga motarasu mono" (What the Elimination of the Large Store Law Will Bring). *Ronsō* (March): 180–87.

Satō, Hiroki. 1996. "Keeping Employees Employed: *Shukkō* and *Tenseki* Job Transfers." *Japan Labor Bulletin* (December 1): 5–8.

——. 1997. "Human Resource Management Systems in Large Firms: The Case of White Collar Graduate Employees." In *Japanese Labor and Management in Transition: Diversity, Flexibility and Participation,* ed. Mari Sako and Hiroki Sato, 104–30. London: Routledge.

Satō, Hiroki, Nagano Hitoshi, and Oki Eiichi. 1996. *Eijiresu Koyō Shisutemu ni kakawaru Shomondai ni Tsuite no Sōgōteki na Chōsa Kenkyū Jigyō Hōkokusho* (A Comprehensive Survey and Research Project regarding Issues Associated with an Ageless Employment System: A Report). Tokyo: Socioeconomic Productivity Center.

Sato, Kazuo. 1997a. "Economic Development and Financial Deepening: The Case of Japan." *Journal of the Asia Pacific Economy* 2, no. 1: 1–27.

——. 1997b. "Corporate Capitalism and Wealth Inequality in Japan." Unpublished paper (September).

Satō Masaaki. 2000. "Toyota wa naze hitorigachi shita ka" (Why Is Toyota Number One?). *Bungei Shunjū,* October, 291.

Satō, Susumu, and Yamauchi Tetsuo. 1994. "Shōhō kaisei o gyakute ni keiretsu no kyōka Susumu" (Circumventing the New Commercial Code, Keiretsu Ties Become Even

Stronger). *Shūkan Tōyō Keizai,* December 31 (a special issue also dated January 7, 1995), 68–71.

Satō Toshiki. 2000. "Shinchūkan Taishū Tanjō kara 20 Nen" (20 years since the Birth of the New Middle Mass). *Chūō Kōron* (May 2000): 68–75.

Saxenian, Analee. 1994. *Regional Advantage: Culture and Competition in Silicon Valley and Route 128.* Cambridge: Harvard University Press.

Sazanami, Yoko, Fukinari Kimura, and Hiroki Kawai. 1997. "Sectoral Price Movements under Yen Appreciation." Unpublished paper.

Sazanami, Yoko, and Wong Yu Ching. 1996. "The Determinants of Intrafirm Transactions and Intrafirm Trade of Japanese MNEs in Asia, Europe and North America." Paper written for the Keio University Keizai Gakkai (December 4).

Schaede, Ulrike. 1995. "The 'Old Boy Network' and Government-Business Relationships in Japan." *Journal of Japanese Studies* 21, no. 2 (Summer): 293–317.

Schattschneider, E. E. 1960. *The Semi-Sovereign People: A Realist's View of Democracy in America.* New York: Holt, Rinehart and Winston.

——. 1963. *Politics, Pressures, and the Tariff: A Study of Free Private Enterprise in Pressure Politics.* Hamden, Conn.: Archon Books.

Scher, Mark J. 1997. *Japanese Interfirm Networks and Their Main Banks.* New York: Palgrave Macmillan.

Schmidt, Vivien A. 2002. *The Futures of European Capitalism.* New York: Oxford University Press.

Schoppa, Leonard. 1997. *Bargaining with Japan: What American Pressure Can and Cannot Do.* New York: Columbia University Press.

——. 2006. *Race for the Exits: The Unraveling of Japan's System of Social Protection.* Ithaca: Cornell University Press.

Schwartz, Frank. 1998. *Advice and Consent: The Politics of Consultation in Japan.* Cambridge: Cambridge University Press.

Science and Technology Agency. 1996. *Kagaku Gijutsu no Shinkō ni kansuru Nenji Hōkoku, Hensei 8 Nendo* (1996 Annual Report on the Promotion of Science and Technology).

——. 2000. *Kagaku Gijutsu Yōran (Science and Technology Handbook).*

Sedgwick, Mitchell W. 1996. "Does Japanese Management Travel in Asia? Managerial Technology Transfer at Japanese Multinationals in Thailand." Working Paper MITJP 96–04, MIT Japan Program.

Seike, Atsushi. 1995. "Nenkō Chingin no Jittai to Henka" (The Status of Seniority wages and Changes in the System). In *Nihon-gata Koyō Shisutemu Yōkai Hōkokusho* (Report on the Dissolution of the Japanese Employment System), ed. Inagami Takeshi. Tokyo: Ministry of Labor.

Seisansei Kenkyūjo. 1997. "Nihon no Seisansei Nobiritsu Kaifuku mo Suru Izen 11-i" (Despite a Recovery in Its Rate of Productivity Increase, Japan Remains #11). *Seisansei Kenkyū* 23 (October).

Seki Mitsuhiro. 1999. *Ajia Shinjidai no Nihon Kigyō* (The Japanese Firm in the New Asian Era). Tokyo: Chūō Kōronsha.

——. 1997. *Kūdōka o Koete: Gijutsu to Chiiki no Saikōchiku* (Beyond Hollowing Out: Technology and Regional Restructuring). Tokyo: Nihon Keizai Shinbunsha.

——. 1993. *Furusetto-gata Sangyō Kōzō o Koete* (Beyond the Full-Set Industrial Structure). Tokyo: Chūōkoronsha.

Seki Takaya. 2005. "Legal Reform and Shareholder Activism by Institutional Investors in Japan." *Corporate Governance* 13, no. 3 (May): 377–85.

Sekimoto, Tadahiro. 1996. "21 Seiki no Zaikaijin ni Tsugu" (Heralding the Arrival of the Businessman of the 21st Century). *Bungei Shunjū* 74, no. 11 (September): 94–104.

Sender, Harry. 1996. "The Sun Never Sets." *Far Eastern Economic Review* (February 1), 46–50.

Sheard, Paul. 1994. "Interlocking Shareholdings and Corporate Governance in Japan." In *The Japanese Firm: Sources of Competitive Strength,* ed. Masahiko Aoki and Ronald Dore. Oxford: Oxford University Press.

——. 2007. "The Japanese Economy: Where Is It Leading in the Asia Pacific? Anatomy of an Abnormal Economy and Policy Failure." In *Japan's Future in East Asia and the Pacific,* ed. Mari Pangestu and Ligang Song. Canberra: Asia Pacific Press.

Sheridan, Kyoko. 1998. "Japan's Economic System." In *Emerging Economic Systems in Asia: A Political and Economic Survey,* ed. Kyoko Sheridan. St. Leonards, Australia: Allen and Unwin.

Shimokawa, Koichi. 1995. "Confronting Hard Times in the Japanese Automobile Industry: The Restructuring Strategy." *Keiei Shirin* (Hosei University) 32, no. 2 (July).

——. 1997. "Restructuring Helps Power Auto Revival." *Nikkei Weekly,* April 14.

Shimotani, Masahiro. 2004. "Recent Changes in Inter-firm Relations in Japan: The Sixth Largest Corporate Complexes." In *The Development of Corporate Governance in Japan and Britain,* ed. Robert Fitzgerald and Etsuo Abe, 191–200. Aldershot, U.K.: Ashgate.

Shiozaki, Yasuhisa. 1999. "Changes in Politics." Speech given to a conference on "Crisis and Aftermath: The Prospects for Institutional Change in Japan," at the Asia/Pacific Research Center, Stanford University, May 3.

Shiraishi, Takashi. 1997. "Japan and Southeast Asia." In *Network Power: Japan and Asia,* ed. Peter Katzenstein and Takashi Shiraishi. Ithaca: Cornell University Press.

Shōkō Chūkin. 1995. "Chūshō kikai kinzoku kōgyō bungyō kōzō jittai chōsa hōkokusho: Dai-go kai" (Fifth Report on the Division of Labor among Small- and Medium-Sized Machinery and Metal-Working Industries).

Singh, Kulwant, Joseph Putti, and George Yip. 1998. "Singapore: Regional Hub." In *Asian Advantage: Key Strategies for Winning in the Asia-Pacific Region,* ed. George Yip, 155–79. Reading, Mass.: Addison-Wesley.

Skocpol, Theda. 1998. "Civic America, Then and Now." Unpublished paper, Harvard University (June).

Small and Medium Enterprise (SME) Agency. 1996. *Chūshō Kigyō Hakusho, Heisei 8-nenban* (Small Business in Japan, 1996). Tokyo: MOF Printing Bureau.

——. 1997. *Chūshō Kigyō Hakusho: Heisei 9-nenban* (Small Business in Japan, 1997). Tokyo: MOF Printing Bureau.

——. 1998. *Chūshō Kigyō Hakusho, Heisei 10-nenban* (Small Business in Japan, 1998). Tokyo: MOF Printing Bureau.

SME Policy Research Group. 1999. *Chūshō Kigyō Seisaku Kenkyūkai Saishū Hōkoku* (The Final Report of SME Policy Research Group). MITI (May).

Smith, Wendy. 1993. "Japanese Management in Malaysia." *Japanese Studies* 13, no. 1: 50–76.

Solis, Mireya. 2004. *Banking on Multinationals: Public Credit and the Export of Japanese Sunset Industries.* Stanford: Stanford University Press.

Sonoda, Hidehiro, 1999. *Toshi Bunka* (Urban Culture). Tokyo: Iwanami Shoten.

Steffensen, Sam K. 1998. "Informational Network Industrialization and Japanese Business Management." *Journal of Organizational Change Management* 11, no. 6: 515–29.

Steinmo, Sven, Kathleen Thelen, and Frank Longstreth. 1992. *Structuring Politics: Historical Institutionalism in Comparative Analysis.* Cambridge: Cambridge University Press.

Stewart, Charles T., Jr. 1985. "Comparing Japanese and U.S. Technology Transfer to Less Developed Countries." *Journal of Northeast Asian Studies* 4 (Spring).

Strange, Susan. 1988. *States and Markets.* New York: Blackwell.

——. 1996. *The Retreat of the State: The Diffusion of Power in the World Economy.* New York: Cambridge University Press.

Streeck, Wolfgang. 1998. "The German Social Market Economy: External Competitiveness and Internal Cohesion." In *Ten Paradigms of Market Economies and Land Systems*, ed. Lee-jay Cho and Yoon Hyung Kim, 59–98. Kyonggi: Korea Research Institute for Human Settlements.

Streeck, Wolfgang, and Christine Trampusch. 2005. "Economic Reform and the Political Economy of the German Welfare State." *German Politics* 14, no. 2 (June): 174–95.

Suehiro, Akira. 1998. "Social Capabilities for Industrialization in Asia: Government Policies, Technology Formation, and Small Business." Paper for the Institute of Small Business Research and Business Administration, Osaka University of Economics (March).

Suehiro, Akira and Natenapha Wailerdsak. 2004. "Top Executive Origins: Comparative Study of Japan and Thailand." *Asian Business and Management* 3: 84–104.

Sugeno, Kazuo, and Suwa Yasuo. 1997. "Labour Law Issues in a Changing Labour Market." In *Japanese Labour and Management in Transition: Diversity, Flexibility and Participation*, ed. Mari Sako and Hiroki Sato, 53–78. London: Routledge.

Sumita, Shōji. 1997. *Yakunin ni Tsukeru Kusuri* (Medicine for Public Officials). Tokyo: Asahi Shinbunsha.

Sunada, Toru, Kiji Michiko, and Chigira Makoto. 1993. "Japan's Direct Investment in East Asia: Changing Division of Labor and Technology Transfer in the Household Electric Appliance Industry." Monograph for the MITI Research Institute (March).

Suzuki, Kazunori. 1997. "Inter-Corporate Shareholdings in Japan: Their Significance and Impact of Sales of Stakes." Unpublished paper for the London Business School, December 10.

Suzuki, T. 1977. *Shōhō to tomoni ayumu* (Retrospective on the Commercial Law). Tokyo: Shōji-hō kenkyūkai. [cited by Hideaki Miyajima in Lonny E. Carlile and Mark C. Tilton, eds., *Is Japan Really Changing Its Ways: Regulatory Reform and the Japanese Economy* (Washington D.C.: Brookings Institution Press, 1998)].

Suzuki, Yukio. 1996. "Fukkatsu suru Nihon Kigyō no Kokusai Kyōsōryoku" (The Resurging International Competitiveness of Japanese Firms). *Zaikai Kansoku* (Nomura Research Institute), May 1.

Szymkowiak, Kenneth. 2001. *Sokaiya: Extortion, Protection, and the Japanese Corporation*. Armonk, N.Y.: M. E. Sharpe.

Tabata, Hirokuni, 1987. "Gendai Nihon no Rōshikankei to Kokka" (Industrial Relations and the State in Contemporary Japan). In *Ken'i-teki Chitsujo to Kokka*, ed. Fujita Isamu. Tokyo: University of Tokyo Press.

Tachibanaki, Toshiaki. 1998. *Nihon Keizai Kakusa: Shotoku to Shisan kara Kangaeru* (Japan's Economic Gap in Terms of Income and Assets). Tokyo: Iwanami Shinsho, 1998.

———. 2000. "'Kekka no Fubyōdō' o Doko made Mitomeru ka" (To What Extent Will We Tolerate the Disparity in Outcomes). *Chūō Kōron* (May 2000): 76–82.

Takahashi, Hiroaki. 1996. "Activities of Japanese Machinery Makers in Southeast Asia." *NRI Quarterly* (Winter).

Takahashi, Masahiro. 1997. "Ajia ni okeru Chiiki no Kokusai Nettowaakuka Shiron" (An Essay on Creating an International Network in Asia). *Keizai Keiei Kenkyū* (March).

Takenaka, Heizo. 1996. "Reference Report to Part II." In *Japan in the 21st Century: Flourish or Fade?*, ed. Fukukawa Shinji. Tokyo: Global Industrial and Social Progress Research Institute.

Tamura, Ei. 1996. "Wagakuni Seizō Kigyō no Kaigai Tōshi no Genjō to Kongo no Hōkō ni tsuite" (The Current State and Future Direction of Foreign Investment by Japanese Manufacturing Firms). *Chūshō Kōko Geppō* (November): 16–22.

Tate, John Jay. 1995. *Driving Production Innovation Home: Guardian State Capitalism and the*

Competitiveness of the Japanese Automobile Industry. Berkeley: Berkeley Roundtable on the International Economy.

Tatsumichi Shingo. 2001. "How Advanced Is Japan's Personnel Management in the IT industry?" *Japan Labor Bulletin,* April 1.

Taylor, Mark Z. 1995. "Dominance through Technology: Is Japan Creating a Yen Bloc in Southeast Asia?" *Foreign Affairs* (November–December).

Tejima, Shigeki. 1996. "Japan's Foreign Direct Investment at the New Stage of Globalization and Its Contribution to the Asian Pacific Region." *Research in Asian Economic Studies* 7 (B).

———. 1997. "Hitotsu no Henkakuki kara Arata na Henkakuki e: Gurōbarizeishon, Riijonarizeishon, Torirenma; Ajia no Tōshi Ukeirekoku no Gaishi Seisaku/Sangyō Seisaku" (From One Change to Another: Globalization/Regionalization, Trilemma, and the Foreign Capital and Industrial Policies of Asian Countries Receiving Investment). *Kaigai Tōshi Kenkyūjohō* (January).

Temin, Peter. "Is It Kosher to Talk about Culture?" *Journal of Economic History* 57, no. 2 (June).

Terry, Edith. 2002. *How Asia Got Rich: Japan, China, and the Asian Miracle.* Armonk, N.Y.: M. E. Sharpe.

Thelen, Kathleen, and Ikuo Kume. 1999. "The Future of Nationally Embedded Capitalism: Industrial Relations in Germany and Japan." Paper prepared for the conference on "Germany and Japan: Nationally Embedded Capitalism in the World Economy," Cologne, June 24–26.

Thompson, E. P. 1971. "The Moral Economy of the English Crowd in the Eighteenth Century." *Past and Present* 50 (February): 76–136.

Thornton, Emily. 1997. "More Cracks in the Social Contract: Strapped Companies Turn More and More to Part-Time Workers." *Business Week* (October 13): 18.

Tiberghien, Yves. 2007. *Entrepreneurial States: Reforming Corporate Governance in France, Japan, and Korea.* Ithaca: Cornell University Press.

Tilton, Mark. 1998. "Regulatory Reform and Market Opening in Japan." In *Is Japan Really Changing Its Ways? Regulatory Reform and the Japanese Economy,* ed. Lonny E. Carlile and Mark C. Tilton. Washington, D.C.: Brookings Institution Press.

———. 2007. "Seeds of an Asian European Union? Regionalism as a Hedge Against the United States on Telecommunications Technology in Japan and Germany." *Pacific Review* 20, no. 3 (September): 301–27.

Tokuhisa, Yoshio. 1997. "Shokigyōka, Autosōsuka de Nihon Kigyō no Gijutsuryoku Kōjō o" (Improving the Technological Capacity of Japanese Firms through the Creation of Start-ups and Outsourcing). *Ekonomisuto* (November 4): 75–76.

Tokunaga, Shojiro, ed. 1992. *Japan's Foreign Investment and Asian Economic Interdependence.* Tokyo: University of Tokyo Press.

Tokyo Chamber of Commerce. 1996. *Wagakuni Seizōgyō no Kyōsōryoku Saikyoku-ka ni Mukete* (Toward the Reinforcement of Competitiveness in Japanese Manufacturing). Report of a Chamber committee on competitiveness (October).

Toyonaga, Mami. 1998. "Change in the Structure of Employment in the Japanese Electric Machine Industry: Do Asian Affiliates Affect Headquarters Employment?" Unpublished paper for the Japan Institute of Labor's "Asian Regional Conference on Industrial Relations," Tokyo.

Tsuru, Kotarō. 1995. *The Japanese Market Economy System: Its Strengths and Weaknesses.* Tokyo: LTCB International Library Foundation.

Tsutagawa Kan. 2004. "Japanese Style Back in Favor." *Yomiuri Shinbun,* February 18.

Tu, Jenn-hwa. 1997. "Taiwan: A Solid Manufacturing Base and Emerging Regional Source of Investment." In *Multinationals and East Asian Integration,* ed. Wendy Dobson and Chia Siow Yue. Ottawa: International Development Research Centre.

Ueda, Tatsuzō. 1996. "Kinyū Shijō no Henka to Chūshō Kigyō" (SMEs and Changes in the Financial Market). In *Shin Chūshō Kigyō-ron o Manabu* (Toward A New Analysis of Small- and Medium-Sized Firms), ed. Tatsumi Nobuharu and Satō Yoshio. Tokyo: Yūhikaku.

Uehara, Masashi. 1999. "Japanese Companies Gave Most Aid to Thai Joint Ventures in Crisis." *Nikkei Weekly* (June 14).

Ueno, Kaori. 1997. "ASEAN sangyō kyōryoku keikaku (AICO) to nikkei jidōsha meikaa no chiikinai senryaku" (The ASEAN Industrial Cooperation Scheme and the Regional Strategies of Japanese Car Manufacturers). *Tokubetsu Keizai Chōsa Repōto, Heisei 8 Nendo.* Tokyo: JETRO.

United Nations. 1998. *World Investment Report 1998: Trends and Determinants.* New York: United Nations.

Upham, Frank. 1987. *Law and Social Change in Postwar Japan.* Cambridge: Harvard University Press.

Urata, Shujiro. 1996a. "Japanese Foreign Direct Investment and Technology Transfer to Asia." Discussion Paper Series No. 4, APEC Study Center of Waseda University and the Institute of Developing Economies, Tokyo (March).

——. 1996b. "Japanese Foreign Direct Investment in Asia: Its Impact on Export Expansion and Technology Acquisition of the Host Economies." Paper prepared for the international workshop on "Foreign Direct Investment, Technology Transfer, and Export-Orientation in Developing Countries," Maastricht (November).

Urata, Shujiro, and Kawai Hiroki. 1996. "Trade Imbalances and Japanese Foreign Direct Investment: Bilateral and Triangular Issues." In *Asia-Pacific Economic Cooperation: Current Issues and Agenda for the Future,* ed. Ku-Hyun Jung and Jang-Hee Yoo, 61–87. East and West Studies Series 39 (Institute of East and West Studies, Yonsei University).

Uriu, Robert M. 1996. *Troubled Industries: Confronting Economic Change in Japan.* Ithaca: Cornell University Press.

Uzzi, Brian. 1996. "The Sources and Consequences of Embeddedness for the Economic Performance of Organizations: The Network Effect." *American Sociological Review* 61 (August): 674–98.

Van Evera, Stephen. 1997. *Guide to Methods for Students of Political Science.* Ithaca: Cornell University Press.

van Wolferen, Karel. 1989. *The Enigma of Japanese Power.* London: Macmillan.

Vestal, James. 1993. *Planning for Change: Industrial Policy and Japanese Economic Development, 1945–90.* New York: Oxford University Press.

Vitols, Sigurt. 2004. "Changes in Germany's Bank-Based Financial System: A Varieties of Capitalism Perspective." Working paper SP II 2004–03 (March), Wissenschaftszentrum Berlin für Sozialforschung.

Vogel, Steven K. 1996. *Freer Markets, More Rules: Regulatory Reform in Advanced Industrial Countries.* Ithaca: Cornell University Press.

——. 1999a. "When Interests Are Not Preferences: The Cautionary Tale of Japanese Consumers." *Comparative Politics* 31, no. 2 (January): 187–207.

——. 1999b. "Can Japan Disengage? Winners and Losers in Japan's Political Economy." *Social Science Japan Journal* 2, no. 1 (April): 3–21.

——. 2003. "The Reorganization of Organized Capitalism: How the German and Japanese Models Are Shaping Their Own Transformations." In *The End of Diversity? Prospects for German and Japanese Capitalism,* ed. Kozo Yamamura and Wolfgang Streeck, 306–33. Ithaca: Cornell University Press.

———. 2006. *Japan Remodeled: How Government and Industry Are Reforming Japanese Capitalism.* Ithaca: Cornell University Press.

Wade, Robert. 1990. *Governing the Market: Economic Theory and the Role of Government in East Asian Industrialization.* Princeton: Princeton University Press.

Waltz, Kenneth. 1979. *Theory of International Politics.* Reading, Mass.: Addison Wesley.

Wan, William P, Daphne W. Yiu, Robert E. Hoskisson, and Heechun Kim. 2008. "The Performance Implications of Relationship Banking during Macroeconomic Expansion and Contraction: A Study of Japanese Banks' Social Relationships and Overseas Expansion." *Journal of International Business Studies* 39: 406–27.

Watanabe, Chihiro, and Martin Hemmert. 1998. "The Interaction between Technology and Economy: Has the 'Virtuous Cycle' of Japan's Technological Innovation System Collapsed?" In *Technology and Innovation in Japan: Policy and Management for the Twenty-first Century,* ed. Martin Hemmert and Christian Oberlander. London: Routledge.

Watanabe, Machiko. 1996. "Jidōsha Sangyō" (The Automobile Industry). *NIRA Seisaku Kenkyū* 9, no. 10.

Watanabe, Osamu. 1987. "Gendai Nihon Shakai no Ken'i-teki Kōzō to Kokka" (The Structure of Authority in Contemporary Japanese Society and the State). In *Ken'i-teki Chitsujo to Kokka (Authoritarian Order and the State),* ed. Fujita Isamu. Tokyo: Tokyo Daigaku Shuppankai.

Watanabe, Shigeru, and Yamamoto Isao. 1992. "Corporate Governance in Japan: Ways to Improve Low Productivity." *NRI Quarterly* 1, no. 3 (Winter): 28–45.

Watanabe, Toshio. 1996. "Higashi Ajia no Naka ni Tokeyuku Nihon" (Japan Is Melding into East Asia). *Asuteion* 42 (Autumn).

Weber, Max. 1946. "Class, Status, and Party." In *Readings from Max Weber,* ed. Hans Gerth and C. Wright Mills. New York: Oxford University Press.

Weidenbaum, Murray, and Samuel Hughes. 1996. *The Bamboo Network: How Expatriate Chinese Entrepreneurs Are Creating a New Economic Superpower in Asia.* New York: Free Press.

Weiss, Linda. 1998. *The Myth of the Powerless State.* Ithaca, N.Y.: Cornell University Press.

Whittaker, D. H. 1997. *Small Firms in the Japanese Economy.* Cambridge: Cambridge University Press.

Williamson, Oliver E. 1975. *Markets and Hierarchies: Analysis and Antitrust Implications.* New York: Free Press.

Winters, Jeffrey A. 1996. *Power in Motion: Capital Mobility and the Indonesian State.* Ithaca: Cornell University Press.

Witt, Michael. 2006. *Changing Japanese Capitalism: Societal Coordination and Institutional Adjustment.* New York: Cambridge University Press.

Yahata, Shigemi. 1996. "Small and Medium-size Enterprises Moving Offshore." *Japan Labor Bulletin* (May 1): 5–8.

Yamada, Bundo, and Kenji Okumura. 1997. "Information Technology, Globalization, and the Strategic Management of Technology." In *Techno-Security in an Age of Globalization,* ed. Denis Fred Simon. Armonk, N.Y.: M. E. Sharpe.

Yamagishi, Toshio. 1998. *Shinrai no Kōzō* (The Structure of Trust). Tokyo: University of Tokyo Press.

———. 1999. *Anshin Shakai Kara Shinrai Shakai e* (From an "Assurance-Based Society" to a "Trust-Based Society"). Tokyo: Chūōkōronsha.

Yamamoto, Takatoshi. 1989. "The Press Clubs of Japan." *Journal of Japanese Studies* 15, no. 2: 371–88.

———. 2002. "Seikai de kyōsō yūi na bunya wa nanni ka" (What Is the Field in Which You Hold a Competitive Advantage?). *Ekonomisuto* (March 5): 18–20.

Yamamoto, Tetsuzo. 1996. "Kikai Buhin Sangyō" (Machinery Parts Industries). *NIRA Seisaku Kenkyū* 9, no. 10: 24–26.

Yamamura, Kozo. 1982. "Success That Soured: Administrative Guidance and Cartels in Japan." In *Policy and Trade Issues of the Japanese Economy: American and Japanese Perspectives*, ed. Kozo Yamamura. Seattle: University of Washington.

———. 1986. "Japan's Deus ex Machina: Western Technology in the 1920s." *Journal of Japanese Studies* 12: 65–94.

———. 1997. "The Japanese Political Economy after the Bubble: Plus Ça Change." *Journal of Japanese Studies* 23, no. 2 (Summer): 291–331.

———. 1999. "Germany and Japan in a New Phase of Capitalism: Confronting the Past and the Future." Paper prepared for a conference on "German and Japanese Capitalism," Cologne, Germany.

———. 2003. "Germany and Japan in a New Phase of Capitalism: Confronting the Past and the Future." In *The End of Diversity? Prospects for German and Japanese Capitalism*, ed. Kozo Yamamura and Wolfgang Streeck. Ithaca: Cornell University Press.

Yamamura, Kozo, and Wolfgang Streeck, eds. 2003. *The End of Diversity? Prospects for German and Japanese Capitalism*. Ithaca: Cornell University Press.

Yamamura, Kozo, and Jan Vandenberg. 1986. "Japan's Rapid-Growth Policy on Trial: The Television Case." In *Trade Issues of the Japanese Economy: American and Japanese Perspectives*, ed. Gary R. Saxonhouse and Kozo Yamamura. Seattle: University of Washington Press.

Yamashita, Shoichi, Takeuchi J., Kawabe N., and Takehana S. 1989. "ASEAN Shokoku ni okeru Nihonteki Keiei to Gijutsu Iten ni kansuru Keiesha no Ishiki Chōsa" (Survey of Japanese Managers on Japanese-Style Management and Technology Transfer to ASEAN Countries). *Hiroshima Economic Studies* 10 (March).

Yamawaki, Hideki. 1984. "Tekkōgyō" (The Steel Industry). In *Nihon no Sangyō Seisaku* (Industrial Policy in Japan), ed. Komiya Ryutarō, Okuno Masahiro, and Suzumura Kōtarō. Tokyo: Tokyo University Press.

Yanagihara, Toru. 1987. "Pacific Basin Economic Relations: Japan's New Role?" *Developing Economies* 25, no. 4 (December): 403–20.

Yashiro Naohiro. 2007. "Kakusa shakai no hannin wa dare da" (Who's to Blame for the Growth in Social Inequality?). *Bungei Shunjū* (April): 282–90.

Yonekura Seiichiro. 2000. "Daihenkaku no jidai ni 'heiji no riron' wa tsūyō shinai" (In a Time of Great Transformation, "Conventional Wisdom" Just Won't Do). *Shokun*, October, 62–73.

Yoshitomi Masaru. 2005. "'Defure ka no keiki kaifuku' o jitsugen shita kigyō no chikara de keiki wa odoriba kara dakkyaku suru" (Thanks to the Strength of Its Firms, Japan Escapes from the Grip of Deflation). *Rinji Zōkangō Ekonomisuto* (Manichi Shinbunsha), February 14.

Young, Michael K. 1984. "Judicial Review of Administrative Guidance: Governmentally Encouraged Consensual Dispute Resolution in Japan." *Columbia Law Review* 84 (May): 923–83.

Zenkoku Kinzoku Kikai Rōdōkumiai. 1997. "Tekisei na Kakaku to Kōsei na Torihiki no Jitsugen o Motomete; Kigyō Jōkyō to Torihiki no Jittai ni kansuru Chōsa Hōkokusho" (Seeking Proper Prices and Fair Trade: The Survey on Corporate Conditions and Transactions). February 2.

Zenkoku Shitauke Kigyō Shinkō Kyōkai (ZSKSK). 1997a. *Datsu Shitauke-gata Kigyō e no Keiei Senryaku: Jirei Bunseki to Sūryō Bunseki ni yoru Teigen* (A Management Strategy for Post-Subcontracting Enterprises: A Proposal Based on Case Study and Quantitative Analysis). March.

———. 1997b. *Shitauke Kigyō ni kansuru Q&A* (Questions and Answers about Being a Subcontractor). March.

Index

Abe, Shinzo, 231
administrative councils, 139
administrative guidance, 1
  in Asia, 147–48
  defined, 49
  and reform, 182, 226
  and relationalism, 63, 111, 114
administrative networks
  as coordinatorship, 99
  extended to Asia, 4, 30–31, 101, 151
  fraying, 207
  positional power and, 98, 144
Aishin, 55, 124, 160–61
Ajiken, 31, 145–46
amakudari, 43, 49–50, 107
  and corruption, 114–18
  and the Japanese financial crisis, 180
  in the new millennium, 230–31
AMEICC, 99, 146–47, 171
American Chamber of Commerce (Tokyo), 233
Americanization, 5, 7, 224
Anti-Monopoly Act
  1997 amendment of, 125–26
  2005 amendment of, 233
  enforcement of, 71 n2, 119–20, 195
  violations of, 232
APEC (Asia Pacific Economic Cooperation), 73
ASEAN (Association of Southeast Asian Nations), 82
  as a region, 159, 207
  regional programs, 83
  trade agreements, 209, 220

ASEAN-4
  defined, 79
  as a region, 82–83, 96, 156–58, 221
Asia Broadband Program, 219
Asian Bond Market Initiative, 220
Asian financial crisis, 143, 169–74, 204, 206–8
Asian Monetary Fund, 171, 219
Asian Talent Fund, 218
Association for Overseas Technical Scholarships, 171
automobile industry
  Asian expansion of, 159–62, 197
  during financial crisis, 84, 170–71
  subcontractors, 96–97, 121–22, 158
  supply networks, 83, 159, 161
  Western acquisition of, 207–8
  See also names of individual automakers

Baburu e Go, 224–25
balance of payment crisis, 61
Bank of Japan, 61–62, 114–15
bankruptcy, 179
  case studies, 151–52
  excess capacity and, 21, 63
  government bailout and, 173, 228
banks. *See names of individual banks*
bid-rigging, 51–52, 119–20, 232–33
bunsha, 190
Burt, Ronald, 16, 25, 176, 255
business-business cooperation, 51–57
  in the 1990s, 118–29, 186
  in the new millennium, 232–38
  regionalization and, 151–63

Cabinet Office, 230, 239
California Public Employees Retirement System, 236–37
Canon, 188
cartels, 21, 51, 63
   case studies, 34–35, 148
   government crack-down on, 119
   intergovernmental, 247
Chiang Mai Initiative, 220
China, 4, 6, 143, 171
   aid to, 80–81, 96
   Dalian, 79, 211
   Japanese manufacturers in, 79, 82–83, 153–54
   local sales in, 216
   the rise of, 171, 204–5, 208–11, 217–21
   subcontractors in, 156
   trading companies and, 99–100
China-ASEAN Free Trade Agreement, 220
China Certification and Inspection Company, 210
CIAJ (Communications Industry Association of Japan), 147–48
Civil War (US), 19
CLM-WG (Cambodia-Laos-Myanmar Working Group), 146–47
companyism, 41, 90
Comprehensive Economic Partnership with ASEAN, 220
computer industry, 63–65, 74, 78–79, 207–8. *See also names of individual computer companies*
construction industry, 51–52, 119, 185, 232
consumer price index, 67
consumers, 33–35, 177, 179
corporate governance, 58
   in the 1990s, 129–30
   in the new millennium, 238–39
   kansayaku style of, 124–25, 239–40
corporations
   academic ties with, 60
   as families, 59
   See also MNCs
corruption, 114–18
cost of living, 67, 108–9, 229
Council on Economic and Fiscal Policy, 230, 245
cross shareholding, 1, 45, 57, 59, 126–29, 235–36
Crozier's dictum, 30–31
cultural analysis, 2, 250

Dai-Ichi Kangyo, 53, 126, 235
dai-risutora, 131
dangō. See bid-rigging

Democratic Party of Japan, 2, 231, 245
deregulation, 107–12, 144–45, 229
developmentalism, 21
Diet
   Anti-Monopoly Act, 125–26, 233
   banks and, 112, 150
   Commercial Code, 124–25, 239
   election laws, 105
   policy development in, 51, 110
   postal savings and insurance system, 229
   Products Liability Act, 182
   public disclosure law, 38
   zoku, 44
distributional change, 106
   in the 1990s, 121–24, 132–35, 139–40
   regionalization and, 144, 155, 164
Dodge Line, 45
dually controlled firm, 58

East Asia, 4 n3
Economic Reform Study Group, 107
e-Japan, 230
Electronic Industries Association of Japan, 147
electronics industry
   Asian expansion of, 82–84, 88–89, 91, 97, 143, 197
   in China, 208
   during financial crisis, 151, 185
   high-tech, 207, 232
   subcontractors, 157–58
   suppliers, 217
   supply networks, 100
   trading patterns of, 76, 215
   Western acquisition of, 207, 215
elites, 14, 26, 30–32, 176–79, 181
embeddedness, 14–15, 23, 247
Emerson, Richard, 26, 255
employment
   case law, 137
   distributional change in, 134–40
   of Japanese-Brazilians, 178
   turnover rate, 135–36
   of women, 133–34, 178, 164, 242
   of young people, 133, 242
   See also lifetime employment; seniority-based wages
Enshakkan Kondankai, 213
enterprise union, 46, 59, 139. *See also* labor unions
entrepreneurs
   business start-up rates, 188–95, 245
   sponsored, 190–91
environmental problems, 35, 37
EPA (Economic Planning Agency), 58, 199

excess competition, 21, 51, 107, 149, 171
exchange networks
  in apparel industry, 23
  power and, 33, 44, 98
  side payments and, 179
  Silicon Valley and, 22 n17
  theory of, 16
Export-Import Bank of Japan, 75, 149–50, 173
Europeanization, 254
European Union, 6–7, 148, 246–47, 252

Fair Trade Commission, 52, 119, 232
familism, 59
FDI (foreign direct investment), 74–78, 96, 149
  convoy-style, 153–56
  effect on trade balance, 197–200
  from the U.S., 203–4
financial bubble, 2, 67, 71, 143, 177, 224–25
Fiscal Investment and Loan Program, 34, 112, 150, 229
flying geese pattern, 4, 81–82, 143, 210
  collapses, 203, 218, 223
foreign aid. *See* ODA
foreign economic policy, 82
Fuji Heavy Industries, 216, 227
Fujitsu, 64, 74, 111, 190–91
Fuyo Group, 53, 125–26, 235

General Agreement on Tariffs and Trade, 45
General Motors, 206
general trading companies, 53, 95, 99–100, 210
  Mitsubishi Corp., 95, 128
  Mitsui Corp., 94–95, 163
Germany, 6–7
  comparative costs in, 48, 229
  in Europe, 246, 252–54
  at the Plaza Accord, 75
  and varieties of capitalism, 43
Gifu Province, 193–94
Global Entrepreneurship Monitor, 188
globalization, 5–6, 246
  threat of, 30, 45
  vs. regionalization, 4, 7–9, 31, 203, 245
golden triangle, 51
Gramsci, Antonio, 28 n25, 30, 255
Granovetter, Mark, 14–16, 22, 255
Gyōten, Toyō, 181

Hamilton, Gary, 255
Hewlett-Packard, 207
Hiraiwa, Gaishi, 107
historical institutionalism, 31–32, 250

Hitachi, 64, 126, 165, 217, 240
Hitachi City, 29, 193–94
Hokkaido Tohoku Development Finance Corporation, 112
hollowing out, 101, 150–52, 164, 196–200, 244
Honda, 158, 165, 170, 215–16, 233
Horie, Takafumi, 223

ICT (information and communication technology), 107, 182–87, 189, 230
iemoto, 61
income distribution, 174, 177–78
Indonesia, 4, 79, 173
  aid to, 80, 96
  automobile industry in, 83, 96–97
  Japanese manufacturers in, 89–90, 157, 166, 168
  JICA advisers in, 147
  subcontractors in, 152
Industrial Competitiveness Strategy Council, 227
Industrial Revitalization Law, 227
industrial sequencing, 81
Information Clearinghouse Japan, 225–26
information disclosure law, 225–26
information hoarding, 26, 34–35, 176
information impactedness, 69, 179
innovation crisis, 175, 182–87, 204
institutional collusion, 69–70
International Monetary Fund, 8, 45, 84, 171, 220
investment race, 62
Isuzu, 215–16
Ito, Masaaki, 195
Itōchu, 99

JAMA (Japan Automobile Manufacturers Association), 147
Japan Bank for International Cooperation, 29, 214
Japan Citizen's Ombudsman Association, 233
Japan Development Bank, 112, 228
Japan Electronic Computer Company, 64
Japan Export-Import Bank, 75, 149–50, 173
Japan Fair Trade Commission, 232–33
Japan Finance Corporation for Small Business, 112, 150, 173
Japan Highway Public Corporation, 232
Japan International Development Corporation, 95
Japan Overseas Development Corporation, 81, 167
Japan Socialist Party, 105

JEMA (Japan Electrical Manufacturers Association), 147
JETRO (Japan External Trade Relations Organization), 99, 148, 167
JICA (Japan International Cooperation Agency), 81
 experts, 96, 147, 172
 soft loans, 213
JNR (Japanese National Railway), 107
JTB (Japan Tobacco Bureau), 107

kanban system, 55
kansayaku, 124–25, 239–40
Kasahara, Hidehiko, 111
Kasumigaseki, 29, 105, 145
Katzenstein, Peter, 8, 246, 252
Keidanren, 73, 95, 107, 129, 135. *See also* Nippon Keidanren
keiretsu, 3, 41, 43, 120
 distribution, 55–57
 domestic vs. Asian, 160–61
 horizontal, 52–54, 93, 124–29, 163
 in the new millennium, 233–36
 studies, 161–62
 vertical, 54–55, 93–94, 120–24, 160
Kirchner, Néstor, 8
Kiyonari Tadao, 188
Knoke, David, 25, 255
Ko, Mishima, 230
Kobe Steel, 236
Koizumi, Jun'ichiro, 26, 39
 cabinet, 213
 reform, 228–32
Kūdōka. See hollowing out

labor-management cooperation, 57–60
 in the 1990s, 129–40, 186
 in the new millennium, 238–44
 regionalization and, 164–69
labor productivity, 71, 74, 113
labor unions, 42–46, 121, 129
 Rengō, 168–69
 See also enterprise union
layoffs, 131–32, 137, 140–41, 164, 170–71, 240–41
LDP (Liberal Democratic Party), 2–3
 Forum to Reconsider Deregulation, 110
 loses power, 105
 side payments, 33–34
 status quo, 37–39
 zoku in, 44
LG Electronics, 208
lifetime employment, 3, 59
 in the 1990s, 135–38
 in the new millennium, 238–44

Livedoor, 223
long-run average costs, 21
Long-Term Credit Bank, 115
lost decade (1990s), 105, 177, 185
Lula (Luiz Inacio da Silva), 8

machinery industry, 121, 124, 166, 184–85
Maekawa Commission, 72
Mahathir bin Mohamad, 206
Malaysia, 4, 172, 206
Manchuria, 24, 79
Marra, David, 238
Matsushita
 in Asia, 76, 97, 143–44, 209, 217
 cross-shareholding of, 236
 industrial cooperation, 119, 232
 protects domestic jobs, 168
 subcontractors, 207
Mazda, 53, 122n28, 132n58, 207, 234
Mercosur, 8
mergers and acquisitions, 203, 207, 254
merit pay, 131, 137–39, 242–43
METI (Ministry of Economy, Trade and Industry), 45, 99
 industrial cluster program, 227
 policies of new millennium, 227
 two-pronged ODA, 213
 See also MITI
Ministry of Health and Welfare, 38, 113–14
Ministry of Foreign Affairs, 213
MITI (Ministry of International Trade and Industry)
 and computer industry, 63–64, 70
 and industrial associations, 147
 liberalization countermeasures, 45–47
 New AID, 146
 role in financial crisis, 171–74
 role in regionalization, 82, 145–50, 198
 and SMEs, 112–13
 venture financing, 195
 See also METI
Mitsuba, 170
Mitsubishi Corporation, 95, 128, 227
Mitsubishi Electric, 64, 159
Mitsubishi Group, 53, 95, 126, 128, 235
Mitsui Corporation, 94–95, 163
Mitsui Group, 53, 94, 235
Mitsui Soko, 99
Miyazawa Initiative, 81, 207, 211
Mizuho Financial Group, 125–26
MMC (Mitsubishi Motors Corp.), 123, 170, 206, 234–35
MNCs (multinational corporations)
 20 percent rule of, 151
 in China, 217

expatriate managers of, 166
interfirm ties among, 93–94
localization of, 90–92, 214
organizational learning in, 86
political ties of, 94–95
regionalization of, 82–85, 143–50
uniquely hierarchical structure of, 87–90
MOF (Ministry of Finance)
  in *Baburu e Go*, 225–26
  during the 1990s, 69, 171
  liberalization countermeasures of, 45–47
  policies of new millennium, 228
  protects industry, 62
  role in regionalization, 145
  scandal within, 114
MPT (Ministry of Posts and Telecommunications), 107, 109n8, 113–14, 118
Murakami, Yasusuke, 20–22, 62

NAFTA, 7, 27, 168–69
Nagano, 37, 226
Nagatachō, 29, 105
Nakasone, Yasuhiro, 72n3, 107
nawabari, 101, 145
NEC, 53, 64, 74, 232
NEC Soft, 218
nenkō jōretsu. *See* seniority-based wages
neohexagon, 51
neoinstitutional economic analysis, 24
network analysis, 14–19, 22–26, 32, 247–48, 255
networks, 13–14
  of affiliation, 41–42
  in the Americas, 251
  China and, 209, 211
  distribution, 56, 99
  in Europe, 252
  exclusionary, 27, 37–38, 51, 100, 181
  financial, 69
  horizontal and vertical, 45
  human, 92, 227
  industrial, 146, 227
  information and, 192
  innovation and, 107
  keiretsu, 147, 155, 161, 194
  labor policy, 44
  open, 194, 249
  other forms of, 60–61
  regional and local, 84, 88, 100
  regulatory policy, 69
  scholarly, 255
  social, 9, 72, 249 (*see also* relational networks)

in the U.S., 19
  See also production networks; supply networks
New Series project, 64
NIEs (newly industrializing economies), 79, 82–83, 196
Nikkei index, 3, 177n2
Nikkeiren, 135, 137, 172. *See also* Nippon Keidanren
Nippon Electronics, 154
Nippon Export and Investment Insurance, 215
Nippon Keidanren, 232
Nippon Steel, 236
Nishi, Kazuhiko, 182–83
Nissan, 112, 180
  in Asia, 165
  during the financial crisis, 170
  and Fuyo group, 126
  subcontractors, 122–23, 234
  in Thailand, 159
norenwake, 190
NTT (Nippon Telegraph and Telephone), 36, 107, 118, 131, 134, 191
Nukazwa, K., 110–11, 181

ODA (official development assistance), 80–81
  change in, 211–14
  during financial crisis, 172
  German, 252
  promotes investment in Asia, 94–97, 146
OECD (Organisation for Economic Cooperation and Development), 213
OEM (original equipment manufacturing), 100
Ogata Sadako, 213
Ōta Ward, 194
Overseas Economic Cooperation Fund, 95

parent firms, 122–24
Pempel, T.J., 5, 41, 44
People's Finance Corporation, 112, 150
Philippines, 80–81, 83, 93–95
Plaza Accord, 75–76
Porite, 154
positional power, 52, 68
  applied, 28–37
  consolidated, 84, 96–102
  declines, 203–5
  defined, 13, 23–28
  in the 1990s, 96–101, 143–44
  and nonelites, 33
  See also selective relationalism
poverty, 177

presidents' club, 53, 128
press clubs, 60, 226
Proctor & Gamble, 207
production networks, 100–101
  in central and eastern Europe, 252
  China at center of, 221
  during financial crisis, 169–74
  extended to Asia, 4, 30–31, 151
  fraying, 207
  from vertical to horizontal, 214–20
  and Honda, 153
  intra-regional trade and, 84
  motivation for extending, 74, 145, 198,
    246
  positional power and, 98, 144
  Toyota and, 83
Products Liability Act, 35, 182
proto-development, 20

quality control circles, 59, 90

rational choice theory, 32–33, 250
Recruit, 37, 244
regionalization
  in Asia, 98, 151–63
  costs of, 181–200
  defined, 6–7, 74
  developmental, 8
  elite, 142, 153–55, 169, 176–79, 181
  in Europe, 246–47
  history of, 74–85
  rearguard, 8
  vs. globalization, 4, 7–9, 31, 203, 245
regulation, 47–48, 107–12. *See also* deregulation
relationalism. *See* selective relationalism
relational networks, 25
  distributional effects of, 176–77
  and foreign investment, 218
  and liberalization countermeasures, 46
  loosening of, 244
  and reassurance, 41
Rengō, 168–69
research and development, 101, 187, 183–
  84, 217–18
reverse imports, 79, 93, 214–15
ringi, 59, 90
risutora, 131, 240

Saeki, Keishi, 224
Sakaiya, Taichi, 230
Sakakibara, Eisuke, 171
Salim Group, 100
Samsung, 208

Sanyo, 137, 154, 217
Schattschneider's dictum, 30–31, 27
Schoppa, Leonard, 4
Seagram, 207
Seki, Mitsuhiro, 73, 151, 153, 215
Sekimoto, Tadahiro, 51
selective relationalism, 14–23, 29, 60–61,
  106, 113
  durability of, 140
  fails, 65–72
  and innovation, 182–87
  motivation for, 250–51
  opportunity costs of, 175–80
  and positional power, 27–37
  reforming, 181–82
  sociological model of, 41–42
  sticky, 200
  three legged stool of, 43, 90
  See also business-business cooperation;
    labor-management cooperation;
    state-industry cooperation
semiconductor industry, 64, 111, 207
seniority-based wages, 43, 59, 90–91
  in the 1990s, 137–38
  in the new millennium, 238, 242
Shanghai Electric, 218
Sharp, 93
shingikai, 50–51, 145
Shōkō Chūkin, 112, 150
shukkō, 131–34, 164–67, 191, 240
shūshin koyō. See lifetime employment
side payments, 19–20, 34, 37, 47, 179
Singapore, 76, 89, 91, 97, 219
SMEs (small and medium-sized enterprises),
  112, 178–79
  case studies of, 193–94
  during the financial crisis, 172–73
  and hollowing out, 150
  and innovations, 187–200
  in Southeast Asia, 78–79, 147
Smoot-Hawley Act, 27
social capital, 18–19, 41, 192
social market, 7
Sogo Co., 228
sōkaiya, 36, 130
South Korea, 18
  Japanese manufacturers in, 88
  rise of, 208–9, 221
  subcontractors in, 157
  technology imports, 85n36
spillovers, 62
start-ups, 188–93
state-industry cooperation, 46–51, 62
  in the 1990s, 107–18, 186

in the new millennium, 226–32
regionalization and, 144–50
steel industry, 63, 120
stock markets
HERCULES, 245
JASDAQ, 219, 245
MOTHERS, 245
Tokyo, 3, 124, 128–30, 236–37, 239
structural change, 106–7
in the 1990s, 124, 134, 135, 139–40
Koizumi and, 38, 228–32
network effect on, 23
in the new millennium, 244–46
outsiders and, 203
regionalization and, 144, 155, 164
structural power, 28
subcontractors
bifurcation of, 120–24
dominance in Asia of, 96–97
motives for expansion, 154–55
regional expansion, 79, 151–63
small, 152–53
in vertical *keiretsu*, 54–55, 94
Sumitomo Group, 53, 63n42
Sumitomo Metal, 63, 227, 236
Sumitomo-Mitsui Bank, 125
sunrise industries, 68
sunset industries, 68
Supachai Panitchpakdi, 209
supply clubs, 54–55, 86, 160–61, 234, 239
supply networks
automobile, 83, 159, 161
during financial crisis, 124
in Ōta Ward, 194
polarized, 122
in SE Asia, 83
Suzuki, 123

Taiwan
Japanese manufacturers in, 90, 153–54, 157
rise of, 207–8, 215–16, 219, 221
suppliers, 84
trading companies in, 99–100
technology transfer, 85–87, 205–6
telecommunications. See ICT
television industry case, 34–35
tenseki, 131–34, 191, 240
TFP (total factor productivity), 65–66
Thailand, 4, 96, 206
aid to, 81, 95–96, 147
automobile industry, 157–60, 170, 216
Eastern Seaboard Development Program, 97–98

electronics industry, 158–59
IMF and, 171
Japanese manufacturers in, 89–90, 94, 100, 154, 167
local managers in, 91
Master Plan for Supporting Industries, 147
supply clubs, 86, 159–62
trade agreements, 209–10
U.S. and European FDI to, 206
three legged stool. *See under* selective relationalism
Tokyo Motor, 227
Tokyo stock exchange, 3, 124, 128–30, 236–37, 239
Toshiba
competition, 221
industrial cooperation, 64, 232
sales growth, 74
town meetings, 26–27
Toyo Engineering, 217
Tōyō Kōgyō. *See* Mazda
Toyota, 54, 83, 94
in Asia, 159, 166, 168, 216–17
corporate governance of, 239
cross-shareholding of, 236
during the financial crisis, 170, 207
industrial cooperation, 119, 123–24
merit pay, 242
subcontractors, 233
supply club, 54–55, 160–61, 239–40
trade agreements
between China and ASEAN, 220
between Japan and U.S., 111
triangular trade pattern, 76, 214
tripolar industrial structure, 153
trust, 15, 19, 41–42, 49, 176
Turkey, 7

unions. *See* enterprise union; labor unions
United States
MNCs in Asia, 207
MNCs in Mexico, 251
occupation of Japan, 44–45
trade policy, 71, 124
u-Japan, 230

varieties of capitalism, 1, 43
venture capital, 191–92
vested interests, 2–3
VLSI project, 64

Washington Consensus, 8
Watanabe, Toshio, 98

Welch, Jack, 58
World Bank, 213

Yahoo! Japan, 244
Yamagishi, Toshio, 255
Yamaha, 215–16

Yamamura, Kozo, 23n18, 43n6, 68, 85, 97
Yawata Steel, 63
Yonekura, Seiichiro, 239

zaibatsu, 44, 52–53, 125
zoku, 44, 50n24

www.ingramcontent.com/pod-product-compliance
Lightning Source LLC
Chambersburg PA
CBHW051953270326
41929CB00015B/2639